W9-AUD-278

H. Peter Chase, M.D.
Barbara Davis Center for Childhood Diabetes
Department of Pediatrics
University of Colorado Health Sciences Center
10th Edition

UNDERSTANDING DIABETES

Barbara Davis Center for Childhood Diabetes
www.barbaradaviscenter.org

Children's Diabetes Foundation at Denver
www.ChildrensDiabetesFdn.org

Children With Diabetes
www.childrenwithdiabetes.com

Juvenile Diabetes Foundation
www.jdrf.org

American Diabetes Association
www.diabetes.org

Appreciation is expressed to Aventis Pharmaceuticals
for underwriting the cost of printing this book through an educational grant.

This edition of the Pink Panther book is dedicated to the Children's Diabetes Foundation and it's Guild. They have made many of the services offered at the Barbara Davis Center possible, and have made life better for many families and children with diabetes.

TABLE OF CONTENTS

Please note: Many parts of this book have been written at an eighth grade level and may be too complex for younger children. The coloring book follows the same outline and may be more appropriate for them. A parent working with a child in reading and understanding parts of this book may also be helpful.

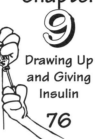

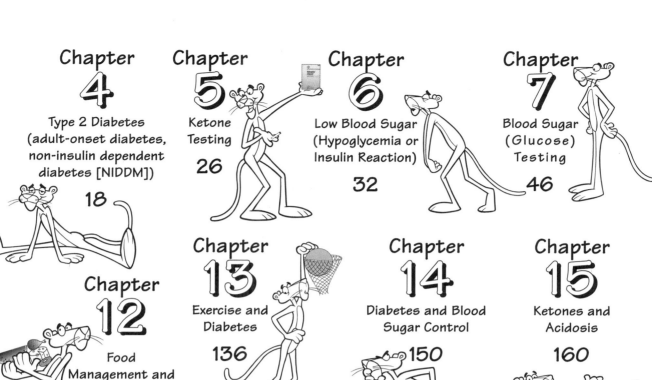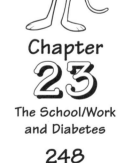

ACKNOWLEDGEMENTS

Appreciation is expressed to:

🐾 Sherrie Harris, BSN, MA, CDE for her help with editing, formatting and typing this edition.

🐾 DeAnn Johnson, BSN, RN, CDE, for her many suggestions in all of the chapters.

🐾 Paula Gutzmer, RN, MN, Sherrie Harris, BSN, MA, CDE and DeAnn Johnson, BSN, RN, CDE, for assistance in formulating the ADA's "Topics," and "Teaching and Learning Objectives" at the beginning of each chapter.

🐾 Proof-readers include Alice Green, Sonia Cooper, Cindie Smith and the entire staff of the Children's Diabetes Foundation.

🐾 Regina Reece for editing and manuscript preparation.

🐾 Finally, appreciation is expressed to Sue Palandri and the entire staff of the Children's Diabetes Foundation for their continued support.

🐾 Book design, graphics and illustrations: Cindy Barton

The author wishes to thank MGM Consumer Products for allowing me to use The Pink Panther™ & ©2002 UNITED ARTISTS CORPORATION. All rights reserved. www.pinkpanther.com

TOPICS FOR THE RECOMMENDED ADA CURRICULUM WITH THEIR RELATED CHAPTERS

TOPIC	CHAPTER LOCATION
Diabetes disease process	1-4
Nutritional management	4, 11 and 12
Physical activity	4, 13 and 25
Medications	4, 8, 9, 21 and 26
Monitoring	1, 4, 5, 7, 14, 20-24 and 27
Prevent, detect and treat acute complications	4-6, 15,16, 23, 24 and 27
Prevent, detect and treat chronic complications	4, 14, 22 and 26-28
Goal setting and problem solving	10, 13, 14 and 18-20
Psychosocial adjustment	10, 17-19, 23-25, 27 and 28
Preconception care, management during pregnancy and gestational management	19, 22 and 27

TEACHING OBJECTIVES:

These are provided with each chapter to assist the person(s) doing the teaching.

LEARNING OBJECTIVES:

These are provided with each chapter to help the learners (parents, child, relatives or self) know the important points.

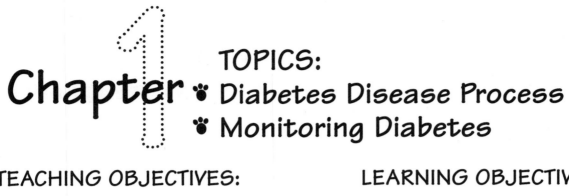

Chapter 1

TOPICS:
- Diabetes Disease Process
- Monitoring Diabetes

TEACHING OBJECTIVES:

1. Design a care plan that reflects the family's lifestyle and the person's educational level/developmental stage (see also Chapters 17, 18 & 19).

2. Design a care plan that allows the person/family to become skilled in the management of diabetes.

LEARNING OBJECTIVES:

Learners (parents, child, relative or self) will be able to:

1. Identify basic management routines.
2. Assist the healthcare provider in developing a diabetes care plan.
3. Check blood sugars as directed by healthcare provider and record results.
4. Communicate blood sugars to healthcare provider.
5. Communicate concerns about high or low blood sugars to healthcare provider.

Chapter 1 THE IMPORTANCE OF EDUCATION IN DIABETES

INTRODUCTION

Families and children need to understand as much as possible about diabetes. The knowledge provided in this book and the skills learned will help them feel more secure about managing diabetes. It will help them manage problems when no doctor is available. It will also help them minimize hospitalizations for diabetes problems. Families who feel they can manage diabetes confidently maintain control, rather than the diabetes controlling them.

This book is written for families when diabetes is a new condition to them. It is also for those who have had the condition for a long time. This book is a reference that can be used with the doctor and diabetes team. It can be used alone as a "refresher" course. Some of the chapters are written to provide very basic information. Other chapters are for readers wanting more in-depth information. Advances are taking place at such a rapid rate that new editions are needed about every three years. Families may choose to bring this book to clinic appointments. It can then be used as a guide for discussion and learning. This is particularly important in the first year after diagnosis.

OUTLINE FOR INITIAL EDUCATION

Initial education is variable based on:

- the day and time of diagnosis
- how sick the person is
- the emotional and physical readiness of the person and family to learn
- hospitalization versus outpatient care
- the availability of appropriately trained educators and healthcare team

It is **essential for both parents** (and often other care-providers) to be present for the initial education. Most families initially come to the clinic for six to eight hours per day for two to four days. We do not expect families to remember all the information the first time. Written guidelines are always given to the family to ensure safety at home. Review and reinforcement of basic concepts occur at each visit. The content of this book should be used for periodic review as needed.

Helpful ways to continue learning are:

- writing down questions and making notes
- video tapes and library books
- parent and child educational group meetings
- our Pink Panther™ *First Book for Understanding Diabetes* provides a synopsis of each of the chapters in this book. Some families start with this book the first week.

The topics considered important for initial diabetes education by the American Diabetes Association (ADA) are outlined at the beginning of this publication. The chapters where each of these topics is covered are also shown. Please let your diabetes healthcare provider know if there are topics which apply to you/your child that are unclear or ones which you would like to spend more time discussing.

CONTINUING EDUCATION

Following initial education, the family usually returns to the clinic:

- in one week
- after four weeks
- after eight weeks
- and then every three months

This may vary for different families and different clinics. Clinic visits every three months should include an evaluation of the family's current diabetes management. Modifications can then be made with feedback from the person and family. Children, who were too young to learn self-care when diagnosed with diabetes, will need on-going education. Clinic visits every three months with the healthcare team can assist in their learning process.

Children who develop diabetes prior to age 10-13 will need to learn specifics about the disease as they are ready. A science project on diabetes is one way to encourage learning and self-discovery. This book can provide information for such a report.

The diabetes nurse educator may start working on chapters in the book with the child alone. This can encourage the child to ask and answer questions. Education from all the diabetes team members should continue with the every three-month clinic visits. We feel a solid educational foundation and the development of good habits will help the person to stay in good diabetes control throughout life. With a supportive family and good habits, the need for later diabetes-related hospitalizations or problems is reduced.

FAMILY RESPONSIBILITIES

Diabetes is a unique disease. It requires on-going communication and assistance between the person and/or significant others in all areas of the day-to-day care. **A knowledgeable and supportive family is very important for good diabetes care.** This is discussed in more detail in Chapter 17, Family Concerns.

Families must assume responsibility for:

- consistency in meals, snacks, shots
- doing blood sugars
- insulin injections (type 1) or oral medicines (type 2)
- blood or urine ketone checks
- ordering and having supplies
- communication with day care/school or work

TOPICS COVERED IN A NEW DIAGNOSIS DIABETES TREATMENT PLAN

1st Day in Hospital or Clinic

Different clinics have different schedules for education of newly diagnosed families. Education at our Center is done primarily in the clinic setting (after discharge if hospitalization was necessary). Day one usually involves learning skills needed for care in the home setting. *These include:*
❑ Blood sugar testing (Chapter 7)
❑ Urine ketone measurements (Chapter 5)
❑ Recognizing the signs of low blood sugar and how to treat (Chapter 6)

We write specific instructions (see Table 2) for the family (meals, snacks, when to test blood or urine and how to record results, and when to phone us) for the period until returning to clinic. The dietitian may discuss ideas for meals and snacks.

Any of the following may be covered:
❑ The Importance of Education in Diabetes (Chapter 1)
❑ What is Diabetes? (Chapter 2)
❑ What Causes Diabetes? (Chapter 3)
❑ Urine Ketone Testing (Chapter 5)
❑ Low Blood Sugar (Chapter 6)
❑ Blood Sugar Testing (Chapter 7)
❑ Insulin (Chapter 8)
❑ Insulin Injections (Chapter 9)
❑ Practice injection technique

Day Two: a.m.
❑ Review above concepts and answer questions
❑ Review insulin and insulin injection technique
❑ Review Low Blood Sugar (Chapter 6)
❑ Normal Nutrition (Chapter 11) and meet with dietitian
❑ Food Management and Diabetes (Chapter 12)
❑ Prescriptions for supplies
❑ Communication plan for the next week

Day Two: p.m.
❑ Causes of low and high blood sugars (Table 3, Chapter 15)
❑ Grief-Adjustment Issues (Chapter 10) and meet social worker
❑ Exercise and Diabetes (Chapter 13)
❑ Diabetes and Blood Sugar Control (Chapter 14)
❑ School and Diabetes and Day Care (Chapter 23)
❑ "Thinking" Scales (Chapter 21)

Day Three:
(variable with Day 2 and 1 Week Visit)
❑ Review above concepts and answer questions
❑ Family Concerns (Chapter 17) and reducing fears of shots and pokes
❑ The Outpatient Management of Diabetes (Chapter 20)
❑ Long-Term Complications of Diabetes - if questions (Chapter 22)

At One-Week/ 1 Month Visit
(may include Day 3 topics)
❑ Review all of the above
❑ Review Ketonuria and Acidosis [Ketoacidosis] (Chapter 15)
❑ Sick-Day Management (Chapter 16)
❑ Research and Diabetes (Chapter 28)
❑ Baby-Sitters and Diabetes (Chapter 24) Vacations and Camp (Chapter 25)
❑ Long-Term Complications of Diabetes - if questions (Chapter 22)
❑ Pregnancy and Diabetes (Chapter 27)
❑ Problem solving and/or quiz

This is a general plan. The timing is varied and length of education depends on the emotional and physical readiness of the family to learn. Also, the plan may change if the person is hospitalized versus when treated only in the clinic. A trend in recent years has been to teach survival skills in the first two days, and to make the visit at one week (when stress is lower) a longer and more in-depth visit.

New Patient First-Night Instructions for _____

A. **The diabetes supplies you will need the first night include** (your nurse will mark which you need):

____ Blood glucose meter	____ Meter test strips	____ Alcohol swabs
____ Ketone check strips	____ Glucose gel & tabs	____ Log book
____ Insulin	____ Syringes	____ Phone contact card

The first night you will either get your insulin injection at our clinic, or you will give the shot at home or where you are staying.

B. *If the insulin is given while at the clinic:*

❏ 1. Humalog® insulin has been given; eat within 10-15 minutes.

❏ 2. Regular insulin has been given, try to eat your meal within 30 minutes – or – have a snack containing carbohydrates on the way home if it will be more than 30 minutes.

3. Allow your child to eat until their appetite is satisfied, avoiding high sugar foods (especially regular sugar pop and sweet desserts).

C. *If the dinner insulin is to be given at home:*

1. Check your child's blood sugar right before your meal. Enter the result into the log book.

2. Check for urine ketones. Enter the result into the log book.

3. Call Dr. _____ at _____ or page at _____ for an insulin dose.
   Give this dose: _____.

4. Draw up and give the insulin injection right before your meal (see Chapter 8). If your child is not very hungry or is tired, you can give the shot after they eat and call the physician with any dose questions.

5. Eat your meal, allowing your child to eat until their appetite is satisfied. Avoid high sugar foods.

D. *Before Bed:*

1. Check your child's blood sugar. Enter the result into the log book.

2. Check for urine ketones. Enter the result into the log book.

3. Call your physician at the numbers listed above if your child's blood sugar is below ____ or above ____, or if urine ketones are "moderate" or "large". If urine ketones are "trace" or "small", have your child drink 8-12 oz of water before going to bed.

4. Give an insulin injection if your physician instructs you to do so. (Dose, if ordered _____.)

5. Have your child eat a bedtime snack. Some ideas for this snack include: cereal and milk, toast and peanut butter, a slice of pizza, yogurt and graham crackers or cheese and crackers. (See Chapter 11, Table 2 in the Pink Panther book for other ideas.)

E. *The second morning before coming to the clinic:*

1. If your physician has instructed you to give the morning insulin at home before coming in, follow the steps listed above (see letter "**C**") for last night's meal dose **before** eating breakfast.

2. If you have been instructed to wait to give the morning dose until after coming to the clinic, do a blood sugar test and a urine ketone test upon awakening (if blood sugar is less than 70, give 4–6 oz of juice promptly).

   Write the blood sugar and urine ketone results in your log book.
   ❏ Eat breakfast at home, and then come to the clinic for your insulin injection.
   ❏ Bring your breakfast to the clinic, and you will eat it after the insulin has been given.

3. Please bring all blood testing supplies and materials you received the first day back to the clinic (including your log book, Pink Panther book, insulin and supplies).

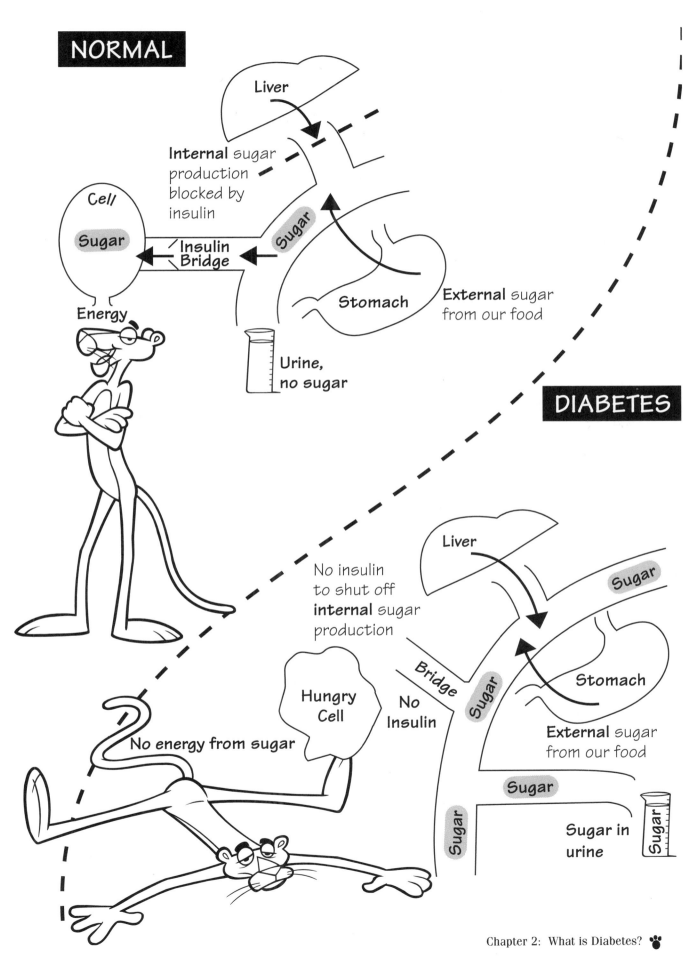

NORMAL

Liver

Internal sugar
production
blocked by
insulin

Cell

Sugar

Energy

Insulin
Bridge

Sugar

Stomach

External sugar
from our food

Urine,
no sugar

DIABETES

No insulin
to shut off
internal sugar
production

Liver

Sugar

Bridge

Sugar

Stomach

Hungry
Cell

No
Insulin

No energy from sugar

External sugar
from our food

Sugar

Sugar

Sugar in
urine

Sugar

Chapter 2

TOPIC: ❦ Diabetes Disease Process

TEACHING OBJECTIVES:

1. Design informational sessions for families in all chapters with consideration for their:

- educational level

- primary language

- culture or ethnicity

- family structure

- learning style

- previous experience with the medical community

LEARNING OBJECTIVES:

Learners (parents, child, relative or self) will be able to:

1. Define the basic disease process of type 1 and type 2 diabetes (also see Chapters 3 & 4).

   a. Define normal and abnormal blood sugars along with HbA_{1c} as part of the diagnosis of diabetes.

   b. Define symptoms of type 1 or type 2 diabetes and compare with the symptoms experienced by the patient at diagnosis.

Chapter 2 — WHAT IS DIABETES?

TYPE 1 (INSULIN-DEPENDENT) DIABETES

Type 1 (also known as insulin-dependent diabetes mellitus [IDDM] or juvenile or childhood) diabetes is the most common type found in children and young adults. **This condition occurs when the pancreas doesn't make enough insulin.**

TYPE 2 DIABETES

There is another kind of diabetes that is sometimes found in overweight pre-teens and teenagers, and is also the most common type of diabetes in adults over age 40 years. It is called **type 2 diabetes**, or sometimes adult-onset or non-insulin-dependent diabetes mellitus (NIDDM). In type 2 diabetes, i**nsulin is still made** in normal or increased amounts (at least initially), but it doesn't work very well in helping the body use sugar. **Insulin cannot be taken in pill form because the acid in the stomach would break it down.**

People who develop childhood (type 1) diabetes are insulin dependent for life. They will always have this type of diabetes. They will not convert to type 2 diabetes as they grow older. Likewise, people with type 2 diabetes do not convert to type 1 diabetes.

In type 2 diabetes, ketones (Chapter 5) may still be present at diagnosis as well as high blood sugars (Chapter 7) and an elevated HbA$_{1c}$ test (Chapter 14). If ketones are present, insulin shots may be started. At a later time, if the antibody tests (Chapter 3) are negative and the blood sugars and HbA$_{1c}$ test have decreased to near normal, the oral tablets may be tried.

WHY WE NEED INSULIN:

- **Insulin allows sugar to pass into our cells so that it can be "burned" for our energy.** The cells are like a furnace, which burn fuel to make energy. Our bodies constantly need energy for all of our body functions, such as allowing our heart to beat and our lungs to breathe. Sugar comes from two places (see drawing at the beginning of this chapter). **"Internal"** sugar comes from our body's own production in the liver or from the release of stored sugar from the liver. This sugar is released into the blood stream. **"External"** sugar comes from the food we eat. It enters the stomach and then moves into the intestine where it is absorbed. When people **do not** have diabetes, the pancreas makes insulin to regulate both internal and external sugar. This means a person without diabetes can eat sugary foods and their blood sugar will remain in the normal range.

When people have type 1 diabetes, the pancreas does not make enough insulin. The blood sugar can't pass into the body's cells to be burned. Instead, the blood sugar rises to a high level and overflows through the kidneys into the urine. When sugar enters the urine, water is pulled from all over the body to go out with the sugar.

*The results are the usual **SYMPTOMS** of diabetes:*

- **Frequent passing of urine**
- **Frequent drinking of liquids:** to make up for water lost in the urine
- **Frequent eating of food:** because the body can't use the food it takes in and is hungry for the energy it isn't getting. This hunger is not always present in children. Sometimes the appetite may even decrease. Ketones (see

Chapter 5) can cause an upset stomach and possible vomiting.

- 🐾 **Weight loss:** when the body can't get sugar into the cells, it burns its own fat and protein for energy. This causes weight loss.

- 🐾 **Changes in behavior:** if the person is getting up frequently at night to pass urine, sound sleep will not occur. This can result in behavioral changes.

- • **A second function of insulin is to shut off the body's internal production of sugar** (see Figure on page 7). This internal sugar mostly comes from the liver. When the insulin level is too low, too much internal sugar is made.

Thus, when there is not enough insulin, the blood sugar level can be high for two reasons:

- 🐾 Too much internal sugar being made

- 🐾 The sugar (from internal production and from external food) cannot pass into the cells

HONEYMOON (GRACE) PERIOD

As stated previously, type 1 (insulin-dependent) diabetes does not turn into type 2 (adult) diabetes as children become adults. According to what we now know, people with type 1 diabetes will need insulin injections for the rest of their lives. Often, there is a honeymoon or grace period that may occur a short time after the onset of diabetes. It commonly starts within two to eight weeks, although not all people have this honeymoon period. During the honeymoon, sugar production is turned off in the liver and a fair bit of insulin is still being made in the islet cells in the pancreas. This is a time when people often think they don't have diabetes. They may be attracted to miracle cures. The honeymoon period may last a few weeks to a few years. During this time, the body may not need much extra insulin. After this period, the body will again need more insulin, although small amounts of insulin may still be made by some. We advise our patients to continue their morning insulin during the grace period, even though they may not need the evening dose. We know from experience that the body will again need more insulin. Usually with growth,

illness or stress there may be a need for more insulin. This need may be evident when the morning blood sugars start to be above the desired range. It is usually hard to begin insulin shots again after having stopped.

The **MOST IMPORTANT RULE** for the patient with diabetes to remember is: **I MUST TAKE MY INSULIN (OR ORAL MEDICINES) EVERY DAY FROM NOW ON. IF I FORGET MY INSULIN/ORAL MEDICINES, MY DIABETES WILL GET OUT OF CONTROL. THERE IS ABSOLUTELY NO WAY I WILL NOT NEED INSULIN EVERY DAY FROM NOW ON IF I HAVE TYPE 1 DIABETES.** Even if I get sick, I still need insulin. I may need more or less insulin, but I must have it every day.
IMPORTANT: The only known difference about people who develop type 1 diabetes is that their bodies don't make enough insulin. *THE PERSON AND EVERY OTHER PART OF THE BODY ARE OTHERWISE COMPLETELY NORMAL.*

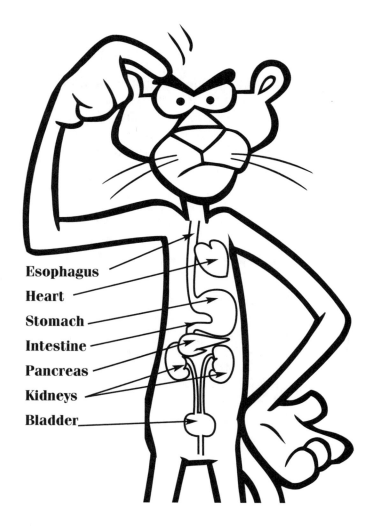

Esophagus

Heart

Stomach

Intestine

Pancreas

Kidneys

Bladder

DEFINITIONS

Bladder: The organ (sac) that collects the water from the kidneys and holds it until it is passed as urine (see the drawing).

Bloodstream: The flow of blood within the blood vessels to and from the different parts of the body.

Cells: The very smallest units of the body. You can only see them with a microscope.

Enzymes: Proteins in liver, muscle and intestine that help make sugar. (There are many enzymes that have other functions.)

Esophagus: The swallowing tube (see the drawing).

External sugar: The sugar taken in from food. Insulin allows the external sugar to pass into the body's cells to be used for energy.

Insulin: The substance (hormone) made by the pancreas that allows sugar to pass into cells.

Internal sugar: The sugar made by the body (or sugar released from stored sugar in the liver). Insulin shuts off the excess production of internal sugar.

Intestine: The part of the GI tract (gut) below the stomach where most sugar (and other foods) are actually absorbed into our blood stream (see the drawing).

Islet cells (pronounced eye-let): The groups of cells within the pancreas that make insulin.

Kidneys: The two organs in the body that remove waste products and water from the bloodstream and make urine (see the drawing).

Pancreas: The organ where insulin is normally made (see the drawing). People who have type 1 diabetes cannot make enough insulin and are thus insulin-dependent.

Stomach: Where the food is collected and processed after it is swallowed (see the drawing).

Type 1 diabetes: (Also called juvenile diabetes or childhood diabetes or insulin-dependent diabetes mellitus [IDDM].) The condition that results when the body cannot make enough insulin. The most common type of diabetes in persons under age 40. Insulin must be taken by shots; pills do not help. Islet cell antibodies are usually present in the blood. This type of diabetes is discussed in detail in Chapter 3.

Type 2 diabetes: (Also called adult-onset diabetes or non-insulin-dependent diabetes mellitus [NIDDM].) The condition in which the body still makes insulin but is unable to use it. This is the most common type in adults over age 40. It also occurs in overweight preteens and teenagers. Pills may be able to stimulate the pancreas to make more insulin or make the person more sensitive to insulin. The pills are not insulin. People with type 2 diabetes do not have islet cell antibodies. This type of diabetes is discussed in detail in Chapter 4.

Urine: Water with wastes passed from the body by the kidneys.

QUESTIONS (Q) AND ANSWERS (A) FROM NEWSNOTES

Q. When our son was diagnosed with diabetes, he had been vomiting and had kept no food down for over 24 hours. Yet his blood sugar was over 1,000 mg/dl (55 mmol/L). How could that be when he had not eaten any sugar?

A. Insulin has several actions in the body. One is to allow all (or any) sugar to pass from the blood stream into cells where it can be burned for energy. A second function, which is emphasized in this Pink Panther book, is to shut off the body's own production of sugar (primarily from the liver). When insulin is not available, as in your son at the time of diagnosis, the liver production of sugar can be enormous. This likely accounted for the high blood sugar even though no sugar had been eaten.

Chapter 3

TOPIC:
🐾 Diabetes Disease Process (type 1)

TEACHING OBJECTIVE:

1. Design an educational plan with the family that will ensure an adequate diabetes knowledge foundation on which to build.

LEARNING OBJECTIVES:

Learners (parents, child, relative or self) will be able to:

1. List two causes each for type 1 and type 2 diabetes.

2. State one major difference in the treatment of type 1 and 2 diabetes.

Chapter 3

TYPE 1 DIABETES

Type 1 diabetes is one of the most common chronic disorders of childhood. It is also the most common form of diabetes to occur in people under age 40. Type 2 is the most common form after age 40. The list of famous people: sport stars, politicians, movie stars and artists, who have type 1 or type 2 diabetes is long. Following diagnosis, children frequently discover classmates who also have diabetes. Their looks, personalities and activities are no different from those of anyone else.

The rate of development of type 2 diabetes has increased in recent years in children age 10 and above. There is also a worldwide increase in type 2 diabetes in adults. This is due primarily to eating high calorie and high fat foods as well as a lack of exercise resulting in excess weight gain.

CAUSES

We know that diabetes is not catching like a cold. We also know that type 1 diabetes isn't caused from eating too much sugar.

Three risk factors seem to be important in determining why a person develops type 1 diabetes:

1. inherited (or genetic) factors

2. self-allergy (autoimmunity)

3. environmental damage (e.g., from a virus or chemical)

1. Inheritance (genetic)

The first important reason seems to be an inherited or genetic factor, such as the way a person inherits the color of the eyes from a mother, father or other relative.

Facts about inheritance:

- People with type 1 diabetes are more likely to

have inherited certain cell types (called **HLA types**). Those who don't have diabetes are less likely to have these HLA types.

- The HLA types are determined by using ***white blood cells*** (WBCs) for typing. Blood types (A, B, AB and O) are determined using red blood cells.

- Nearly all people with type 1 diabetes have an HLA type **DR3** or **DR4**.

- Fifty-three percent of people with type 1 diabetes have one DR3 and one DR4, **with one of these coming from each parent.**

- Only 3% of people without diabetes have this DR3/DR4 combination. This combination makes a person more likely to develop diabetes. This is especially true when they have a relative with diabetes.

- Over half of the families (up to 90% in one study) have no close relative with type 1 diabetes. Perhaps a family has a DR3 or a DR4 gene, but no family member has ever married into a family with the other DR gene. If a family member with a DR3 gene then marries into another family carrying the DR4 gene, the child may end up with the DR3/DR4 combination. They may then be at high risk for diabetes.

- It is now known that there are also different genes that help to protect a person from developing diabetes.

- Children from a family who have a child with diabetes have a greater chance of developing it than without a family history. A brother or sister of a child with diabetes has about a 1 in 20 (5%) chance of developing diabetes.

- The cause is not completely due to heredity. We know this from studies of identical twins. When one identical twin gets diabetes, only in half of the cases does the other twin also develop the disease. If it were entirely due to heredity, both twins would always develop it. We don't completely understand the inheritance factors. We do believe that <u>both</u> mother and father transmit the tendency to develop diabetes to their child.

2. Self-allergy (autoimmunity)

The second cause that seems to be important in type 1 diabetes is self-allergy (or autoimmunity). Normally, our immune systems protect our bodies from disease.

Facts about self-allergy (autoimmunity):

- In the case of type 1 diabetes and other autoimmune diseases such as lupus, arthritis and multiple sclerosis, the immune system turns against a body part.

- There can be evidence of this allergic reaction found in the blood. The allergic reaction is against the cells in the pancreas (islet cells) that make insulin. Most Anglo and about half of Hispanic and African-American children show this allergy when they develop diabetes. The evidence in the blood is called an antibody or, more specifically, an **"islet cell antibody" (ICA).** We now know that some people can have this antibody present in their blood for many years before they need insulin.

- Other diabetes antibodies called biochemical antibodies ("GAD" antibodies, insulin autoantibodies [IAA] and ICA 512 antibodies) can now be measured. They are easier to measure and have also been found in the blood of people who are developing diabetes.

- Identifying these antibodies in the blood has made it possible to screen people who are at risk to develop diabetes. This screening has lead to research trials (see Chapter 28) which will try to prevent diabetes. We believe it is important for brothers, sisters and other relatives to have this screening.

- The antibodies gradually disappear from the blood after the onset of type 1 diabetes. Within one year, many people will no longer have them.

- People who develop type 2 diabetes (previously called adult-onset) do not have these antibodies, even if they are under age 21 at onset.

MICROSCOPIC PHOTOGRAPH OF PANCREATIC ISLET:

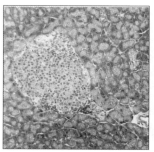 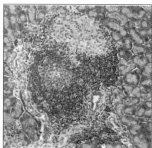

The photo on the left shows a normal islet (center) surrounded by other pancreatic tissue. This other tissue is responsible for making digestive enzymes. The photo on the right is from a diabetic animal. The white blood cells (WBCs) have invaded and destroyed the islet.

3. Environmental (virus or chemical)

A third factor may also be important. This environmental factor may either be a virus or something in the food we eat. This factor may be the bridge between the genetic (inherited) part and the allergic reaction.

An example of the sequence of events might be:

- A person *inherits* the tendency for diabetes.

- This tendency might allow a virus or a part of a protein (peptide) to injure the islet cells.

- Part of the damaged islet cell may then be released into the blood.

- The body would then make islet cell antibodies (an allergic or autoimmune reaction).

- The damage can attract white blood cells (WBCs) to the area of the islet. These now active WBCs produce chemicals, which further injure the other islet cells.

- Anything that activates the WBCs in the future (viral infections, certain foods, stress, etc.) may result in more of the islet cells being destroyed.

We now know that most people who get diabetes don't just suddenly develop it. They have been in the process of developing it for many years, sometimes even from birth. Most likely many viral infections and other factors result in damage and destroy a few more islet cells. As more and more islet cells are destroyed the person moves closer to having diabetes (see Figure below where diabetes is represented by the broken line).

TYPE 2 (ADULT-ONSET) DIABETES: Chapter 4 explains type 2 diabetes in more depth.

The three main risk factors for type 2 diabetes are:

1. **Overweight**

2. **Insulin insensitivity**

3. **Inheritance (genetics)**

1. **Overweight (obesity):** is an important risk factor for type 2 (adult-onset) diabetes. It is not a cause of type 1 diabetes.

2. **Insulin insensitivity:** Insulin does not seem to work normally in the person with type 2 diabetes. Initially it can still be made in normal or above-normal amounts. This is different from type 1 diabetes, where insulin cannot be made at all or is made in small amounts. Later, people with type 2 diabetes may also have reduced insulin production. They will then need insulin shots.

3. **Inheritance (genetics):** Type 2 diabetes also has a strong inherited (genetic) cause. People with type 2 diabetes do not have the same association with the HLA genes as do people with type 1 diabetes. They also do not make islet cell antibodies. The causes of the two types of diabetes seem to be completely different.

Figure

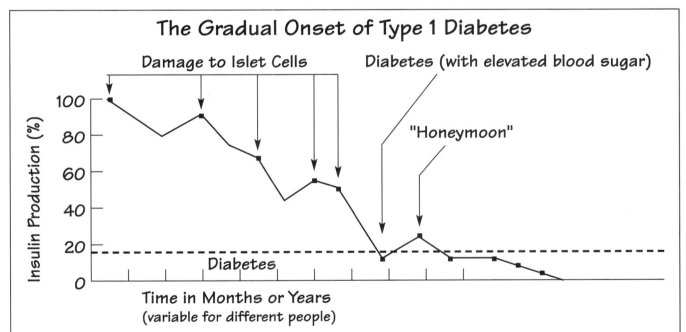

The Gradual Onset of Type 1 Diabetes

Damage to Islet Cells   Diabetes (with elevated blood sugar)

"Honeymoon"

Insulin Production (%)

100, 80, 60, 40, 20, 0

Diabetes

Time in Months or Years
(variable for different people)

It is now believed that diabetes develops gradually, over many months or many years. It does not just come on suddenly in the week or two before the elevated blood sugars. Many insults (represented by the arrows in this Figure) likely result in further damage until the diagnosis of diabetes is made. The insults may include viral infections, stress, chemicals in the diet, or other agents. These agents may work by "activating" white blood cells in the islets to make toxic chemicals that cause injury to the insulin-producing cells (beta cells). However, a "genetic-predisposition" (inherited factors) must be present for the process to start.

DEFINITIONS

Allergy: A special reaction of the body to some material. This is similar to what happens if you are allergic to something that makes you sneeze.

Antibody: The material we measure in the blood if someone has an allergy (example: milk antibodies might be present if someone has a milk allergy).

Autoimmunity (self-allergy): The process of forming an allergic reaction against one's own tissues. This happens in diseases such as lupus and arthritis. People with type 1 diabetes make an antibody against their islet cells (where the insulin is made).

Genetic (inherited): Features, such as eye color, that are passed from both parents to children.

HLA type: The way to group cell types just as red blood cells are grouped into A, B, AB and O blood types. HLA stands for Human Leukocyte Antigen. A leukocyte is another name for a white blood cell. The white blood cell is the type of cell used in HLA typing.

Identical twins: Twins that come from the same egg. All their features (genetics) are exactly alike.

Islet cell (pronounced eye-let): The groups of cells within the pancreas that make insulin.

Islet cell antibody: The material we measure in the person's blood to show that they have had an allergy against the cells in the pancreas (the islet cells) that make insulin.

QUESTIONS (Q) AND ANSWERS (A) FROM NEWSNOTES

Q. My daughter was in a car accident the week before the onset of her diabetes. Could that have caused the diabetes?

A. It is now accepted that diabetes comes on gradually over many months or many years. It is not just brought about by one event. After initial damage occurs to the islets in the pancreas (where insulin is made), islet cell antibodies may be positive, indicating that some damage has occurred. We have followed many people with positive islet cell antibodies. Some have not needed to start insulin treatment for as long as ten years.

After the initial damage, many factors may cause activation of white blood cells (WBCs) in the islets. These factors may include some viral infections, content of the diet or even stress. When the WBCs in the islets are activated by these factors, they produce toxic chemicals that destroy a few more islets each time. Gradually, a person gets closer to having full-blown diabetes. Thus, the stress of the automobile accident may have been the final precipitating event, but it was most likely only one of several insults over many years.

Chapter 4

TOPICS:

- Diabetes Disease Process (type 2)
- Medications (type 2 diabetes)
- Nutritional Management (also see Chapters 11 and 12)
- Physical Activity (also see Chapter 13)
- Monitoring (checking blood sugars and ketones; also see Chapters 5 and 7)
- Prevent, Detect and Treat Acute and Chronic Complications (also see Chapter 22)

TEACHING OBJECTIVES:

1. Present the basic concepts of type 2 diabetes and management.

2. Introduce the medications to be used including dosing and side effects.

3. Assess current dietary habits and develop an individual nutritional management program.

4. Assess current activity level and develop an individualized exercise program.

5. Discuss monitoring blood sugars, ketones and laboratory tests.

6. Introduce acute and chronic complications.

WITH SPECIAL THANKS FOR THE SUGGESTIONS OF:

- Lawrence Dolan, MD
- Georgeanna Klingensmith, MD
- Philip Zeitler, MD

LEARNING OBJECTIVES:

Learners (parents, child, relative or self) will be able to:

1. State two differences between type 1 and type 2 diabetes.

2. Identify the name, dose, schedule and side effects of medication(s) to be used.

3. Identify the individualized nutritional management program (see Chapter 12).

4. Work with healthcare provider to develop an exercise program (see Chapter 13).

5. Identify time frames for monitoring blood sugars, ketones and laboratory tests.

6. List two possible acute and two possible chronic complications.

Chapter 4

TYPE 2 DIABETES (ADULT-ONSET DIABETES, NON-INSULIN DEPENDENT DIABETES [NIDDM])

This is the most common type of diabetes in adults over age 40. It is also becoming more common in overweight pre-teens and teenagers. The rates per 1,000 people are higher in people of Hispanic, Native-American or African-American heritages. It also occurs in all Anglo populations and is often referred to as a "disease of lifestyles." Past ancestors, by necessity, were very active for thousands of years. We now live in a world of automobile travel, television, computers and video games. The main exercise many people now receive is walking from their car or bus into work or school. Schools also no longer have the resources to offer daily exercise. In addition, high calorie fast foods have become a major part of our meals and snacks. The result has been a great increase in the incidence of type 2 diabetes in the U.S. and worldwide. Data from Cincinnati, OH suggests the incidence in 10 to 19 year olds increased from 0.7/100,000 in 1982 to 7.2/100,000 in 1994 (10 fold increase).

DIFFERENCES BETWEEN TYPE 2 AND TYPE 1 DIABETES

Type 2 diabetes

☙ Normal or increased amounts of insulin are made initially. (In type 1 the insulin levels are low or absent.) Despite the normal or increased amount of insulin being present, the insulin cannot act normally to keep blood sugars in the desired range. Later the amount of insulin made may also decrease in type 2 diabetes. This happens as the pancreas fails to keep up with the body's higher demands for insulin. The person still has type 2 diabetes. The two types of diabetes are very different. One type does not turn into the other type.

☙ Islet cell antibodies (ICA) **ARE NOT PRESENT**. (In type 1, ICA are usually present.)

Usually it is fairly easy to decide which type of diabetes a person may have by doing these blood tests. Measurement of insulin and C-peptide, an insulin related protein, as well as ICA may help in deciding between type 1 and type 2 diabetes. However, sometimes it takes following the person with diabetes for a while to clarify the diabetes type.

CAUSES

☙ Inheritance (genetics)

Type 2 diabetes has a stronger inherited risk than type 1. In most cases, a parent and/or grandparent will also have the disease. In the case of identical twins, if one twin develops type 2 diabetes, the other twin has an 80% chance of also developing the disease. (In type 1, an identical twin has a 35-50% chance.) There are some Native-American tribes in which half of the adults have type 2 diabetes.

In type 2 diabetes, there are different inherited (genetic) defects, which vary between families. There is not just one common defect in all families. It is also **NOT** inherited in relation to the HLA system as is type 1 diabetes (Chapter 3).

☙ Lifestyle

As mentioned above, most (not all) people with type 2 diabetes are overweight and don't have very active lives. About 20% of adults presenting with type 2 diabetes are not overweight. This group often has an inherited (genetic) defect which causes the insulin resistance. The corresponding number for adolescents is unknown.

Insulin resistance usually occurs with excess weight and decreased physical fitness. Insulin resistance means the insulin doesn't work to allow sugar to pass into the cells as it would normally (Chapter 2). In some cases this happens along with a darkening of the skin. The most common areas for this darkening are the neck, armpits and/or the elbows (called acanthosis nigricans). The excess weight and skin color changes are associated with insulin resistance. By losing weight (eating fewer calories and exercising more), the sensitivity to insulin may again return. The dark skin coloring may also lessen or disappear. Over time insulin production for people with type 2 may decrease low enough to make insulin injections necessary. A long-acting insulin given at bedtime such as Humulin N®, Novolin N® or Lantus® may work to bring the a.m. fasting blood sugar into range.

DIAGNOSIS

People with type 2 diabetes can go several years with high blood sugar levels without signs of diabetes. Then, with an illness or stress and less effective function of the pancreas, symptoms begin.

How it can be discovered

✔ Sometimes sugar is found in the urine during a routine check-up. There may not be any signs or symptoms.

✔ The increased urination and drinking of fluids may be absent or mild with type 2 diabetes.

✔ Weight loss can occur (though variable).

✔ Increasing fatigue may be present.

✔ During an illness, blood sugar levels (and/or ketones) may become very high. The illness may be a deep skin infection (abscess) or a yeast infection.

✔ Numbness/tingling in the toes: damage to the nerves caused by high blood sugars over time (neuropathy: Chapter 22).

✔ Trouble with vision (blurry/frequent change of glasses) due to swelling of the lens of the eye from high blood sugars.

Specific testing for diabetes:

- if a blood sugar value is very high (e.g., > 200 mg/dl or 11.1 mmol/L), the glucose tolerance test (Table 1) may not be needed.

- the hemoglobin A_{1c} (HbA$_{1c}$) test is elevated (Chapter 14)

- oral glucose tolerance test (OGTT): a fasting test (no food for 10 hours). After a fasting blood sugar is drawn, the person then drinks a high sugar drink (Glucola®) within 5 minutes. Blood samples are drawn every 30 minutes for two hours. See Table 1 for blood sugar values.

- high (or normal) insulin or C-peptide levels (C-peptide: a side product when insulin is made in the body; see Definitions in the back of this chapter). These tests are sometimes better done after the body's metabolism has returned to normal (2-3 weeks after diagnosis).

OGTT BLOOD SUGAR VALUES (mg/dl and mmol/L)

	NORMAL		BORDERLINE		DIABETIC	
	mg/dl	mmol/L	mg/dl	mmol/L	mg/dl	mmol/L
FASTING	< 126	6.1	110-126	6.1-7.0	> 126	>7.0
TWO HOURS AFTER DRINKING THE GLUCOLA	< 140	7.8	140-200	7.8-11.1	> 200	>11.1

TREATMENT

The treatment of type 2 diabetes is initially like that for type 1. The family must learn as much as they can, as diabetes is a family disease. (Education is stressed in Chapter 1.) Blood sugar checking is essential (Chapter 7).

The family must initially learn to give insulin shots (Chapters 8 and 9) if:

- ketones are present (Chapter 5)

- symptoms of urination, thirst and weight loss are severe

- or if there is uncertainty about the diabetes type

Lifestyle Changes

Dietary treatment is **very important** (Chapters 11 and 12). Lowering calorie, fat and carbohydrate intake is essential. Food management is discussed in detail in Chapter 12. The family **must** work with a knowledgeable dietitian. Exercise is **equally important** (Chapter 13). The goal should be at least 30 minutes of moderate exercise every day.

Insulin Shots

Most people with type 2 diabetes who present with ketones will initially be treated with insulin shots. Some who are able to lose 10 or more pounds can sometimes come off insulin shots and try oral medicines (Table 2). However, they may need to return to insulin shots in later years.

It is important to remember that during times of illness, especially if ketones return, insulin shots may again have to be given. Some people with type 2 diabetes will always need to take insulin shots. Others may be able to take oral medication for the first few years. Eventually, those taking the oral medication may need to take insulin shots. Which medication is used and for how long depends upon blood sugar levels and success with changing the lifestyle.

Oral Tablets

It is important to remember that the oral tablets are **NOT** insulin. If taken orally, insulin would be destroyed by the stomach acid. The tablets are medicines that make the person more sensitive to their own insulin. Some of the medicines also make the pancreas release extra amounts of insulin. (Table 2 lists some of these medications.)

1. Metformin (glucophage): the medication we most frequently try first. In addition to helping to control blood sugar levels, it may help with weight loss.

- Main side effect: upset stomach, diarrhea, vomiting, bloating.

  ** Important:
  Lactic Acidosis is a rare side effect which can occur if Metformin is not stopped when a person has the stomach flu or a severe illness. It can also happen during an x-ray procedure using dyes, and during episodes of vomiting, diarrhea, pneumonia or with lung diseases.

  ◆ Dosing
- start low with 500 mg (0.5 gm) once daily

- after 1 week, try this dose twice a day (at breakfast and dinner)

- after the 3rd week, if needed, try 2 tablets (1 gm) in the morning and 1 tablet (0.5 gm) at dinner

- the 4th week, if needed and stomach upset isn't a problem, try 2 tablets (1 gm) both at breakfast and dinner

- Some people can use the long-acting form. This can be taken in the morning with the dose gradually increased. As noted above, it is important to know a person is taking Metformin if they become ill. Metformin needs to be stopped during times of severe illness or with vomiting or diarrhea. (It is often best to take insulin shots during an illness. Consult your doctor or nurse.) There have been cases of lactic acidosis in people receiving Metformin who became seriously ill.

2. Other Oral Medications

Different physicians have their medication of first choice. The sulfonylureas (Table 2) have been around the longest. They act to make the person's own pancreas secrete more insulin. Low blood sugar (Chapter 6) is a possible side effect.

Two of the newest agents are ACTOS® and Avandia® (Table 2). They belong to a class called thiazolidinediones and act to increase the body's sensitivity to insulin. Their most dangerous side effect is liver toxicity. Liver function tests should be done before starting either medication and then every 2-3 months.

Monitoring for Complications

Acute: Low blood sugars are less frequent with type 2 than with type 1 diabetes. However, they can occur. They are most frequently associated with the sulfonylurea and meglitinide medications (Table 2). Treatment is explained in Chapter 6.

Ketone production is also less frequent with type 2 than with type 1 diabetes. However, they can occur during times of illness. If a person is receiving oral medications, they usually need to return to using insulin shots when ketones are present.

Chronic: Blood pressure elevations and/or blood lipid abnormalities (high cholesterol and/or triglyceride; Chapter 11) must be checked regularly. Treatment should be considered for any abnormalities.

Type 2 diabetes can be present for years prior to diagnosis. It is recommended that eye and kidney testing be done initially and then annually. This is explained in Chapter 22, but should include annual eye exams by an eye-specialist. It should include annual urinary microalbumin tests for the kidneys (Chapter 22). Evidence has shown that, as with type 1 diabetes, good control of blood sugars (as monitored by the HbA_{1c} test every 3 months – Chapter 14), will help to prevent eye and/or kidney damage.

COMMONLY USED ORAL HYPOGLYCEMIC MEDICATIONS

Name	Action	Initial Dose	Maximum Dose	Side-effects
1. Metformin (Glucophage)	Reduces liver secretion of glucose; may help reduce weight	0.5–1 gm	2 gms	Stomach upset; acidosis with illness
Metformin XR (Glucophage XR)	a long acting form of Metformin	(dose same as above)		

2. Sulfonylureas stimulate the pancreas to make more insulin.

Name	Action	Initial Dose	Maximum Dose	Side-effects
a. Chlorpropamide (Diabinese)		125-250 mg	500 mg	Low blood sugar, dizziness
b. Glyburide (Diabeta) (Micronase)		2.5-5.0 mg	20 mg	Skin rashes, headache and stomach upset
c. Glypizide (Glucotrol)		5 mg	40 mg	" "
d. Glucotrol XL (extended release)		5 mg	20 mg	" "

(Others include Amaryl, Glynase, Orinase and Tolinase.)   "   "

3. Thiazolindinediones: help muscle cells respond to insulin better.   **For Both:**

Name	Action	Initial Dose	Maximum Dose	Side-effects
a. Pioglitazone (ACTOS)		15 mg	45 mg	Stuffy nose, headache, liver problems, weight gain
b. Rosiglitazone (Avandia)		4 mg	8 mg	

Must follow liver function tests initially and every 2-3 months.

4. Meglitinides: stimulate early insulin release with meals.

Name	Action	Initial Dose	Maximum Dose	Side-effects
a. Nateglinide (Starlix)		60 mg (30 minutes before each meal)	120 mg	Diarrhea, nausea, low blood sugar
b. Repaglinide (Prandin)		0.5 mg (30 minutes before each meal)	16 mg	Stuffy nose, low blood sugar, chest pain

Successful treatment of type 2 diabetes may require the use of combinations of agents. Some examples are:
a. A sulfonylurea and glucophage (e.g., Glucovance: combination of glyburide and glucophage)
b. Glucophage and a thiazolidinedione
c. A sulfonylurea and a thiazolidinedione
d. A meglitinide and glucophage
e. Insulin and any of the oral agents

NOTE: *There are many other good oral agents which are preferred by some physicians, but were not included on this listing due to space.*

DEFINITIONS

C-peptide: An insulin-related protein. It is split off from proinsulin when the active insulin is formed.

Lifestyle changes: In this chapter, this means changing a sedentary (little exercise) lifestyle and decreasing high calorie, high fat, high carbohydrate food intake (e.g., fast foods). The changes must include at least 30 minutes of moderate exercise each day. They must also include a reduction in calorie, fat and carbohydrate intake.

Oral glucose tolerance test (OGTT): Blood sugar levels before and after drinking a high sugar drink. It is considered the "gold standard" test to diagnose diabetes when the diagnosis is uncertain. (Normal values are in Table 1 in this chapter.)

Oral hypoglycemic agents: These are pills which help to make the body more sensitive to insulin or to release more insulin. However, they are **NOT** insulin. Table 2 gives the names of a few of these agents.

Type 2 diabetes: (Also called adult-onset diabetes or non-insulin-dependent diabetes [NIDDM]). The condition in which the body still makes insulin, but is unable to use it. This is the most common type in adults over age 40. It is also becoming increasingly common in youth, particularly in those who are overweight.

Exercise is important.

Chapter 5

TOPIC:
- ❣ Monitoring (ketones)
- ❣ Prevention, Detection and Treatment of Acute Complications (How and when to test for ketones)

TEACHING OBJECTIVES:

1. Discuss when ketone measurement should be done.

2. Introduce method to be used for measuring ketones.

3. Present the appropriate time to call the healthcare provider.

LEARNING OBJECTIVES:

Learners (parents, child, relative or self) will be able to:

1. Define ketones and the importance of ketone testing.

2. Identify and demonstrate when and how to test for ketones.

3. State the appropriate time to call the healthcare provider.

Chapter KETONE TESTING

KETONES

Ketones are chemicals which appear in the urine and blood when body fat is used for energy. Ketones are a side product of fat breakdown (see Chapter 15).

Body fat is used for energy...

• when there is not enough insulin to allow sugar to be burned as energy in the body.

• when not enough food has been eaten to provide energy.

Ketone testing is **VERY** important. A method of testing for ketones must be kept in the home (and taken on trips) at all times.

We usually teach families how to do the urine ketone test on the first day of diagnosis of diabetes. Frequent urine ketone tests are important in the first few days after diagnosis to determine if enough insulin is being given to turn off ketone production. **Turning off ketone production is the first goal in the treatment of newly diagnosed diabetes**

managed in the outpatient setting. This usually takes one or two days after starting insulin.

The second goal is to lower blood sugar levels (done primarily by turning off internal sugar production in the liver). This usually takes one or two weeks after starting insulin. Giving insulin helps to accomplish both goals.

REASONS FOR TESTING FOR KETONES

It is important to test for urine or blood ketones because they can build up in the body. This can result in one of the two emergencies of diabetes, acidosis or ketoacidosis (see Chapter 15). In the past, it was only possible to test for urine ketones. The Precision Xtra™ meter is now available to do a home fingerstick test for blood ketones. The diabetes care provider should be notified when the urine ketone test shows moderate or large ketones or if the blood ketone test is above 0.6 mmol/L.

COMPARISON OF BLOOD BETA KETONE AND URINE KETONE READINGS *

Blood (mmol/L)		Urine
< 0.6		negative
0.6 to 1.5		small to moderate
1.6 to 3.0		usually large
≥ 3.0	↔ **go directly to the E.R.** ↔	**very large**

* The blood and urine ketone values do NOT always agree. The urine may have been in the bladder for several hours. The blood levels tell what the ketones are at the moment the test is done. (Also read the second Q and A at the back of this chapter.)

The healthcare provider should be called for all values > 0.6 mmol/L in the blood or if the urine ketones are moderate or large.

Usually extra insulin is taken to help make the ketones go away. If the ketones are not detected early, they will build up in the body and ketoacidosis will result. This is particularly true during illnesses. Early detection of ketones and the treatment with extra Humalog or NovoLog® insulin can help prevent hospitalizations for ketoacidosis (see Chapter 15). Hospitalizations for ketoacidosis are still listed as the number one reason for hospitalizing children in the U.S. with known diabetes. **It is our belief that these hospitalizations for ketoacidosis are completely preventable. To accomplish this, the ketone testing must be done, the diabetes care provider called when indicated, and extra shots of insulin given.**

WHEN TO TEST FOR KETONES

Ketones must always be checked if the blood sugar is high (above 240 mg/dl [13.3 mmol/L] fasting, or above 300 mg/dl [16.6 mmol/L]) during the day. They must also be checked ANYTIME THE PERSON FEELS SICK OR NAUSEATED (especially if he/she vomits, even once). **If the person is sick, ketones can be present even when the sugar is not high.**

CALL YOUR DIABETES CARE PROVIDER NIGHT OR DAY IF MODERATE OR LARGE URINE KETONES ARE PRESENT OR FOR BLOOD KETONES ≥ 0.6 MMOL/L. TELL THE PERSON ANSWERING THE PHONE THAT THE CALL IS URGENT.

People who have been recently diagnosed with diabetes usually need to check ketones twice daily (or more often if they are positive). After the first few days, if all ketone checks have been negative, daily testing of ketones is not needed.

People who take only one insulin injection per day should do routine morning blood or urine ketone tests to see if their insulin is lasting a full 24 hours. Morning ketones will usually be present if an insulin injection is needed in the evening.

If the morning blood sugars vary between very high and very low values, check morning ketones. This will be discussed in more detail in Chapter 6, Low Blood Sugar. Morning ketones can be a sign of a low blood sugar during the night followed by rebounding or bouncing back to a normal or high level by morning.

WHAT TEST MATERIALS ARE AVAILABLE?

Testing for Urine Ketones

The two strips that are most frequently used in checking for urine ketones are the Ketostix® and the Chemstrip K®. If the child is not yet toilet trained, it is usually best to press a test strip (see section on Ketostix) firmly against the wet diaper. It is also possible to place cotton balls in the diaper where the diaper is wettest. Drops of urine can then be squeezed from the cotton ball.

❧ Ketostix

The Ketostix (or Ketodiastix® with the sugar check) is reliable for urine testing IF THEY ARE CAREFULLY TIMED WITH A SECOND HAND ON A CLOCK. The Ketostix are cheaper than the Ketodiastix and it is not necessary to do the urine sugar, as a blood sugar is more accurate. There is a place on the side of the bottle to write the date the bottle is opened. The strips are then good for six months. Individually foil-wrapped Ketostix will not expire for two or three years. This gets around the problem of having to throw any unused Ketostix away once the bottle has been open for six months. Ask your pharmacist to order them if he/she does not have them. The Bayer product number for ordering is 2640 (20 foiled strips).

The following procedure must be followed exactly:

1. Completely cover the colored square on the end of the strip by dipping into FRESH urine. Then immediately remove the strip from the urine. We prefer that the urine be collected in a cup and that the strip then be timed and read by two people. This prevents errors due to color blindness or psychologic factors. A supply of small paper cups might be kept in the bathroom medicine cabinet for this purpose.

2. Gently tap the edge of the strip against the side of the urine container to remove excess urine.

3. Compare the test area closely with the corresponding color chart. The timing is **very** important. READ KETONES AT **EXACTLY** 15 SECONDS AFTER DIPPING THE STRIP. HOLD THE STRIP CLOSE TO THE COLOR BLOCK AND MATCH THE COLORS CAREFULLY. These tests must always be timed with the second hand of a clock. Counting is NOT accurate enough.

4. Immediately record the result of the ketone test as negative, small (15), moderate (40), large (80) or large-large (160) in the notebook so that it is not forgotten.

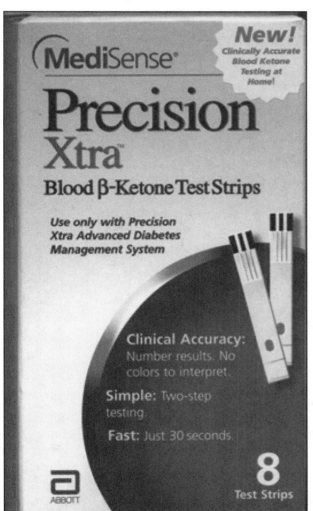

Chemstrip K

The Chemstrip K (or Chemstrip uGK® with the urine glucose check) is the second method that can be used to check for urine ketones. The only difference from the instructions for the Ketostix is in the timing. Chemstrip K must be timed for one minute. Read as negative, small, moderate or large at exactly one minute.

Testing for Blood Ketones

The Precision Xtra™ Meter is the only meter which allows testing for blood beta ketones. Four blood ketone strips come in each box of blood sugar strips. They can also be purchased in boxes of 8 foil wrapped beta ketone strips (see scan of box).

Steps:

1. The red control strip must first be inserted to calibrate for beta ketones. Make sure the calibration code on the red calibration strip matches the code on the ketone strip.

2. Open a strip and place it into the meter with the 3 black bars facing up.

Push the strip completely into the test port of the meter.

3. After washing and drying the hand, lance the finger.

4. Place a drop of blood into the purple hole on the strip.

5. The result is then displayed on the meter in 30 seconds.

We suggest interpreting the readings as follows (in mmol/L):

< 0.6   = normal

0.6 – 1.5   = call a healthcare provider

> 1.5   = serious and call healthcare provider and state the call is urgent

> 3.0   = **Go directly to the Emergency Room. Have someone take you!**

DEFINITIONS

Chemstrip K: Strips for measuring urine ketones (acetone). They are also available as Chemstrip uGK (for urine ketones and sugar).

Ketoacidosis (Acidosis): What happens in the body when not enough insulin is available. Blood sugar is usually high at this time. Moderate or large ketones are present in the urine as well as in the body. This is the subject of Chapter 15.

Ketostix: Strips for measuring urine ketones (acetone). They are also available as Ketodiastix (for urine ketones and sugar).

Ketones (Acetone): The chemicals that appear when not enough insulin is present and fat is broken down. Acetest tablets, Ketostix or Chemstrip K measure urine ketones. The Precision Xtra measures blood beta ketones.

mg/dl: Milligrams of material in a measured amount (100cc). Blood sugar (glucose) levels are expressed in these terms in the U.S., but they are usually expressed as mmol/L in Europe. It is possible to convert mg/dl to mmol/L by dividing by 18 (or multiplying by 0.0555). The opposite is done to go from mmol/L to mg/dl. A conversion table for glucose values is in the Appendix.

mmol/L: Method of measuring the amount of a material (sugar or ketones) in the blood. This method is usually used in Europe. See mg/dl for conversion factor for sugar (and the table in the Appendix).

Void: Passage of urine.

QUESTIONS (Q) AND ANSWERS (A) FROM NEWSNOTES

Q. Why are you now advising that we buy the foil-wrapped rather than the bottles of Ketostix for measuring urine ketones?

A. You will note that on the side of a bottle of Ketostix, you are asked to write in the date the bottle is opened and to dispose of the bottle six months later. Sometimes people forget to do this. Once the bottle is open, moisture and other factors result in a gradual loss of sensitivity. Often, a flu episode will start in the middle of the night. As one looks at the date on the side of the bottle, if the strips have been open longer than six months, they are unreliable. Similarly if a date was not recorded, it is usually necessary to assume that the strips have been open more than six months. They then must be discarded. Then one has to go looking for an open pharmacy in the middle of the night. The foil-wrapped Ketostix avoids this problem. They may have an expiration date two years away. The foil wrapped Ketostix can be divided and placed with a color copy of the chart at school or daycare.

Ketone measurements are **VERY** important. A method for ketone testing **MUST** be in the home at all times. It is **ONLY** by measuring the ketones that one can know if moderate or large urine ketones or high levels of ketones in the blood are present. If present, the physician must be called immediately. This may prevent a life-threatening episode of ketoacidosis (Chapter 15).

Q. We recently obtained a Precision Xtra meter that measures the blood ketones as well as the blood sugars. How do the blood ketone measurements compare with the urine ketone measurements? When do we need to call our doctor or nurse?

A. Like a blood sugar measured on a meter, the blood (serum) ketone value gives the ketone level at the time the test is done. The urine ketone measurement, like a urine sugar, can be hours behind. (The urine collected is since the last void.) The blood ketone value has the potential to be better than the urine ketone measurement.

I am not aware of studies comparing the serum ketone (primarily beta-hydroxy butyric acid) with the urine ketone (primarily acetoacetic acid) levels. The company notes that levels below 0.6 (all values are in mmol/L) are considered "normal" levels, in the 0.6 to 1.5 range are considered "moderate" and levels from 1.6 to 3.0 are considered "high" (probably similar to "large" urine ketones). Levels above 3.0 should be considered dangerous with a need to head to a hospital (DKA – Chapter 15). It is most beneficial when sequential blood levels are done throughout the day so that the family can know if values are increasing, staying the same or decreasing. The test is particularly helpful when a person cannot void frequently due to dehydration, or when a person does void for the first time in a number of hours, so that it is not possible to tell if the urine ketone measurement represents the current level. It would be wise to routinely call the diabetes care provider when values above 0.6 are obtained. As an added note, please remember to check the calibration code when you use a new batch of the ketone strips. The red calibration stick needs to match the code on the ketone strip you are using.

Chapter 6

TOPIC:
☙ Prevention, Detection, and Treatment of Acute Complications (hypoglycemia – low blood sugar)

TEACHING OBJECTIVES:

1. Present the symptoms, causes, and treatment of mild, moderate and severe hypoglycemia.

2. Identify the appropriate time to contact the healthcare provider.

LEARNING OBJECTIVES:

Learners (parents, child, relative or self) will be able to:

1. Define mild, moderate and severe low sugar symptoms, causes and treatment.

2. State the appropriate time to contact a healthcare provider.

Chapter 6

LOW BLOOD SUGAR (HYPOGLYCEMIA OR INSULIN REACTION)

HYPOGLYCEMIA (LOW BLOOD SUGAR)

There are two emergency problems in blood sugar control for people with diabetes. The first, discussed in this chapter, is low blood sugar or hypoglycemia. (The second, discussed in Chapter 15, is acidosis or ketoacidosis.) Low blood sugar comes on quickly and must be treated by the person, family or friends. Early treatment helps prevent a more severe reaction and possible hospitalization.

Any time a person has received a shot of insulin, or an oral diabetes medicine, there is a chance of a low blood sugar reaction. The family of a person with newly diagnosed diabetes must know the signs and symptoms of hypoglycemia before going home the first night.

A normal blood sugar is 70-120 mg/dl (3.9-6.6 mmol/L). The DCCT (Chapter 14) defined a low blood sugar as a value < 50 mg/dl (<2.7 mmol/L). For purposes of this book, **we define a true low blood sugar as < 60 mg/dl (<3.2 mmol/L)**.

CAUSES OF LOW BLOOD SUGAR

Hypoglycemia (low blood sugar) occurs because the body doesn't have enough sugar to burn for energy. The level of sugar in the blood falls too low. Sometimes it is called an **insulin reaction**, a **reaction** or a **low**.

Frequent causes are listed below:

- Meals and snacks that are late or missed
- Extra exercise that burns more sugar than usual

- An insulin or oral medicine dose that is too high
- An insulin dose peaking at a different time than usual
- Giving a shot into muscle which results in rapid absorption of insulin
- Making a mistake in the drawing up and giving of an insulin dose
- Taking a bath or shower (or hot tub) soon after taking a shot of insulin. (The blood vessels in the skin dilate from the hot water and cause insulin to be rapidly absorbed. It is always wise to wait to take an insulin shot after a shower, bath or hot tub.)

Prevention of low blood sugars (lows) is much wiser than having to treat the lows. When too many lows occur, the stored adrenaline (epinephrine) is drained. When this occurs, the usual symptoms of a low may not occur. In addition, over treatment (eating too much) can cause a high blood sugar and can increase the HbA_{1c} value (Chapter 14). Paying attention to the seven causes of lows listed above will help to decrease the number of low blood sugars.

SYMPTOMS OF LOW BLOOD SUGAR

Usually the body gives a warning when low blood sugar or an insulin reaction is developing. **DIFFERENT PEOPLE GET DIFFERENT WARNINGS.**

These signs are the most common warnings of an insulin reaction:

- **Hunger:** the person may either feel hungry or have an upset stomach (nausea)
- **Shakiness:** the person's hands or body may feel shaky

- **Sweatiness:** the person may sweat more than usual (often a cold sweat)
- **Color:** the face may become pale, gray or red
- **Headache**
- **Confusion:** the person may feel or look spacey, or may appear dazed
- **Drowsiness:** the person may yawn, feel sleepy, or may have trouble thinking clearly; preschoolers frequently get sleepy
- **Behavioral changes:** changes in behavior are quite common; often the person may cry, act intoxicated, or they act angry, or they may feel weak or anxious
- **Double vision:** the person may see double or the pupils of the eyes may get bigger; the eyes may appear glassy; the whites of the eyes may look blood shot
- **Loss of consciousness**
- **Seizure or convulsion:** both loss of consciousness and convulsion occur late in the reaction. They are usually the result of not treating a reaction quickly enough.

With an insulin reaction, you may experience confusion or drowsiness.

The first four initial symptoms are due to the output of the "fight or flight" hormone, adrenaline (epinephrine is another name). Later symptoms are more related to the lack of sugar to the brain. Sugar is the main source of fuel for the brain. If the low sugar continues too long, the brain can be harmed. **It is particularly important to prevent severe low blood sugar in young children.** The brain grows very rapidly in the first four years of life.

NIGHTTIME LOWS

People usually wake up with symptoms (infants may just cry) when lows occur during the night. *The symptoms may be the same as during the daytime although there are sometimes special clues:*

- **Inability to sleep or waking up alert**
- **Waking up sweating**
- **Waking up with a fast heart rate**
- **Waking up with a headache**
- **Waking up feeling foggy-headed or with memory loss**
- **Unusually high blood sugar or positive urine ketones (possible rebounding)**

IF ANY OF THESE DO OCCUR, TEST YOUR BLOOD SUGAR IMMEDIATELY. If low, treat appropriately and call the doctor or nurse the next day. Also think about what was different the previous day (extra exercise, extra insulin, less food, etc.). This will allow planning ahead to prevent a low with a similar cause in the future. Preventing minor lows during the night is very important. More than half of severe lows occur during the night.

RECOGNIZING A LOW BLOOD SUGAR

It is important to recognize a low blood sugar at the earliest possible time. By doing this, the reaction will not progress to a severe reaction. The common symptoms are listed, but they can vary from person to person. The early warning signs of a reaction are due to the release of a hormone called adrenaline. Most people make it when they are excited or scared. Another name for this "fight or flight" (excitatory) hormone is epinephrine. It causes shakiness, sweating, dilated pupils, a rapid heart rate and other symptoms. Some people tend to have only mild reactions and can easily detect symptoms. This seems to be more common in the first few years after diagnosis. Others may have more difficulty detecting symptoms. This seems to happen to people who have had diabetes longer or whose blood sugars run at more normal levels. A term, **"hypoglycemic unawareness"** is sometimes applied to this condition, and it is discussed later in this chapter. Sometimes this is due to less adrenaline being available. In some cases, the lack of symptoms may be due to a slow or less dramatic fall in blood sugar levels, such as from 70 to 50 mg/dl (3.9 to 2.7 mmol/L) rather than from 170 to 50 mg/dl (9.5 to 2.7 mmol/L). Some people are less likely to detect low blood sugar in the morning because the sugar has fallen gradually during the night. Thus, adrenaline release and its symptoms did not occur. Symptoms are more likely to occur with a greater and faster fall of a blood sugar level.

Different children learn to tell if they have low blood sugar at different ages (see Chapter 18). It may be possible to train young children (or older people who have difficulty detecting low blood sugars) to recognize certain signs.

Parents may frequently need to remind a young child …

> Remember how you felt shaky (or whatever the feeling was [one toddler would say, "There's a tiger in my tummy."]) and you came and told me? You did a good job! Remember to tell a grown up if you feel that way again.

Ask the child how they feel when a low is found. This will reinforce their awareness of the symptoms. For very young children, the parent can often tell when the child has low blood sugar by the type of cry or fussiness he/she presents. Young children may be unaware of lows because they are busy playing. It is critical for adults to be aware of the need for snacks. A snack is especially important when a child discontinues naps during the day. It can be compared with an adult adding a new exercise program.

PREVENTING INSULIN REACTIONS (THINKING AHEAD)

It is important to prevent lows. This allows the stores of epinephrine and glucagon to build up so they are available when needed.

Considerations in preventing insulin reactions:

🐾 **Snacks can be important when**

✔ heavy physical exercise or all day exercise is planned: hiking, skiing, etc.

✔ the bedtime blood sugar is below 150 mg/dl (8.3 mmol/L).

✔ a person has a low, but be careful not to eat in excess.

🐾 **Insulin:**

✔ Reduce the dose of insulin which will be acting during the exercise period.

✔ Take the insulin injection AFTER a hot shower, bath or hot tub.

✔ For some people, with careful insulin dose adjustments, or using Lantus insulin or an insulin pump, a snack may not be needed.

✔ If doing corrections for high blood sugars at bedtime or during the night, use half the usual dose.

🐾 **Blood sugar:**

✔ Doing extra blood tests before, during and after periods of exercise will help to prevent lows and plan for future activity.

✔ Knowing a blood sugar level can help decide the amount of treatment needed.

False Reaction

A rapid fall in blood sugar can also cause an adrenaline release and symptoms. This can happen even if a low blood sugar does NOT occur. We call this a false reaction. The symptoms of low blood sugar occur, but the blood sugar is not low. A common example is when children eat lunch at school. Their blood sugar rises to a value of perhaps 250 mg/dl (13.9 mmol/L) after eating. They then go outside to play and the sugar might fall to 150 mg/dl (8.3 mmol/L) fairly rapidly. Adrenaline is released and the symptoms of having a reaction occur. Yet their blood sugar is 150 mg/dl (8.3 mmol/L) and they DO NOT HAVE LOW BLOOD SUGAR. It was just the rapid fall in blood sugar that caused an adrenaline release and made them feel like they were having a reaction. Since the sugar is not truly low, they do NOT need to drink sugar pop or juice, which will only raise their blood sugar. They might feel better if they ate some solid food, such as crackers or fresh fruit. It is important to remember that THE ONLY WAY TO TELL IF SOMEONE HAD A RAPID FALL IN BLOOD SUGAR OR A TRULY LOW BLOOD SUGAR IS BY DOING A BLOOD SUGAR TEST. Whenever possible, a blood sugar test should be done when the symptoms of low blood sugar occur.

TREATMENT FOR A LOW BLOOD SUGAR (INSULIN REACTION)

The general rule is to GIVE SUGAR IN SOME FORM AS FAST AS POSSIBLE. If the reaction is not severe, do a blood sugar test first. If you are not able to do a blood sugar, then just give milk, juice or sugar pop. A person with diabetes won't get sick from excess sugar. It will just cause high blood sugar and then be passed in the urine. Insulin reactions come quickly and should be treated at once by the person, parent, friend or teacher.

Different forms of sugar can be carried to treat low blood sugar. PEOPLE WITH DIABETES SHOULD CARRY SUGAR PACKETS OR GLUCOSE TABLETS IN THEIR POCKETS AT ALL TIMES FOR EMERGENCIES. Candy is too tempting. It also may be taken by other children. A special pocket for sugar packets can be sewn inside of gym shorts. Some people carry them in a jogger wallet attached to a shoe. Others slip packets in high stockings. It is often best to wrap the packet in foil or a plastic bag in case of leaks. Insta-Glucose™ comes in a tube and looks like toothpaste. It is available in most pharmacies. A tube of clear cake gel or honey tube from the grocery store will also work. After taking in some sugar and liquids, the person should wait 10 minutes and then eat a sandwich or other longer-lasting solid food. The liquid sugar will

be absorbed more quickly if the person waits before eating the solid food. Gradually, each person will become familiar with the type of reactions that occur. The person will learn how severe the reactions tend to be, when they are most likely to occur and how best to treat them.

Eventually, as a person becomes more familiar with diabetes, it may be possible to treat the various reactions differently. Remember, when possible, it is always wise to do a blood sugar if the reaction is not severe. If the level is above 60 mg/dl (3.2 mmol/L), it may be possible to treat the reaction with fresh fruit and solid food rather than milk, juice or sugar pop. **ALSO, REMEMBER THAT IT TAKES TEN MINUTES FOR THE BLOOD SUGAR LEVEL TO RISE, AND IT IS WISE TO WAIT FOR AT LEAST TEN MINUTES TO RETURN TO NORMAL ACTIVITY.** Some sources of quick-acting sugar with appropriate amounts for people of different ages are given in Table 1.

SOURCES OF QUICK-ACTING SUGAR (GLUCOSE) FOR HYPOGLYCEMIA

FOOD	AGE		
	5 years or less (10 gms)	**6-10 years (10-15 gms)**	**over 10 years (15-20 gms)**
Glucose Tabs (4 gms each - check label; some = 5 gms)	2	3-4	4-5
Instant Glucose (31 gm tube)	1/3 tube	1/3-1/2 tube	1/2-2/3 tube
Cake gel (1 small tube = 12 gms)	1 tube	1 tube	1-2 tubes
Apple juice (1/2 cup = 15 gms)	1/3 cup	1/3-1/2 cup	1/2-2/3 cup
Orange juice (1/2 cup = 15 gms)	1/4-1/2 cup	1/2-3/4 cup	3/4-1 cup
Sugar (1 tsp = 4 gms)	2 tsp	3-4 tsp	4-5 tsp
Honey (1 tsp = 5 gms; do not use if child is less than two years old)	2 tsp	2-3 tsp	3-4 tsp
Regular pop (1 oz = 3 gms)	3 oz	4-5 oz	5-6 oz
Milk (12 gms/cup)	3/4 cup	1 cup	1 1/2 cup
LIFE-SAVERS® (2.5 gms each)	4	4-6	6-8
Skittles® (1 gm each)	10 pieces	10-15 pieces	15-20 pieces
Sweet Tarts® (1.7 gms each)	6 pieces	6-8 pieces	8-12 pieces
Raisins (1 Tbsp = 7 1/2 gms)	1-2 Tbsp	2 Tbsp	2 1/2 Tbsp

Possible variations on the usual treatment for reactions follow:

🐾 **Mild Reaction:** (such as hunger at an unusual time, shakiness or irritability): If possible, do a blood sugar test. If below 60 mg/dl (3.2 mmol/L), give a glass of milk, a small glass of juice or sugar pop (4 oz). Wait 10 minutes for absorption of the liquid sugar and then give solid food (crackers, sandwich, fresh fruit, etc.). If the blood sugar is above 60 mg/dl (3.2 mmol/L), give just solid food.

🐾 **Moderate Reaction:** (very confused or spacey, very pale or very shaky): Give Insta-Glucose, Reactose™, Monojel™ or any source of simple sugar, such as sugar pop or juice. One-half tube of the Insta-Glucose can be placed between the cheeks and gums, and the person should be told to swallow. Do a blood sugar test as soon as it is possible. Always check for the risk of choking. Repeat the blood test after 10 minutes to make sure it is above 60 mg/dl (3.2 mmol/L). If not, repeat the initial treatment and wait another 10 minutes. Once the blood sugar has risen above 60 mg/dl (3.2 mmol/L) give solid food.

🐾 **Severe Reaction:** If the person is completely unconscious, it is risky to put the concentrated sugar around the gums. It could get into the airway. It is better to just give glucagon as instructed in Table 2 in this chapter. Remember to do the blood sugar level as soon as possible. If the person does not improve after 10-20 minutes, it may be necessary to call 911 to get extra help. A second dose (same amount) of glucagon (from the same vial) can also be given. In the preliminary part of the Diabetes Control and Complications Trial (DCCT; Chapter 14), one of every 10 people (10%) receiving standard treatment had a severe reaction each year. One of four people (25%) on intensive treatment (including insulin pumps) had a severe insulin reaction each year. Every family must have glucagon available and know how to use it (see Table 2). Our current hypoglycemia video may be helpful in understanding how to use glucagon. It is wise to call the diabetes care provider prior to the next insulin injection for possible dose reductions.

We are concerned about any blood sugar below 60 mg/dl (3.2 mmol/L). When these are obtained in routine testing, the insulin dose or snacks should be changed so that further low values do not occur. In a child under five years old, we are concerned about values below 70 mg/dl (3.9 mmol/L). When values are below these levels at the time of an insulin injection, we usually recommend not giving the usual amount of Humalog or NovoLog insulin (at least until after eating). If two or three values below 60 mg/dl (3.2 mmol/L) are present at the same time of day in the same week, a decrease in insulin dose is probably needed. CALL THE DIABETES CARE PROVIDER IF HELP IS NEEDED.

🐾 **Hypoglycemic Unawareness:** Sometimes low blood sugars will be found during routine testing, and the person will not have had symptoms. This may be due to a very gradual fall in the blood sugar, or in young children, because they have not learned to recognize the symptoms. Some adults with very strict sugar control do not release adrenaline and may have the problem medically referred to as **"HYPOGLYCEMIC UNAWARENESS."** In this case, they must not aim for such strict blood sugar control. Sometimes the insulin dose can be lowered. After blood sugars have been higher for two or three weeks, it may be possible to again recognize low blood sugars.

🐾 **One-sided Weakness (paralysis):** It is not known why, but on rare occasions some people experience weakness (or paralysis) on one side of the body with a severe insulin reaction. This can last for one to 12 hours, but eventually clears. It is particularly worrisome to doctors in emergency rooms. They often insist on a very expensive evaluation to prove that a stroke has not occurred.

GLUCAGON INJECTIONS - WHEN TO AND HOW TO

🐾 Use only when a person is unconscious or having a seizure.

🐾 Keep in a convenient and known place. Store in a refrigerator during hot weather. Protect from freezing.

🐾 Keep a 3cc syringe available or use the fluid-filled syringe in the emergency kit. An insulin syringe and needle can also be used (preferably a 1.0cc syringe). Some people tape the syringe to the kit so they have this readily available (see video on hypoglycemia).

🐾 If you have the emergency kit, the fluid does not need to be withdrawn from bottle 1 (diagram below) as it is already in the syringe.

🐾 Withdraw from the mixed glucagon bottle:

(Estimate if using the emergency kit syringe.)

　0.3cc for a child less than six years old

　0.5cc for a child 6-18 years of age

　1.0cc for an adult over 18 years of age

🐾 If using the syringe that comes in the emergency kit, inject into deep muscle (in front of leg or upper, outer arm) though it is OK to inject into the subcutaneous fat. If the glucagon is drawn into an insulin syringe then give it just as you would an insulin shot. If a blood sugar has not yet been done, it can be done now.

🐾 Wait 10 minutes. Check blood sugar. If still unconscious and blood sugar is still below 60 mg/dl (3.2 mmol/L), inject second dose of glucagon (same amount as first dose).

🐾 If there is no response to the glucagon, or if there is any difficulty breathing, call paramedics (or 911).

🐾 As soon as he/she awakens, give sips of juice, sugar pop or sugar in water initially. Honey may help to raise the blood sugar. After 10 minutes, encourage solid food (crackers and peanut butter or cheese, sandwich, etc.).

🐾 Notify diabetes care team of severe reaction prior to next insulin injection (so dose can be changed if needed). Complete recovery may take 1-6 hours.

Please copy this page as often as you wish. Tape a copy to the box of glucagon.

1. Insert 1/2cc of air into fluid bottle (1cc won't fit).

2. Draw out 1cc of fluid from bottle.

3. Inject the 1cc of fluid into bottle with tablet. Mix.

GLUCAGON

Glucagon is a hormone made in the pancreas like insulin. However, it has the opposite effect of insulin and raises the blood sugar level. It is rarely needed, but we ask families to keep it handy. The expiration date on the box should be checked regularly and, if outdated, a new bottle should be obtained. If a very severe reaction occurs and the person loses consciousness, glucagon should be given promptly. It can be stored at room temperature. It should not reach a temperature above 90° or below freezing. It can be taken in a cooler with the insulin and blood sugar strips for trips away from home.

Use of Glucagon

1. Severe Low Blood Sugar

Glucagon comes in a bottle containing 1 mg as a tablet or powder. There is a syringe containing diluting solution in the emergency kit. The method for giving glucagon is shown in Table 2. **This table may be copied and attached to the glucagon kit.**

Sometimes vomiting will occur after a severe reaction. This may be from the person's own glucagon output or from the glucagon that was injected. It usually does not last very long, and if the blood sugar is above 150 mg/dl (8.3 mmol/L), it is not a big problem. If the person is lying down, the head should be turned to the side to avoid choking. Urine or blood ketones should be checked (see Chapter 5) as they can sometimes also form. If the family is concerned about the ketones, if the blood sugar did not rise, or if the vomiting continues, the diabetes care provider should be called.

2. Low Blood Sugar and Vomiting

Sometimes the blood sugar can be low (< 60 mg/dl [3.2 mmol/L]) and the person cannot keep any food down. Glucagon can be mixed (Table 2) and given just like insulin – using an insulin syringe. The dose is one unit per year of age.

For example: a five-year -old would get 5 units or a 10 year old would get 10 units.

If the blood sugar is not higher in 20-30 minutes, the same dose can be repeated. This treatment has saved many ER visits for our clinic patients.

DELAYED HYPOGLYCEMIA

Delayed hypoglycemia is also discussed in Chapter 13 on exercise. It usually occurs from 4-12 hours after exercise, however it can occur up to 24 hours after the exercise. For some people, blood sugars can be high after exercise. This is due to the normal response of releasing adrenaline during exercise. Adrenaline causes sugar to come out of the liver and raise the blood sugar. At some point after the exercise, the adrenaline levels go back down (sometimes not until the time of sleep), and the sugar moves back into the muscle and liver. The result can be a low blood sugar or **"delayed hypoglycemia."**

Prevention involves lowering the insulin dose. This must be done after heavy exercise even though the blood sugar may be high. Taking extra carbohydrate at bedtime (even with high blood sugar) may also be helpful. Exercise is essential for the heart and cardiovascular system. Therefore, it is important to always be thinking about how to best prevent post-exercise lows.

REBOUNDING (REACTIVE HYPOGLYCEMIA OR SOMOGYI REACTION)

Occasionally the blood sugar will become low during the night. The person will put out hormones (epinephrine and glucagon) to raise the blood sugar. These hormones may also result in ketone output in the urine. The person may not have any symptoms during the night, or they may complain of night sweats or a morning headache. Rebounding should be considered if the morning blood sugar varies frequently from being very low to being very high (and possibly even having intermittent morning ketones). Rebounding should also be considered if a person is on a very large insulin dose (above 1.5 units/kg or 0.75 units/lb body weight). Table 3 summarizes when to consider rebounding. A person may experience only one or two of the six factors listed in the table.

If rebounding is suspected, it is important to check the blood sugar level during the night (usually between midnight and 4 a.m.) for

Table 3

WHEN TO CONSIDER REBOUNDING

- Variable (very low to very high) morning blood sugars
- Intermittent morning urine ketones
- Night sweats
- Morning headaches
- Stomachaches/nausea
- Large insulin dosage (above 1.5 units/kg or 0.75 units/lb body weight)

several nights to make sure the values are not low. Table 2 in Chapter 7, Blood Sugar Testing, gives blood sugar levels to aim for at bedtime (before the bedtime snack) and in the morning. If bedtime blood sugar values are below the desired ranges, extra food should be eaten at bedtime to prevent low blood sugars during the night. If the values are VERY low at bedtime (e.g., below 60 mg/dl or 3.2 mmol/L), the value should be rechecked during the night. If bedtime or morning values are below the desired ranges two or more days in a week, the insulin dose working at that time should be reduced (see Chapter 21, Adjusting the Insulin Dose). The diabetes care provider should be called during office hours if there are further questions.

RECORD ALL INSULIN REACTIONS

Record insulin reactions in your record book. Many families circle all values <60 mg/dl (3.2 mmol/L). Try to identify and record the cause of any low or high blood sugars (Table 4). If more than two mild insulin reactions occur in a short time period, call the diabetes care provider to adjust the amount of insulin. It is usually possible to call during office hours, but if a severe reaction occurs, call the care provider prior to giving the next regularly scheduled insulin shot.

MEDICAL IDENTIFICATION

In case of a severe insulin reaction, EVERYONE needs to know about the diabetes. This includes teachers, strangers, police, co-workers, friends and medical personnel. The person with diabetes should wear a bracelet or necklace with this information. A card in the wallet is not good enough; this may not be found by paramedics. A diabetes ID card can also be stapled to the registration of the car in the glove compartment. Bracelets or necklaces can be found at most pharmacies or medical supply houses.

The MedicAlert Foundation
(provides MedicAlert tags)
P.O. Box 1009
Turlock, California 95381

The MedicAlert tag includes a number that can be called 24 hours a day for information concerning both the person and the doctor. The minimum charge for the bracelet or necklace and keeping the information readily available 24 hours per day is $35. Then the annual membership renewal after the first year is $15.

There is a second company called MediCheck that provides stainless steel bracelets or necklaces for a donation of $25 or more. The person's name, address, phone number, condition (Diabetes) and the doctor's name and phone number can all be put on the neck tag or bracelet for this price. In this case, the doctor is called and not MediCheck.

MediCheck International, Inc. Foundation
800 Lee Street
Des Plaines, Illinois 60016

An application is in Appendix 2 in the back of this book.

Dog tags (similar to the ones soldiers wear) have gained in popularity and instructions for ordering them are in Appendix 2 in the back of the book. A bracelet, necklace or medallion with your personal medical information (name, condition and medications) can be engraved and ordered through the American Medical

Identifications, Inc. The prices for an identification tag start at $21.95.

American Medical Identifications, Inc.
P.O. Box 925617
Houston, Texas 77292

Colorful sports bracelets are sometimes preferred and can be ordered from FIFTY 50 PHARMACY. The cost per bracelet is $16.95 plus $3.50 for shipping. Mail your order with payment to:

FIFTY 50
1740 South IH35, Suite 112
Carrollton, Texas 75006
Phone: 800-746-7505

Medical charms are also popular. These work well for attaching to the toddler shoe laces. The addresses are:

medicharms@missbrooke.com
http://www.missbrooke.com
P.O. Box 558
Bryant, Arkansas 72089
Phone: 888-417-7591

For those who desire additional choices, see http://www.tah-handcrafted-jewelry.com

For people who will not wear a necklace or bracelet, a watch or shoe tag may be the next best choice.

Toddlers should not wear a neck chain (too risky), but they often do well with ankle bracelets, charms or a medallion laced in the shoe. The sports bracelet described above works quite well around the ankle.

SOME FACTORS THAT CHANGE THE BLOOD SUGAR

Lowers:

🐾 Insulin

🐾 Hot bath, showers or hot tubs may increase insulin absorption and cause a low blood sugar

🐾 Exercise, although for some people, the values may be higher immediately following exercise

🐾 Less food or eating late

Raises:

🐾 Sugar intake

🐾 Glucagon

🐾 Hormones such as glucagon, adrenaline, growth hormone and cortisol (prednisone); their action is opposite to that of insulin

🐾 Illness (which may cause ketones)

🐾 Rapid growth; teenagers usually require more insulin with increased growth

🐾 Menstrual periods (may cause ketones)

🐾 Emotions such as anger and excitement; some younger children can have lower blood sugars with extra excitement

🐾 Inhalers given for asthma which have epinephrine derivatives in them

DEFINITIONS

Adrenaline (epinephrine): The excitatory hormone. This is released with a low blood sugar or a rapid fall in blood sugar, which then causes the symptoms of low blood sugar (shaking, sweating and pounding heart).

Glucagon: A hormone also made in the pancreas (like insulin) that causes the blood sugar to rise. It is available to inject into people when they have severe (unconscious) insulin reactions.

Hypoglycemia: The term used for a low blood sugar (insulin reaction).

Hypoglycemic unawareness: The term used to describe low blood sugars without the person having any warning signs or symptoms.

Insta-Glucose, Monojel, or Reactose: Source of concentrated sugar that can be purchased. It can be given to a person in case of low blood sugar.

Ketoacidosis (Acidosis): What happens in the body when not enough insulin is available. Blood sugar is usually high at this time. Moderate or large ketones (acetone) are present in the urine. See Chapter 15.

Rebounding (Somogyi reaction or bouncing): The process of blood sugars falling to low levels and then rebounding to high levels. Ketones may sometimes be present when this occurs.

Seizure (convulsion): Loss of consciousness with jerking of muscles. This can occur with a very severe low blood sugar (insulin reaction).

QUESTIONS (Q) AND ANSWERS (A) FROM NEWSNOTES

Q. Do we still need to keep glucagon?

A. YES.

The current statistic (from three studies) is that 4% to 13% of standard insulin-treated patients have one or more severe episodes of hypoglycemia each year. With intensive insulin therapy in the DCCT, 25% (one in four) of subjects had a severe reaction each year. Glucagon should be given anytime there is loss of consciousness without being able to arouse the person. If paramedics are to be called, it is still wise to give the glucagon before they arrive.

The biggest change in giving glucagon is that two studies have shown it will work just as fast when given subcutaneously (the same place as insulin) as when given into muscle. People used to think it always had to be given into muscle.

The Eli Lilly Company Glucagon Emergency Kit comes with the diluting solution already in the syringe ready to be injected into the bottle with the powdered glucagon for mixing. The syringe and needle they provide can then also be used for the subcutaneous or intra-muscular injection (either is fine).

Some people have rebounding, a high blood sugar and even ketones after glucagon. Vomiting can also occur, but these side effects can be handled.

Q. Since I have changed to three injections of insulin per day, and my Hemoglobin A_{1c} has come down, I don't seem to feel low blood sugar reactions. Is this common?

A. Unfortunately, this is not unusual. It is called hypoglycemic unawareness. People on intensive insulin therapy often do not make the counter-regulatory hormones as effectively as they did previously . Adrenaline (epinephrine) output is sometimes reduced in people with very tight sugar control. This is probably the most important hormone, which normally increases with low blood sugar and then causes the symptoms (shakiness, sweatiness, rapid heart beat, etc.). Sometimes it is possible to reduce the insulin dose to let the blood sugars run a bit higher for two or three weeks in order to regain the ability to feel low blood sugars.

Other hormones which normally help to raise the blood sugar may also have reduced output following intensive insulin therapy. Production of the hormone glucagon, made in the pancreas like insulin (normally), is reduced in most people who have had diabetes for longer than one year. Therefore, it also may not be available to help raise the blood sugar. It is important to let your diabetes care provider know if you are having low blood sugars without symptoms.

Q. We were recently told at a clinic visit that our child should not be given insulin just prior to a hot bath, shower or hot tub. Would you please explain the reason for this?

A. The hot bath or shower (or hot tub) increases the blood flow to the skin. As more blood flows to this area, more insulin is rapidly taken up by the blood (probably primarily Humalog, NovoLog or Regular insulins). This can then result in a severe low blood sugar. The answer is to **always take the insulin after the hot shower or bath.** The bath or shower should not be taken in the 30-90 minutes after Humalog/NovoLog or in the four hours after taking Regular insulin. This may help to prevent a severe low blood sugar.

Wait to take your shot after a bath or shower.

Chapter 7

TOPIC:
🐾 Monitoring Diabetes
(testing blood sugar)

TEACHING OBJECTIVES:

1. Present glucose testing concepts (rationale, testing times, frequency and desired ranges for the individual).

2. Provide instruction for the meter of choice.

3. Discuss how to trouble shoot problems with their meter.

4. Introduce the concept of recording blood sugars and observing trends.

LEARNING OBJECTIVES:

Learners (parents, child, relative or self) will be able to:

1. Describe rationale for blood sugar testing and list testing times, frequency and their desired ranges.

2. Demonstrate use of meter including setting time and code when necessary.

3. Locate and state the 1-800 number listed on the meter to call for problems.

4. Choose and apply a method for recording blood sugars and recognizing trends.

Chapter 7

BLOOD SUGAR (GLUCOSE) TESTING

MEASURING BLOOD SUGARS

The ability of people (or families) with diabetes to check blood sugar levels quickly and accurately has changed diabetes management more than anything else in the past 20 years. Prior to this, diabetes was primarily managed by measuring urine sugars, which were very unreliable. The people in the intensive treatment group of the Diabetes Control and Complications Trial (DCCT) did at least four blood sugars every day (see Chapter 14). They were able to achieve excellent diabetes control as a result of frequent blood sugar testing, more frequent dosages of insulin and following a dietary plan. The improved glucose control was shown to reduce the risk for the eye, kidney and nerve complications of diabetes. Clearly, for people who are able to check blood sugars more frequently, improved sugar control

is now possible. The Standards of Diabetes Care (see Chapter 20) recommends "frequent blood-glucose monitoring" (at least 3-4 times per day). This is a reasonable goal for all people with diabetes.

WHY DO SELF BLOOD-GLUCOSE MONITORING?

There are many reasons why measuring blood sugars at home has become a "cornerstone" of diabetes care. A few of these will be discussed here (and are listed in Table 1):

🐾 **Safety:** A big reason for the use of blood sugar testing relates to safety. Almost no one feels all the low blood sugars that occur (and very young children may not report feeling any lows). Checking the blood sugar before the bedtime snack may help in choosing ways to prevent low blood sugars during the night.

Figure 1: Blood Sugars

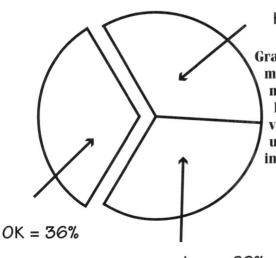

High = 35%

OK = 36%

Low = 29%

Graphs can be obtained from some of the blood sugar meters when they are brought to the clinic. This young man had a HbA$_{1c}$ (see Chapter 14) of 7.1%, but was having too many lows. We like no more than 14% of values to be low and for less than 50% to be above the upper range (see suggested ranges for different ages in Table 2).

Improving sugar control: Studies have clearly shown that testing a minimum of four blood sugars daily and using the results wisely can result in improved sugar control. This results in a reduced risk for diabetic eye, kidney and nerve complications.

Adjusting the insulin dosage: If regular blood sugars are checked, and the results are recorded to look for patterns of lows or highs, the insulin dosage can be adjusted as needed. People who take Humalog/NovoLog insulin before meals should use the blood sugar level (along with the amount of food and planned exercise) to decide how much insulin to take.

Managing illness: Being able to check blood sugars at home when a person is sick (or before or after surgery) allows for safe management at home. In the past, people with diabetes were sometimes kept in the hospital because accurate blood sugars could not be done at home.

To understand the effects of various foods, exercise or stress: By checking a blood sugar two hours after eating a certain food or doing a certain amount of exercise, one can better plan the insulin dose the next time. Pizza, for example, tends to raise blood sugars more than other foods for some people. If this is found to be true, extra Humalog or NovoLog insulin can be considered for the next time it is to be eaten. Similarly, some people raise their blood sugar with a certain exercise, whereas others do not. Knowing the blood sugar value after doing the exercise a few times will help in future planning.

To separate a rapid fall in blood sugar from a truly low blood sugar value: Some people report frequent symptoms of an insulin reaction (see Chapter 6). This occurs when the blood sugar falls rapidly (for example from 300 to 150 mg/dl [16.6 to 8.3 mmol/L]) or when a low blood sugar truly occurs. A blood sugar test at the time of a reaction will help determine whether the symptoms are due to a rapid fall **(false reaction)** or a seriously low blood sugar. We consider a truly low blood sugar to be **below 60 mg/dl (3.2 mmol/L)** or in a preschooler, **below 70 mg/dl (3.9 mmol/L)**. Sugar can be given if the level is low, but it is not needed if the symptoms are just due to a rapid fall in sugar. If the level is between 60 and 100 mg/dl (3.2 and 5.5 mmol/L), it is often helpful to eat food that is not high in sugar. These differences will not be known unless a blood sugar level is tested at the time of the insulin reactions.

To know the blood sugar level immediately: A blood sugar test will give immediate results when the value is important to know. For example, a child may be irritable and the cause may be unknown. A blood sugar test will quickly help the parent decide if the irritability is due to a low blood sugar level or another cause. Another person may have an important event and just want to know the blood sugar prior to the event.

Blood sugar testing gives people a "sense of control" over their diabetes: Many people feel better knowing how their blood sugars are running. However, it is important to remember that there may not always be an exact relationship between the blood sugar level and what one expects it to be. There are always unknown factors that result in occasional high or low levels. This can be very upsetting for the person who expects blood sugars to always be in the target range. It is important not to become discouraged when blood sugars do not always match the expected results. Questions or concerns about the blood sugar tests should be discussed with the diabetes team.

As an indicator to do a urine or blood ketone test: A fasting blood sugar above 240 mg/dl (13.3 mmol/L) or a value above 300 mg/dl (16.6 mmol/L) during the rest of the day should indicate a need for a blood or urine ketone test. (Some meters now even flash this advice.) Testing for blood or urine ketones when the blood sugar is high may help to prevent an episode of ketoacidosis (see Chapter 15).

Table 1

REASONS FOR BLOOD SUGAR (GLUCOSE) TESTING

- Safety
- Improve sugar control
- Adjust the insulin dosage
- Manage illnesses
- Understand the effects of various foods, exercise or stress
- Determine a rapid fall in blood sugar from a truly low blood sugar value
- Know the blood sugar level immediately
- Sense of control
- Indicate a need to test for urine or blood ketones

WHEN TO DO BLOOD SUGAR TESTS

We now encourage people to do at least four blood sugar tests every day. When four blood sugar tests are done each day, they are often scheduled before breakfast, before lunch, before the afternoon snack or before dinner and before the bedtime snack. Occasional values should also be done two hours after meals and during the night. The blood sugar goals for before meals and two hours after meals are shown in Figure 2 and Table 2. Suggested bedtime and nighttime values are given in Table 2.

1. Pre-breakfast:

The morning blood sugar test reflects the values during the night and is probably the most important blood sugar related to diabetes control. As shown in the figure in Chapter 2, this value reflects the "turning off" of internal sugar production by the liver. The short-acting insulin dosages at breakfast and dinner are sometimes based, at least in part, on blood sugar results at these two times.

2. Pre-lunch:

A blood sugar test before lunch helps to decide if the morning Humalog (NovoLog) and/or Regular insulin dosage is correct. For people using morning NPH insulin, it may also be having an effect at this time. Some families routinely request that a test be done prior to eating lunch. For some children (and schools),

this is not a problem and can be done without interfering with the child's normal school life. Other families (or children) prefer to only do blood sugars at school if the child is feeling "low." This is discussed in more detail in Chapter 23, The School and Diabetes.

3. Pre-dinner:

The test before dinner reflects the dose of morning NPH or Lente insulin. It may also reflect afternoon sports activities and an afternoon snack. A test should not be done unless it has been at least two hours since food was eaten. Otherwise, the result will be high from the food eaten in the previous two hours. If it is time for dinner and the person had an afternoon snack one hour earlier, it may be best to just wait and do the test prior to the bedtime snack. If this is a common occurrence, change to doing the blood sugar tests BEFORE the afternoon snack. Some youth, who like a large afternoon snack, will now routinely use Humalog (NovoLog) to cover the rise in blood sugar. The dinner value will then tell if the dose given was correct.

4. Bedtime:

The blood sugar test prior to the bedtime snack is important for:

- people who tend to have reactions during the night
- children who play outside after dinner
- anyone who did not eat well at dinner

knowing if the short-acting insulin dose given at dinner is correct

As can be seen in Table 2, suggested bedtime blood sugar values are given for the different ages. **If the values are below the values in brackets (two stars), doing a blood sugar check during the night is wise.** These values may be different for a given person.

5. After meals:

In recent years, more emphasis has been placed on doing a blood sugar two hours after eating a meal. The highest blood sugars of the day occur after meals and these values add to the HbA_{1c} value (Chapter 14). More people are now using carbohydrate counting. They may inject insulin prior to meals based on their expected carbohydrate intake (Chapter 12). The blood sugar two hours after the meal tells if the **I**nsulin to **C**arbohydrate ratio (**I/C** ratio – Chapter 12) and estimated carbohydrates are correct. **The sugar values listed in Table 2 by age can also be the goals for two hours after meals.** We would recommend that families try to check one value two hours after each meal once or twice weekly.

6. Nighttime:

It may be necessary to occasionally do blood sugar tests in the middle of the night (see Chapter 6 on Low Blood Sugar) to make sure the value is not getting too low. The diabetes care provider may suggest this if very erratic results are noted for the morning blood sugars.

A nighttime blood sugar is particularly important for people who tend to have reactions (low blood sugars) during the night. More than half of the severe low sugars occur during the nighttime hours. Many families will routinely do a test during the night. Others choose to do a test once weekly. It is important to test on nights when there has been extra physical activity. The extra activity might be a basketball game in the evening. For a younger child, it might be playing hard outside on a nice summer evening. The best time to do a check varies with each person. For some, between midnight and 2 a.m. is the best. For others, the early morning hours are the most valuable – perhaps when a parent is

getting ready for work. Table 2 also gives suggested values for during the night.

HOW TO DO SELF BLOOD SUGAR TESTS

FINGER-POKING

A finger-poking (lancing) device is used to get the drop of blood. There are many good devices on the market, and these can now often be set at different depths for different people. The adjustable pokers are particularly good for young children who have tender skin and may not need much lancing depth.

The hands should be washed with warm water (to increase blood flow and to make sure they are clean). Any trace of sugar on the finger

Figure 2:

Blood Sugar Levels in mg/dl (mmol/L)

400-800 (22.2-44.4)	Very High
200-400 (11.1-22.2)	High
GOAL	
80-200 (4.4-11.1)	Under 5 years
70-180 (3.9-10)	5-11 years
70-150 (3.9-8.3)	12 years and up
70-120 (3.9-6.6)	Normal
below 60 (below 3.2)	Low

SUGGESTED BLOOD SUGAR LEVELS

Table 2

Age (years)	Fasting (a.m.) or no food for 2 hours		Bedtime (before bedtime snack or during the night)	
	mg/dl	**mmol/L**	**mg/dl**	**mmol/L**
Below 5	80-200	4.5-11.1	Above 150*[80**]	8.3*[4.4**]
5-11	70-180	3.9-10.0	Above 120*[70**]	6.6*[3.9**]
12 and above	70-150	3.9-8.3	Above 100*[60**]	5.5*[3.2**]

*If values are below these levels, milk or other food might be added to the solid protein and carbohydrate bedtime snack.
**If values are below these levels, the test should be rechecked between midnight and 2 a.m. If this happens more than once within a week, either reduce the dinner Humalog /NovoLog or Regular insulin or call the diabetes care provider for advice.

Note: A normal fasting blood sugar (or when no food has been eaten for two hours) for people without diabetes is between 70 mg/dl (3.9 mmol/L) and 120 mg/dl (6.6 mmol/L).

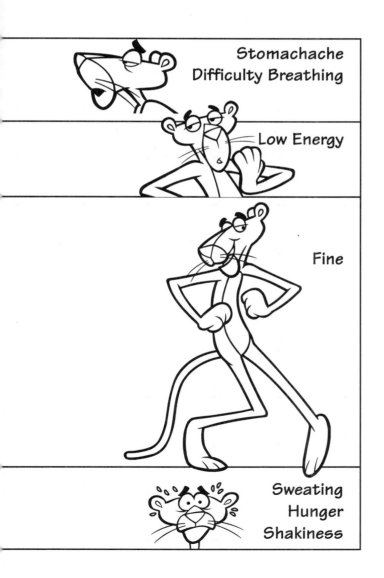

Stomachache
Difficulty Breathing

Low Energy

Fine

Sweating
Hunger
Shakiness

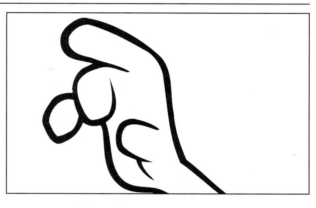

may give a false elevated reading. We do not recommend routinely wiping with alcohol because any trace of alcohol left on the skin will interfere with the chemical reaction for the blood sugar test (Table 3). Alcohol also dries and toughens the skin. Occasionally, when away from home (e.g., camping, picnics), it is necessary to use alcohol-free travel wipes to cleanse the finger. Air dry the finger before doing the blood sugar check.

It is often helpful to place the finger to be used on a table top (to prevent the natural reflex of withdrawing the finger and not getting an adequate poke). The side of the finger should be used rather than the fleshy pad on the fingertip, which is more painful. If the drop is not coming easily, hold the hand down to the side of the body to increase the blood in the finger. OBTAINING TOO SMALL A DROP OF BLOOD THAT FAILS TO FILL THE STRIP IS ONE OF THE MOST COMMON ERRORS AND CAUSES INACCURATE RESULTS. If the fingers become sore, the toes may be used.

ALTERNATE TESTING SITES

Many children are now poking sites other than the fingers or toes. These sites are used as they may not hurt as much. The poker must be 'dialed' to the maximum depth to get enough blood. The most common site is the forearm. Meters approved for the arm include The FreeStyle™, the One Touch Ultra® and the Sof-Tac™. The FreeStyle is also approved for use on the fleshy pad of the hand, the upper arm, the thigh and calf. The main problem has been that the blood flow through the arm is slower than through the fingertips. The slower blood flow means the blood sugar value from the arm is 10 minutes **behind** the fingertip. It is important to rub the site to be used on the arm prior to doing the stick. The rubbing will increase the blood flow in the area. The person may feel low or have a low value from a finger stick, but the arm level will not be low. We advise families to use the fingertip if feeling low. Also, people who do not feel their lows (hypoglycemic unawareness; Chapter 6) should always use their fingertips for blood sugars. **Remember** to change the lancet everyday. A sharp lancet will lessen injury to the site and help prevent an infection.

BLOOD SUGAR (GLUCOSE) METERS

Some of the desirable features in selecting a meter are listed in Table 4. The meter chosen should meet the person's needs. Some people leave a meter at school or at work. If testing is done on more than one meter, try to use no more than two different brands. Families tend to prefer small meters that are easy to slip into a pocket. They also prefer meters that

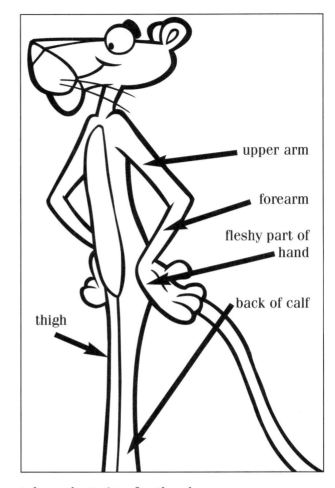

upper arm

forearm

fleshy part of hand

back of calf

thigh

take a short time for the glucose determination. Particularly for younger children, the need for only a small amount of blood is helpful. Most of the strips now have a capillary action to pull the blood into the strip. This may be helpful for a small child who has difficulty holding still. For some people, accuracy in cold, heat, high humidity or high altitude is important. If a strip has been in a

COMMON PROBLEMS CAUSING INACCURATE BLOOD SUGAR TEST RESULTS

Table 3

- Finger is not clean and dry (sugar on finger will raise result; alcohol will interfere)
- Adding more blood after the first drop has been put on pad (now ok for some meters)
- Meter parts are dirty (e.g., with dried blood)
- Codes on strips and meters are not matched (some meters now read the codes automatically)
- Too small a drop of blood on pad
- Strips have expired

DESIRED FEATURES OF BLOOD GLUCOSE METERS

Table 4

- 🐾 Accurate (in environment where it is to be used)
- 🐾 Storage of at least the last 100 values
- 🐾 Able to be downloaded at clinic and/or at home
- 🐾 Small in size
- 🐾 Short determination time
- 🐾 Small drop of blood (± capillary action of strip)
- 🐾 Cleaning is easy or not necessary
- 🐾 A control solution or strip can be used to check for accuracy
- 🐾 Strips are paid for by the family's insurance

cooler or refrigerator (most strips spoil at above 90° or if they freeze), they should always be brought to room temperature before using.

Often the main reason one meter is selected over another in the U.S. is that the family's health insurance will pay for that meter and its strips. The glucose strips usually add up to a cost of $2-3 (U.S.) per day, and so insurance coverage is important. The cost of strips is usually a more important factor than the cost of the meter.

It is important with most meters to test a control strip or solution at regular intervals to make sure reliable results are being obtained. Some clinics with a more accurate meter may wish to intermittently check the family's meter with the clinic's. Some common problems causing inaccurate blood sugar test results are shown in Table 3.

We do request that families choose a meter with a memory for at least the last 100 glucose values. **The meter(s) must always be brought to the clinic visit** so that it can be downloaded. The values as well as graphs, such as the pie-chart (Figure 1), can be printed. Some families like to download their blood glucose results in their homes. Research from our Center showed that if at least half of the blood sugar values are below the upper limit of the goal for the age (see Figure 2 and Table 2), the HbA_{1c} values will usually be in the desired range for the age (see Chapter 14). During the "honeymoon" phase (Chapter 2), or when one still makes much of

their own insulin, most of the blood sugars will be in the desired range for age. For other people with diabetes, it is a reasonable goal to try to get half of the blood sugar values at any time of day within range for that person's age.

Most meters read within 10% of a hospital laboratory determined value. Most of the meters currently on the market read the sugar in the plasma (the clear part of the blood). Other meters like the Profile™, read whole blood sugar (including the red cells which have a lower sugar level). As a result, meters reading plasma glucose usually give values that are 15% higher than for meters reading whole blood glucose. Thus, results from different meters are often not comparable.

The visual method for Chemstrip bG® strips (for those not using a meter) is included in the Appendix at the end of this Chapter.

🐾 RECORD KEEPING

Examples of daily record sheets are included in this chapter. The pages record either the last one week or the last two weeks of blood sugars. Many families will now fax the page to their diabetes care provider at regular intervals. If this is done, make sure the insulin dosages and instructions for return fax or phone contact are included. These sheets may be copied and stored in a notebook to bring along to clinic visits. Keeping good records to look for patterns in blood sugars is essential. It is wise to keep written records even if your meter is able to store results (these may be lost if the meter malfunctions). **Patterns of high or low blood sugars will be missed if results are not recorded.** It is important to note all reactions and possible causes. Some people also circle all values below 60 mg/dl (3.25 mmol/L) or put a star on days of reactions so that these can be easily noted by the diabetes care providers. If times of heavy exercise are recorded, it may be possible to see the effects of exercise on blood sugars. Illnesses, stress and menstrual periods may increase the blood sugar and should be noted. It may be helpful to record what was eaten for the bedtime snack or any evening exercise to see if these are related to morning blood sugars. Hopefully, occasional tests will also be done at the time(s) when routine tests are not usually done. Also included is a place to record urine or blood ketone checks, as newly diagnosed people must check their ketones frequently. Ketone checks are essential with any illness **or** anytime the blood sugar level is above 240 mg/dl (13.3 mmol/L) fasting or over 300 mg/dl (16.6 mmol/L) during the day. We realize, however, that most people will not need to routinely check ketones after the period of new diagnosis.

The insulin dose can be recorded with the units of short-lasting insulin on top (e.g., 5H or 5R) and the units of intermediate-acting insulin on the bottom (e.g., 15N).

Good record keeping and bringing the results to clinic visits allow the family and diabetes team to work together most effectively to achieve good diabetes management.

❀ NON OR MINIMALLY INVASIVE GLUCOSE MONITORING

As discussed in Chapter 28, two minimally invasive meters are now available. Both are accurate and read subcutaneous (not blood) glucose levels, which are about ten minutes behind the blood glucose levels. This is generally not a problem.

The two devices currently available are:

1. The Continuous Glucose Monitoring System® (CGMS) by MiniMed was approved by the FDA in 1999. This system involves the insertion of a small plastic tube with a needle that is then removed. It can stay in place for three days (like the insulin pump cannula). It is usually put under the abdominal skin. Readings are done every ten seconds and are summarized every five minutes. It may lead to a "bionic" pancreas someday (Chapter 28).

2. The GlucoWatch®, by Cygnus, pulls extra-cellular fluid from under the skin by a small current from a battery within the watch. As discussed in Chapter 28, it is completely non-invasive in that a needle is not put through the skin. However, many people have temporary areas of irritation, either from the pad under the watch (where the fluid is drawn) or from the adhesive material around the outer edges of the watch. The watch is removed first and then the sensor pad. It is important to remove the sensor pad gently. One patient in the trial used Unisolve™ pads to help loosen the adhesive or allowed the sensor to soak off in the shower. Both worked well. Using the second-generation watch, after a two-hour equilibration period and one blood sugar determination, the watch can check six glucose readings per hour for 13 hours. Any reading is cancelled if there is excessive sweating.

The person wearing the watch can read the glucose levels as they are done. There is also an alarm that can be set for a desired level of high or low glucose values.

Some of the Uses of These Devices are:

✔ Helping to monitor sugar levels more closely for people who have had severe hypoglycemia. (Blood sugar testing will still be necessary, but this will allow values between the blood sugar tests to be evaluated.)

✔ Providing frequent glucose levels when changing people from two shots per day to intensive insulin therapy (multiple shots of insulin or an insulin pump).

✔ Monitoring glucose levels when a medicine is needed such as prednisone (steroids greatly increase blood sugars).

✔ Attempting to improve glucose control in people whose HbA$_{1c}$ level (Chapter 14) is too high.

✔ Checking to make sure sugar levels during the night are not too high or too low.

✔ Monitoring sugar levels during illness or after surgery.

✔ Monitoring sugar levels after periods of strenuous exercise.

Even with the limitations of the CSGM system and of the GlucoWatch, as discussed in this chapter and in Chapter 28, they represent important advances.

SUMMARY

Whichever method of blood sugar testing you use, WRITE DOWN THE TIME OF THE TEST, THE DATE, HOW YOU FEEL AND THE BLOOD SUGAR VALUE. BRING THESE RESULTS TO CLINIC APPOINTMENTS. Samples of daily record sheets are found in this chapter. If the results are consistently outside of the desired range, change your insulin dose or call, mail or fax your test results to your diabetes care provider to obtain help. **Don't wait for your next scheduled appointment.** The use of blood sugar testing adds an extra expense to diabetes management. In most cases, insurance companies will help to cover this expense. Most doctors and nurses believe diabetes control can be improved through the use of blood sugar testing.

It is necessary for the whole family to be supportive in this effort. Family members must never show displeasure when a reading is high, or testing will become a negative experience. The only response is, "**THANK YOU FOR DOING THE TEST.**"

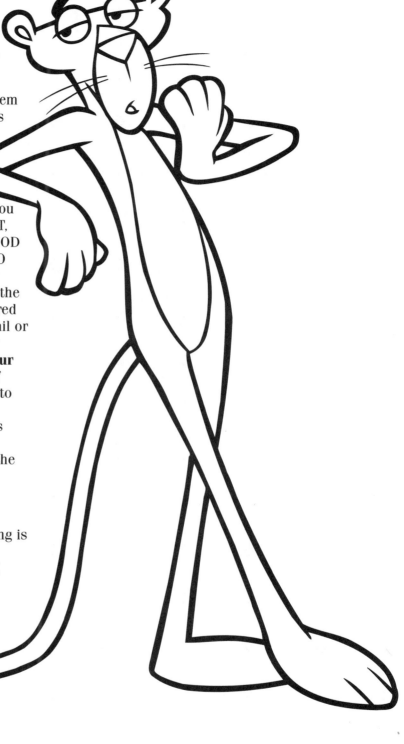

Daily Record Sheet

Name _____

Fax To _____ At _____

Bring these results to your clinic visit

		Breakfast		Lunch		Dinner		Bedtime		Comments: Reactions, exercise, illness, bedtime snack
		Results	Insulin Dose	Results	Insulin Dose	Results	Insulin Dose	Results	Insulin Dose	
Sun	Time									
	BG/Ket									
Mon	Time									
	BG/Ket									
Tues	Time									
	BG/Ket									
Wed	Time									
	BG/Ket									
Thurs	Time									
	BG/Ket									
Fri	Time									
	BG/Ket									
Sat	Time									
	BG/Ket									
Sun	Time									
	BG/Ket									
Mon	Time									
	BG/Ket									
Tues	Time									
	BG/Ket									
Wed	Time									
	BG/Ket									
Thurs	Time									
	BG/Ket									
Fri	Time									
	BG/Ket									
Sat	Time									
	BG/Ket									

Reminder: 1. Make sure insulin doses are included under the Insulin Dose Heading.
2. How to reach you: FAX _____ or Phone _____
    if by phone, best time to reach you:_____ (between 8 a.m.- 5 p.m.)
3. Person to be reached:_____

Daily Record Sheet

Name _____

Fax To _____ At _____

Bring these results to your clinic visit

	Breakfast		Lunch		Dinner		Bedtime		Comments: Reactions, exercise, illness, bedtime snack
	Results	Insulin Dose	Results	Insulin Dose	Results	Insulin Dose	Results	Insulin Dose	
Sun Time									
BG/Ket									
Mon Time									
BG/Ket									
Tues Time									
BG/Ket									
Wed Time									
BG/Ket									
Thurs Time									
BG/Ket									
Fri Time									
BG/Ket									
Sat Time									
BG/Ket									

Reminder: 1. Make sure insulin doses are included under the Insulin Dose Heading
2. How to reach you: FAX _____ or Phone _____
if by phone, best time to reach you:_____ (between 8 a.m.- 5 p.m.)
3. Person to be reached:_____

Concerns:

_____

_____

_____

_____

_____

_____

_____

_____

_____

_____

_____

_____

_____

The Daily Record Sheets may be photocopied as often as desired.

DEFINITIONS

DCCT: Diabetes Control and Complications Trial. This trial was completed in June 1993 and clearly showed that eye, kidney and nerve complications of diabetes were related to glucose control.

Glucose: The scientific name for the sugar in the blood or urine.

Insulin reaction (hypoglycemia): Another term for a blood sugar level that is too low. See Chapter 6.

Monitoring: As used in this chapter, keeping track of and following blood sugar levels at home and writing them down in a record book.

Self blood-glucose monitoring: Checking one's own blood sugar rather than going into a clinic or hospital to have the tests done.

Subcutaneous: Under the skin (but not in a blood vessel).

QUESTIONS (Q) AND ANSWERS (A) FROM NEWSNOTES

Q. What is the best range for my blood sugars?

A. This is not an easy question to answer. It depends on the individual person and family as well as the age of the person with diabetes. Most textbooks list a normal fasting level (or when no food is taken for two or more hours) as 70-120 mg/dl (3.9-6.6 mmol/L). It is unrealistic for most people with diabetes to aim for normal non-diabetic sugar levels. Understanding Diabetes (the Pink Panther book) suggests ranges by ages:

Under five years old: 80-200 mg/dl (4.5-11.1 mmol/L)

5-11 years old: 70-180 mg/dl (3.9-10.0 mmol/L)

12 years old and above: 70-150 mg/dl (3.9-8.3 mmol/L)

However, these are "generally suggested ranges" for fasting or if there is no food intake for at least two hours, and they do not take

individuals or families into account. For example, a 10 to 11-year-old who does blood sugar testing regularly so that the chances of unrecognized low blood sugars occurring are unlikely, and who does not have severe insulin reactions (e.g., unconscious episodes), can probably safely aim for a level of 70-150 mg/dl (3.9-8.3 mmol/L). The reason for aiming for the lower level would be so that the glycohemoglobin (HbA$_{1c}$) levels may be lower with a reduced long-term likelihood of complications.

On the other hand, an adult who has severe episodes of unrecognized hypoglycemia might be wiser to try to achieve the middle range of 70-180 mg/dl (3.9-10.0 mmol/L). This might help to reduce the severe insulin reactions.

It is generally wise to discuss the level of blood sugar to aim for with your physician at each clinic visit.

Q. Should bedtime blood sugar values be in the same range as morning blood sugars?

A. No!
Table 2 in Chapter 7, Blood Glucose Testing, lists suggested blood sugar levels for the morning and bedtime. We ask that values be 50-70 mg/dl (2.7-3.9 mmol/L) higher at bedtime for the three age groups in comparison to the morning values.

This is particularly important for the spring and early summer. As the good weather comes and children play outside in the evening, it is important to reduce the pre-dinner Humalog or NovoLog insulin and to check the blood sugar before the bedtime snack. If the blood sugar value is below the suggested lower limit for the age, an additional snack should be given (and the insulin dose further reduced the next afternoon). Levels are also suggested in Table 2 for when it would be wise to check another blood sugar during the night. It is only by constant monitoring that some families are able to prevent severe insulin reactions in their children.

Q. With the data from the DCCT being in everything we read about diabetes, what can we do to improve glucose control for our 17-year-old son? His morning blood sugars are fine, but he is extremely variable (60-340 mg/dl or 3.2-18.9 mmol/L) before dinner.

A. Blood sugars before dinner are influenced by lots of factors. *For example*:

🐾 The size and sugar content of the afternoon snack

🐾 If it has been two hours without food intake when the blood sugar is done

🐾 Exercise, which makes some people's blood sugar higher due to adrenaline (epinephrine) output while causing other people's to become lower

One helpful practice is to do a blood sugar before the afternoon snack. If the value is high, the snack can be limited to low carbohydrate foods such as diet pop, popcorn, string cheese, carrots, celery, etc. Then see if the value is down by dinner. Obviously, if the value is low, calories are needed. Each family has to decide (on the basis of exercise, school lunch, stress, etc.) what a low value is at that time of day for their child.

Another alternative might also be considered. I know a 17-year-old (whose father asked this question) whom I would guess is going to eat regardless of the blood sugar level! He might take some Humalog or NovoLog insulin if the value is above a certain level to hold him until dinner. In this boy's case, I suggested he take four units of short-acting insulin if the blood sugar is 150-200 mg/dl (8.3-11.1 mmol/L) and six units if greater than 200 mg/dl (11.1 mmol/L). The dose would vary for different sized people and different sized appetites.

A third alternative which works for many people is to exercise for 30 or more minutes (shooting baskets, riding an exercise bike or doing other activities). This brings the sugar down for many people, and the exercise is obviously important for many other reasons.

I should also stress that with the DCCT data and the push for better control, more frequent blood sugar monitoring and extra insulin when the value is high may be the key for many people. Sometimes the extra shot may be in the afternoon or at lunch. This adds extra pressure to families who have children 13 years old or above (as studied in the DCCT), but the results will be rewarding in the long run.

Q. Do I need to test my child's blood sugar every morning at 2:00 a.m.?

A. For most children, this is NOT necessary. Occasional checks during the night (e.g., once every one or two weeks) are helpful. *Special circumstances that make nighttime checks important are:*

🐾 **An illness.** A sick child who may not have eaten well during the day, or who had urine ketones and/or extra (or less) insulin secondary to the illness.

🐾 **A low pre-bedtime snack blood sugar.** If values are below 80 mg/dl (4.4 mmol/L) in a preschooler, below 70 mg/dl (3.9 mmol/L) in a 5 to 12-year-old, or below 60 mg/dl (3.2 mmol/L) in a person age 12 or above, the blood sugar should be checked later (when the parents go to bed or during the night) to make sure the value has risen. This is recommended in Table 2 in Chapter 6. It might also be good to give an extra snack (or a larger amount) at bedtime.

🐾 **Variable morning blood sugar levels.** When some morning blood sugar values are low (e.g., below 60 mg/dl [3.2 mmol/L]) and other values are high (e.g., above 200 mg/dl [11.1 mmol/L]), many care providers suggest doing a value during the night to make sure "rebounding" from low values is not causing the high values. Other care providers believe that rebounding is very unlikely and that the difference in morning values is due to other factors such as variability in insulin absorption.

🐾 **Frequent low blood sugars during the night.** If a child is awakening two or more times during the week with symptoms of low blood sugar, it may be wise to routinely do some middle-of-the-night blood sugars to make sure this is not happening more frequently. The physician caring for the child should also be called.

🐾 **If blood sugars are fluctuating without explanation.** A more intensive testing schedule for a week or more, including early a.m., can often determine where the insulin dosage needs to be adjusted.

Q. With all of the good glucose meters having memories of blood sugar values which can be printed out in clinic, do I still need to write down every blood sugar value?

A. Unfortunately, the answer is **YES**. It is just as important to write values down now as it was when meters did not have memories. It is important to look for "trends" in blood sugar levels in order to know when to make changes in insulin dosages. If a person or family does not do this, they are not doing a good job of home diabetes management. One of my top "pet peeves" in diabetes care is to have a patient (or family) who does blood sugars and constantly has values that are too high or too low, but they don't make changes between clinic visits or fax the values to a diabetes care provider who can make suggestions.

Our general rule of thumb is that if more than half of the values at any time of day are above the upper level (usually 180 for 5-11 years old or above 150 if 12 years or older), an increase in the insulin dose is needed. For example, if an 11-year-old has all morning values above 180 mg/dl (10 mmol/L) for a week, the evening long-lasting insulin should be increased by one unit. Similarly, if the pre-dinner values are all above 180 mg/dl (10 mmol/L) for a week, the morning long-lasting insulin dose should be increased by one or two units. If the values are not being recorded in such a way that values done at the same time of day can be easily compared, it is possible that these trends will be missed. The opposite is also true; if there are more than one or two values in a week below 60 mg/dl (3.24 mmol/L) at any time of the day, the insulin dose working at that time can be reduced. If there is a question whether doses should be changed, the fax page in this Chapter can be faxed to the

healthcare provider (most schools and work places now have fax machines). The faxing of the blood sugars saves valuable doctor/nurse time in having to sit at a phone and write down results. Our Center now averages over twenty patient faxes per day, and it is considered part of the service of the quarterly (every three months) clinic visits.

For the young child or teen who does not want to write values down, it is often acceptable for the parent to push the "M" (memory) button at the end of the day and record the values. This is a way for the parents to stay involved and most teenagers agree to accept this help. The parent is often the family member who does the faxing to the healthcare team as well.

Q. Are blood sugar levels after meals important?

A. Blood sugar levels after meals have previously been largely ignored by children's doctors and families. Yet, the highest blood sugars of the day occur in the 1-2 hours after meals. Recent data shows that these high values affect the HbA_{1c} and are also important in relation to many of the later complications of diabetes. Thus, a new recommendation in this edition of the Pink Panther book is to check the blood sugar two hours after each of the meals at least once weekly.

Part of the problem in the past was that there was not a rapid acting insulin to help to lower the sugars after meals. Now Humalog/NovoLog insulin fills the need. Many of our teens working for improved glucose control (a lower HbA_{1c} level) will now take a shot of Humalog/NovoLog insulin with lunch or with their afternoon snack. If this is done consistently, it can be just as effective as using an insulin pump. The disposable insulin pens are easy to carry and often work effectively for this purpose.

Q. Our family does everything by e-mail now. Is there a way I can get the blood glucose fax sheets from Chapter 7 of the Pink Panther book on my computer?

A. Yes, this can now be easily done. Families wanting to use these forms to e-mail to their doctor or nurse, can get them from these links:

The Barbara Davis Center home page is at: http://www.barbaradaviscenter.org. Then go to Books Online, to Understanding Diabetes, and you can then e-mail them to your doctor and nurse at the Center. The e-mail address at my clinic is:

_____

It is <u>essential</u> for you to give phone numbers and the time to get back to you as it is often best to actively discuss the blood sugars and insulin doses.

Please note: depending on the resolution of your monitor, the lines on the sheets may not appear continuous. They will, however, print out accurately.

APPENDIX 1 FOR CHAPTER 7

VISUAL METHOD TO DO BLOOD SUGARS USING CHEMSTRIP bG Strips

The nurse educator will explain how to use the strip. There are several products available for doing blood sugar tests. The Chemstrip bG strips can be used without a meter by comparing the color change of the strip to a color chart. They also may be used with several blood sugar meters. Chemstrips can be cut in half (lengthwise) for visual reading (not meter reading) to save some money.

The directions for using the Chemstrip bG strips are on the side of every can but will be summarized here:

🐾 Place a large drop of blood on the white-yellow pad at the end of the strip, covering the entire pad (essential if the strip is to be meter-read). Do not add a second drop of blood if the first drop was not large enough. The strip can still be visually read.

🐾 Note the time on the second hand of a clock as the drop is put on the strip. If using a meter, push the timer button. A clock with a second hand or a digital timer must always be used for visual reading.

🐾 After EXACTLY 60 seconds, wipe off all visible blood with a dry cotton (or rayon) ball. Wait another 60 seconds and then compare the colors to those on the side of the can. If a meter is being used, place the strip in the slot at 100-110 seconds. This allows drying time before inserting the strip into the meter.

🐾 In contrast to the directions on the can, we suggest using only the green block at the top of the strip if this block turns color. If it doesn't, only the blue (lower) block is used when comparing to the colors on the side of the can. We do not recommend trying to average the results of the two blocks.

🐾 When the green color is darker than the 240 mg/dl (13.3 mmol/L) comparison block, it is necessary to wait another minute before comparing the color on the strip with the three blocks in the second row on the can. Some meters also have a way to do a later reading.

🐾 Values can be estimated when colors of the strip are between those of the blocks on the can.

🐾 The Chemstrip bG strips hold their color for two hours after the test so others can check to see if they agree with the reading. The strips can also be dated and put back in the can if it is desired to keep them longer than two hours.

🐾 If the meter will not read the strip (the Accu-Chek II gives an "S -" reading), it can still be read visually. Reasons for a meter not giving a reading are outlined in Table 3 in this Chapter.

🐾 Remember to always record the results of the test in your book and to bring your record book with you to clinic visits.

Note: *Problems with visual readings can result from improper timing, wiping too hard or too lightly and not using the correct material (dry cotton or rayon) for doing the wiping.*

APPENDIX II FOR CHAPTER 7

SOME METERS WITH PROGRAMS TO ALLOW DOWNLOADING AT HOME

PROGRAM AND COST	VENDOR/ADDRESS PHONE/WEBSITE	METER SUPPORT
In Touch Diabetes Management: free with connecting cable; cable = $19.99	**LifeScan, Inc.**, 1000 Gibraltar Drive, Milpitas, CA 95035, 800-382-7226, http://www.lifescan.com/lsprods/intouch.html	One Touch Ultra
Precision Link: connecting cable = $50.00	**MediSense, Inc.**, 4A Crosby Drive, Bedford, MA 01730, 800-527-3339, http://www.abbottdiagnostics.com	Precision Xtra
WinGlucofacts: software can be downloaded from website (http://www.bayerdiag.com) Bayer Glucometer Dex connecting cable = $29.95; Glucometer Elite XL connecting cable = $29.95	**Bayer Corp.**, 511 Benedict Avenue, Tarrytown, NY 10591, 800-348-8100, http://www.glucometerdex.com http://www.glucometerelitexl.com http://www.glucometerstore.com	Bayer Glucometer Dex
Accu-Chek Compass: software = $29.99 connecting cable = $30.00	**Roche Diagnostics,** 9115 Hague Road, P.O. Box 50457, Indianapolis, IN 46250-0457, 800-858-8072, http://www.accu-chek.com	Accu-Chek® Complete
Camit for Windows 1.1: $59.95 (including cable)	**Roche Diagnostics,** Same as above	Accu-Chek Advantage, Easy, and Accu-Chek III
FreeStyle Connect Data Management System with cable = $75.00	**Therasense,** 1360 South Loop Road Alameda, CA 94502, 510-749-5400, http://www.therasense.com	FreeStyle

Chapter 8

TOPIC: ❧ Medications (Insulin)

TEACHING OBJECTIVES:

1. Describe insulin and what it does in the body.

2. Present the types of insulins to be used and their actions.

3. Discuss the schedule for insulin injections.

4. Identify who and when to call for insulin doses.

LEARNING OBJECTIVES:

Learners (parents, child, relative and self) will be able to:

1. State why the body needs insulin.

2. List the specific types of insulins to be used and their actions (onset, peak and duration).

3. State the schedule for insulin injections (including before or after meals).

4. Identify who and when to call for insulin doses.

Chapter 8 INSULIN: TYPES AND ACTIVITY

INSULIN

Before insulin was discovered in 1921, there was little help for people who had type 1 diabetes. Since then, millions of people all over the world have been helped by insulin.

Insulin is a hormone made in the pancreas, an organ inside the abdomen (see picture in Chapter 2). Special cells called "beta cells" make the insulin. These cells are located in a part of the pancreas called the "islets" (pronounced eye-lets). When a person has type 1 diabetes, there is a loss of the cells which make insulin. Other cells in the pancreas and throughout the body continue to work normally.

Most people with diabetes now use human insulin. The human insulin does not come from humans, but has the same "make-up" as human insulin. It is produced by bacteria (Lilly) or by yeast (Novo-Nordisk) using "genetic engineering." There are no known advantages of one brand of insulin over another brand.

WHAT IT DOES

Food (carbohydrate) is converted to sugar for the body's energy needs. The insulin allows the sugar to pass from the blood into the cells. There it is burned for energy. The body cannot turn sugar into energy without insulin (see diagram in Chapter 2). Insulin also turns off the making of sugar in the liver (see Chapter 2). If insulin is not available, the sugar builds up in the blood until it spills into the urine.

People who have type 1 diabetes can't make enough insulin. These people have to get the needed insulin through injections. **Insulin cannot be taken as a pill, because the stomach acid destroys it.** People who have type 2 diabetes still make insulin. They can

take pills to help them make even more insulin or to be more sensitive to their own insulin. However, these pills **are not** insulin. There are no known vitamins, herbs or other medications which can take the place of insulin injections.

TYPES OF INSULIN

Several companies make many different types of insulins.

The three broad classes of insulin are:

1. "short-acting" (such as Humalog, NovoLog and Regular)

2. "intermediate-acting" (such as NPH [N], Lente and Ultralente)

3. "long-acting" such as Lantus®

Insulin action (when it begins working, when it peaks in activity and how long it lasts) may vary from person to person. The action may also vary from one day to the next in the same person. The site of the shot and exercise may influence the insulin action as well. Average times of action for different insulins are shown in Table 1.

1. Short-Acting Insulins (last 4-9 hours)

Humalog/NovoLog insulin is fast in onset of activity (10-15 minutes). It has its peak activity in 30-90 minutes and lasts four hours. The figures show the activities of the short acting insulins.

Our experience at the time of writing this chapter is mainly with Humalog insulin. NovoLog (made by Novo-Nordisk) has similar action. Thus, although the name Humalog may be used alone in this Chapter, NovoLog has similar activity. We may also use Humalog/NovoLog to indicate the insulin used may be either one.

Humalog/NovoLog insulin has several advantages over Regular insulin:

☙ It starts to work in 10 minutes rather than in 30-60 minutes. It can be taken just prior to eating rather than 30 minutes before meals. It also can be given after meals to allow for carbohydrate counting or "picky" eaters. It peaks in activity as the food is absorbed. On the other hand, Regular insulin peaks after the food is mostly absorbed.

☙ The blood sugar levels two hours after meals are lower when it is taken prior to meals.

☙ Because it does not last as long, there is less danger of lows during the night.

☙ Use of Humalog after meals in toddlers who eat varying amounts can help to prevent hypoglycemia as well as food struggles (Chapter 18).

The main disadvantage of the Humalog/NovoLog insulin is its shorter time of action. Regular insulin can be mixed with the Humalog insulin (with either one going into the syringe first). This can extend the period of action. The intermediate-acting insulin can also be added to the same syringe. We have used the term "insulin cocktails" to refer to the mixing of three or more insulins in the same syringe. This is discussed in more detail in Chapter 21.

It is fine to use Humalog/NovoLog just before a meal on one day when one plans to eat right away. On another day, if the meal will not be eaten right away, Regular insulin (same dosage) can be taken.

Regular insulin begins to act approximately 30-60 minutes after being injected. It has its peak effect 2-4 hours after the injection and lasts 6-9 hours. There is again, considerable variability in these times from person to person.

Humalog/NovoLog and Regular insulins can be combined in the same syringe. It does not matter which of the two insulins goes into the syringe first. They should **both** be drawn up **before** the intermediate-acting insulin (see Chapter 9). Using both Humalog and Regular insulin together allows for an immediate effect on the blood sugar and food about to be eaten (from Humalog/NovoLog). The Regular will cover for a later snack or meal. Examples of

mixtures of Humalog/NovoLog and Regular insulin are given in Chapter 21.

It is important to remember to avoid taking a warm shower (or bath) or getting into a hot tub for one to two hours after taking insulin. The warm water increases the blood flow to the skin and causes the insulin to be absorbed faster. This faster rate of absorption could cause a low blood sugar.

2. Intermediate-acting insulins (last 10-20 hours)

✔ **NPH (N)** insulin is made with a protein that allows it to be absorbed in the body more slowly. The letters NPH stand for **N**eutral **P**rotamine **H**agedorn. Protamine is the protein added to the insulin to make it longer-acting. Hagedorn is the name of the man who developed it. Human NPH has its peak activity 4-8 hours after the injection in most people. If it is taken in the morning, the peak action comes before supper. Human NPH insulin lasts an average of 13 hours. The peak in NPH insulin activity and the duration of activity may vary for some people. NPH insulin can be premixed with Regular insulin without changing the activities of either insulin. (NPH is now called "N" on the bottles.)

✔ Human **Ultralente** insulin lasts 15-18 hours and, for some people, up to 24 hours. It has some peak in activity which occurs later than for NPH insulin. It is sometimes taken at dinner as the intermediate-acting insulin to turn off sugar production in one's own body ("internal" sugar production by the liver - see Chapter 2) during the night. This is shown in the figures that follow. The methods to adjust all insulin dosages are discussed in Chapter 21.

✔ **Pre-mixed Insulins:** The pre-mixed insulins are used primarily by people who do not wish to draw the insulins from separate vials prior to injecting.

• **Lente** insulin is a pre-mixed combination of seven parts of Ultralente insulin and three parts Semilente (a short-acting) insulin (see Table 1).

• **70/30®** and **Mixtard®** similarly, different combinations of pre-mixed NPH and Regular insulin are available. The most frequently used are 70/30 and Mixtard, both of which have 70% NPH and 30% Regular insulins. The usual times of activity are shown in Table 1.

- **Humalog mix 75/25** (Lilly) is also a combination of a rapid (25%) and an intermediate-acting (75%) insulin. The rapid-acting portion is a bit "blunted" when compared with the usual Humalog peak. Some people require a third injection of 75/25 at lunch or bedtime for better control.

3. Long-acting insulin (lasts 20-24 hours)

✔ **Lantus (Insulin Glargine)** insulin became readily available in the U.S. in May, 2001. It is a clear insulin that lasts 24 hours with almost no peak (the first true basal insulin). Its profile is similar to the basal insulin (the insulin that stops sugar output from the liver) put out by a normal pancreas. It is often compared with the basal insulin of an insulin pump (Chapter 26).

Advantages of Lantus:

- Its consistency in absorption and activity make it more predictable. NPH and Ultralente vary in their peak activity even in the same person from one day to the next. Lantus insulin has less variability.

- Because it is a clear insulin, it does not need to be turned up and down to mix. There is no settling and insulin concentrations do not vary from one shot to the next.

- Reduction of low blood sugars: initial studies at our Center have shown a decrease in very low blood sugars when compared with using NPH, Lente and Ultralente insulins. This is due to less of an activity peak as well as consistent absorption.

Disadvantages of Lantus:

- No other insulin can be mixed in the same syringe. It is more acidic (pH 4.0) than other insulins (pH 7.4). If Lantus is mixed with another insulin, both lose activity.

- When using Lantus, three or more shots per day of a short-acting insulin may be needed.

- Because it is clear and has a purple cap, care must be taken not to confuse it with the short-acting insulin, Humalog.

Four ways we are currently using Lantus insulin:

1. Lantus is taken in the evening (6-10 p.m.). Humalog is taken before each meal. The pre-meal insulin is usually given with an insulin pen (see Figure 1). The advantage of taking Lantus at 9-10 p.m. is that its activity can decrease after 20-24 hours. This is a time (6-10 p.m.) when the dinner Humalog is working, and so the decrease won't matter. If the activity of the Lantus lessens after 20 hours, the dinner Humalog/NovoLog will cover this time period.

For those teens who prefer having fewer time periods to inject insulin, the Lantus and Humalog/NovoLog can both be given at dinner. They MUST be given in separate syringes or pens. This may help prevent forgetting the Lantus shot later in the evening.

For infants or those who have trouble with shots, Lantus can be given after they are sleeping (usually in the buttocks). This should be discussed between the family and the healthcare provider. It is best used this way with the permission of the child.

2. Lantus is taken either at dinner or in the evening as above. A mixture (in the same syringe) of NPH and Humalog/NovoLog (sometimes also Regular) is taken prior to breakfast. This works well for children who are not ready to take a noon shot at school. The NPH insulin may also help to cover an afternoon snack. Some people who take a noon shot still do better with a small amount of NPH insulin in the morning. This may be because Humalog/NovoLog taken at noon is gone by 4 p.m. We usually start with about one-third of the previous morning dose of intermediate-acting insulin.

3. Some younger children do better getting their Lantus in the morning. Insulin activity can then fall off in the early morning hours of the next day. A separate morning shot of Humalog/NovoLog and NPH may be required. A third shot of Humalog/NovoLog prior to dinner is also usually needed.

4. Some prefer to divide the Lantus into two separate doses. If Lantus is given twice, 25% of the day's dose is given in the a.m. and 75%

in the p.m. This may involve five shots of insulin per day, giving Humalog/NovoLog before each meal. Dividing the Lantus dose in this way may give more insulin activity during the daytime.

Lantus Dose: the <u>starting</u> dose is often half the total units of intermediate-acting insulin taken per day (a.m. and p.m.).

For example:

If 40 units of NPH insulin was taken in the morning and 20 units of ultralente insulin was taken at dinner, a total of 60 units of intermediate-acting insulin was taken per day. We would then start the person on 30 units of Lantus insulin.

This dose can then be increased or decreased depending on morning blood sugars.

The goal for the morning and pre-dinner blood sugar value is:

Under 5 years of age:
80-200 mg/dl (4.5-11.1 mmol/L)

5-11 years of age:
70-180 mg/dl (3.9-10.0 mmol/L)

12 years and above:
70-150 mg/dl (3.9-8.3 mmol/L)

Once the Lantus dose is set, if sugar values are too high during the day, Humalog and NPH (usually about one-third the previous morning NPH dose) can be added in the morning. The dose of morning NPH is increased until the pre-dinner blood sugars are within the ranges listed above.

Lantus is not for everyone. If the HbA_{1c} (Chapter 14) is good and there is not a problem with frequent lows, a change is probably not needed. ("If it's not broken, don't fix it.") Similarly, if the child or family is not ready for three or four shots per day, Lantus should not be considered. It is expensive (up to $60 [U.S.]/bottle), and it is important to make sure the HMO or insurance company will pay for it.

Figure 1: Use of Lantus Insulin

Two of the most common methods of using Lantus insulin:

In the first example, Lantus is used as the basal insulin and Humalog (H) or NovoLog is taken prior to meals.

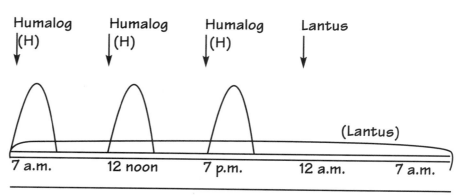

In this second example, NPH and Humalog (H) or NovoLog are taken in one syringe in the a.m. Humalog is taken alone at dinner. Lantus (alone in the syringe) is taken either at dinner, at bedtime or in the a.m.

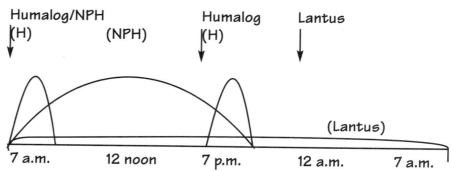

INSULIN ACTIVITIES

Type of Insulin	Begins Working	Main Effect	All Gone
SHORT-ACTING (lasts 4-10 hours)			
Humalog/NovoLog	10-15 minutes	30-90 minutes	4 hours
Regular	30-60 minutes	2-4 hours	6-9 hours
INTERMEDIATE-ACTING (lasts 10-20 hours)			
NPH	1-2 hours	3-8 hours	12-15 hours
Ultralente	2-4 hours	6-14 hours	18-20 hours
LONG-ACTING (lasts 20-24 hours)			
Lantus (Insulin Glargine)	1-2 hours	2-22 hours	24 hours
PRE-MIXED INSULINS			
Lente	1-2 hours	3-14 hours	18-20 hours
70/30 NPH/Regular	30-60 minutes	3-8 hours	12-15 hours
75/25 NPH/Humalog	10-15 minutes	30 minutes-8 hours	12-15 hours

HOW OFTEN IS INSULIN GIVEN?

One Injection Per Day

A few people have good blood sugar control by taking insulin once a day. This is particularly true during the "honeymoon" period that occurs shortly after diagnosis. The new Lantus insulin is the first true "basal" insulin and is usually taken at dinner or bedtime. It has very little "peak" and lasts a full 24 hours (see Table 1). One injection a day of Lantus might be used during this "honeymoon" period. Some people with type 2 diabetes who need insulin may do well with one injection of Lantus each day. The combination of insulins usually used is an intermediate-acting insulin (Lente, Ultralente or NPH) and a short-acting insulin (Humalog, NovoLog or Regular). The two types of insulin are combined in one syringe for a single injection to provide insulin activity over several time periods. The morning shot of NPH, Lente or Ultralente insulin has its main activity in the afternoon. These insulins do not last through the night. Thus, two injections per day are usually necessary.

People who take one insulin injection per day may do better on two injections per day if they:

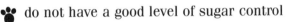 do not have a good level of sugar control

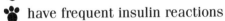 have frequent insulin reactions

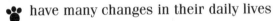 have many changes in their daily lives

Two Injections Per Day

Most people obtain better sugar control using two or more injections of insulin per day. (The exception may be during the honeymoon period.) Most doctors now believe it is best to treat all patients with type 1 diabetes with two or more injections per day. When a person receives two injections per day, there are four (or more) small peaks of insulin activity (see Figure 2 for diagrams of two shots each day). Each of the small peaks in insulin activity can be adjusted to fit the person's schedule.

During adolescence, diabetes control may become more difficult. Teens usually need more insulin. The sex and growth hormones make it more difficult for insulin to work. These hormones also seem to increase the likelihood of blood vessel changes in people with diabetes. Because of this, better sugar control is an important goal at this time. This goal can often be achieved more easily with three or more injections of insulin per day.

Figure 2: Two Injections Per Day

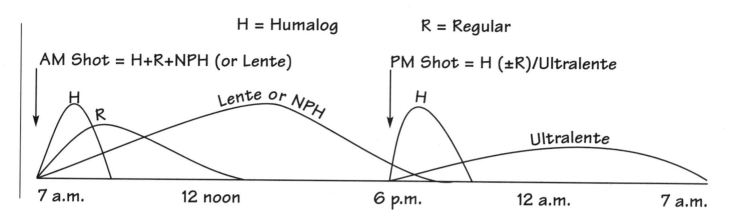

H = Humalog   R = Regular

AM Shot = H+R+NPH (or Lente)   PM Shot = H (±R)/Ultralente

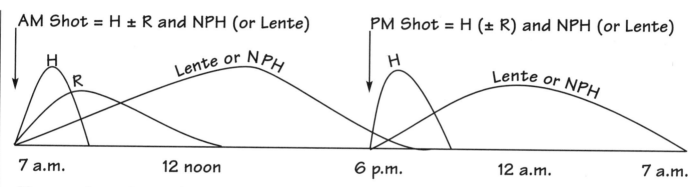

AM Shot = H ± R and NPH (or Lente)   PM Shot = H (± R) and NPH (or Lente)

Many people receive two injections per day of NPH or Lente as their intermediate-acting insulin. They can then take Humalog or Regular or both with the NPH or Lente (see figure above).

Either NPH, Lente or Ultralente insulins can be used as the intermediate-acting insulin when two or three injections of insulin are taken each day. We will sometimes even mix NPH and Ultralente in the same syringe (see Chapter 21, Insulin Cocktails). If Humalog/NovoLog and Regular insulin are also being used, there could be four insulins in the same syringe. NPH insulin is often used in the morning. The peak in activity helps allow the food eaten during the day to be used for energy. Ultralente is sometimes used at dinner as it lasts a few hours longer than NPH. It may be more likely to last during the night. When only Humalog/NovoLog (not Regular) insulin is used in the dinner shot with Ultralente (or NPH), there is less risk for low blood sugars between 10 p.m. and 2 a.m.

Three or More Injections Per Day

Most people over age 12 now receive three (or more) shots of insulin each day (see Figure 3). In addition, most people using Lantus as their basal insulin, take at least three shots per day. This is often called **intensive diabetes management**.

Intensive diabetes management involves:

* Three or more shots of insulin per day (or use of an insulin pump)

* Checking blood sugar levels four or more times per day

* Paying attention to food intake

* Frequent communication with the healthcare provider

Figure 3: Three Injections Per Day

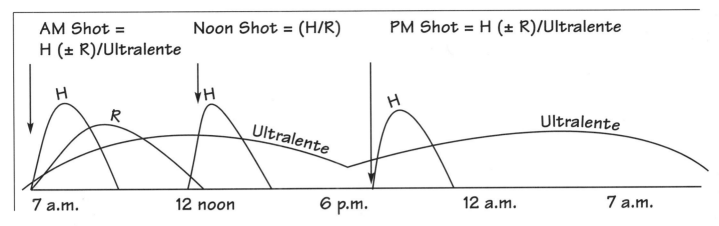

AM Shot =
H (± R)/Ultralente

Noon Shot = (H/R)

PM Shot = H (± R)/Ultralente

H

R

Ultralente

H

H

Ultralente

7 a.m.   12 noon   6 p.m.   12 a.m.   7 a.m.

The above diagram shows Humalog (± Regular) and Ultralente in the morning and at dinner, with Humalog (± Regular) at lunch.

The diagram below demonstrates Humalog (and/or Regular mixtures) with NPH or Lente insulins in the morning, Humalog (and/or Regular) at dinner, and NPH (or Lente) at bedtime.

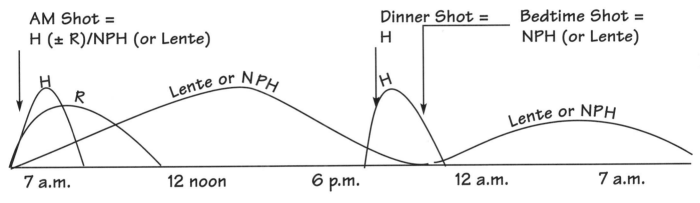

AM Shot =
H (± R)/NPH (or Lente)

Dinner Shot =
H

Bedtime Shot =
NPH (or Lente)

H

R

Lente or NPH

H

Lente or NPH

7 a.m.   12 noon   6 p.m.   12 a.m.   7 a.m.

A third regimen for people taking three shots per day is to use Humalog/Regular with NPH or Lente in the morning, a shot of Humalog at 3:30 p.m. to cover "grazing" in the afternoons and Humalog and Ultralente at dinner (see below). A modification of this third regimen (not shown) is to take a mixture of Humalog and Regular at 3:30 p.m. to cover the afternoon snack and dinner and then to take the longer-acting insulin - NPH, Lente or Ultralente at bedtime.

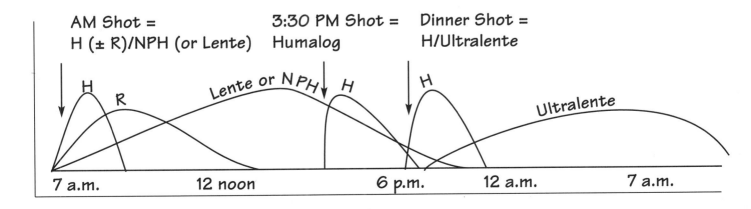

AM Shot =
H (± R)/NPH (or Lente)

3:30 PM Shot =
Humalog

Dinner Shot =
H/Ultralente

H

R

Lente or NPH

H

H

Ultralente

7 a.m.   12 noon   6 p.m.   12 a.m.   7 a.m.

Three common regimens for using three or more shots per day are:

1. Before each meal: Humalog/NovoLog
Before dinner/bedtime: Lantus

OR

2. Before breakfast: Humalog/NovoLog and NPH
Before dinner: Humalog/NovoLog
Before dinner/bedtime: Lantus

3. Before breakfast: Humalog/NovoLog (or Regular) and NPH or Ultralente
Before noon meal: Humalog/NovoLog (or Regular)
Before dinner: Humalog/NovoLog (or Regular) and NPH or Ultralente
Before bedtime: NPH if not given before dinner

AMOUNT OF INSULIN

Insulin is measured in "units" per cc (ml). All U.S. insulin now contains 100 units per cc (ml). It is called U-100 insulin. Standard insulin syringes hold either 3/10cc (30 units), 1/2cc (50 units) or 1cc (100 units). The 3/10cc syringes have larger distances between the unit lines and are easier to use if it is necessary to measure small doses.

Insulin dosage is based on body weight, blood sugar test results, exercise planned and food intake. After the initial diagnosis and treatment, people are usually started on approximately 1/4 unit of insulin per pound (1/2 unit per kilogram [kg]) of body weight per day. The dose is then gradually increased as needed up to 1/2 unit per pound body weight (1 unit per kg body weight). After a few weeks to months, many children go into a "honeymoon" or "grace" period when very little insulin is required (see Chapter 2). Frequent telephone contact with the diabetes team is important when the honeymoon starts. The insulin dosage must then be reduced to prevent low blood sugars. We generally recommend continuing the injections during this period. After the honeymoon, most people gradually increase to an average insulin dosage of 1/2 unit per pound body weight (1.1 units per kg body weight). During the teenage growth spurt, the growth hormone level is high and blocks insulin activity. The insulin dosage may

increase to 1.5 units per kg body weight (0.7 units/pound). The dosage then goes back down after the period of growth is over. Insulin dosages can be adjusted to fit the person's lifestyle and needs.

For example, seasonal changes are common.

🐾 In the winter: when it is cold outside, children do not go out to play after dinner. They may need more Humalog/NovoLog (or Regular) insulin before the evening meal.

🐾 In the summer: when they go outside to play after dinner, the evening Humalog/NovoLog (or Regular) insulin dose often can be decreased. Chapter 21 deals with how to adjust insulin dosages.

INTENSIVE DIABETES MANAGEMENT

Intensive diabetes management refers to the routine use of more than two shots of insulin per day (or insulin pump therapy). It was discussed above under "Three or more Injections per Day." It also includes frequent blood glucose monitoring (four or more times per day). It requires careful adjustment of food intake. Frequent contact with the healthcare provider is often necessary. Some of the insulin regimens are are shown in Figures 1 and 3.

The Diabetes Control and Complications Trial (DCCT) research proved that sugar control "closer to normal" helps to prevent the complications of diabetes (Chapter 14). More individuals are selecting intensive diabetes management. The goal of intensive management is to keep the blood sugars closer to normal than can be done with one or two injections per day. For intensive therapy to be safe, frequent blood sugar tests are needed. When people tell us they are ready for intensive management, we often test their commitment by first asking them to do four blood sugar tests per day for one month. It is pointless to recommend intensive management until people decide that they are ready and willing. Insulin pumps have become safer and more popular in recent years. Chapter 26 discusses insulin pump use.

INSULINS WE FREQUENTLY USE

Type	Name	Color of Box or Cap	Manufacturer
Humalog	Humalog	Purple Cap	Lilly
Regular	Humulin-R	White Box With Black Print	" "
NPH	Humulin-N	" "	" "
Lente	Humulin-L	" "	" "
Ultralente	Humulin-U	" "	" "
Humalog Mix	75/25	" "	" "
Regular	Novolin-R	White Box With Blue Markings	Novo-Nordisk
NPH	Novolin-N	" "	" "
Lente	Novolin-L	" "	" "
Regular (Pen)	Novolin R PenFill	" "	" "
NPH (Pen)	Novolin N PenFill	" "	" "
NovoLog	NovoLog	Orange cap	" "
Insulin Glargine	Lantus (clear)	Purple cap, tall bottle	Aventis

DEFINITIONS

Analog: A new form of insulin with a slightly different make-up that results in different times of onset and duration of activity. Humalog is an example of an insulin analog modified to have rapid onset of activity.

Beta cells: The cells in the islets of the pancreas which actually produce insulin.

cc (cubic centimeter; same as ml or milliliter): A unit of measurement. Five cubic centimeters (cc) equals one teaspoon; 15cc equals one tablespoon; 30cc equals one ounce; 240cc equals one cup.

DCCT: The Diabetes Control and Complications Trial. A very large research trial that showed that better sugar control reduced the likelihood of the eye, kidney and nerve complications in people over age 13 with type 1 diabetes.

Hormone: A chemical found in the blood and made in certain glands. An example is insulin that is produced by the pancreas.

Humalog insulin (insulin lispro): This is synthetically made insulin with two amino acids in the insulin molecule, lysine and proline, reversed in order. As a result, the insulin molecules do not bind as tightly to each other and the insulin has a more rapid onset of action (10-15 minutes) and a shorter duration of meaningful activity (about four hours).

Insulin pump: A machine designed to give a preset steady (basal) injection of insulin throughout the day, as well as before-meal supplements (boluses) which are regulated by the user. Current pumps do not stop injecting insulin when blood sugars are low.

Lantus insulin (Insulin Glargine): A new basal insulin that is flat in activity and lasts 24-hours. It has an acid pH and cannot be mixed with any other insulin (all have a nuetral pH).

NovoLog insulin: a rapid-acting synthetic insulin (made by the Novo-Nordisk company) which has activity very similar to that of Humalog (see above).

QUESTIONS (Q) AND ANSWERS (A) FROM NEWSNOTES

Q. I know I'm supposed to take my insulin and then wait to eat, but there's no way. My life just isn't that structured. I inject right before I eat. Would Humalog insulin work better for me than Regular insulin?

A. You're in good company. Most people don't wait the recommended 30-60 minutes between injecting Regular insulin and eating. In one survey, 90% of the respondents didn't wait.

Humalog is the no-wait insulin. It starts acting much more quickly than Regular, so you take it right before you eat. It starts working about the time the glucose from your meal hits your bloodstream. In contrast, if you inject Regular right before you eat, the glucose from your meal will hit your bloodstream way before the Regular does, and your glucose level will be high after the meal. So if you prefer to inject right before you eat, you're going to get better blood glucose control with Humalog than with Regular.

Q. I sometimes have low sugars in the middle of the night. Do you have any suggestions to prevent this?

A. People who use Regular at dinner time and who tend to have hypoglycemic episodes between 10 p.m. and 2 a.m. will likely have fewer lows when they change to Humalog/NovoLog. This is because Humalog/NovoLog lasts only about four hours. A shot taken at 6 p.m. won't be active in the middle of the night. In contrast, Regular insulin may still be lowering the blood sugar 6-10 hours later, and sometimes even 14 hours later. Our research shows that the total number of hypoglycemic events is reduced by half in people taking Humalog compared with Regular insulin users. The frequency of nighttime lows, in particular, is reduced. A consistent bedtime snack is also helpful.

Q. What are the main advantages of the insulin analogs, Humalog or NovoLog? Should everyone just switch to it?

A. First, the advantages: Humalog/NovoLog is quick-acting and starts working in 10 minutes. With the human Regular insulin, we ask people to wait 30-60 minutes to eat after taking their shot. This would allow insulin to work as the food was absorbed, rather than first sending the blood sugar to 300-500 mg/dl (16.6-27.7 mmol/L). Unfortunately, this was inconvenient and most people (90% in one survey) just took their shots and ate. The high blood sugars in the hour or two after eating added to higher HbA_{1c} values at clinic visits. Now, with Humalog/NovoLog, the waiting is not necessary. People can take their shots and immediately eat their meals. This will result in lower blood sugars in the two hours after meals as well as less guilt from not following rigid instructions.

A **second** major advantage of Humalog/NovoLog is that it only lasts four hours. When people take human Regular insulin before supper, it is not unusual to get late peaks of activity (and hypoglycemia) between midnight and 2:00 a.m. This will not happen with Humalog/NovoLog as activity is gone in four hours. Our research showed the total number of low blood sugars to be reduced in half in people using Humalog. The lows from midnight to 6:00 a.m. were particularly reduced.

Q. Should everyone switch to Humalog/NovoLog?

A. The answer is definitely **NO**.

It is a prescription medication and the switch should be made with the help of healthcare providers at the time of clinic visits. A recent example of a person who should not switch was that of a college student who wanted to take his insulin shots in the dorm room and then walk across the street to stand in line to eat at the cafeteria. It would be likely that this person would be experiencing low blood sugars before the first bite was ever eaten if he was using Humalog/NovoLog. Another example of someone who should not switch is a teenager who receives two shots of insulin daily but who does not eat breakfast!

It is fine to use Humalog/NovoLog at one meal and human Regular at another meal on the same day. As people learn more about how Humalog/NovoLog works in their body, they will likely use "THINKING SCALES" (see Chapter 21) more and more. For example, they may use Humalog/NovoLog on Saturday morning when getting up a bit late with a high blood sugar (and planning to eat right away). Or, they may use Regular insulin on another morning when the blood sugar is low and there will be six hours between breakfast and lunch. Or, they may use a mixture of the two insulins in the same situation when the morning blood sugar is high! All kinds of alternatives will now be possible!

Q. How do you decide when someone is ready for intensive diabetes management?

A. This is a decision that is made by the person with diabetes and the diabetes care provider. Intensive management takes extra time and effort; the patient has to be ready to make this commitment (not the parents). It involves taking insulin shots before meals, adjusting for carbohydrate intake and doing frequent blood sugar monitoring to determine if insulin dosages are correct. We often start by asking the person to do a minimum of four blood sugar tests per day and ask them to bring the values to the clinic in one month. Motivation to proceed can then be discussed.

Chapter 9

TOPIC:
❧ Medications: Insulin Mixing and Administration

TEACHING OBJECTIVES:

1. Demonstrate technique for mixing and drawing up insulin.

2. Identify age appropriate injection sites.

3. Instruct injection technique.

4. Observe family members/self giving insulin injection.

WITH SPECIAL THANKS FOR THE SUGGESTIONS OF:

- Paula Gutzmer, RN, MN
- DeAnn Johnson, RN, BSN, CDE

LEARNER OBJECTIVES:

Learner (parents, child, relative or self) will be able to:

1. Complete accurate demonstration for mixing and drawing up insulin.

2. Choose two age appropriate sites for injections.

3. Demonstrate correct injection technique using saline.

4. Demonstrate correct injection technique using insulin.

Chapter 9

DRAWING UP AND GIVING INSULIN

WHERE TO INJECT THE INSULIN

Insulin is injected into the fat layer beneath the skin. Proper techniques must be learned so that the insulin is not injected too close to the outer skin (which may cause a lump, pain or a red spot) or too deep into the muscle (which may cause pain and insulin to be absorbed too quickly). If the injections are given in the recommended areas (see diagram of the Pink Panther), it is very unlikely that a large artery or vein will be entered. The only problem if this were ever to happen would be that the insulin would last only a matter of minutes rather than hours. Also, it is not true that injecting a bubble of air into someone (even into an artery or vein) would harm them. These are common, but unnecessary worries.

INJECTION SITES

The best places to give insulin are the abdomen, arms, thighs and buttocks. Rotation of injection sites used to be a frequent area of conflict between parents and children. It is now possible to select two or three of the usual four areas for injections (arms, thighs, abdomen, buttocks) and to skip areas that are not well tolerated. Injections should be moved around within the sites that are used (example: six to nine areas in each thigh site). If there are swollen (hypertrophied) areas, injections should not be given into these sites, as the insulin may be absorbed at a different rate.

Insulin is absorbed more rapidly from the abdomen than from the arm, and more rapidly from the arm than from the thigh or buttock. However, the differences are not great for most people. Some people who do notice a difference will use one site for morning shots and another site for dinner shots. For example, the abdomen or arm might be used in the morning when more rapid insulin uptake is desired. The thigh or buttock might be used in the evening when less rapid insulin uptake is desired so that the insulin will last through the night.

There is some increase in uptake of insulin when the shot is given in an area that is then exercised. Injecting into an arm or leg which will be used in an activity may result in low blood sugars during exercise. Therefore, if you are to play tennis, don't inject into the arm that will be used to swing the racquet. More blood will go to this arm during the exercise and more insulin will be absorbed into the blood. A low blood sugar could occur.

Insulin should also not be injected just prior to a bath, shower or hot tub. The warm water will draw more blood to the skin, causing a rapid absorption and resulting in a serious low blood sugar.

INSULIN SYRINGES

(See picture diagram of insulin syringes and Table 1)

There are now several brands of disposable insulin syringes with varying needle widths (measured in gauges with a larger number for a thinner needle) and varying lengths. The needles are thin and are sharp for easy insertion. If money is short, the syringes can be reused. Others feel it is best to only use the syringe one time. They note the needle may be dulled as a result of going through the rubber stopper on the insulin vial. If dulled, then it might cause more tissue damage. There is also the possibility of infection when reusing syringes.

The amount of insulin the syringe will hold varies. There are 3/10cc and 1/2cc syringes for people using less than 30 or 50 units of

Injection Rotation Chart

Chapter 9: Drawing Up and Giving Insulin

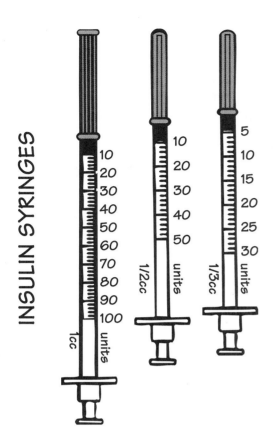

INSULIN SYRINGES

1cc units — 10 20 30 40 50 60 70 80 90 100

1/2cc units — 10 20 30 40 50

1/3cc units — 5 10 15 20 25 30

insulin per injection, or 1cc syringes for those using more than 50 units per injection (see drawings). The B-D Ultra-Fine II short needles are just 5/16 inch in length (compared with the usual 1/2 inch length) and at 30 gauge are very thin. The Precision™ Sure-Dose™ 0.3cc syringe (30 gauge needle by 3/8 inch length) can measure insulin in half units. It is a MediSense product of Abbott Laboratories. This syringe can be helpful for young children.

DRAWING UP THE INSULIN

You will be shown how to draw the insulin into the syringe. YOU SHOULD LEARN BY PRACTICE AND FORM GOOD HABITS FROM THE START. When possible, wash your hands first. The picture diagrams show how to draw up insulin and give an injection. Our families often start by doing "air" shots into a doll or mannequin. The next practice step is drawing up sterile salt water (saline) and doing the injection into each other. This helps family members to realize how little the pain is from the shots. In addition, Table 1 gives a checklist to follow. The nurse will go over the checklist with you at regular intervals.

These are the steps:

🐾 Get everything together: alcohol, insulin and a syringe.

🐾 Wash your hands.

🐾 Push the plunger of the disposable syringe up and down before drawing in the insulin. This will help soften the rubber at the end of the plunger and smooth the plunger action.

🐾 Wipe the top of the insulin bottle(s) with alcohol and allow to air dry.

🐾 Insert the needle through the rubber top of the bottle of short-acting (Humalog/NovoLog or Regular) insulin with the bottle sitting upright on the table. Turn the bottle (with the needle inserted) upside down. To remove any air bubbles, draw out about 5 more units of insulin than needed and push back into the bottle. This can be repeated several times as needed until air bubbles are cleared. "Flicking" the syringe barrel with the finger is not recommended as it can cause the needle to bend. After the air bubbles are gone, adjust the top edge of the rubber plunger to be in line with the exact number of units needed. The needle can then be removed from the vial and held or the cap put on the needle. Some families leave the needle in the short-acting insulin bottle until the intermediate-acting insulin is mixed. Others hold the syringe in one hand while mixing the intermediate-acting insulin (turning up and down 20 times) with the other hand.

🐾 If also receiving an intermediate-acting insulin (NPH, Lente, Ultralente) at this time, it can be drawn into the same syringe. First prepare the insulin by turning the bottle back and forth to mix. Some people roll the bottle between the palms of their hands. The bottle should be turned or rolled 20 times to mix thoroughly. Avoid touching the rubber stopper of the vial if it has already been wiped with alcohol.

🐾 Remove the cap from the syringe containing the short-acting insulin. Insert the needle into the bottle of the intermediate-acting insulin while the bottle is upside down. This prevents air from the intermediate-acting insulin vial getting into the syringe. With the bottle turned upside down, slowly draw the number of units of the intermediate-acting insulin needed. The total number of units in the syringe will be the sum of the short-acting units plus the intermediate-acting units.

🐾 Venting the insulin bottles:

In the past, we instructed families to inject air into the insulin bottles with each dose. This was to prevent a vacuum from developing, which would pull the insulin drawn out, back into the bottle.

In recent years, most of our families have preferred to "vent" their insulin bottles once a week. This is done by first removing the plunger from the syringe barrel. With the insulin vial sitting upright on the table, insert the needle into the rubber stopper and allow air to equalize in the insulin bottle. This will remove any vacuum which may be inside the bottle. Pick one consistent day of the week to vent the bottles.

Some families may prefer to inject the air when drawing up the insulin. This is particularly true when large doses are being given. The amount of air injected into a bottle equals the number of units of insulin being withdrawn. The air should be added to the intermediate-acting insulin bottle first. The rubber stopper of the bottle should first be cleaned with alcohol. With the bottle sitting upright, insert the needle into the bottle and push in the air within the syringe. Remove the needle from the bottle.

Draw air into the syringe again, the amount equal to the dose of the short-acting insulin. With the short-acting bottle upright on a table, insert the needle and push in the air. Leave the needle in the bottle and turn upside down. Follow the steps outlined above to withdraw the insulin doses required.

The people who make insulin recommend changing insulin vials every 30 days if the bottle is kept at room temperature. This is due to the possible growth of bacteria. Blood sugars should be watched carefully when the insulin bottle is almost empty. If the blood sugars start to be unusually high or low, the last bit of insulin should be discarded. Some people prefer to just routinely discard the insulin when it only fills the neck of the turned bottle. The expiration date on the bottle should always be checked and the insulin discarded if that date is reached. Unopened, refrigerated insulin is good until the manufacturer's expiration date on the top of the box.

In summary, BE PRECISE ABOUT THE DOSAGE. An overdose can cause an insulin reaction or low blood sugar. If you ever take an incorrect dose, be sure to notify your diabetes care provider. It is wise to have the morning and afternoon dosages posted on the refrigerator or some obvious place to prevent confusion. Children below age 10 do not usually have the fine motor abilities and concern for accuracy to draw up insulin by themselves (see Chapter 18).

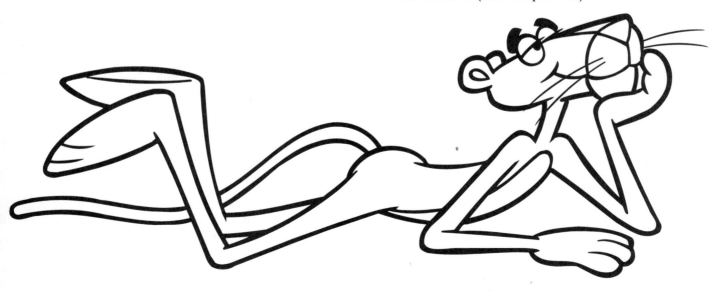

Table 1

DRAWING UP INSULIN

A. Gather supplies: Insulin, syringe, alcohol wipe for tops of bottles, log book with current tests and insulin dosage (please record each blood sugar result in log book after each test).

B. Technique:

- Know correct insulin dosage (based on "thinking" scales if appropriate)

- Wipe tops of insulin bottles with alcohol swab

- Either "vent"* the bottles weekly (smaller doses) or put air into the long-acting (cloudy) insulin with the bottle upright and remove the needle. Put air in the clear insulin and leave the needle in.

- Draw up clear (short-acting) insulin, get rid of air bubbles and remove the needle

- Mix cloudy (intermediate-acting) insulin vial by gently turning the bottle up and down 20 times; this ensures that the insulin gets well mixed

- Slowly draw up cloudy insulin into syringe, making sure not to push any insulin already in the syringe back into the vial

- If insulin vials have been in the refrigerator, you can warm up the insulin once it is mixed in the syringe by holding the syringe in the closed palm of your hand for 1-2 minutes; it will be less likely to sting if brought to room temperature

- Give insulin injection

- **Remember** if you are using the new Lantus insulin, **NO OTHER INSULIN CAN GO INTO THE SYRINGE WITH THIS INSULIN**. Also, it is a clear insulin and doesn't need to be mixed.

An option now used by some people is to not put air into the bottles, but to just "vent" the bottles to remove any vacuum once weekly (see text).

HOW TO INJECT THE INSULIN

(See Table 2 and picture diagrams)

* Clean the site of injection with soap and water (or an alcohol swab if camping or in a hospital). Alcohol dries and toughens the skin and is not routinely recommended.

Lift the skin and fat tissue between the thumb and the first finger. **If you are using the B-D ULTRA-FINE II (0.3, 0.5 or 1.0cc) syringe with short needles (5/16 inch) and the fat in the area of injection is adequate, the needle can be inserted at a 90° angle.** If there is not much fat, a gentle pinch should still be used during the injection. Touch the needle to the skin, holding the syringe at a 45° angle (or less) for the 1/2 inch needles. It is generally best to push the needle all the way into the skin. If the needle is not in far enough, the insulin may not be injected into the fatty layer. If it goes into the layer directly under the skin rather than into the fatty layer, it will sting and may cause a bump or redness and itching. If the needle is not close to the fingers holding the skin, the gentle pinch can continue to be held during the injection of the insulin.

* Inject the insulin by pushing the plunger down with a SLOW and steady push as far as it will go. Some people like to wait a few seconds to let the insulin "spread out" after each five units of insulin is injected. A smooth injection is important. AFTER THE INSULIN IS IN, WAIT FIVE TO TEN SECONDS BEFORE REMOVING THE NEEDLE. COUNT SLOWLY TO FIVE. THIS WILL HELP TO PREVENT INSULIN LEAKAGE FROM THE INJECTION SITE. A loss of one drop of insulin may be equal to two to five units. Loss of insulin is a common reason for variations in the blood sugar levels. If "leak-back" continues to be a problem move to a new site. Also, two units of air can be drawn into the syringe after removing the needle from the insulin bottle. Then flick the side of the syringe with a finger to make the air rise up under the plunger. The air will then be injected after the insulin and will help to prevent "leak-back."

* After the injection, place a finger or dry cotton swab over the site of injection. Hold for a few seconds to prevent any bleeding. Rub the site gently to close the needle track. Some bleeding may occur after the needle is pulled out; this is not harmful, although some insulin may be carried out with the blood. Press the dry cotton firmly on the site. Some people put their finger over the site where the needle came out and rub gently. The finger should be clean.

* The plastic syringes are recommended for one time use only by the manufacturer. The needle becomes dull after one use and may be more painful by the second or third shot. If they are to be reused, after giving the injection, push the plunger up and down to get rid of any insulin left in the needle. Wipe the needle off with an alcohol swab. Put the cap over the needle and store the syringe and needle in the refrigerator until ready for the next use.

* Table 2 provides a summary for injecting the insulin.

GIVING THE INSULIN

Table 2

- Choose injection site; use a good site rotation plan

- Make sure the site is clean

- Relax the chosen area

- Lift up the skin with a "gentle-pinch"

- Touch the needle to the skin and gently push it through the skin. Use a 45° angle for the 1/2 inch or 5/8 inch long needle or a 90° angle for the 5/16 inch (short) needle. If there is not much fat, a gentle-pinch should still be used with the short needles.

- If the fingers holding the skin are not close to the needle, the gentle-pinch can continue to be held during the injection

- Push the insulin in slowly and steadily

- Wait 5 to 10 seconds to let the insulin spread out

- Put a finger or dry cotton over the site as the needle is pulled out. Gently rub a few times to close the track.

- Put pressure on the site if bruising or bleeding are common

- Observe for a drop of insulin ("leak-back"); note in record book if a drop of insulin is present

A. Wash hands

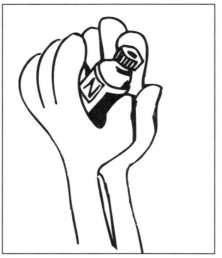

B. Warm and mix insulin

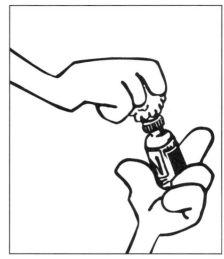

C. Wipe top of insulin bottle with alcohol

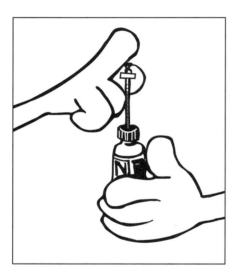

D. Air = insulin dose in units

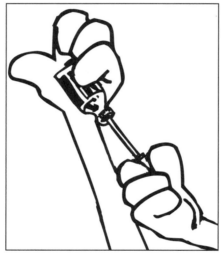

E. Pull out dose of insulin

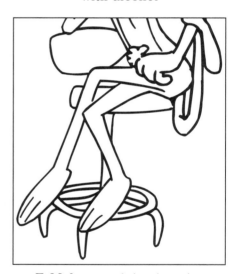

F. Make sure injection site is clean

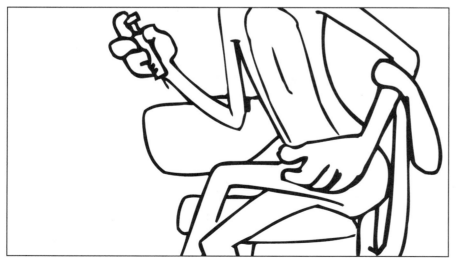

G. Pinch up skin and fat tissue if using 5/8 inch needle. **Go straight in (no pinch) if using the 5/16 inch (short) needle.**

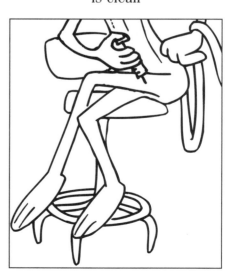

H. Inject insulin at 45° (5/8 inch) or 90° (5/16 inch needle)

WHEN TO INJECT THE INSULIN

Regular and NPH insulins can be premixed and are even sold in bottles of premixed combinations. Lente insulins bind Regular insulin and should not be mixed together until it is time to give the shot. NPH insulin binds Humalog/NovoLog insulin, so they should not be premixed. Humalog/NovoLog and Ultralente (or Lente) can be premixed. If insulin is mixed in a syringe prior to giving the shot (premixed), it will be necessary to roll the syringe between the hands to mix it thoroughly.

With Regular insulin, it is best to take the shot 30 to 60 minutes before eating. This allows the Regular insulin to start working at the time food is eaten. It will prevent the blood sugar from going very high in the half-hour or hour after eating. When the pre-meal blood sugar level is known, the time can be varied between the shot and eating the meal, as shown in Table 3. It has been our experience that using a time scale such as this can improve blood sugar control.

Other people routinely use Humalog/NovoLog insulin and they must eat immediately after taking their shot. An exception is with the toddler or a picky eater who has variable food intake, when it is better to wait to give the shot until after seeing how much food has been eaten (see Chapter 17). Giving insulin after the meal is also used when people/families are carb counting. This can be done when people are limiting carbs to maintain or reduce their current weight. Such people are usually teenage girls who decide to diet or people with type 2 diabetes.

STORAGE

Ideally, insulin should be stored in the refrigerator and warmed to room temperature prior to giving the shot. Some people keep the bottles they are using at room temperature (except in a very hot summer). It will not be as likely to sting or to cause red spots after injection if it is kept at room temperature. After drawing up insulin that has been in the refrigerator, the filled, capped syringe can also be warmed in the closed palm of your hand to avoid stinging. A drawer in the kitchen might

be identified for storage of all diabetes supplies. Research has shown that if insulin is stored at room temperature, it loses 1.5% of its potency per month (after one month 1cc U-100 insulin would have 98.5 units of insulin rather than 100 units). For most people, this small change would not make a difference (9.85 units rather than 10.0 units). One of the insulin manufacturers wrote: **"Insulin vials currently in use may be kept at room temperature for 30 days, in a cool place and away from sunlight."** Insulin will spoil if it gets above 90° or if it freezes.

Insulin bottles (or pens) cannot be left in a car in the hot summer or the cold winter. If insulin has spoiled, sometimes clumps will then be seen sticking to the sides of the intermediate-acting insulin bottle. That bottle and the accompanying bottle of short-acting insulin should not be used if this occurs. Unfortunately, the short-acting (clear) insulins do not have any telltale signs when they spoil. A clear insulin should be thrown away if it becomes cloudy. It may have bacteria (germs) growing in it. We have also suggested throwing away bottles of insulin that have been opened for three or more months, even if refrigerated. Families using low dosages of a particular insulin may find it more effective to draw out of 300 unit insulin cartridges (for Humalog/NovoLog, Regular or NPH insulins). If blood sugars rise, (for no other reason) after using the current insulin vials for longer than one month, replace them.

INSULIN PENS

Use of insulin pens has increased greatly in recent years. In the U.S., this is related to people wanting an easy method to take supplements of short-acting insulins (Humalog/NovoLog) with food intake during the day. In Europe, many people use pre-mixed insulins from the time of diagnosis and may not even learn to draw up mixtures of insulins. If they use pre-mixed short and intermediate-lasting insulins (e.g., 70/30 NPH/Regular), they cannot then change the individual insulin dosages for food intake and exercise.

There are now several types of pens available:

🐾 Lilly Pre-filled Disposable Pens:

Lilly disposable pens for Humalog, Humulin NPH, 70/30 NPH/Regular and Humalog Mix 75/25 insulins are readily available. The pens are simple to use and will take a small B-D 31 gauge (5/16 inch) Ultra-Fine III® needle or a NovoFine® 30 gauge (1/3 inch) disposable needle.

Using a new needle each time, instructions for using the pen are as follows:

1. Wipe the cap on the insulin chamber with an alcohol pad

2. Remove the paper tab and screw the needle onto the pen

3. Turn the dose knob until the larger arrow lines up below the tiny magnifying glass

4. Pull back on the plunger and dial in a two unit priming dose

5. Push the plunger in all the way while holding the needle pointed upward (to fill the needle with insulin)

6. Repeat steps 3 and 4 to dial in the desired insulin dose

7. Assuming body fat is adequate and a short needle is being used, angle at 90° to inject this dose under the skin; keep the plunger pushed down all the way for approximately five seconds after hearing a "click"

With any pre-filled insulin pen, rub the injection site with the finger as the needle is removed. This helps to close the track from the needle and reduce leak-back. Reuse of pen needles is not recommended as the needle dulls and can cause tissue damage at the injection site. By leaving a pen needle on the device, bacteria may enter the cartridge and contaminate the insulin.

🐾 Cartridge Pens

The **NovoPen® 3.0** from Novo Nordisk and the B-D pen offer the chance to use cartridges of Regular, NPH, 70/30 NPH/Regular or Humalog/NovoLog insulins. There are not cartridges of Lente or Ultralente insulins. The cartridges contain 3.0 ml of insulin (300 units) and are replaced into the pen when the cartridge is empty. The NovoPen 3.0 delivers a

dose of 2 to 70 units. The B-D pen has a maximum dose of 30 units. There is also a **BD Pen Mini®** which has a 1.5 ml cartridge for Humalog (no other 1.5 ml insulin cartridges are available). It can deliver 1/2 unit dosages. A colorful pen from Novo Nordisk will soon be on the market in the U.S. It is called the **Novo-Junior®** and can also deliver 1/2 unit doses. It takes the 3 ml insulin cartridges so it can be used with any Novo Nordisk 3.0 insulin cartridge available.

The directions for the NovoPen 3.0 are, once again, fairly simple:

1. Remove the cap (the part with the pocket clip) and unscrew the silver bottom to drop the cartridge of insulin down into the holder (metal cap first). Make sure the piston rod is flat (even) at the end of the top of the plunger. Then screw the silver bottom back on tightly.

2. Wipe the rubber stopper with alcohol, remove the paper tab from the needle and screw the needle on the end of the pen (until tight).

3. Turn the dial to one or two units. Pull off both needle caps and, holding the needle upward, push the button on the end to see if insulin comes out. If not, repeat the procedure until insulin appears (to get rid of all air). Do this with each usage of the pen.

4. For giving the shot, starting at "0," turn the dial-a-dose selector to the required dose, lift up the skin (as directed earlier) and insert the needle at a 90° angle (assuming adequate fat). Press the button on the end down firmly to deliver all insulin. Wait five seconds, pull the needle out and rub gently. Place the small plastic cover over the needle and put the cap with the pocket clip back on the pen.

The **Innovo®** is a new pen from Novo Nordisk with new features. It takes 3 ml (cc) NovoLog cartridges from the Novo Nordisk company only. It requires a standard pen needle which screws on to the end of the cartridge. A user manual and Quick guide comes with the Innovo. These give very clear directions, so they won't be repeated here.

Two of the features are:

1. It tells when your last shot was given and how much was taken. The clock is divided into four quarters. There are three dots within each quarter. Each dot represents one hour. The dose of the last injection appears below the clock.

2. As the plunger is pressed, segments of a circle appear. These segments gradually meet forming a complete circle. This closed circle indicates the entire dose has been given. In the past, families have been concerned that if a drop was left on the needle, the full dose was not given. This should no longer be a concern.

The **InDuo**™ is a pen/meter combination from Novo Nordisk. The Innovo pen is combined with the Ultra meter. Some people will appreciate having both a meter and an insulin pen in one device. Visit the following web site address: http://www.induo.com for more information.

Pen Needles

Becton, Dickinson and Company (BD) now has three pen needles on the market. *They are:*

Name	*Length (inches)*	*Width (mm)*
BD Original	1/2	12.7
BD Short	5/16	8
BD Mini	3/16	5

The BD Mini was introduced in 2002. It is not necessary to pinch the skin when using this needle. The BD Mini can be used with pens made by BD, Lilly and NovoNordisk.

PROBLEMS THAT MAY ARISE WITH INSULIN INJECTIONS

🐾 Hypertrophy (swelling) of Skin

Swelling of the skin or hypertrophy, occurs when too many injections are given in one area over a period of months to years. People like to give shots in the same spot because nerve endings (pain) are dulled after a few injections. You can inject insulin into the body anywhere there is enough fat under the skin. Usually there isn't fat over the joints and bones, so these areas are not used. **If swelling in an area does occur, you should not give further injections in that area until the swelling is gone.** This may take several months and varies for different people. **The swelling will alter the uptake of insulin.**

🐾 Skin Dents (atrophy or lipoatrophy)

You may develop "dents" at the injection site. This is different from skin swelling, and is due to a loss of fat in that place. "Denting" is now very rare when human insulin is used. When dents do occur, it is possible to help them go away. To inject into the dented area, pick the skin up at the side of the dent. Slide the needle under the center of the dent. If you inject human insulin four times in a row each week, the dent will gradually go away. This may take several weeks.

PRE-MEAL BLOOD SUGAR AND TIME TO WAIT BEFORE EATING

		Time to Wait Before Eating (Minutes)	
Blood Sugar Level		**Type of Insulin**	
mg/dl	**mmol/L**	**Regular**	**Humalog/NovoLog**
above 200	above 11.1	60	10
151-200	8.4-11.1	45	5
80-150	4.5-8.3	30	don't wait
60-80	3.2-4.5	don't wait (take the shot & start eating right away)	don't wait (take the shot & start eating right away)
< 60	< 3.2	eat first (consider reducing the short-acting insulin)	eat first (consider reducing the short-acting insulin)

🐾 Plugged Needle

Occasionally, a small piece of fat or the insulin (particularly Ultralente insulin) will plug the end of the needle during the injection. Sometimes it is possible to pull out the needle a little and then push the needle back into a slightly different place. If you still cannot push down the plunger to finish the injection, you will have to pull the needle completely out of the skin. **NOTE VERY PRECISELY THE UNITS OF INSULIN REMAINING IN THE SYRINGE.** After you fill a new syringe with the total insulin dose as originally drawn, discard the amount of insulin you have already injected. Inject the rest into another site. An advantage of the Lantus insulin is syringe needles no longer become plugged.

🐾 Giving the Wrong Insulin Dose

"To err is human" is very true. If the morning insulin dose is accidentally given in the evening, usually an excess of insulin results. This results in a very long night, as the person must be awakened every two or three hours, blood sugars checked and extra juice and food must be given. Obviously, if the blood sugar is low, more frequent checks will be needed.

🐾 Bleeding After the Injection

A small capillary blood vessel is probably hit with every injection. Sometimes a drop of blood or a bruise under the skin will be seen after the injection. This will not cause any problem except for the possible loss of some insulin with the blood. Some people are upset by the bruises. As noted earlier in this chapter, place a dry piece of cotton or a clean finger over the injection site and rub gently after removing the needle. This will usually stop any bleeding. Sometimes applying pressure for 30 to 60 seconds will help to reduce bruising.

🐾 Injecting Insulin Into Muscle

If a person is very thin or very muscular, there may be little fat under the skin. Injections may go into the underlying muscle, causing more rapid absorption of insulin and low blood sugar. There may then be less insulin to act later in the day, resulting in high blood sugar. Injections into the muscle are most likely to occur if the syringe is held at a 90° angle to the body (unless the short needles are used). Sometimes extra pain will occur when shots go into muscle, but this is not always the case. Thus, the pain is NOT a good indicator of shots given into muscle. If injecting into muscle is a problem, it may be necessary to pull the skin away from the muscle and insert the needle into the "tent" below (while still holding the pinch of skin). Since the entire pinch is not being held, just the upper tip, the insulin should not leak-back. This technique can be taught by your diabetes nurse. Occasionally, it may be helpful to give an injection in the presence of your diabetes care provider to have your injection technique checked. If the patient is newly diagnosed and has very little body fat, the buttocks may be the safest place for injections.

🐾 Injection Devices

Some people have difficulty pushing the needle through the skin. Others would like to inject in a difficult to reach area such as the buttocks, but can't. Placing the syringe in an injection device such as the **Inject-Ease®** (B-D) or the B-D **Automatic Injector®** may help with both of these problems. After putting the syringe in the device and pushing a button, the needle is automatically pushed through the skin very quickly. It is still necessary to push down on the plunger of the syringe to inject the insulin. If the 1/2 inch needles are being used, it may still be important to hold the device at a 45° angle with the skin lifted to prevent shots into the muscle. However, the depth can be changed by using an adapter, so for some sites, this is not a concern. The Inject-Ease has a cap for 30 unit syringes with short needles. If 50 or 100 unit syringes are to be used with long needles, the extra rings can be added and the cap and the needles then resemble the short needles. Injections are then made at a 90° angle to the skin. It is still important to count before removing the needle and to briefly rub the site to close the needle track and prevent "leak-back." Other devices are available (such as the **Ulster Auto Injector®**) that push both the needle through the skin and push down on the plunger of the syringe to inject the insulin. Finally, there are air-pressure devices that "blow" the insulin into the body. These are expensive, but may be covered, at least in part, by insurance. They are most useful for people with needle phobia or those who cannot adjust to the insulin shots. The insulin dose may need to be changed since part of the insulin from air-pressure injections usually goes into muscle. More irregular blood sugar values may result. If you wish to see any of these devices, you should ask your diabetes nurse educator.

DEFINITIONS

Atrophy (or Lipoatrophy): Areas of fat loss under the skin which appear as "dents" in the skin. Although they are believed to be due to a form of insulin allergy, they can occur in areas where insulin has never been injected.

Buttocks: The seat; the part of the body that one sits on.

Hypertrophy: Areas of swelling of the skin, which occur in places where too many shots are being given. Injecting insulin in areas of hypertrophy may cause altered insulin absorption.

Leak-back: The leaking out of a drop of insulin after the insulin injection is completed. This can be a cause of variation in day-to-day blood sugar levels.

Needle phobia: The intense fear of needles. Working with a social worker or psychologist around "needle desensitization" may help this, as well as use of injection devices.

QUESTIONS (Q) AND ANSWERS (A) FROM NEWSNOTES

Q. I often note that a drop of insulin comes back after I withdraw the needle when giving the morning insulin to my child. Is this of any importance and what can I do to prevent it?

A. We are frequently asked this question. We call this "leak-back." One drop of insulin is equivalent to 1/20th of 1 ml of insulin. As 1 ml contains 100 units (U-100 Insulin), each drop would contain approximately five units of insulin. This can be a significant amount and it is therefore important to try to avoid the loss of the insulin following injections.

The six main methods to prevent this loss are listed below:

1. Letting go of the lift of skin before injecting the insulin so that pressure is not forcing the insulin out from under the skin at the same time it is being injected.

2. Making sure the needle is in the full length and that one does not start to pull the needle out until after the injection is completed.

3. Making sure there is not excessive pressure on the site of injection. For example, if the child is sitting on a chair, he/she should sit on the edge of the chair when injecting in the leg rather than on the back of the chair where the pressure beneath the leg might force the insulin out of the injection site. Having the leg straight rather than bent at the knee may also result in less pressure.

4. Injecting the insulin slowly.

5. Routinely counting for five seconds or longer (as is needed) after the insulin is injected before removing the needle.

6. Rubbing the needle track for two or three seconds as the needle is removed to "close off" the track.

If these six principles are followed, it is unusual for drops of insulin to leak-back.

Q. My teenager read about the air-pressure device to give insulin without having to use needles. Should we be considering one of these for her?

A. The latest models of the air-pressure injectors are greatly improved over the earlier models. The new models are simpler and are much easier to clean.

We have had mixed reactions from the families that have tried the air-pressure injectors. One complaint has been that the insulin did not last as long. This is probably due to some of the insulin being given into muscle. Irregular blood sugars may result. A second problem has been bruising of the skin when the intensity was set high enough to make sure a drop of the insulin was not left on the skin. Expense has been another problem, with most models costing between $600-$800. Insurance will sometimes cover a part of this.

The families, which have seemed to like the device the most, are those with very young children. When a two- or three-year-old undergoes much stress with needle injections, it may be reduced by using the air-pressure injectors. Also, when fear of needles (needle phobia) is a real problem, the air-pressure injector may help. It is not for everyone, but some people do seem to benefit.

Q. We notice that when we give the shot to our daughter in the upper outer arm, she frequently has a low blood sugar at school that morning, but is then very high before dinner. Is this possible?

A. It sounds like you are injecting the shot into muscle. This is common in the deltoid muscle (upper lateral arm) area as there is not much fat. I would guess that you are also going straight in (not at a 45° angle) with the 1/2-inch needle, which almost always results in the insulin being given into muscle. When the insulin does go into muscle, it is absorbed more rapidly so that low blood sugars are common. Then there is not enough insulin left to have its normal effect 6-10 hours later. Sometimes, use of the short needles (5/16 inch) helps to prevent injections into muscle.

Q. We just gave our son his afternoon shot and accidentally gave the morning dose rather than the afternoon dose. What should we do?

A. We hear this question almost every week. The answer is to eat more at dinner and at the bedtime snack (pizza is particularly effective). In addition, it is wise to set the alarm for every two or three hours, get up, do a blood sugar and give extra juice or food. If the value falls to very low levels (below 70 mg/dl or 3.9 mmol/L), it is necessary to stay up and keep doing the blood sugars every 20 or 30 minutes until the value is above 120 mg/dl or 6.7 mmol/L. This problem can be handled and, in our experience, has never required hospitalization or resulted in a severe insulin reaction. Some families find that having the a.m. and p.m. insulin doses taped to the front of the refrigerator can be a helpful reminder. It may also be a good way to communicate or remember recent dosage changes. It is also effective to routinely have a second person check the dose.

Q. Lately, our needle has plugged halfway through the shot several times. What causes this and what should we do?

A. The plugging may be due to a small piece of fat getting into the needle. Occasionally, the insulin can also cause the plugging, particularly Ultralente insulin (Lente insulin is 70% Ultralente). Some people have also noted a greater likelihood of plugging with one brand of syringes compared to another, so you might consider a different brand and see if it makes a difference.

As noted in bold print in the section on "Plugged Needles" in this chapter, if plugging does occur, note precisely the number of units of insulin remaining in the syringe. It is then necessary to start over with a new syringe. Draw up the full injection dose of insulin and discard the extra down to the number of units of insulin still needed. Then inject this as with any shot.

Chapter 10

TOPIC: Psychosocial Adjustment

TEACHING OBJECTIVES:

1. Reflect with the family typical adjustment feelings associated with diagnosis and encourage expression of feelings.

2. Provide information relating to additional support services.

LEARNING OBJECTIVES:

Learners (parents, child, relative or self) will be able to:

1. List two feelings of adjustment associated with diagnosis.

2. Describe how to access additional support services.

Chapter 10 FEELINGS AND DIABETES

INTRODUCTION

This chapter deals with the normal feelings people have when they learn that a family member has diabetes. (Chapter 17 will cover other family concerns related to diabetes that may occur.) The emotions that one deals with at the diagnosis of diabetes are common with the onset of any serious medical condition. They are present in some form in all families who have a family member with diabetes. If families do not deal with the way they feel at the time of diagnosis, the feelings may linger and cause problems for many years. In our Clinic, we ask **EVERY** newly diagnosed family to meet with the clinical social worker or psychologist to discuss these feelings. Dealing with the feelings openly at the time of diagnosis will help with long-term adjustment.

CONFUSION OR SHOCK, are common feelings for families. Some families feel like giving up when diabetes is diagnosed. They feel there is no hope and that this is the end of everything. The person that they thought was "perfect" will now be "different." The person will never be the same. This kind of sadness is similar to the process of mourning. The family mourns the loss of the person's health. These feelings are very natural. Diabetes may be the worst thing that has happened to the family. If the family learns as much as possible about the cause and the management of diabetes, and talks together about their feelings, everyone will do much better.

Because of the shock, it is often hard for families to think about what the medical team is saying in regards to diabetes. Sometimes they will ask to have things repeated. The medical team understands what the family is going through and is happy to go over the information several times. Because of the shock, and often a lack of sleep, many clinics

teach only survival skills in the first day or two. They can then go into more depth at the one-week visit.

DENIAL is often expressed in comments such as, "This can't happen to us," or "This can't be happening to my child; there must be a mistake in the diagnosis." As a result, a family may want to seek second opinions from other doctors, hoping to be told that their family member doesn't have diabetes. This denial may make the person's and the family's struggle to adjust to the diagnosis much longer and more difficult. It may even interfere with medical treatment and education. Some family members may want to deny that they have any feelings at all about the diagnosis. Family members may not want to talk about the diabetes. If this happens, the person with diabetes may feel alone and the family members may not be able to help each other through a very stressful time. Sometimes people try to hide their feelings to be "strong" for a newly diagnosed person. Doing this may cause the person to feel that others don't care. IT IS IMPORTANT FOR CLOSE FRIENDS AND FAMILY TO SHARE THEIR FEELINGS ABOUT THE DIABETES.

SADNESS is a feeling that can be felt by any family member. Any member may cry, feel depressed or feel hopeless. One teenager, shortly after she was diagnosed as having diabetes, began to cry each time she talked about living with diabetes and giving daily shots "for the rest of my life." A mother did well for three months after she learned her child had diabetes. She helped manage the diabetes and also cared for her other children. After three months, she began to cry often and had trouble caring for her family. It was important for this mother to share her feelings and to talk about her sadness. When she did, she began to feel better. A father expressed much sadness when his son was diagnosed with diabetes. Several days later, after discussing exercise and diabetes, he felt much better as he realized his son would still be able to participate in sports activities. Feeling sad is normal and brief periods of sadness can reoccur years later (see adjustment in this chapter).

ANGER is a feeling many families have. They may vent the anger toward the doctors, nurses, God, a husband or wife, the person who has diabetes, other family members or even themselves. The person with diabetes often feels, "Why me? Why did I have to get diabetes? Did I do something wrong?" It is important for the person with diabetes to know it isn't their fault that they developed diabetes. He or she may feel anger toward other healthy family members or toward others for no apparent good reason. The anger may be expressed or it may be buried. Such anger, although it seems to have no basis, is a very normal feeling. It is important to find positive ways to let it out. This may be through talking with others or through sports or other activities. If it lasts for a long time, the person and family may have a hard time managing the diabetes. When these feelings are too strong or last a long time, family or individual counseling may be helpful.

FEAR may be felt by all the family members. The parents or spouse may fear the extra responsibilities and expenses associated with diabetes. Parents also fear not being able to manage the diabetes and doubt their abilities. Brothers and sisters may fear they might have or might get diabetes. The person with diabetes may fear such things as injections, hospitalizations or death. He/she may fear being different from friends or family. Many of the fears may not be realistic. The family members should talk about their fears, both with each other and with the diabetes team. Then they can learn which fears are not realistic. If fears and concerns are shared with other people, they don't get "bottled-up" inside. This makes them easier to manage.

GUILT is a feeling common to many family members. Parents often feel that they "gave" their child diabetes. This idea occurs even though parents have been told that autoimmunity (self-allergy), viral infections and other unknown factors are important in causing diabetes. We do not completely understand why someone develops diabetes. There is no proven way at this time to prevent it. Earlier diagnosis after the beginning of symptoms would not have prevented the diabetes from developing or changed the way diabetes is treated. One mother felt that because there was diabetes in her family, and not in her husband's, he must be blaming her for their child's diabetes. After months of worry and concern, she finally shared her feelings with her husband. He had not felt that way at all. Some young children feel that their diabetes is a punishment for bad behavior. Some family members may feel that "eating too much sugar" caused the child's diabetes. It didn't! These ideas can cause unnecessary guilt for everyone.

ADAPTATION OR ADJUSTMENT to the diagnosis of diabetes takes a long time. In an earlier edition of this book, the word "acceptance" was used. A knowledgeable parent related: "I won't accept the diagnosis, but I'll adapt or adjust to it." Often one parent will have stronger or more obvious feelings than the other parent. It helps to talk and share feelings within the family and with members of the diabetes team. We have every newly diagnosed family meet with a member of our psychosocial staff. As the person and family live with diabetes, they become more used to it. They will feel more sure that they can manage it. Fears that have no reason will go away. Sadness and anger may still come and go at times. The family may feel sadness when the person is hospitalized or when they see pictures of the person before the diagnosis. Sometimes the parent may feel very sad for a moment, such as when kissing the child at bedtime. These feelings decrease with time. The continued love for the family member is the most important feeling and does not change.

As the family adjusts, the members begin to feel more hopeful. They may want to help in diabetes research studies or help diabetes support groups raise money. It is important not to look at diabetes as the end of the world. If all family members have a positive attitude, life with diabetes will be much easier. Fitting diabetes care into as normal a lifestyle as possible is a major goal.

DEFINITIONS

Adjustment (adaptation): Gradually learning to live with something (such as the diagnosis of diabetes).

Denial (deny): A refusal to believe something. A person may refuse to believe that he or she has diabetes.

Diagnosis: The process of finding that a person has a disease.

Guilt: A feeling that one caused something to happen.

QUESTIONS (Q) AND ANSWERS (A) FROM NEWSNOTES

Q. Why is the Pink Panther character used in the educational manual, Understanding Diabetes?

A. Having a family member develop diabetes is often the most traumatic event that has happened to a family. If a child were pictured to demonstrate a side effect, such as hypoglycemia, it might be harder for a family member to accept than a picture of the Pink Panther having a reaction. Also, a bit of humor at this time of intense emotions can often be a big help.

Chapter 11

TOPIC: ❦ Nutritional Management

TEACHING OBJECTIVES:

1. Present basic nutritional components including carbohydrates, protein and fat.

2. Introduce the importance of carbohydrate intake in diabetes management.

3. Present nutritional guidelines for fat/cholesterol intake and desired blood lipid ranges.

LEARNER OBJECTIVES:

Learner (parents, child, relative or self) will be able to:

1. List three major food components and give an example of each.

2. Explain the effect of carbohydrate intake on blood sugar levels.

3. Describe a dietary method to lower blood cholesterol/lipid levels.

WITH SPECIAL THANKS FOR THE SUGGESTIONS OF:

- Michelle Hansen, MS, RD, CDE
- Darcy Owen, MS, RD, CDE
- Gail Spiegel, MS, RD, CDE
- Markey Swanson, RD, CDE

Chapter 11 NORMAL NUTRITION

TYPES OF NUTRIENTS

Families of a newly diagnosed person with diabetes are usually overly concerned and worried about what someone with diabetes should eat. They shouldn't be, as **the ideal diet for someone with diabetes (type 1 or type 2) is really just a healthy diet from which all people would benefit.** This chapter is meant to be a review of normal nutrition, which will help to improve the entire family's nutrition. It will be a good introduction to Chapter 12, Food Management and Diabetes. It will also make some of the words used by the dietitian easier to follow.

Foods provide different nutrients necessary for growth and health. If you know about these nutrients, you can help your family eat the right foods. Learning to read food labels will help you to know what you are buying at the grocery store.

Types of nutrients include:
1. protein
2. carbohydrate
3. fat
4. vitamins and minerals
5. water
6. fiber

Our bodies need some of all of these nutrients but in differing amounts.

🐾 Protein

Protein is important for muscle and bone growth. However, eating extra protein does **not** cause increased muscle growth. Muscles only grow as a result of proper exercise. Foods high in protein include milk, yogurt, meats, fish, chicken, turkey, egg whites, cheese, cottage cheese, beans and nuts. In addition to fish being a good source of protein, the fish oils (fat) are believed to help prevent heart disease (see "Fat" in this chapter). Protein should provide 10-20% of the total caloric intake. Protein from animal sources is a **complete** protein. This means it contains all of the essential building blocks of protein called amino acids.

Adults can receive adequate protein eating only a vegetarian diet, but this is more difficult for growing infants and children. Many people do not realize that protein also is available from non-meat sources. Dried beans, legumes, nuts and seeds are fairly good sources of protein.

Most people eat more protein than they need. In a review of three-day diet records from our clinic, the young men were getting approximately three times, and the young women two times the amount of protein needed. High protein intake usually results in high animal fat intake, which may be bad for the heart. It may also provide an extra stress for some people's kidneys.

It is important to choose low-fat grades of meat and poultry. Low fat meats may be graded as **lean** or **choice** for lower grades of fat. *Two examples of reducing the fat content of the diet are:*

1. removing the skin from poultry

2. buying meats which do not have a lot of visible fat

Fat is higher in calories than other foods, which can lead to weight gain. High fat intake also increases the risk for heart disease (this is discussed in more detail below under "Fat"). Most fast food is high in fat (hamburgers, cheeseburgers, french fries).

🐾 Carbohydrate

Carbohydrate is the food source we are most concerned about for people with diabetes.

This is because it is changed to blood sugar. Carbohydrate is important mainly as an energy source for the body. Each gram of carbohydrate supplies four calories.

It used to be believed that sugar, which is a carbohydrate, was rapidly absorbed and starchy carbohydrates were slowly absorbed. This is an easy concept to explain and to believe, but it is **NOT** true. Research has shown that there is no difference in absorption of a sugar as compared with a starchy carbohydrate. This is because the intestine has such high levels of digestive enzymes that starchy carbohydrate is rapidly broken down to sugar. Thus, **"a carbohydrate is a carbohydrate, is a carbohydrate..."**. They all effect blood sugar levels in a similar way.

What is important is:

1. **how much** carbohydrate is eaten

2. **when** the carbohydrate is eaten

3. **with what** the carbohydrate is eaten

4. **if adequate insulin activity is available** at that moment to allow the sugar to pass into the cells to be used for energy.

Insulin is essential to allow sugar to pass into the cells of the body to be burned for energy. **The balance between all carbohydrate eaten and the insulin dosage is one of the major keys to diabetes management.** These concepts will be discussed in detail in the next chapter, Food Management and Diabetes.

Some examples of carbohydrate foods are:
✔ breads
✔ cereals and grains
✔ crackers
✔ fruits
✔ beans (baked, refried, black, kidney, etc.)
✔ vegetables
  • starchy (1/2 cup approximately 15 gm carbohydrate): corn, peas, potatoes and yams
  • non-starchy (1/2 cup approximately 5 gm carbohydrate): green beans, asparagus, broccoli, celery, cabbage, cauliflower and carrots
✔ milk and yogurt (also contain fat and protein)
✔ most desserts

More detailed knowledge about starches and sugars, both of which are carbohydrates, is helpful.

Starch: Starch is a substance made up of hundreds of sugar units. The sugar from starch is now known to be absorbed as quickly as from table sugar (when each is taken alone without other foods). Sources of starch are breads, noodles, pasta, rice, cereals and starchy vegetables such as corn, peas, potatoes and legumes.

Sugar: The U.S. Dietary Guidelines recommend that all people should limit (processed) sugar intake to less than 10% of calories. A diet high in sugars contributes to dental cavities and provides few vitamins and minerals. Often high sugar foods also contain large amounts of fat. A nutritious diet does not contain large amounts of high sugar foods. There are many different kinds of sugar found in foods. Some sugar is often added to foods as a sweetener and may not be noticed unless labels are read. The names for sugars often end in "—ose." Some of the common sugars are listed below.

✔ **Glucose:** Glucose is the name for the main sugar in our body. When we talk about blood and urine sugar, we really mean glucose. Table sugar is half glucose and half fructose. Corn sugar is primarily glucose. Another name for glucose is dextrose

✔ **Fructose:** Fructose is sometimes called "fruit sugar" as it is the main type of sugar found in fruits. It is sold in pure granulated form and is a part of many food products. Fructose has the same number of calories per gram as table sugar (sucrose). The liquid form is sweeter than table sugar, but the taste is the same in baked products. Generally, only one-half to one-third the amount of fructose needs to be used to have the same degree of sweetness as table sugar.

"High-fructose" corn syrup is different from pure fructose and contains large amounts of sucrose. People with diabetes need to be aware of how much of this is eaten.

✔ **Sucrose or table sugar:** The body breaks down sucrose to glucose and fructose. Foods high in sucrose and glucose include cake, cookies, pie, candy, soft drinks and other desserts.

✔ **Lactose or milk sugar:** Lactose is found in milk and yogurt. Children and adolescents should drink three to four 8 oz glasses of milk per day for calcium and vitamin D.

✔ **Syrups:** Corn syrup, corn syrup solids, high fructose syrups, maple syrup, sorghum syrup and sugar cane syrup are all primarily glucose and must be consumed carefully by people with diabetes.

Fat

Fat is an important energy source and is needed for growth. However, fat should provide only 25-30% of total caloric intake. A major emphasis in nutrition in the past decade has been the reduction of the total daily fat intake and lower dietary cholesterol intake. Dietary cholesterol intake should be < 300 mg/day. People with high LDL cholesterol levels (Table 1) may benefit from lowering dietary cholesterol to < 200 mg/day. Reducing cholesterol and saturated fat intake is discussed as the sixth principle of food management for a person with diabetes in the next chapter. Higher fat and cholesterol intakes may lead to elevated blood fat levels (cholesterol and triglycerides: Table 1) and a higher risk for heart disease. People may consume as much as 40-50% of calories from fat rather than the recommended 25-30%. Fried food eaten in fast-food restaurants is usually very high in fat. Fat has more calories (nine calories per gram) than protein or carbohydrate (four calories per gram). Thus, it is more likely to lead to weight gain and obesity. Most effective long-term weight reduction programs emphasize limiting total fat intake.

The main fats in the diet are divided into three types:

✔ **monounsaturated** (high in olive and canola oils)

✔ **polyunsaturated** (most vegetable oils)

✔ **saturated** (mainly animal fats)

It is important to eat more of the monounsaturated and polyunsaturated fats than the saturated fats. **Less than 10% of total calories eaten per day should be from saturated fat.** Increasing the intake of monounsaturated fats (e.g., olive oil and canola oil) can help prevent heart disease.

There are high amounts of polyunsaturated fat in most vegetable oils (coconut and palm are exceptions). Margarines made from vegetable oils are also polyunsaturated. In general, the softer or more liquid a fat is at room temperature, the less saturated it is. For example, liquid margarine is a better choice than stick margarine, and vegetable oil is better than vegetable shortening.

The saturated fats include most animal fats such as the fat in meats, cheese, milk, butter and lard. Chicken, turkey and fish are lower in saturated fat than beef or pork, particularly when the skin is removed. Chicken, turkey and fish also contain some polyunsaturated fat.

Blood Lipids

High levels of the two main blood fats (lipids), **cholesterol** and **triglyceride**, can lead to early aging of the large blood vessels. These vessels carry blood to the heart, legs and other body parts. Other causes of early aging of large blood vessels are diabetes, tobacco use, high blood pressure, lack of exercise and being overweight. As people with diabetes already have one risk factor (by having diabetes), they do not need another. Research from the Barbara Davis Center has shown that children with poorly controlled diabetes have higher blood cholesterol and triglyceride levels than children who have good diabetes control or who don't have diabetes. In addition to poor diabetes control, eating foods high in total fat, animal (saturated) fat or high in cholesterol often results in higher blood cholesterol levels.

In addition to cholesterol levels, the proteins which carry cholesterol in the blood (lipoproteins) are also important. The **LDL cholesterol** (often referred to as the "**bad cholesterol**") carries the cholesterol into the blood vessel wall. Therefore, this level needs to be low. When cholesterol builds up in the blood vessel wall, hardening of the arteries (atherosclerosis) or a heart attack is more likely to occur. The **HDL cholesterol ("good cholesterol")** carries the cholesterol out of the blood vessel wall. This level should be

high. Desired levels for people with diabetes are shown in Table 1. Since diabetes alone is a risk factor for heart disease, the desired levels shown in Table 1 are lower for people with diabetes than for the general population.

We recommend a low fat diet that allows no more than 30% of total calories from fat. Cholesterol intake should be < 300 mg/day. We also recommend limiting intake of foods that are high in animal (saturated) fat. Suggestions for changes are shown in Table 2. Reduction of total fat, animal (saturated) fat and cholesterol intake are good nutrition practices whether a person does or doesn't have diabetes. Trans-fatty acids are similar to saturated fatty acids. Hydrogen has been added back to make them less liquid. They are found in solid margarines, commercial cookies, crackers and other foods.

Suggestions for good nutrition include eating:

- fish and poultry (with the skin removed)
- cold-water fish (salmon, tuna), with omega-3 fatty acids, at least twice weekly
- milk with no more than 1% fat
- canola, olive, corn, safflower or soy oils should be used for salads and cooking

Other suggestions for improving the fat content of food choices are shown in Table 2.

RECOMMENDED LEVELS (mg/dl) FOR LIPIDS AND LIPOPROTEINS

Lipid Type	Desired Level**	Borderline	Abnormal***
Cholesterol	<200 (<170)†	200-240 (170-199)	>240 (>200)
LDL Cholesterol*	<100 (<110)	100-130 (110-129)	>130 (≥130)
HDL Cholesterol*	>40	35-40	<35
Triglyceride*	<130	130-150	>150 (>120)

* Preferably drawn after fasting overnight. If fasting overnight is not possible, then at least four hours after eating.

** Desired level for a person with diabetes

*** Abnormal value for anyone, with or without diabetes

† Values in parentheses are recommended values for children as defined by the National Cholesterol Education Program for Children and Adolescents.

MAKING FOOD CHOICES FOR FAT CONTENT

Food Group (Amount)	Decrease	Instead Choose
Meat, Poultry, & Fish (≤5-6 oz per day)	Beef, pork, lamb, regular ground beef, fatty cuts, spare ribs, organ meats	Lean beef, pork, lamb (lean cuts), well-trimmed before cooking
	Poultry with skin, fried chicken, fried fish, fried shellfish, regular luncheon meat (e.g., bologna, salami, sausage, frankfurters)	Poultry without skin, fish, shellfish, processed meat - prepared, from lean meat (e.g., sliced turkey from the deli)
Eggs (≤2 yolks per week)	Egg yolks: If high blood cholesterol, limit to two per week (includes eggs used in cooking and baking)	Egg whites (two whites can be substituted for whole egg in recipes), cholesterol-free egg substitute
Dairy Products (2-3 servings per day)	Whole milk (fluid, evaporated, condensed), 2% fat milk (low-fat milk), imitation milk, whole milk yogurt, whole milk yogurt beverages, regular cheeses (American, blue, Brie, cheddar, Colby, Edam, Monterey Jack, whole-milk mozzarella, Parmesan, Swiss), cream cheese, Neufchatel cheese	Milk - skim, 1/2%, or 1% fat (fluid, powdered, evaporated) Yogurt - nonfat or low-fat yogurt or yogurt beverages; cheese: low-fat natural or processed cheese
	Cottage cheese (4% fat)	Low-fat or nonfat varieties of cottage cheese
	Ice cream	Frozen dairy dessert - ice milk, frozen yogurt (low fat or nonfat), nonfat ice cream
	Cream, half & half, whipped cream, nondairy creamer, sour cream	Low-fat coffee creamer, low-fat or nonfat sour cream
Fats and Oils (≤6-8 teaspoons per day)	Coconut oil, palm kernel oil, palm oils	Polyunsaturated oils - safflower, sunflower, corn, canola*, olive*, peanut
	Butter, lard, shortening, bacon fat, hard margarine	Margarine - made from unsaturated oils listed above, light or diet margarine, especially soft or liquid forms (e.g., Parkay Squeeze™)

* High in mono-saturated fats.

Adapted from Powers, MA; Handbook of Diabetes Medical Nutrition Therapy, Aspen Publishers, Inc. Gaithersburg, MD, 1996 p. 354.

Vitamins and Minerals

These are important for growth, formation of blood cells, healthy skin, good vision, strong teeth and bones. Fruits and vegetables are rich in vitamins. Vitamins E and C have antioxidant properties that may be important in preventing heart or blood vessel disease. Minerals are found in milk, meats and vegetables. Calcium is a mineral that is important for the bones and teeth. People who do not drink milk may need to take a calcium supplement. Many foods (e.g., cereals, waffles) are now fortified with calcium. Children ages 1–3 years need 400 mg of calcium per day and those who are 4–10 years need 800 mg of calcium per day. Most people 10-20 years old need 1300 mg of calcium per day.

Zinc is a mineral that is lost in the urine in proportion to sugar in the urine. Zinc is important for growth. Some children with diabetes may grow better with a zinc supplement.

Sodium is also a mineral, which, in some "salt-sensitive" people, may relate to higher blood pressure. It is now recommended that all people limit their sodium to no more than 3000 mg (1 1/4 tsp of table salt) per day. If the blood pressure is elevated, this amount should be even lower (2400 mg of sodium or about 1 tsp of table salt). Salt in the food we eat (e.g., chips, hamburgers, hot dogs and convenience foods) is often "hidden" but may be a significant source of salt.

Generally, people who eat a well-balanced diet do not need extra vitamins. If a child does not eat a balanced diet (e.g., not liking yellow or green vegetables), a vitamin supplement may be helpful. Also, vitamins and minerals often are recommended in the month following onset of diabetes as the body rebuilds. In general, "mega" doses of nutrients should be avoided, and the vitamins should not contain more than 100% of the recommended daily allowance (RDA). The fat-soluble vitamins (A, D, E and K) are stored in the body and excessive doses can be harmful. If you do take vitamins, choose a multi-vitamin with trace minerals that includes zinc and iron.

Water

Water is the most important nutrient for the survival of humans. It makes up much of the blood, the body fluids and the body's transport system. It serves as a coolant, shock absorber and waste remover. It has many other important functions. Since the body is made-up of about two-thirds water, it is important to drink a lot of it. We recommend at least six 8 oz glasses of liquid per day, including allowed juices and milk. When a person with diabetes is spilling urine ketones, it is important to drink more water and sugar-free liquids. This helps to replace body fluid loss.

Fiber

Dietary fiber is the part of plants ("roughage" or "bulk") that is not digested and is not absorbed into the body. Foods vary in the amounts and kinds of fiber they contain. Fiber in the diet supplies bulk (without calories) and roughage which helps satisfy the appetite and keep the digestive system running smoothly. In people with type 2 diabetes, increased fiber intake has been helpful in slowing the absorption of sugar. Fiber has not been as helpful in lowering blood sugar levels in people with type 1 diabetes.

Fiber often is divided into two types. The first is **water-soluble fiber**, such as parts of oats and beans, seeds, citrus fruits and apples. These may help lower the blood cholesterol levels. They also may help reduce the blood sugar levels after meals in people with type 2 diabetes. The other type, **water-insoluble fiber**, such as parts of wheat bran, most grains, nuts and vegetables, helps prevent constipation and may help other digestive disorders. Based on the Food Guide Pyramid (see Figure), the minimum intake of fruits and vegetables is "5-a-Day." The Eat 5-a-Day campaign was developed by The Produce for Better Health Foundation in cooperation with the National Cancer Institute. This includes 2 servings of fruits and 3 of vegetables. The current recommendation is to eat between 20 grams and 35 grams of fiber in the daily diet.

An example of fiber in breakfast might be: a serving of the cereal with 2.5 grams of fiber, two slices of whole wheat bread and a whole banana. The fiber intake would be 8.1 grams. Most of us need to increase our fiber intake.

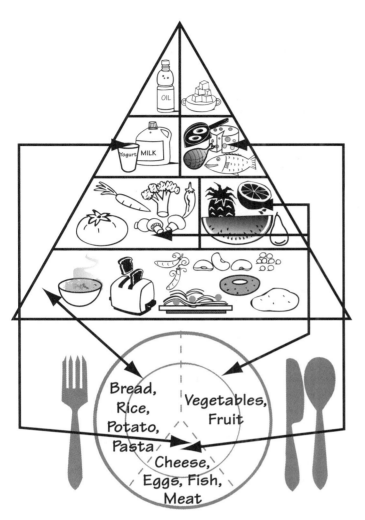

The Daily Plate of Food.

What does your plate for a day look like?

Look at the food guide to see if you need to:

• Eat more starchy foods (e.g., bread, rice, potato and pasta)

• Eat more fruits and vegetables

• Eat less protein and fat (particularly red meat)

Food Groups/Food Guide Pyramid

Foods are often divided into groups or exchanges (see Chapter 12). The common divisions include the milk and yogurt, meat, grains and starchy vegetables, non-starchy vegetables, fruit and fat groups. The milk and meat groups are important sources of protein, and the milk group is a major source of calcium and vitamin D. Milk also has carbohydrate. Some of the minerals such as iron and zinc are high in the meat groups. Vitamins and fiber are generally highest in the fruit and vegetable groups. Be aware that some foods from each of the food groups should be eaten daily to have a well-balanced diet. The food pyramid (see Figure) is now usually used as a guide to good nutrition (rather than food groups).

Three-day Food Record

It is good to keep a three-day food record once a year. This will show you if you are eating the right foods. Write down all foods and the amounts you eat for three days as shown in the Appendix in this Chapter. The dietitian can then review the record and suggest changes if needed. Chapter 12 emphasizes the use of food records for carbohydrate counting. While you are doing the recording, you will need to give accurate information. If you feel you need more help with instructions, ask your dietitian.

SWEETENERS
(Sugar-substitutes)

Many foods are now available which contain sweeteners that either do not raise the blood sugar or which may cause less of an increase than a similar amount of table sugar. They are divided into the **nutritive sweeteners** (including table sugar), which do provide calories and carbohydrate, and the **non-nutritive sweeteners**, which essentially provide no calories or carbohydrate.

 Nutritive Sweeteners

These include all sugars and all sugar-alcohols. Sugars contain four grams of carbohydrate and 16 calories per level teaspoon. The two main sugars used as sweeteners are sucrose (table sugar) and fructose. Both are discussed earlier in this chapter under Carbohydrates, and both cause an increase in blood sugar levels. High-fructose corn syrup is a combination of both sugars and raises the blood sugar more than pure fructose. Foods sweetened with fruit juices, dates or raisins may have the label "no added sugar." This is misleading as there is sugar in these food-additives.

The sugar alcohols include sorbitol, xylitol, mannitol and others (often ending in "—ol"). They provide about two grams of carbohydrate and eight calories per teaspoon. They are more slowly absorbed than sugar, and eating an excessive amount can cause diarrhea. They are often found in "sugar-free" candies.

Non-nutritive Sweeteners

The non-nutritive (or "artificial") sweeteners do not provide any calories or carbohydrate. *The five currently on the market are:*

1. Saccharin: Saccharin is 200-700 times sweeter than table sugar. It is found in Sweet'N Low®, other table top sweeteners and in some diet drinks.

2. Aspartame: Aspartame is 200 times sweeter than table sugar. It is broken down into aspartic acid, methanol and phenylalanine. (Rare patients with a condition called phenylketonuria cannot metabolize phenylalanine and cannot eat foods with this sweetener.) People have suggested that the methanol (or its breakdown product, formaldehyde), could be bad for one's health, but there is **NO SCIENTIFIC DATA TO SUPPORT THIS IN HUMANS**. The products that contain aspartame include: Equal®, NutraSweet®, diet pop, sugar-free JELL-O®, Kool-Aid®, ice cream, Crystal Light® and many others. Use in moderation is generally advised (no more than two diet pops per day!).

3. Acesulfame-K (Ace-K): Ace-K is 200 times sweeter than table sugar. It is approved for use as a table-top sweetener (Sweet-One® or Sunnette®) and for use in chewing gum, desserts, beverages and other products. It is used in PEPSI-ONE®, along with aspartame.

4. Sucralose: Sucralose was approved for use in 1998 and is 600 times sweeter than sugar. It is used as a table-top sweetener (Splenda®) and is found in RC Cola®, in Ocean Spray Lightstyle Juices® and in Log Cabin® Sugar-Free Syrup.

5. Stevia: Stevia is a natural alternative sweetener from the herb, Stevia Rebaudiana. It is 300 times sweeter than sugar.

LABEL READING

Label reading has become easier for people in the U.S. as the law requires labeling of the nutrient content of products. Smart buyers can learn a lot about the foods they are considering buying by learning to read labels. The information that can be gained from reading a label is discussed in Table 3.

If you are interested in the carbohydrate content for carbohydrate (or "carb") counting (see Chapter 12), it is listed under "total carbohydrate" on most labels. In the U.S., one carbohydrate choice is considered to be 15 grams of carbohydrate. The counts are approximate so that a food having 12 grams may be rounded off to one choice. For high fiber foods (>5 gm), the grams of fiber (which are not absorbed) can be subtracted from the grams of total carbohydrate. Carbohydrate counting is discussed in detail in the next chapter.

Table 3

READING A NUTRITION LABEL

The serving size is shown at the top. It is important to observe the serving size. (This is often less than the amount people eat. If you eat two cups rather than one, you would need to double all of the daily values eaten.) The total calories and the calories from fat per serving are routinely given and are important.

The total fat includes all types of fat (saturated, polyunsaturated and monounsaturated). The total fat, saturated fat and cholesterol content are all important in relation to heart disease and it is wise to look for lower fat choices.

The saturated fats for the entire day should be under 10% of the total calories per day. For someone eating 2,000 calories per day, this would mean under 200 calories from saturated fat or under 22 grams (nine calories per gram).

†The percent of daily values for fat, carbohydrate and protein are listed on the label based on a 2,000-calorie daily intake. More active people will need more calories, in which case these amounts should be figured based on calories actually eaten.

For those who count carbohydrates, one helping of this cereal has 15 grams of carbohydrate, which is one carbohydrate choice (or count). If one cup of white milk (any type) is added, then one additional carbohydrate choice must also be added so that there would be a total of two carb choices. The sugars include those found naturally in the food as well as those added to the food. Both are included in the grams of "Total Carbohydrate."

The recommended daily amounts for cholesterol, sodium (salt) and fiber stay the same for the 24-hour period for the three caloric intakes.

The ingredients are usually included on the label in order of the amount present.

Nutrition Facts

Serving Size 1.0 Cup (120g)
Servings Per Container   8

Amount Per Serving

Calories 130   Calories From Fat 60

                 % Daily Value †

Total Fat 6.5g	10%
Saturated Fat 2.5g	12%
Cholesterol 30mg	10%
Sodium 240mg	10%
Total Carbohydrate 15g	5%
Dietary Fiber 2.5g	10%
Sugars 3g	
Protein 3g	6%

Vitamin A 10%		Vitamin E 5%	
Calcium 15%		Iron 5%	

†Percent Daily Values are based on a 2,000-calorie diet. Your daily values may be higher or lower depending on your calorie needs:

Calories:	2,000	2,500	3,200
Total Fat (g)	65	80	107
Sat Fat (g)	20	25	36
Cholesterol (mg)	300	300	300
Sodium (mg)	2,400	2,400	2,400
Total Carb (g)	300	375	480
Fiber	25	30	37

Calories per gram:

Fat 9   Carbohydrate 4   Protein 4

Ingredients: Whole wheat, oat bran, raisins, gelatin, malt, flavoring, vitamins, and minerals.

FAST-FOOD RESTAURANTS

It is difficult to eat at fast-food restaurants and not eat foods high in animal fat, calories and salt. Eating at fast-food restaurants goes against good nutrition principles and may be bad for the heart. In addition, meals are usually low in vitamin-containing fruits and vegetables. Some fast-food restaurants are now trying to provide healthier food choices (salads, leaner meat and deep-frying in vegetable oils rather than animal fat). However, eating at fast-food restaurants should be limited.

ALCOHOL

We hesitate to discuss alcohol under normal nutrition. It is, of course, illegal for children and adolescents to use alcohol prior to reaching the legal drinking age in a particular state or country. We do not condone alcohol use for children or adolescents. However, exposure often begins prior to the legal drinking age. Education is important regardless of the age.

Blood sugars may initially be elevated after drinking alcohol; beer, for example, contains a fair amount of carbohydrate. However, the more dangerous effect of alcohol is the lowering of the blood sugar level (as much as 6-12 hours later). The alcohol prevents the other foods stored in the body from being converted to blood sugar.

If alcohol consumption is to occur, some general rules are listed below:

✔ Use alcohol only in moderation. Sip slowly and make one drink last a long time.

✔ Eat when drinking alcohol. Never drink on an empty stomach.

✔ A low blood sugar is the main worry - and a bedtime snack (solid protein and some carbohydrate) must be taken after drinking in the evening even if the bedtime blood sugar level is high.

✔ The next morning, get up at the usual time, test blood sugar, take insulin, eat breakfast and then go back to bed if you feel ill. "Sleeping-in" can result in a bad reaction.

✔ NEVER drink and drive. Ask a friend who has not been drinking to drive, or call someone to come and get you.

A college student, helping to teach our College Workshop course to newly-graduated high school seniors, had a useful recommendation regarding college parties. He noted that if he had a cup in his hand, no one tried to push further drinks. In contrast, if his hands were empty (no glass), he received a lot of pressure. The answer was to hold the same cup all evening and to just have fun!

APPENDIX FOR CHAPTER 11

THREE-DAY FOOD RECORD FORM

Instructions for completing food record form:

1. Please write down everything you eat or drink for three days. This includes meals and snacks. Often it's easier to remember what you eat if you record your food intake at the time you eat it.

2. Include the amount of food or beverage eaten. Also include the method of preparation (baked, fried, broiled, etc.), as well as any brand names of products (labels can also be enclosed). Use standard measuring cups or spoons. Record meat portions in ounces after cooking. If you do not have a scale, you can estimate ounces. The size of a deck of cards is about equal to three ounces of meat.

3. Be sure to include items added to your food. For example, include salad dressing on salad, margarine or butter on bread.

4. Include any supplements you take (vitamin, mineral or protein powders). Write down the name of the supplement, what it contains and the amount taken. Include a copy of the label, if possible.

5. Please include meal and snack times, blood glucose values, amount of insulin, type of food, amount of food, grams of carbohydrate and any activity or exercise. Put a star next to any blood sugar that is two hours after a meal.

The following is an example of how to complete your food record. Please record what you eat on the forms on the following page. The forms can then be faxed or mailed to your diabetes care provider. *An example for the start of a day follows:*

Time	Blood Glucose	Insulin	Food (include amounts)	Carbs	Activity
8:00	170	3H/10N	Cheerios-3/4 cup	15 gms	
			Skim milk-1/2 cup	6 gms	
			Orange juice-1 cup	30 gms	
10:00	160*				Jog-20 min.

THREE-DAY FOOD RECORD FORM

Name:_____   Home Phone: _____

Date(s): _____   Work Phone: _____

Dietitian: _____   Best time to be reached: _____

Time	Blood Sugar	Dose: Insulin/ Oral Meds	Food (include amounts)	Carbs	Activity/Other (illness, stress, menses, etc.)

This page may be copied as often as desired. (We prefer three separate days of records.)

DEFINITIONS

Acesulfame-K: An artificial sweetener which does not need insulin to be absorbed by the body. It is available as Sweet-One when used as a sweetener at the table.

Artificial sweetener: A very sweet substance (many hundreds of times sweeter than table sugar) used in very small amounts (and thus having almost no calories) to make foods or drinks taste sweet.

Aspartame: An artificial sweetener which does not need insulin to be absorbed by the body. It is available as a tablet or powder called "Equal" or "NutraSweet."

Calorie: A measurement of the food taken into the body for energy.

Caloric intake: Refers to the energy from foods that are eaten.

Carbohydrate: One of the main energy nutrients. It supplies energy for the body and is further divided into sugars and starches. Carbohydrates are found in all fruits and vegetables, all grain products, dried beans and peas, milk and yogurt. *Carbohydrates include:*

✔ **Starch:** Carbohydrates such as starchy vegetables, pasta, whole grain breads and cereals.

✔ **Sugar:** Carbohydrates such as table sugar, honey, *the four sugars listed below and others*:

1. Fructose: The type of sugar found in fruit. It does not require insulin in order for the body to use it.

2. Glucose: The main type of sugar found in the blood and urine. It is this sugar that is elevated in people with diabetes. Table sugar is half glucose.

3. Lactose: The main sugar found in milk. It needs insulin to be used completely.

4. Sucrose: Table sugar or "granulated sugar" - the body breaks it down to glucose and fructose. The glucose needs insulin to be used.

Cholesterol: A fat present in foods from animals. It is also made in our body. Our blood cholesterol level results from our own body's production (85%) and from the animal products we eat (15%). A high blood cholesterol level (>200 mg/dl) results in a greater risk for heart disease.

Cup (c): A measure of volume of eight ounces or 240cc (ml). Two cups equal one pint. Four cups equal one quart.

Dextrose: Another name for glucose.

Dietetic: This just means that at least one part of the food has been changed (e.g., salt, sugar or fat). It does not necessarily mean the sugar has been removed!

Exchange: Division of foods into six groups. Each exchange within the six groups contains a similar amount of carbohydrate, protein, fat and calories.

Fat: One of the energy nutrients. *Total fat includes:*

✔ **Polyunsaturated fat:** Fat found mainly in vegetable oils.

✔ **Monounsaturated fat:** Fat that has one double bond. It is high in olive and canola oils. When large amounts (3 Tbsp) are consumed each day, blood cholesterol levels will be lower.

✔ **Saturated fat:** Fat found mainly in animal foods.

Cholesterol and Triglyceride: Fats present in foods and in our bodies. High cholesterol and triglyceride blood levels for many years are a cause of "clogged" blood vessels and heart attacks.

Fiber: The parts of plants in food that are not absorbed by the body.

Gram (gm): A unit of weight in the metric system; 1000 grams is equal to 1 kg. There are 448 grams in one pound and 28 grams in 1 oz. Carbohydrate, protein and fat in foods are measured as grams. Information can be obtained from label reading.

✔ One gram of carbohydrate provides four calories.

✔ One gram of protein provides four calories.

✔ One gram of fat provides nine calories.

✔ **Ounce (oz):** A unit of weight equivalent to 28 grams. It is also equal to 30cc (ml) of water.

Mannitol: A sugar alcohol that is used in foods to give a sweet taste. It does provide calories, but doesn't increase the blood sugar as much as sucrose. Too much will cause diarrhea or an upset stomach.

Protein: One of the energy nutrients. It is found in meat, eggs, fish, milk, yogurt and, in lesser amounts, in vegetables and other non-meat products (e.g., nuts, seeds, beans, etc.).

Registered Dietitian (R.D.): A person trained to help you with your diet. He/she has a minimum of a four year college degree in nutrition or a related area, has completed an internship and has passed a national exam.

Saccharin: An artificial sweetener (e.g., Sweet'N Low) which needs no insulin and provides no calories.

Sorbitol: A sugar alcohol that is used in foods to give a sweet taste. It does provide calories, but does not increase the blood sugar as much as sucrose.

Tablespoon (Tbsp): A measure of 3 tsp or 15cc (ml). It is equal to 15 grams (1/2 oz) of water. There are 16 tablespoons of sugar (sucrose) in one cup.

Teaspoon (tsp): A measure of 5cc (ml). It is also equal to five grams of water.

QUESTIONS (Q) AND ANSWERS (A) FROM NEWSNOTES

Q. What is fiber and what is its value in the diet?

A. Fiber is generally defined as the part of food that is not broken down by the enzymes in the intestine. In the past 50-100 years, the food industry has moved toward the purification of foods, leaving out the parts our bodies cannot absorb and assuming they were of no value. It was forgotten that man had developed over millions of years eating much fiber in his foods. Then in the 1960s, two British epidemiologists noted that African natives had little or no problem with appendicitis, cancer of the colon, obesity, gallstones, adult diabetes, hemorrhoids, constipation, diverticulitis, gallbladder disease and several other diseases which were fairly common in industrialized countries. They developed the "fiber hypothesis" and gave reasons why each of these diseases could be related to a low fiber intake.

Some of the physiological effects of fiber are to prolong the time it takes food to leave the stomach, to shorten the transit of food through the rest of the intestine, to reduce fat absorption and to increase stool weight and bulk. Pressure in the colon is generally reduced.

The effect of fiber in the diabetic diet primarily relates to the delay in food leaving the stomach. For example, sugar (such as in sugar pop) eaten with a high-fiber food (such as whole wheat bread) might slowly trickle from the stomach for slow absorption with a mild increase in the blood sugar. When the same food (sugar pop) is consumed alone, it all passes immediately into the intestine for immediate absorption. (We measured one boy's blood sugar after consuming sugar pop alone, watching it rise from 250 to 450 mg/dl [13.9 to 25 mmol/L] in 30 minutes.)

Although fiber sounds like a blessing for the diabetic diet, it has been more useful in type 2 diabetes than in type 1 diabetes. So many things affect the person with type 1 diabetes, particularly insulin dose and exercise, that altering one part of the diet (fiber) and expecting miraculous changes in diabetes control has not been realistic.

Increasing fiber intake should still be a goal for all children and young adults. The high-fiber foods are mainly vegetables, bran or whole grain cereals, whole wheat or rye bread and fruits. A minimum of 3 servings of vegetables and two servings of fruit should be in all our diets. This will meet the current "Eat 5-A-Day" minimum. The "Eat 5-A-Day" program was developed by The Produce for Better Health Foundation in cooperation with the National Cancer Institute. At least twice this many fruits and vegetables, plus all whole wheat and rye bread and daily exchanges of beans, would be required for the high-fiber, high-carbohydrate diet.

It is unrealistic to think of requiring our teenagers to eat the high-carbohydrate, high-fiber diet when one survey showed that half of all U.S. teenagers eat less than one serving of fruit or vegetable per day. They are not even near the eight "exchanges" of fruits and vegetables (combined) currently recommended for all teens, much less the higher quantities required for the high-fiber diet. The question, "Where's the beef?" missed the point entirely for our teenagers. They eat too much hamburger already! The real question is, "Where are the fruits and vegetables?"

Fortunately, children with diabetes do far better than most teenagers. This is because of the teaching they regularly receive in the diabetes clinic and meeting with the dietitians on a regular basis. Families who come to clinic should take advantage of this opportunity for their youth to learn about good nutrition.

Q. Why do you check the blood cholesterol levels each year on the people seen at the Clinic?

A. Blood cholesterol levels (and when possible, triglyceride and lipoprotein levels) are one of the best predictors of who will have heart problems later in life. When someone with diabetes becomes older, this becomes an important concern. The two other big risk factors for coronary artery disease are tobacco use and high blood pressure. Needless to say, no one with diabetes should smoke, and blood pressures should be checked at regular clinic visits.

Research from the Clinic was among the first to show that children with diabetes have an increased problem with elevated blood cholesterol levels. When the high levels are found, the first concern always relates to the diabetes control. If the control is poor (high hemoglobin A_{1c} level), the high cholesterol may be secondary to the poor diabetes control. If the diabetes control is good and the blood cholesterol level is still high, the next thing to consider is diet. Although most people immediately think of eggs and cholesterol intake, it is even more important to reduce the animal fat (saturated fat) and to increase the vegetable fats, fowl and fish (sources of polyunsaturated and monounsaturated fats) in the diet than it is to reduce the cholesterol intake. We call the ratio of polyunsaturated to saturated fat intake the P/S ratio. It is also important to reduce total fat intake and possibly to increase the intake of monounsaturated oils.

Q. More has been in the newspapers of late about the dangers of NutraSweet (aspartame). Do we need to stop using it?

A. A recent news article mentioned a five-year-old boy who became "inconsolably and wildly emotional" after drinking NutraSweet products. We have not heard of similar instances in our Clinic, although a few people have complained of headaches and stomachaches after high NutraSweet intake. Children with a rare inherited condition (phenylketonuria) cannot consume NutraSweet because it contains phenylalanine. We have only one known patient in our Clinic with both diabetes and phenylketonuria, so this is fortunately a rare combination.

As emphasized by our dietitians in an earlier issue of NEWSNOTES, moderation is probably the answer for now. We generally suggest restricting the diet pop to no more than two per day. Common sense should also be used in watching the number of other foods consumed each day which contain NutraSweet. However, if you think you or your child has specific symptoms after consuming NutraSweet products, you should share this information with your dietitian.

Chapter 12

TOPIC: 🐾 Food Management and Diabetes

TEACHING OBJECTIVES:

1. Present the principles of food management related to diabetes.

2. Explain the significance of carbohydrates (carbs) in diabetes management.

3. Discuss types of meal planning approaches including carb counting.

WITH SPECIAL THANKS FOR THE SUGGESTIONS OF:

- Michelle Hansen, MS, RD, CDE
- Darcy Owen, MS, RD, CDE
- Gail Spiegel, MS, RD, CDE
- Markey Swanson, RD, CDE

LEARNING OBJECTIVES:

Learner (parents, child, relative or self) will be able to:

1. List three objectives of food management.

2. Describe examples of carbohydrate (carb) containing foods and their effect on blood sugar levels.

3. Explain the type of food plan you will be using.

Chapter 12

FOOD MANAGEMENT AND DIABETES

Food is one of the major influences on blood sugar levels in people with diabetes. As discussed in Chapter 2, the body (particularly the liver) also makes sugar (internal sugar), which adds to the blood sugar. Other sugars (external sugars) come from the food we eat. Recommendations for the use of sugars for people with diabetes have changed. It has gone from avoidance to allowing sugar within the context of a healthy meal plan. As discussed in Chapter 11, the right amount and types of food are essential for normal growth and health. **TYPE 1 (INSULIN-DEPENDENT) DIABETES CANNOT BE TREATED WITH DIET ALONE.** In contrast, type 2 diabetes can sometimes be treated with diet and exercise alone.

OBJECTIVES OF FOOD MANAGEMENT

No matter which of the food plans are used, the objectives of food management are the same:

* to balance insulin and carb intake in order to keep the blood sugars as close to normal as possible

* to keep the blood fats (cholesterol and triglycerides) and lipoproteins (LDL and HDL) at desired levels

* to improve the overall health by maintaining the best possible nutrition

* to help avoid long-term complications

* to help attain normal growth and development for children and appropriate weight for everyone

* to help prevent severe hypoglycemia

It is amazing how often we hear parents comment, "My child with diabetes is the healthiest in our family BECAUSE HE/SHE EATS THE BEST." Although this is not proven, it may be true. Good nutrition for a person with diabetes is really just a healthy diet from which **all** people would benefit.

Views on food management for people with diabetes have changed considerably. There was a time when some diabetes care providers believed every family should rigidly be given an ADA exchange food program.

In 1994, the Position Statement of the ADA stated:

"Today there is no one 'diabetic' or 'ADA' diet. The recommended food program can only be defined as a dietary prescription based on nutrition assessment and treatment goals. Medical nutrition therapy for people with diabetes should be individualized, with consideration given to usual eating habits and other lifestyle changes."

This has been the philosophy of the 10 editions of this book over the last 27 years.

The DCCT (Chapter 14) also contributed to our knowledge about food and diabetes. In the DCCT, six main nutrition factors were found that contributed to better sugar control (lower HbA_{1c} levels).

The six main nutritional factors were:

1. following some sort of a meal plan

2. avoidance of extra snacks

3. avoidance of over-treatment of low blood sugars (hypoglycemia)

4. prompt treatment of high blood sugars when found

5. adjusting insulin levels for meals

6. consistency of night snacks

The DCCT did **NOT** report that one type of meal plan was any more effective than another.

Three of the major meal planning approaches we use to help people manage diabetes are discussed below. In recent years, carb counting has become more popular. We tend to emphasize this plan. Most families now start with a constant carb food plan. Some families will change from one plan to another or use a combination of plans that works for them.

TYPES OF MEAL PLANNING APPROACHES

Different types of meal planning approaches have been used for people with diabetes for about 4,000 years. They are talked about in an ancient scroll called the "Ebers Papyrus" which was written about 2000 B.C. In 1993 the DCCT showed that people with diabetes who followed a dietary program had better sugar control than those who didn't. There are now many types of food management plans for people with diabetes. All food management plans require people to pay attention to carbs. Over 90 percent of carbs eaten are converted into blood glucose over the next one to two hours. Meats (protein) and fat have very little conversion to blood sugar. All three of the food plans discussed below pay special attention to carbs.

The three approaches used most commonly in our Clinic are:

1. ***Constant Carbohydrate Meal Plan***

2. ***Carbohydrate Counting Meal Plan***

3. ***Exchange Meal Plan***

The clinic caring for the person with newly diagnosed diabetes may prefer one type of meal planning approach over another. It may be unnecessary to read about the other approaches, at least initially. The purpose of all meal plans is to achieve better control of blood sugar levels. The method that works best for one person may not be the best for someone else.

Any of the three meal planning approaches can work. No single approach has been proven better than any other in achieving good blood sugar control. It is up to each clinic and family to eventually decide which approach works best for them. Some families will switch from one approach to another or combine parts of each to fit their needs. Many families initially use the constant carb food plan. They then move to adjusting short-acting insulin for carbs eaten (carb counting) as they gain confidence, knowledge and carb counting skills. It is important to meet with a registered dietitian to develop a meal plan that meets your lifestyle.

1. CONSTANT CARBOHYDRATE (CARB) MEAL PLAN

CAREFUL MANAGEMENT OF CARB INTAKE MUST BE PART OF ANY OF THE PROGRAMS. IT IS IMPOSSIBLE TO EAT VARYING AMOUNTS OF CARBS (WITHOUT CHANGING THE INSULIN DOSAGE) AND KEEP THE BLOOD SUGAR FROM FLUCTUATING UP OR DOWN. Knowing how many carbs are being eaten is important in all three of the meal plans.

The amount of insulin (usually two or three shots per day) is kept relatively constant from day-to-day. This is done to match relatively consistent food intake. **The amount of carbs (types can vary) is kept about the same for each meal and each snack from one day to the next.** Often families begin by using the constant carb meal plan. They then move to counting carbs as they gain confidence and knowledge.

Labels must be read to know the grams (gm) of carbs being eaten (see Chapter 11). The dietitian may give a range of carbs for each meal. This might be 45 to 60 grams for a pre-teen. A teenage boy might have a range of 60 to 150 gm/meal. **CONSISTENCY IS THE KEY.** The constant carb meal plan is formed around the 10 principles discussed in this chapter.

The amount of food eaten at a meal or snack can vary with:

✔ expected exercise

✔ insulin taken

✔ blood sugar level

More carbs may be needed for fun activities such as sports, hiking and biking. For work related activities, such as ranching and farming, more carbs may also be needed. However, the normal eating pattern of the child and the family should stay the same as much as possible.

Families often ask, "How many carb choices (or counts or exchanges) are appropriate for me/my child?" They can count carbs even if insulin adjustments are not being made to match the carb intake. This helps to keep the carbs eaten at each meal consistent. The numbers of carb choices to be eaten at each meal can be estimated by looking at Table 4 under the Exchange Meal Plan. Approximate numbers of calories needed per day can be calculated from the formula in that section (or ask your dietitian). The usual number of carb choices for each of the three meals for the level of calories per 24 hours can be seen in the dark print in Table 4.

2. CARBOHYDRATE (CARB) COUNTING MEAL PLAN

Carb counting involves counting the grams of carbs and giving a matching dose of insulin. It allows for greater freedom and flexibility in food choices. It is not possible to count carbs without learning to read food labels (Chapter 11). Carb counting is both similar to and different from the other two meal planning approaches.

Comparison to the Constant Carbohydrate Meal Plan:

Similarity …

✔ It emphasizes carb intake and on keeping protein and fat relatively consistent.

Difference …

✔ It presumes that carb intake (and insulin dose) will vary, thus providing more flexibility and greater safety from hypoglycemia.

Comparison to the Exchange Meal Plan:

Similarity …

✔ similar sized "exchanges" of carbs are used

Difference …

✔ protein and fat exchanges are not used

Tables 1 gives summaries of foods equaling one carb choice (count). One carb choice is the amount of each food equal to 15 grams of carb. It may be helpful to copy Table 1 initially and carry it in a wallet or purse.

Carb counting involves counting the grams of carbs to be eaten and taking a matching amount of insulin.

Two Approaches:

Some people prefer to just think of the number of grams of carbs.

1. When converting to an Insulin to Carb ratio (**I/C** ratio) one usually thinks in grams of carbs. Thus, the conversion to 15-gram choices is not really needed. An example of an **I/C** ratio is 1 to 15 (1/15). This refers to one unit of insulin per 15 gm of carbs eaten (or to be eaten). Carb counting was greatly aided by the food labeling laws (Chapter 11). They require the grams of total carbs be given on the label of most every food.

2. Others prefer to convert each 15 gm unit to one carb choice.

More detailed quantities of various foods equaling one carb choice (e.g., 15 grams of carb) are given in Table 2. The total grams of carbs to be eaten are divided by 15 to get carb choices (15 grams of carbs equals one carb choice or count). The units of short-acting insulin (Humalog/NovoLog or Regular) are then adjusted at every meal to match the carb choices (units of 15 grams of carb). The amount of exercise and the blood sugar level must also be considered.

Getting Started (Restarted)

First:

We ask families to keep precise food, insulin, blood sugar and activity records for at least three days. (See the Three-Day Food Record Form in the Appendix of Chapter 11. This page can be copied as desired.)

After completing the form (as accurately as possible), fax it to your dietitian for analysis. The dietitian, working with your doctor or nurse, will then make suggestions for Insulin to Carb (I/C) ratios. The more blood sugars you can do prior to meals and two hours after meals, the better the advice she/he can give. It is also important to include all doses of insulin or oral meds that were taken.

Every person is different in his or her need for short-acting insulin. The same person may vary from one time of day to another.

✔ Some people can use one unit of short-acting insulin per 15 grams of carb (one carb count) for all meals and snacks. This is an I/C ratio of 1/15.

✔ Others might need:

• breakfast - one unit of insulin for each 15 grams of carb

• lunch - one unit of insulin for every 30 grams of carb (I/C ratio of 1/30 or l/2 unit per 15 grams carb)

• dinner - one unit of insulin per 10 grams of carb (I/C ratio of 1/10 or 1.5 units per 15 grams carb)

Humalog/NovoLog dosages for meals are best adjusted by measuring blood sugar levels two hours after the meal. The same sugar levels suggested in Chapters 7 and 21 can also apply for the desired values two hours after eating. If the values are not in the desired range for age two hours after eating, the Insulin to Carb (I/C) ratio will need to be changed.

✔ **If the blood sugar value is consistently high**, more insulin is needed for the grams of carb in the I/C ratio. An example would be to change from 1/15 (1 unit/15 gm carb to 1/10 [1 unit/10 gm carb]).

✔ **If the sugar level is below the lower limit**, a lower amount of insulin is needed. An example would be to change from an I/C ratio of 1/15 (1 unit/15 gm carb) to an I/C ratio of 1/20 (1 unit/20 gm carb).

Call your healthcare provider to help you make adjustments.

Second:

After calculating the dose of insulin for the carb choices, the final dose must be adjusted considering a correction factor (Chapter 21), exercise and any other factors (illness, stress, menses, etc.). Some people subtract one unit

if the blood sugar is below 70 mg/dl (3.9 mmol/L) or add one unit if the blood sugar is above 200 mg/dl (11.1 mmol/L).

Third:

Careful record keeping for the first one or two weeks is essential (possibly using Table 5 in Chapter 26 to record the blood sugar, carb count and insulin dose). Checking blood sugars two hours after meals allows one to see if the insulin to carb ratio used for a given meal resulted in the correct insulin dose.

Fourth:

It is then important to review the records with the dietitian and physician to decide the best I/C ratios to use at different meals.

Fifth:

Carb counting is most difficult for combination foods such as soups, casseroles and foods with many ingredients. The grams of carbs can be calculated from the amounts of each of the ingredients. (The amount is then divided by the number of servings.)

Sixth:

It may be necessary to estimate the grams of carbs when eating out. This could be done on the basis of the grams in the same food prepared at home. Obviously, this does not always work (some cooks add more sugar!). Doing a blood sugar two hours after the meal helps to make a better guess the next time.

The booklet, *Nutrition in the Fast Lane*, from Eli Lilly & Co. gives grams of carbs (and other nutrients) for over 1000 menu items. It includes data on foods served by 30 of the top fast-food restaurants (see Resources in this chapter). The booklet, *Fast Food Guide*, from BD is also helpful for carb contents of foods in fast-food restaurants.

Some degree of thinking (just like the "thinking scales" in Chapter 21) is obviously necessary for carb counting. However, once the best dosages are determined, the process becomes very automatic. Most people who use an insulin pump use carb counting to determine the bolus of insulin to be taken with any food intake (see Chapter 26). Use of carb counting allows people to better observe the relationship between factors affecting the blood sugar and insulin dosage. In England (and the entire U.K.), carb counting (using 10 gram carb choices) has been used successfully for many years. A summary of 15-gram carb equivalents in foods frequently eaten is given in Tables 1 and 2. In addition, Table 3 gives carb counts of foods that are high in carbs.

How Many Carb Choices?

Table 4 lists exchanges for different numbers of calories eaten per day. If uncertain how many calories per day are needed, this is discussed in Table 4. As the exchange diets used 15 gm carb exchanges, the numbers suggested in dark print for each of the different caloric diets, would also refer to the carb-counting food plan. Thus, the "1" indicates 1 carb choice (count) of 15 gm; the "2" equals 2 carb choices or 30 gm, etc. This table then shows the number of carb choices at each time of day for a given caloric intake.

ONE CARBOHYDRATE (CARB) COUNT OR CHOICE*

1 Starch = 1 Fruit = 1 Milk = 15 grams Carbohydrate = 1 CARB Choice

Food Group	Carbohydrate Content	Portion Sizes
Starch/Grains	15 gms	1 slice bread 1 six inch tortilla 1/2 cup pasta 1/2 bagel 1/2 hamburger bun 1/2 cup peas or corn 1 small potato (3 oz) 1/3 cup rice 1/3 cup cooked dried beans
Fruit	15 gms	1 piece fruit (small to med.) 1/2 cup canned fruit 1/2 cup fruit juice 1/4 cup dried fruit 1 cup berries or melon
Milk	12 gms	1 cup skim, 1%, 2% or whole milk 8 oz plain yogurt

*These are not exact but are close enough for most people.

NOTE: This half-page may be copied and carried in the wallet as needed.

Table 2

CARBOHYDRATE CONTENT OF FOODS

Amount of Starches/Grains that equal 15 grams carbohydrate

Food	Serving Size
Bagel	1/2 small (1 oz)
Beans, cooked, dried, canned	1/3 cup
Bread, white, whole wheat, rye	1 slice (1 oz)
Corn, cooked	1/2 cup
Crackers	4-6
English muffin	1/2
Graham crackers	3 squares
Hamburger bun	1/2 bun
Popcorn	3 cups
Pasta, cooked	1/2 cup
Peas, cooked	1/2 cup
Potato, baked	1 small (3 oz)
Potato, mashed	1/2 cup
Rice, cooked	1/3 cup
Roll (dinner, hard)	1 small
Tortilla (6" corn or 8" flour)	1

Fruits
15 grams carbohydrate

Food	Serving Size
Apple, small	1 (4 oz)
Applesauce, unsweetened	1/2 cup
Banana	1 small banana or 1/2 large
Blueberries	3/4 cup
Canned fruit, light or juice packed	1/2 cup
Cantaloupe, melon	1 cup cubed
Cherries, sweet, fresh	12 (3 oz)
Fruit juice	1/2 cup (4 oz)
Grapefruit, medium	1/2
Grapes, small	17
Orange, small	1 (6 1/2 oz)
Pear, large, fresh	1/2
Raisins	2 Tbsp
Strawberries	1 1/4 cup whole berries
Watermelon	1 1/4 cup cubes

Milk/Yogurt
12 grams carbohydrate

Food	Serving Size
Milk (skim, 1%, 2%, whole)	1 cup (8 oz)
Yogurt (see "Other Carbohydrates" list)	

Other carbohydrates on the next page

Other Carbohydrates
(Table 2 Continued)

Food	Serving Size	Carbohydrate gms
Brownie, small unfrosted	2" square	15 gm
Cake, unfrosted	2" square	15 gm
Cake, frosted	2" square	30 gm
Chicken noodle soup	1 cup (8 oz)	15 gm
Cookie, (sandwich or chocolate chip)	2 cookies	15 gm
Cookie, medium (homemade)	1 cookie	15 gm
Cupcake, frosted	1 small	30 gm
Doughnut, plain cake	1 medium (1.5 oz)	20 gm
Doughnut, glazed	3 3/4 in. (2 oz)	30 gm
French fries, thin	20-25	30 gm
Granola bar	1	20-25 gm
Ice cream (regular, light, fat free)	1/2 cup	20 gm
Jam or jelly, regular	1 Tbsp	15 gm
Macaroni and cheese	1 cup (8 oz)	30 gm
Noodle casserole	1 cup (8 oz)	30 gm
Pie, fruit, 2 crusts	1/6 pie	45 gm
Poptart, unfrosted	1	35 gm
Potato chips	12-18 (1 oz)	15 gm
Pizza	1 slice (1/4 of 10")	30 gm
Pudding, regular	1/2 cup (4 oz)	25 gm
Syrup, light	2 Tbsp	15 gm
Syrup, regular	1 Tbsp	15 gm
Tomato soup (made with water)	1 cup (8 oz)	15 gm
Tortilla chips	6-12 (1 oz)	15 gm
Yogurt, light	1 cup (6-8 oz)	15 gm

*The carbohydrate amounts listed on this handout are estimates. If the food you are eating has a food label check the Nutrition Facts for the accurate amount of carbohydrate in that product.

Measurement Key

3 tsp = 1 Tbsp   4 ounces = 1/2 cup

4 Tbsp = 1/4 cup   8 ounces = 1 cup

5 1/3 Tbsp = 1/3 cup   1 cup = 1/2 pint

SUGAR CONTENT OF SOME
HIGH-CARBOHYDRATE FOODS

Food Item	Size Portion	Sugar Content* (teaspoons)	"Carb" Choices	GM Carb
Beverages				
Cola drinks	12 oz can	10	3	50
Rootbeer	12 oz can	7	2	35
7-Up®*	12 oz can	9	3	45
Grape, orange, apple juice	6 oz can	5	1.5	25
Dairy Products				
Sherbet	1 scoop	9	3	45
Ice cream cone	1 scoop	3 1/2	1	17
Chocolate milk shake	10 oz glass	11	4	55
Milk	8 oz glass	4	1	15
Chocolate milk	8 oz glass	9 1/2	3	52
Fruit yogurt	8 oz cup	9	3	45
Cakes and Cookies				
Angel food cake	4 oz piece	7	2	35
Chocolate cake, plain	4 oz piece	6	2	30
Chocolate cake, w/frosting	4 oz piece	10	3	50
Sugar cookie	1	1 1/2	1/2	7
Oatmeal cookie	1	2	1	10
Donut, plain	1	4	1	20
Donut, glazed	1	6	2	30
Desserts				
JELL-O	1/2 cup	4 1/2	1 1/2	22
Pastry	4 oz piece	4	1	20
Apple pie	1 slice	7	2	35
Berry pie	1 slice	10	3	50
Chocolate pudding	l/2 cup	4	1	20
Candies				
Chocolate candy bar	1 1/2 oz	2 1/2	1	12
Chewing gum	1 stick	1/2	-	2
Fudge	1 oz square	4 1/2	1/2	22
Hard candy	1 oz	5	2	25
LIFE-SAVERS®	1	1/3	-	1 1/2
Marshmallow	1 piece	1 1/2	1/2	7
Chocolate creme	1 piece	2	1	10
Miscellaneous				
Jelly	1 Tbsp	3	1	15
Strawberry jam	1 Tbsp	3	1	15
Brown sugar	1 Tbsp	3	1	15
Honey	1 Tbsp	3	1	15
Chocolate sauce	1 Tbsp	3	1	15
Karo Syrup®	1 Tbsp	3	1	15

*3 tsp = 1 Tbsp = 1 carb count = 15 grams of carbs

Carbohydrate Counting Resources:

For those wanting more detailed information on carb counting or on carb quantities in foods, there are now entire books written on these subjects.

1. *Counting Carbohydrates*, by Brackenridge, B.P., Fredrickson, L. and Reed, C. Available from Medtronic MiniMed, 18000 Devonshire, Northridge, CA 91325 (1-800-933-3322)

2. *Calories and Carbohydrates* (11th Edition), by Barbara Kraus, Penguin Books, 1995

3. *The Complete Book of Food Counts* (4th Edition), by Corinne Netzer, Dell Publishing, 1997

4. *Food Values of Portions Commonly Used* (17th Edition), by Pennington and Church, Lippencott-Raven Publishers, 1998

5. *The Diabetes Carbohydrate and Fat Gram Guide*, by Lea Ann Holzmeister, 1997

6. *Nutrition In the Fast Lane* (condensed version), Eli Lilly and Co., 1999

7. *Carbohydrate Counting*, by A. Daley, B. Barry, S. Gillespie, K. Kulkarni and M. Richardson. The American Diabetes Association and the American Dietetic Association (1-800-366-1655 or 1-800-232-3472)

    Level 1: Getting Started

    Level 2: Moving On

    Level 3: Using Carbohydrate/Insulin Ratios

8. *Fast Food Guide*, Becton Dickinson Consumer Health Care, Franklin Lakes, NJ, 07417-1883 (http://www.bd.com/diabetes)

9. *Complete Guide to Carb Counting*, by H.S. Warshaw and K. Kulkarni, 2001

10. *Exchanges for All Occasions*, by Marion J. Franz, IDC Publishing

11. *The Doctor's Pocket Calorie, Fat and Carbohydrate Counter*, by Allan Borushek, Family Health Publications

12. *Carbohydrates, Calories and Fat*, by Dr. Art Ulene, Avery Publishing

Websites

http://www.calorieking.com

http://www.cyberdiet.com

3. EXCHANGE MEAL PLAN

If you/your child is newly diagnosed and your dietitian has already met with your family and recommended a different food management plan, it may not be necessary to spend time on this section.

In the exchange food program, foods are grouped into one of six food lists. Foods in each of the six lists having similar sources of calories. The foods within a group can be traded for one another as they have similar caloric, protein, carb and fat content.

The exchange diet and carb counting both consider 15 gm carb as one exchange or one carb choice (count). Exchange tables can be useful when doing carb counts. Table 4 in this chapter gives common carb counts for the three daily meals for different caloric intakes. (Calculation of caloric intake is described under Calculating Calories.)

Note: The **dark numbers** show the number of carbohydrate choices (15-gram amounts) for the number of calories/day for each of the 3 main meals and 3 snacks. The numbers not in dark print represent non-carb exchanges.

EXAMPLES OF EXCHANGES
FOR DIFFERENT CALORIC DIETS

Calories/24 hrs.	1200	1500	1800	2000	2200	2500	2700	3000	3500
BREAKFAST									
Meat	0	0	1	1	1	1	1	1	1
Bread	1	1	2	2	2	3	3	4	5
Fat	0	0	1	0	0	1	1	1	1
Fruit	1	2	2	2	2	2	2	2	2
Milk	1	1	1	1	1	2	2	2	2
Carb Choice Totals	3	4	5	5	5	7	7	8	9
LUNCH									
Meat	1	1	1	2	2	3	3	3	5
Bread	2	2	2	3	3	3	4	4	6
Vegetable	0	0	1/3	1/3	1/3	1/3	1/3	1/3	1/3
Fat	1	1	1	1	1	1	2	2	2
Fruit	1	1	2	2	2	2	2	2	2
Milk	1/2	1	1	1	1	1	1	1	1
Carb Choice Totals	3.5	4	5	6	6	6	7	7	9
DINNER									
Meat	2	2	2	3	3	3	3	4	5
Bread	1	2	2	3	3	3	3	4	6
Vegetable	1/3	1/3	1/3	1/3	1/3	1/3	1/3	1/3	1/3
Fat	0	1	1	1	1	1	1	1	2
Fruit	1	1	1	1	1	2	2	2	2
Milk	1/2	1	1	1	1	1	1	1	1
Carb Choice Totals	3	4	4	5	5	6	6	7	9

Snacks (also included in the total calorie count)

10:00 a.m.	fresh fruit (small apple, orange, banana or half a medium banana)
3:00 p.m.	1500-2400 cal: **1** bread, **1** fruit
	2500-3500 cal: **2** bread, **1** fruit
9:00 p.m.	1200-2400 cal: **1** bread, 1 meat
	2500-3500 cal: **2** bread, 1 meat

These plans are all 30% fat or less

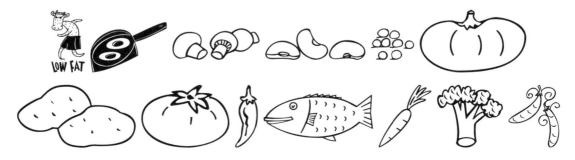

The exchange food program was initially developed for weight control and is still effective for this purpose. Many families, in which someone has just been diagnosed with diabetes, will initially learn the exchange food program. They are able to gain a feeling for how much of which foods to eat. As they feel more comfortable with this plan, they may then gradually change to the constant carb meal plan. In the exchange food program, the number of calories to be eaten each day is initially chosen. Examples of how many of each of the six types of exchanges to eat each day for the number of calories are shown in Table 4. A brief summary of the three food groupings (carbs, meat and fat) is given in the Appendix at the end of this Chapter. Foods in each sub-group contain similar numbers of calories and similar amounts of carb, protein and fat.

CALCULATING CALORIES

In the exchange food program, a caloric level that is appropriate for the age, size and activity of the person is prescribed. Most children under age 14 years need 1,000 calories per day plus 100 calories for each year of age. For example, a five-year-old would need 1,500 calories:

5 years x 100 = 500 cal/day

500 + 1,000 = 1,500 cal/day

The dietitian changes the calories into exchanges. The exchanges are then divided into meals and snacks (Table 4). This meal plan allows both consistent carb intake and a variety of foods. In addition to working with a dietitian, buying the ADA booklet *Exchange Lists for Meal Planning* (see Appendix for ordering address) would be helpful.

In Canada, the Good Health Eating Guide (GHEG) was developed by the Canadian Diabetes Association to have six food groups. They are slightly different from the U.S. Fruits and vegetables are combined into one group and each serving is equivalent to 10 grams of carb and one gram of protein. The sixth food group is the extras (free foods).

CHOOSING A MEAL PLAN APPROACH

One type of meal plan has not been shown to be better for people with diabetes than another. The best meal plan for your family is the one that fits your lifestyle. All three programs work. You could take parts of each program and develop a meal plan suitable for your eating habits and lifestyle. Many families change from one type of program to another to fit their needs at the time. **HOWEVER, THERE MUST BE SOME PROGRAM OF FOOD MANAGEMENT**. Initially, after evaluating your family's eating patterns, it may be wise to let the dietitian help choose the best food program for your family.

TEN PRINCIPLES OF FOOD MANAGEMENT FOR ALL FOOD PLANS

The ten principles listed below are important in all three plans. They would be helpful for any person to follow.

1. EAT A WELL-BALANCED DIET

2. EAT MEALS AND SNACKS AT THE SAME TIME EACH DAY (variable depending on food plan being used)

3. USE SNACKS TO PREVENT INSULIN REACTIONS

4. BALANCE CARB INTAKE AND INSULIN CAREFULLY

5. AVOID OVER-TREATING LOW BLOOD SUGARS

6. REDUCE CHOLESTEROL AND SATURATED FAT INTAKE; REDUCE TOTAL FAT INTAKE

7. MAINTAIN APPROPRIATE HEIGHT AND WEIGHT

8. INCREASE FIBER INTAKE

9. AVOID FOODS HIGH IN SALT (SODIUM)

10. AVOID EXCESSIVE PROTEIN INTAKE

1. Eat a Well-balanced Diet

A well-balanced meal plan is a step toward good health for everyone in the family. It is particularly important in supporting the growth of children. If you understand normal nutrition (Chapter 11), you can help your family have a well-balanced meal plan. Most people have a period of weight loss prior to being diagnosed with diabetes. Starting insulin treatment allows the body to regain weight. Usually the individual's appetite is ravenous for about one month. The body is returning to its usual growth pattern. The appetite then returns to normal. Most individuals can then self-regulate their caloric intake without a set number of calories being prescribed for each day. The exchange food program can help in following a recommended caloric intake.

A well-balanced meal plan is currently considered to contain:

✔ 10-20% of calories from protein

✔ 50-60% from carbs

✔ 25-30% from fat

Meals should be balanced and contain:

✔ a rich source of carbs (fruits, vegetables and whole grains)

✔ a moderate amount of protein (milk, cheese, yogurt, meat, poultry, fish, egg white, nuts and seeds)

✔ a limited amount of fat (butter, egg yolk, animal fat, etc.)

An excess of animal fat may result in higher blood fats and a greater risk for heart disease later in life. A high-protein diet is harmful to the kidneys for people who have either early or advanced kidney damage from diabetes. Working with the dietitian will help assure intake of the recommended balance of foods.

2. Eat Meals and Snacks at the Same Time Each Day

For people following a constant carb or exchange program and using relatively constant insulin dosages, it is important to eat meals and snacks at the same time each day. Use of an insulin pump or the new Lantus insulin gives more flexibility. This is especially true when either is used with adjusting insulin for carb counting. Carb counting allows a person to take insulin to match carbs when they are eaten. There can be more flexibility in the timing of meals and snacks as well as in the number of carbs eaten.

3. Use Snacks to Prevent Insulin Reactions

Snacks help to balance the insulin activity. Peaks in insulin activity vary from person to person. You will learn from experience when you need a snack. It may be before lunch, in the late afternoon or at bedtime. Discuss your need for snacks at your clinic visits. Young children often have a mid or late morning snack. Teens and adults may not always need a morning snack. Mid or late afternoon snacks are eaten by most people with (or without) diabetes. Most children with diabetes need a bedtime snack. Some adults only use a bedtime snack if their blood sugar is below 150 mg/dl (8.3 mmol/L). Once it is decided which snacks you need, TRY TO BE CONSISTENT. Suggestions for daytime and bedtime snacks are given in Tables 5 and 6.

The type of snack is also important. Fruits are good for a morning or afternoon snack. Proteins with fat, such as cheese or meat, delay absorption. A SOLID SNACK CONTAINING PROTEIN, FAT and CARBS IS BEST FOR BEDTIME. Uncooked cornstarch may be broken down slower than other carbs and helps some children prevent lows during the night. Two cornstarch recipes are given in Table 7. Your dietitian can suggest other cornstarch recipes, or you can buy cornstarch snack bars (usually $1.00 each) from several companies.

4. Balance Carb Intake and Insulin Carefully

It is recommended that about half of the food we eat come from carbs. As insulin must be available to utilize most carbs, it is important to learn to balance your insulin with carb intake. Tables 1, 2 and 3 list the carb contents of different foods. It is known that the rise in blood sugar after eating is dependent upon the total amount of carbs eaten and not the form of carbs. It has been pointed out that, **"a carbohydrate is a carbohydrate, is a carbohydrate..."**

We know the most important factors are:

A. how much carb is eaten

B. when the carb is eaten

C. with what the carb is eaten

D. having adequate insulin available when the carb is eaten. Each will be discussed in more detail.

A. How much carb is eaten

Some meals are much higher in carbs than other meals. At breakfast, a meal of eggs, bacon and toast would have fewer carbs than a plate of pancakes. Similarly, a meal of meat, vegetables and salad would have fewer carbs than one of spaghetti and garlic bread or of pizza. More insulin will be required to handle a meal high in carbs compared with one low in carbs.

B. When the carb is eaten

Large amounts of carbs should not be consumed between meals unless additional insulin is given. An extreme example is using a regular (sugar) pop (40 grams of carbs) as a morning or afternoon snack.

One boy with diabetes brought a can of regular sugar pop (10 tsp of sugar, see Table 3) to our clinic with him, freely admitting that he still drank regular pop. We measured his blood sugar before drinking the pop (180 mg/dl or 10 mmol/L) and one hour later (450 mg/dl or 25 mmol/L). The liquid sugars cause the fastest rise in the blood sugar.

When extra carbs are eaten, it is best to take extra Humalog/NovoLog or Regular insulin. The carb counts of some high carb foods are shown in Table 3.

C. With what the carb is eaten

A research project was done at our Center on children with diabetes. The children came in on four consecutive Saturday mornings for breakfast. This project evaluated four different breakfasts varying in sugar or protein and fat content. The blood sugars peaked later and remained higher for a longer time when fat was added (whether extra sugar was added or not).

High fat meals (e.g., pizza, Chinese food, fast foods) will delay the absorption of carbs and the blood sugar may stay elevated longer. When this is observed, extra short-acting insulin can be given the next time. DIFFERENT FOODS AFFECT EACH PERSON DIFFERENTLY. EXPERIENCE IS THE BEST TEACHER.

Research on the effects carbs have on blood sugar levels is often studied by giving the carb by itself. Then, blood sugar levels are measured to see how much the level rises ("glycemic-index"). However, the effects of other foods are very important. The best way to find out the effect of a given carb is to check the blood sugar, eat the food and/or meal and check the blood sugar again in two hours.

D. Having adequate insulin activity when the carb is eaten

Eating extra carbs is possible if extra

Humalog/NovoLog or Regular insulin is added. Measuring the blood sugar two hours after the meal will determine if the insulin dose used was appropriate.

On special occasions, such as birthday parties, the person with diabetes can consume extra carbs. Extra sugar **will not make the person ill and will not cause acidosis**. Not taking extra insulin may result in higher than usual blood sugar and more frequent urination as the sugar passes into the urine. Often the extra activity or excitement at a party balances the extra carb intake.

It is generally healthier to allow a person to fit in a sweet food on an "as-needed" basis. Allowing this can prevent the sneaking of candy or treats. This can be planned for a time when adequate insulin is available. We encourage the entire family to get used to eating foods without a "sugary" taste. **To allow for better nutrition, avoid having non-nutritional foods (Table 3) such as donuts, cookies, cake, etc. in the home. If they are there, they will be hard to avoid.** Most have no nutritional value except adding calories. This will result in better nutrition for the entire family.

There are several alternatives for handling holidays and parties where there are a great number of concentrated sweets. Halloween focuses on candy and is a special problem for young children.

Some suggestions for Halloween trick-or-treating candy:

✔ The child can select a few for his/her regular treats, and give or throw the rest away. If sweets are to be eaten, it is best to eat them when insulin is working. The dose of Humalog/NovoLog or Regular insulin for that meal can then be increased.

✔ Taking the treats to a sick friend or a child in the hospital is a nice option.

✔ Another option is to "sell" the candy to the parents. The money can then be spent to purchase something the child wants.

It is important not to become upset with a child if he/she does eat extra sweets. The stress of the parent being upset can raise the blood sugar more than the sweets (see Chapter 17 on Family Concerns). Instead, discuss the incident with the child and try to find compromises.

HEALTHY DAYTIME SNACKS

Snacks, besides being fun to eat, help prevent low blood sugar levels and provide energy between meals. Typical snacks are usually 1-2 carb choices or 15-30 grams of carb. Below are some low-fat snack ideas to try.

15 grams of carb or one carb choice

1 small apple or orange	18 small pretzel twists
2 popcorn cakes	1/2 small bagel with fat-free cream cheese
8 oz or 1 carton light yogurt	3 cups air popped or low-fat microwave popcorn
1 1/2 graham crackers	4-5 vanilla wafers, 5-6 saltine crackers
1/2 cup low-fat ice cream	1 fruit juice bar
2 Tbsp raisins	1/2 cup unsweetened applesauce
1/2 cup sugar-free pudding	1 fruit roll-up

30 grams of carb or two carb choices

1 small bagel with fat-free cream cheese	1 oz baked tortilla chips with 1/4 cup salsa
1 low-fat granola bar	1 large banana or 2 pieces of fruit (small)
4 oz individual fruit cup and 1 cup skim milk	1 cup Cheerios® with 1/2 cup skim milk
	1/4 cup dried fruit
2 caramel corn cakes	1 cereal bar
15 baked potato chips	14 animal crackers and 1/2 cup skim milk
2 fig cookies and 1 cup skim milk	

SPECIAL SUGGESTIONS

- Encourage fresh fruit rather than juice as a routine snack (unless blood sugar is low)

- Sugar-free flavorings (e.g., sugar-free cocoa or milk flavorings) can be added to milk

- If the child is still hungry after the snack, offer water, popsicles made using diet pop or Kool-Aid or sticks of sliced fresh carrots or celery placed in a dish with cold water and ice cubes

- Don't make issues of "food jags" or eating "crazes"; they usually pass (if not emphasized)

TWO GOOD SUMMER DAYTIME SNACKS

Yogurt creamsicles

Combine:

1/2 cup plain skim milk yogurt (1/2 carb)

1/2 cup fruit juice concentrate, undiluted (3 carbs)

Freeze in popsicle molds until solid.

The total mixture = 3 carb choices

Fruit popsicles

Blend:

1 cup fresh fruit: berries, peaches or bananas (2 carbs)

1/2 cup apple juice concentrate, undiluted (3 carbs)

Freeze in popsicle molds until solid.

The total mixture = 5 carb choices

POSSIBLE BEDTIME SNACKS

Bedtime snacks play an important role in blood sugar control for people with type 1 diabetes. A snack which includes food sources of carbohydrate and protein is helpful in maintaining blood sugar levels throughout the night. A typical snack includes 15 grams of carbohydrate and 7-8 grams of protein, but this can vary depending on age, blood sugar levels and activity throughout the day. Most protein also contains some fat, which results in food staying in the stomach longer. Examples of foods containing 15 grams of carbohydrate and 7-8 grams of protein are listed below:

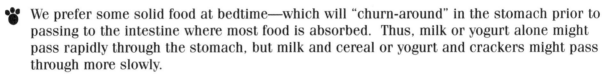

<u>15 grams of Carbohydrate</u>	plus	<u>7-8 grams of Protein</u>
1 slice of bread		2 Tbsp peanut butter
1 - 6 inch tortilla		1/4 cup grated cheese
6 saltine crackers		1 string cheese
3 cups popcorn		1 oz of meat or 1 egg
12 small pretzels		2 Tbsp sunflower seeds
3/4-1 cup cereal		1/4 cup peanuts
5 vanilla wafers		1 cup milk*
		8 oz of no-sugar-added yogurt*

Yogurt and milk provide about 15 grams of carbohydrate as well as protein.

We prefer some solid food at bedtime—which will "churn-around" in the stomach prior to passing to the intestine where most food is absorbed. Thus, milk or yogurt alone might pass rapidly through the stomach, but milk and cereal or yogurt and crackers might pass through more slowly.

Adjustments in carbohydrate amounts can be made based on what the blood sugar is at bedtime.

Here are some guidelines to follow:

- If blood sugar is 150-200 mg/dl (8.3-11.1mmol/L), have **15-20** grams of carbohydrate and 7-8 grams of protein.

- If blood sugar is 100-150 mg/dl (5.5-8.3 mmol/L), have **25-30** grams of carbohydrate and 7-8 grams of protein.

- If blood sugar is less than 100 mg/dl (5.5 mmol/L), have **30-45** grams of carbohydrate and 7-8 grams of protein.

Table 7 gives possible recipes for cornstarch snacks.

TWO CORNSTARCH RECIPES TO USE FOR BEDTIME SNACKS*

Table 7

Corny "O"s**

1/2 stick butter or margarine
1/2 cup chocolate chips
1/2 cup peanut butter
5 cups Cheerios
1 cup cornstarch
1/2 cup powdered sugar

1. Melt butter and chocolate chips, add peanut butter

2. Pour mixture over Cheerios

3. In a paper sack, combine cornstarch and powdered sugar. Add Cheerios mixture and shake until Cheerios are completely covered.

Quantity:	10 servings
Serving size:	1/2 cup
Carb	34 gms/serving
Protein	5 gms/serving
Fat	14 gms/serving

Developed by Michelle Hansen, MS, RD, CDE
** Not for children under 2 years old*

"Corny Cookies"

12 Tbsp (3/4 cup) peanut butter
3 Tbsp honey
1/4 cup cornstarch
2 cups cornflakes

1. Stir together peanut butter, honey and cornstarch

2. Form into balls, about 1 Tbsp size, and roll in crushed cornflakes

3. Flatten balls with a tumbler and chill

Quantity:	1 dozen
Serving Size:	1 cookie
Carb	13 gms/1 cookie
Protein	4 gms/1 cookie
Fat	8 gms/1 cookie

Serving size:	2 cookies
Carb	26 gms/2 cookies
Protein	8 gms/2 cookies
Fat	16 gms/2 cookies

5. Avoid Over-treating Low Blood Sugars

Avoiding the over-treatment of low blood sugars (hypoglycemia) was one of the factors found in the DCCT to relate to better sugar control (a lower HbA_{1c} level). The problem is how to accomplish this. Only a person who has had a truly low blood sugar can know the feeling of being "ravenously hungry" and wanting to eat everything in sight (and so the person does). For many years, people thought "rebounding" to be the cause of the high blood sugar after hypoglycemia. Only in recent years was it realized to be primarily due to excessive eating after the low blood sugar.

Chapter 6 discusses the treatment of hypoglycemia and emphasizes:

1. checking the blood sugar to see how low the value is and repeating this at 10-minute intervals to see if the value is rising

2. drinking one cup of milk (8-10 oz), 1/2 cup of juice or four ounces of sugar pop

3. or taking 1/2 tube of Instant Glucose or 4 dextrose tablets (e.g., 15 grams of carb or one "carb" count). Wait 10 minutes and do the second blood sugar level.

4. if the value has **not** risen, repeat the process using 15 grams of carb or one "carb" choice every 10 minutes until a rise does occur

5. if the blood sugar is rising after 10 minutes and is above 60 mg/dl (3.2 mmol/L)

✔ eat solid food, such as two or three crackers with peanut butter or cheese

✔ if it is close to mealtime, just eat the next meal

Not eating too much, but enough to raise the blood sugar, is tricky. It can vary from person to person or from one time to another for the same person. Careful monitoring of blood sugar levels is essential.

6. Reduce Cholesterol and Saturated Fat Intake; Reduce Total Fat Intake

Cholesterol and triglyceride are two of the major fats present in our blood.

Cholesterol is found in many foods, but it is particularly high in:

✔ egg yolks
✔ organ meats
✔ large portions of high-fat red meat (e.g., prime rib)
✔ Cholesterol is found in animal products only.

*There is **no cholesterol** in:*

✔ fruits
✔ vegetables
✔ cereals
✔ grains
✔ beans
✔ nuts
✔ seeds

The eating of saturated fat in animal products like meat, cheese and whole milk may raise blood cholesterol levels even more than eating high cholesterol foods. This is discussed in more detail in the previous chapter on Normal Nutrition. Blood cholesterol and triglyceride levels can also be high if blood sugar levels are too high.

The blood cholesterol level should be checked once a year (fasting is not necessary). If your doctor has not checked your blood cholesterol level, you could request that this be done. Suggested levels for people with diabetes are given in Table 1 of Chapter 11. If a high level is found, the dietitian can make suggestions to help lower it. The average American now eats 400-450 mg of cholesterol per day. This should gradually be reduced to about 300 mg per day. Table 2 in Chapter 11 gives suggestions for reducing fat and cholesterol intake. Each egg has about 213 mg of cholesterol. Egg white is a good source of protein. Some people now just eat the whites, which have no cholesterol.

Triglyceride levels for a given person tend to be variable. They are related to the diabetes control at the time, the amount of exercise in the previous week and other factors. It is necessary to be fasting for accurate triglyceride and lipoprotein (LDL and HDL)

determinations. Fasting is sometimes dangerous for people with diabetes (e.g., driving across town with no food intake). We now often draw a "lipid panel" once yearly when it has been three to four hours since the last meal (Chapter 11).

7. Maintain Appropriate Height and Weight

Normal growth is important for children and teenagers. An important part of clinic visits is to make sure the height and weight are increasing appropriately. Research has shown that if blood sugar control is poor during the teenage years, final adult height will be less.

About 30% of people with type 1 diabetes and 80% of people with type 2 diabetes are overweight. Preventing excessive weight gain by staying active and eating nutritionally is important. If you have questions about weight management, meet with a registered dietitian.

We discourage the use of quick weight loss diets and diet pills. They do not teach a person to eat correctly. When the fad diet is over, the weight is almost always regained. It is much wiser to work with a registered dietitian to learn healthy eating habits and to develop a plan to gradually reduce weight. It is important for parents to be careful not to be critical or to emphasize a child's weight gain. It can make the problem worse and lead to eating disorders or missed shots. If a parent has concerns, it might be better to express them to the dietitian or to other diabetes team members.

8. Increase Fiber Intake

Fiber is the roughage in our food that is not absorbed into the body. Many of us don't have enough fiber in our diets. Adding fiber may slow the rise in blood sugar levels for children with diabetes. The blood sugar may not be as high two hours after eating an apple (one carb choice) as it is two hours after drinking 1/2 cup (four ounces) of apple juice (one carb choice). Extra fiber is good for people, particularly in helping to avoid constipation. Raw fruits, vegetables, legumes, high-fiber cereals and whole wheat breads are the most effective high-fiber foods.

9. Avoid Foods High in Salt (Sodium)

If a person has borderline high blood pressure, a high salt intake may bring out this tendency. People who eat at fast food restaurants have a higher salt intake. Those who have early kidney damage seem to be more likely to have an increased blood pressure from high salt intake.

Foods higher in salt are:

✔ many canned soups
✔ frozen vegetables in sauces
✔ fast foods
✔ many snack foods (especially chips)

Some health authorities recommend that all people eat under 3,000 mg of sodium (1 1/4 tsp of table salt) each day.

Increased blood pressure is an important risk factor for both the eye and the kidney complications of diabetes as well as heart attacks. Therefore, it is important not to eat large amounts of salt. If the blood pressure is elevated, 2,400 mg (approximately 1 tsp of table salt) or less per day is recommended. This can be discussed with the dietitian.

10. Avoid Excessive Protein Intake

It is difficult to avoid an excess of protein when someone has been told not to eat excessive amounts of sugar, animal fat and salt. Many teenagers eat four to six times the quantity of protein needed. This is particularly true for those who frequently eat or snack at fast-food restaurants. Athletes should not consume protein (amino acid) supplements. Only exercise builds muscle - not protein supplements. Extra protein is bad when kidney damage is present, as it presents an extra load for the kidneys. It is still unclear whether or not high protein intake contributes to the kidney complications of diabetes. The best method to reduce protein intake is to decrease portion size (e.g., smaller meat portions). Meats, eggs and cheese can be eliminated from breakfast and the morning and afternoon snacks. However, we recommend that the bedtime snack include carbs, protein and fat as they may help to keep the blood sugar at a reasonable level during the night.

SUMMARY

The key to food management in diabetes is constant thinking and matching insulin to carb intake. The entire family must help with this.

Important points:

✔ There is no difference in the effect of a simple sugar compared with a starch in raising the blood sugar level.

✔ A person with diabetes can eat almost any food in moderation if it is worked into the meal plan.

✔ A person with diabetes can eat foods with simple sugars in them. The simple sugar should be eaten at a time when adequate insulin is present.

✔ Nutritious carb choices should be encouraged whenever possible.

✔ Frequent blood sugar testing (e.g., two hours after eating various foods) is encouraged to determine how a given food affects any individual.

✔ Blood sugar testing when an insulin reaction occurs is important in avoiding over treatment of lows. The excessive eating with a hypoglycemic reaction (or just the psychological feeling of hunger) is a major concern in controlling blood sugar levels.

Remember: Food management for people with diabetes does not mean a restrictive diet, but rather a healthy eating regimen that family and friends can also enjoy.

APPENDIX FOR CHAPTER 12

SUMMARY OF EXCHANGE LISTS

The purpose of this food list is to give examples of food exchanges and the concept of the "exchange food program." A more complete reference is *Exchange Lists for Meal Planning*, 1999 update published by the **American Diabetes Association and the American Dietetic Association, P.O. Box 930850, Atlanta, GA 31193.** The cost is $1.75, plus $4.99 for shipping and handling (or less if purchased in quantities). In general, the idea of the exchange food program is to develop "equivalents" in each food group that are similar to each other in amounts of sugar and in calories. Nutrition instruction should be given by a dietitian or nutritionist. The food groups, with examples of foods that have similar values in each of the groups, are listed on the following pages.

CARBOHYDRATE GROUP

Starch/Bread List: One bread exchange contains about 15 grams of carbohydrate and three grams of protein (80 calories).

Examples are:

✔ one slice of bread
✔ 1/2 hamburger or hot dog bun
✔ 3/4 cup of unsweetened cereal
✔ 1/2 cup noodles
✔ three cups popcorn
✔ crackers (six small saltines, two squares of graham crackers, three of most other crackers)
✔ one pancake or waffle (5 inch)
✔ 15 potato or corn chips

The vegetables included in the bread exchanges are:

✔ corn (1/2 cup or one ear)
✔ white potato (one baked or 1/2 cup mashed)
✔ yam or sweet potato (1/4 cup)
✔ green peas (1/2 cup)
✔ squash (1/2 cup)
✔ lima beans (1/2 cup)

Fruit List: One fruit exchange contains about 15 grams of carbohydrate (60 calories) and essentially no fat or protein.

Examples of one fruit exchange are:

✔ grape juice (1/3 cup)
✔ apple or pineapple juice (1/2 cup)
✔ orange or grapefruit juice (1/2 cup)
✔ one small apple, orange, pear or peach
✔ 1/2 banana
✔ 1/2 cup berries
✔ 1/3 of a small cantaloupe
✔ one cup of watermelon

Milk List: One milk exchange is the quantity equal to about eight grams of protein or 32 calories, and 12 grams of carbohydrate or 48 calories (with a trace of fat for a total of 90 calories).

Examples of one milk exchange are:

✔ one cup of skim or non-fat milk
✔ one cup of 1% milk (also includes 1/2 fat exchange)
✔ one cup yogurt made from skim milk
✔ one cup of yogurt from 2% milk (also includes one fat exchange)
✔ one cup 2% milk (also includes one fat exchange)

Vegetable List: One-half cup of most vegetables (cooked or raw) has about 5 grams of carbohydrate and two grams of protein (25 calories)

Examples are:

✔ one-half cup of most vegetables (cooked)
✔ one cup raw vegetables

Raw lettuce may be taken in larger quantities, but salad dressing usually equals one fat exchange. Some raw vegetables are higher in carbohydrate, equal to 15 grams carbohydrate and two grams protein, and should be considered equivalent to one bread exchange in quantity. These include corn and potatoes and are listed in the Bread Exchanges.

MEAT AND MEAT SUBSTITUTE GROUP

The three groups are:

1. Very Lean and **Lean** meat - one ounce of the lean meats contains seven grams of protein and three grams of fat (55 calories).

The best of the **Lean Meat** groups are:

✔ poultry (chicken and turkey without the skin)
✔ fish
✔ lean pork
✔ USDA Select or Choice grades of lean beef
✔ 1/2 or 1% fat cottage cheese

2. Medium Fat Meat group - one ounce equals seven grams of protein and five grams of fat (75 calories).

Some examples are:

✔ one ounce of ground beef
✔ most cuts of beef, pork, lamb or veal
✔ one ounce of low-fat cheese
✔ one egg

3. High Fat Meat group - one ounce equals seven grams of protein and eight grams of fat (100 calories).

This group includes:

✔ sausages
✔ spare ribs
✔ most regular cheeses
✔ processed sandwich meats

FAT GROUP

Fat is necessary for the body and is particularly important during periods of fasting (overnight), when it is very slowly absorbed. One fat exchange contains five grams of fat (45 calories).

This group includes:

• monosaturated and polyunsaturated fats are better for us than saturated fats.

One exchange includes:

✔ 1 tsp margarine or 1 tsp of any vegetable oil (except coconut)

• saturated fat

One exchange includes:

✔ 1 tsp butter
✔ one strip of bacon
✔ 1 Tbsp of cream

DEFINITIONS

ADA: American Diabetes Association.

"Carb count or choice": 15-gram equivalent of carb used to determine the units of short-acting insulin to be taken.

Carbohydrate (carb) counting: A meal plan in which counting the grams of carb to be eaten (and considering the blood sugar level and any planned exercise) is used to adjust the dosage of Humalog/NovoLog or Regular insulin prior to meals.

Cholesterol: One of the two main blood fats. High levels are related to a greater chance for heart attacks later in life.

Constant carbohydrate diet: A meal plan in which the amount of carb is kept consistent from day-to-day to match a relatively consistent dose of insulin.

DCCT: Diabetes Control and Complications Trial, which ended in June, 1993. It showed that good glucose control helped to prevent the eye, kidney and nerve complications of diabetes.

Exchange diet: A meal plan in which foods are grouped into one of six food lists having similar nutritional composition. Caloric intake and number of exchanges are set, but foods within a food group can be exchanged with one another.

Glycemic index: A ranking of foods based on the rise in blood sugar when that food is given alone (with no other food).

Tablespoon (Tbsp): A measure of 15cc (ml) or three teaspoons. It is equal to 15 grams (1/2 oz) of water.

Teaspoon (tsp): A measure of 5cc (ml). It is also equal to five grams of water.

Triglyceride: One of the two main blood fats. High levels are believed to be related to a greater risk for heart attacks later in life for people with diabetes.

QUESTIONS (Q) AND ANSWERS (A) FROM NEWSNOTES

Q. Is there any way to know if the pop received at fast-food restaurants, theaters and other places is truly "sugar-free" or the regular sugar-containing pop?

A. This question is asked frequently and the answer is "yes." Probably the cheapest way to test is by using the Test-Tape®, a roll of yellow tape from which a piece can be dipped into the pop. It turns green if there is sugar in the pop. The Diastix® (the sugar-only part of KetoDiastix), or the distal sugar block on KetoDiastix will also change color if there is sugar present. Unfortunately, it is more common for the wrong pop to be served than most people realize, probably in the range of 20% of the time (one glass in five). As sugar pop is one of the most concentrated sources of sugar (approximately 10 tsp per can), it usually raises the blood sugar level to the 200-400 mg/dl (11.1-22.2 mmol/L) level. This is especially true if it is consumed without other foods, which slow the absorption of the sugar, or at a time when Humalog/NovoLog or Regular insulin is not taken to allow the sugar to enter the cells.

Q. How important is a diet in relation to my HbA$_{1c}$ and my blood sugar control?

A. The best answer to this comes from the DCCT data (*Diabetes Care* 16:1453, 1993). They found that patients in their intensive treatment group (mean HbA$_{1c}$ = 7.1%) who followed a meal plan over 90% of the time had an average HbA$_{1c}$ level that was 0.9% lower than those who followed a meal plan less then 45% of the time. As the HbA$_{1c}$ difference in the intensive treatment group was 1.8% (7.1% vs. 8.9%), this suggests that half of the difference was related to following a food plan.

Other factors that were important in relation to a lower HbA$_{1c}$ level were:

• doing a prompt correction when a high blood sugar was found

• adjusting the insulin for meal size

• not eating extra snacks

• avoiding over treatment of low blood sugars (hypoglycemia)

Our Clinic always has dietitians available at the time of clinic visits. Our preference in food management at this time is the use of carb counting. Since we know carbs are the nutrients that are converted to blood sugar, patients need to learn how to match insulin dosage with carb intake. We even offer a Thursday or Friday afternoon class once a month just on carb counting. We ask that all families meet with a dietitian at least once a year. If a family has not done this, they can request to do so at their clinic visit.

Chapter 13

TOPICS:
- Physical Activity
- Goal Setting and Problem Solving

TEACHING OBJECTIVES:

1. Discuss the importance of exercise as a critical component of diabetes management.

2. Explain exercise recommendations and precautions for people with type 1 or type 2 diabetes.

WITH SPECIAL THANKS FOR THE SUGGESTIONS OF:

- Michelle Hansen, MS, RD, CDE
- Jane E. Reusch, MD

LEARNER OBJECTIVES

Learner (parents, child, relative or self) will be able to:

1. List three reasons why exercise is important.

2. Develop an exercise plan which includes monitoring of blood sugars, use of snacks and medication adjustments.

Chapter EXERCISE AND DIABETES

INTRODUCTION

Many of the people with the best-controlled diabetes are those who exercise regularly. Exercise should be a normal part of life for everyone. We strongly encourage regular exercise for anyone who has diabetes, even if this means making a special effort to plan daily exercise. Young people from our Clinic have participated in almost every sport: football, baseball, golf, track, swimming, wrestling, dancing, skiing, basketball, soccer, weight lifting, horseback riding, jumping rope, jogging and tennis. In the Figures in Chapter 14, Diabetes and Blood Sugar Control, **EXERCISE** is listed as one of the "Big 4" factors to help attain good sugar control. This is true for people with either type 1 or type 2 diabetes.

Many former and present professional athletes have diabetes. Professional baseball players with diabetes include Bill Gullickson (pitcher) and Ron Santo (third base). Gary Hall, Jr. won 4 medals (2 gold) in the 2000 Olympics. He had been diagnosed with diabetes one year earlier and he became the top swimmer in the

world. Professional football players include Kenny Duckett (wide receiver), Johnathon Hayes (tight end), Wade Wilson (quarterback) and Jay Leuwenberg, who was an All-American center for the University of Colorado in the 1990s and then went on to play professional football. In the U.K., Gary Mabbott has type 1 diabetes and is a star football (American soccer) player. Hockey player Bobby Clarke, a former player of the Philadelphia Flyers, developed diabetes at age 15. He won the award for outstanding player in the National Hockey League twice. Billy Talbert began playing tennis at age 12, two years after he developed diabetes. Because of the diabetes, he had been told by his doctor that he could no longer play baseball. He became one of the best tennis players in the world, winning 37 national tournaments and being captain of America's winning Davis Cup Team and a member of the Tennis Hall of Fame. When he was in Denver to instruct youth with diabetes about tennis, we asked Billy why he felt he had no complications after over 40 years with diabetes. He replied, "I have gotten some exercise every day of my life in which it has been possible."

THE IMPORTANCE OF EXERCISE

- **Exercise helps burn excess sugar**
- **Exercise helps people feel better**
- **Exercise helps maintain proper body weight**
- **Exercise helps keep the heart rate (pulse) and blood pressure lower**
- **Exercise helps keep blood fat levels normal**
- **Exercise improves insulin sensitivity**
- **Exercise may help maintain normal blood circulation in the feet**

THE IMPORTANCE OF EXERCISE

Exercise is important and helps people with or without diabetes in the following ways (Table 1):

🐾 Exercise Helps Burn Excess Sugar

Physical exercise helps the body burn more sugar. Insulin is still needed to allow the sugar to be burned but usually in reduced amounts. Insulin levels automatically decrease during exercise in people who do not have diabetes. Stored sugar in the muscle as well as sugar released from the liver is "burned" by the muscle during exercise. The old belief that people should not exercise if they have high blood sugar is wrong. Exercise usually helps lower the blood sugar. IT IS ONLY WHEN KETONES ARE PRESENT THAT PEOPLE SHOULD NOT EXERCISE.

🐾 Exercise Helps People Feel Better

There is a feeling of "well-being" and pride that comes from being in good physical condition. Many people just seem to feel better when they exercise daily. They tend not to tire as easily. Some people even say they are happier.

Teenagers get much of their support from friends. Friends often are made during sports activities. Exercise can give people the opportunity to mix with others. Some people like to watch TV and eat snacks that raise the blood sugar level. Exercise is a good way to improve a bad mood and to change a bad habit. In this way, exercise serves a double purpose.

🐾 Exercise Helps Maintain Proper Body Weight

Exercise is important, not only for people with diabetes, but for everybody. For thousands of years, people had to hunt for food and were very active. In the last 100 years, modern machines have made it possible for people to live with almost no exercise. This lack of activity has led to new health problems such as obesity, type 2 diabetes and heart trouble. THE ONLY WAYS TO PREVENT OBESITY ARE TO EXERCISE AND TO EAT MODERATELY. Exercise helps burn excess calories and prevents obesity. A recent national study in the U.S. (The Diabetes Prevention Program)

showed exercise helped to prevent diabetes in people at high risk for type 2 diabetes. A person who keeps a normal weight is also less likely to have a heart attack later in life.

🐾 Exercise Helps Keep the Heart Rate (pulse) and Blood Pressure Lower

The heart is helped by exercise for many reasons. The heart of a person who is in good physical shape can do the same work with fewer heartbeats. An average heart rate (pulse) is 80 beats per minute. Many people who exercise regularly will have values in the 60s. Blood pressure tends to be lower in people who exercise. Thus, the heart doesn't have to pump as hard. Lower blood pressure helps prevent heart attacks later in life. It is also important in preventing the eye and kidney complications of diabetes (see Chapter 22 on complications). Exercise helps to build extra blood vessels in the heart. This lets more blood flow to the heart.

🐾 Exercise Helps Keep Blood Fat Levels Normal

We have discussed the importance of reducing cholesterol and saturated (animal) fat in the diet in Chapters 11 and 12. Many people with type 1 and type 2 diabetes have high levels of the blood fats, cholesterol and/or triglycerides. These high blood fat levels can lead to early aging of blood vessels. Exercise and good blood sugar control are the best ways to reduce blood triglyceride levels. One study showed that triglyceride levels could be reduced greatly after only four sessions of running 40 minutes a day. Exercise may also help remove cholesterol from blood vessel walls by increasing HDL (high density lipoprotein; see Chapter 11). Lowering the blood fat levels improves the health of blood vessels (including those supplying blood to the heart) and lessens the risk of heart attacks.

🐾 Exercise Improves Insulin Sensitivity

The only way humans can increase insulin sensitivity is by exercising. As a result of exercise, the person is more sensitive to insulin, the insulin can work more efficiently, and a lower daily dose is usually required. Regular exercise (and weight loss) allows some people with type 2 diabetes to stop insulin injections and change to oral medication. It is now believed many of the beneficial effects of exercise on the risk of heart disease, particularly in type 2 diabetes, are due to improvements with insulin sensitivity. It is important to exercise regularly and vigorously.

❧ Exercise May Help Maintain Normal Blood Circulation to the Feet Later in Life

Data from the Pittsburgh Diabetes Registry showed that when boys with diabetes played in high school sports, they were more likely to keep normal foot circulation in later years. It is likely that the boys who were active in high school were also more apt to be active in later years. The same findings likely apply to females; although in the 1950s, when this study was begun, not many high school athletic programs were available for girls. It is important to get boys and girls with diabetes started in a sports activity at a young age so that they will be good enough to make a sports team (whether they are a star or not) as a teenager. However, it doesn't have to be a team sport. Any activity, such as walking, biking, swimming, playing or running is helpful. Most younger children are constantly active so that exercise is not a problem in the younger age group.

TYPE 2 DIABETES AND EXERCISE

Although exercise is important for all people, it is **essential** for people with type 2 diabetes. It is also important for those people who are at high risk for type 2 diabetes. The Diabetes Prevention Program (DPP) studied 3,234 people with impaired (not diabetic; see Chapter 4) glucose tolerance tests. (They were close to having type 2 diabetes.) **The DPP showed that 30 minutes of activity per day (five days per week) combined with a low-fat diet reduced the risk of developing diabetes by 58%.**

Why don't people with type 2 diabetes or those at high risk get into exercise programs? *Some reasons might be:*

✔ Psychological/stress /can't find the time

✔ Started too fast in the past (must start slowly)

✔ Too painful in the past (forgot stretching and "working-up" gradually)

✔ Lack of motivation (TV, computer games more fun)

✔ Not aware of the importance of exercise for good health

Whatever the reason, if the person is unable to achieve a lifestyle modification on his or her own, it may be helpful to join a supervised exercise and/or weight loss program. Counseling could be helpful as well. The cost of NOT modifying the lifestyle is just too great!

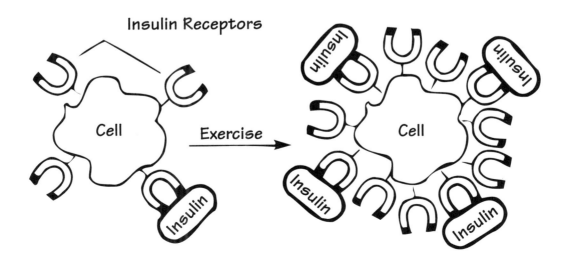

Insulin Receptors

MANAGING EXERCISE IN PEOPLE WITH DIABETES

Now that you know seven of the many reasons why exercise is important for a person with diabetes, you should ask yourself some questions.

Which Kinds of Exercise are Best?

THE BEST EXERCISE IS THE ONE YOU LIKE. Different strokes for different folks! If you hate to jog or swim, but you do it because you are told to, you probably won't exercise regularly. Swimming five days a week in an outdoor pool is fun in the summer, but it may be more difficult to do in the winter. You may need to choose a different exercise, such as jumping rope or riding an exercise bicycle, in the winter.

Only aerobic exercises help heart fitness. Aerobic exercises include most continuous activities (such as jogging, walking, swimming or bicycling) that are done for a period of 30 minutes or longer. Many training programs use machines at health spas that feature continuous aerobic activity rather than short bursts of activity followed by a rest (a non-aerobic activity). When activities such as weight lifting are done in short bursts with rests in between, they are considered strength building, not aerobic.

Boxing is the only activity in which we have asked youth not to participate. The high incidence of eye injuries is not needed by a person who has diabetes (which can also cause eye problems). In addition, the high incidence of brain damage makes boxing dangerous for people with or without diabetes.

Careful diabetes management to prevent low blood sugar levels (as discussed in this chapter) is important in all activities. It is particularly important for those in which there is an associated danger (e.g., scuba diving). Fortunately, dangerous activities are not generally used for daily aerobic activity.

When Should I Exercise?

The best time to exercise will vary with your schedule. Think ahead and make changes in insulin doses and snacks to help prevent low blood sugars. Children like to play after school, and most organized sports activities take place at that time. This is the time when most intermediate-acting insulins are having their main effect so taking extra care to prevent low blood sugar is important. When possible, pick an exercise time, preferably the same time each day, and adjust the snacks and insulin dose to fit the exercise. YOUR DIABETES MANAGEMENT CAN BE ADJUSTED TO SUIT YOUR LIFESTYLE. YOUR LIFESTYLE DOES NOT HAVE TO BE ADJUSTED TO FIT YOUR DIABETES.

When Should I Not Exercise?

If blood or urine ketone levels are elevated, exercise can raise the sugar or ketone level even higher. Thus, it is not good for you to exercise when you have ketones. Remember to check ketones before exercising if you are not feeling well.

How Should I Get Started?

The best way to make exercise a part of everyday living is to begin early in life. Older children may not be as willing to begin a regular exercise program. Exercise should be part of the normal routine. Many people prefer TV or computer games instead of exercise, and the parent may have to encourage exercise. The parent can reward the child for good behavior with exercise activities such as skating and swimming. It is helpful if the parent can have fun with the child in the activity. Jogging, walking or jumping rope is good for parents too! Whenever a child has a parent's attention and company, the time quickly becomes a reward. A child of any age will often pick up the parent's exercise behaviors. The parent needs to be a good example by exercising regularly even if it is not with the child. Exercising with a friend(s) can be fun. Friends can help each other continue the exercise plan.

When beginning a new exercise program, it is always best to START SLOWLY and gradually extend the time and amount of exercise. This will result in fewer sore muscles and a better chance to continue the program. Recommendations for people over 35 years old or who have other risk factors are discussed under "Age and Exercise".

How Often and How Far?

How often should the person with diabetes exercise? THIRTY MINUTES OF AEROBIC EXERCISE, AT LEAST FIVE TIMES PER WEEK, IS NOW CONSIDERED IDEAL. The more exercise a person gets, the more fat that is "burned." Some people burn more calories with their exercise than others. This is partly related to how hard and how long the person exercises. For example, a person who runs at a rate of seven minutes per mile burns 300 calories in 30 minutes. However, if the person runs at 11 minutes per mile, 200 calories are burned in 30 minutes. If weight loss is one of the goals, it may be necessary to work harder or for a longer period to reach the desired goals.

It is wise to check the pulse immediately (for 10 seconds, and multiply by six) after stopping the activity. If the pulse is more than 160 beats per minute, the exercise has probably been too strenuous. Another rule of thumb is 220 minus the age of the person as the upper limit for the heart rate.

How Can I Prevent Low Blood Sugar (hypoglycemic) Reactions During Exercise?

It is essential to prevent low blood sugar reactions during exercise. This can be done in several ways.

✔ Check blood sugars before, during and after the exercise

The best way to know how any exercise affects a person is to check blood sugars before, during (when possible) and after the exercise. Once a pattern is detected (e.g., "swimming always makes my blood sugar fall" or "softball doesn't seem to affect my blood sugar"), more accurate insulin and food changes can be made. Sometimes blood sugars go up with exercise. This may be because of output of the hormones glucagon and adrenaline (epinephrine), which is a normal response in people with or without diabetes. These hormones cause sugar to be released from liver which stores and raises the blood sugar for varying periods of time. Therefore, don't be overly concerned about a high number immediately following an activity. Wait one to two hours and recheck the blood sugar to see if it has fallen. Keeping good records is important so when a similar exercise is done

at a similar time of the day (with the same insulin peaking) and with a similar starting blood sugar level, the best plans for insulin changes and food can be made. A suggested exercise record is shown in Table 2. The overall effect of activity is to lower blood sugar levels.

Some people become frustrated with the "ups and downs" of blood sugars during exercise. It is important to remember, **"DIABETES IS A COMPROMISE."** One must put up with the changes in blood sugars in return for the better health of the heart, blood vessels and the entire body.

✔ Eat before heavy exercise

If you are going to exercise around mealtime, you should eat the meal first. When possible, allow a half-hour for digestion. Liquids such as milk and juices are absorbed most rapidly and generally prevent low blood sugar reactions for the next 30-60 minutes. Solid foods, such as those eaten at mealtime, are digested more slowly and usually provide protection for at least two to three hours. When it is possible to choose the exercise time, try to begin the exercise 30-60 minutes after a meal or snack (and omit or reduce the Humalog/NovoLog). Table 3 gives suggestions for snacks for people who take insulin.

✔ Have extra snacks available during exercise

THE PERSON WITH DIABETES MUST ALWAYS HAVE A SOURCE OF SUGAR AVAILABLE. Parents have sewn pockets in basketball shorts, jogging pants and other clothes to hold three sugar packets, three sugar cubes or three glucose tablets for a possible emergency. Joggers' wallets on shoes work nicely. A sandwich or similar snack should be available nearby, as a sugar packet may last only a few minutes. It is helpful for the coach or instructor to have a tube of instant glucose or some other emergency source of sugar.

It is often difficult to guess the amount of a snack necessary for a particular activity. If the exercise is in the hour after a meal, an extra snack may not be needed. If a person is physically unfit, the blood sugar may drop more rapidly than if the person is physically fit. It is very useful to monitor the blood sugar to determine what the correct snack is for each child. If the blood sugar is low (e.g., below 100 mg/dl or 5.5 mmol/L), a larger snack is needed than when the blood sugar is high. **IN FACT, EXERCISING CAN BE A VERY EFFECTIVE WAY TO LOWER A HIGH BLOOD SUGAR (AS LONG AS URINE KETONES ARE NOT PRESENT).** Blood sugars may actually increase slightly during the first hour of exercise because the body releases the hormones glucagon and adrenaline. Blood sugars may then decline. The type of snack can be varied depending on the expected length of the activity. IN GENERAL, THE MORE RAPIDLY ABSORBED CARBOHYDRATES, SUCH AS MILK OR JUICE, ARE USED FOR SHORT-TERM ACTIVITIES. More food is added, such as crackers or bread, if the activity is to last longer. THE SNACK THAT KEEPS THE BLOOD SUGAR UP THE LONGEST IS ONE THAT INCLUDES PROTEIN AND FAT ALONG WITH THE CARBOHYDRATE. This might be a cheese or meat sandwich with a glass of juice. It is wise to check the blood sugar after the activity to help decide what to use for a snack the next time. Extra foods taken during the exercise period can help keep blood sugars in the normal range (see Table 3). **Experience is the best teacher!**

It is a good idea to keep packets of cheese and crackers in the glove box of the car to eat before or after an activity. This is especially important if the distance is great between home and the activity.

"DELAYED HYPOGLYCEMIA" refers to low blood sugars several hours after the exercise is over. These may occur three to four hours or up to 12 hours after exercise. Some people with type 2 diabetes who are not in good physical condition may experience delayed hypoglycemia. This may happen up to 24 hours after the exercise. The result may be a low blood sugar in the middle of the night. It may happen because extra sugar in the blood goes back into storage in the muscle. Hormone changes with sleep (e.g., lower adrenaline levels) may also be important.

It is best prevented by:

1. Extra carbohydrate at the next meal or snack (even when the blood sugar is above-range)

2. A longer-lasting snack (including solid carbohydrate, protein and fat) at bedtime

3. Reducing the insulin dose (see below)

✔ **Reduce the insulin dosage**

Before trying an activity for the first time, discuss any changes that might be needed in insulin dosage with your diabetes care provider. The insulin dose is easy to decrease if you know which insulin is having its main effect during the time of exercise. If on two shots per day, the day is divided into four periods, and one of the insulins is most active in each period (see Chapter 21, Adjusting The Insulin Dose). You should reduce the insulin that is most active during the period of heavy exercise. If exercise is in the evening, it is also wise to reduce the dinner or evening Lantus dose by 10-20%. The figures in Chapter 8 show which insulin acts during each of the four periods.

If extra morning exercise is planned, you can reduce or even leave out the morning Humalog/NovoLog or Regular insulin. If late afternoon exercise is planned, you can reduce the morning NPH or Lente insulin by 10-50%. NPH or Lente insulin is never left out entirely. Similarly, Lantus insulin in the evening may be reduced by a few units when heavy exercise occurs after dinner. People reduce insulin by different amounts. **EXPERIENCE IS THE BEST TEACHER.**

You should reduce the insulin that is active during the period of exercise. Suppose you are receiving 30 units of NPH insulin in the morning and you have a soccer game in the afternoon. You might reduce the dose by 10-20% (three to six units). You would then receive 24-27 units of NPH insulin.

If strenuous exercise is planned for all day, both the morning NPH and the short-acting insulins can be reduced. The evening insulin dose may also need to be reduced to prevent "delayed hypoglycemia." If strenuous exercise is planned for the evening, the evening Humalog/NovoLog or Regular insulin can be reduced or omitted. One reason the evening NPH might be decreased is for overnights at friends' homes when a child may be staying up later than usual. More activity and excitement burn more sugar, and less insulin may be needed. You may have to try a few times before you find the best way to reduce your insulin for activities. Keep careful records and discuss them at clinic visits. Blood sugar tests before and after exercise can help you make these decisions.

✔ Changing the short-acting insulin

Most low blood sugars from Humalog/NovoLog occur in the first 90 minutes after injection. Thus, if exercise is planned in the first hour after eating, it would be better to use Regular insulin only (no Humalog) if a pre-meal shot is being taken. In contrast, if heavy exercise (e.g., a soccer game) is to occur two to four hours after eating (when Regular insulin is peaking), it would be better to use only Humalog as the short-acting insulin. It is OK to use Humalog insulin on one day and to use Regular insulin at the same time on another day. It is important to THINK AHEAD as to which insulin might be better on a given day. People with type 2 diabetes who tend to get low with exercise may also need to change their medicines (particularly if receiving sulfonylurea meds – see Chapter 4) when exercising.

✔ Change the injection site

The choice of where you inject the insulin can help prevent low blood sugars. Exercise increases blood flow into the part of the body that is moving. The increased blood flow takes up more insulin. When a person with diabetes exercises, the blood insulin level may increase; whereas insulin levels decrease in non-diabetics during exercise. If you inject insulin into an arm or leg that you will use heavily during exercise, your body may absorb the insulin too rapidly. If you are going to run, don't inject insulin into the leg. If you are going to play tennis, avoid the tennis arm. The abdomen is a good site for most strenuous exercise days.

✔ Make sure others know

It is important that coaches and teammates are aware of the diabetes. A team manager may be a good person to carry extra sugar snacks. It is helpful if the coach can have at least some awareness of the diabetes and

know the symptoms and treatment of low blood sugar. A letter is included at the end of this chapter that you are welcome to copy as often as you like to share with coaches. Remember that when a low blood sugar occurs during a sporting event, it is important to rest for at least ten minutes to let the blood sugar rise. The coach should be aware of this.

EXERCISE RECORD

Table 2

Day and date	Insulin or Oral meds (time taken)	Type of exercise	Time of day (start/end)	Pre-exercise blood sugar	Snack(s) eaten (and times)	Blood sugars during/after exercise (and times)	Hypoglycemic episodes (and when)

This page may be copied as often as desired.

EXTRA FOOD TO COVER EXERCISE*†

Expected length of exercise	Blood sugars mg/dl	mmol/L	Examples of foods
A. Short (15-30 minutes)†	<80	<4.4	8 oz Gatorade or milk** or 4-6 oz juice**
	80-150	4.4-8.3	A fresh fruit (or any 15 grams carbohydrate **)
	>150	>8.3	None
B. Longer (30-120 minutes)†	<80	<4.4	8 oz Gatorade or milk** or 4 oz juice plus 1/2 sandwich
	80-150	4.4-8.3	8 oz Gatorade or milk plus fresh fruit
	>150	>8.3	1/2 sandwich**
C. Longest (2-4 hours)*†	<80	<4.4	8 oz Gatorade or 4 oz juice, whole sandwich
	80-150	4.4-8.3	Fruit, whole sandwich
	>150	>8.3	Whole sandwich

*Remember to also drink water, Gatorade or other fluids (one 8 oz glass for **A**, two 8 oz glasses for **B**, and three 8 oz glasses for **C**) before or during the exercise to prevent dehydration. This table is for a moderate degree of exercise (e.g., walking, bicycling leisurely, shooting a basketball or mowing the lawn). If heavier exercise (e.g., jogging, bicycle race, basketball game or digging in the garden) is to be done for the same amount of time, then more food may need to be added. Amounts vary for different people and the best way to learn is to do blood sugars before and after the exercise and keep a record of the blood sugar values (see Table 2).*

** *Each of these represent 15 grams of carbohydrate which will last for about 30 minutes of moderate exercise. A sandwich with meat or other protein lasts longer.*

† *May also need to reduce insulin dosage*

SUGGESTIONS FOR EXERCISING SAFELY

Table 4

- 🐾 Eat before heavy exercise

- 🐾 Have extra snacks available during exercise; some people use Gatorade, 4-8 oz, for every 30 minutes of vigorous exercise

- 🐾 Always carry sugar

- 🐾 Reduce the insulin dose

- 🐾 Consider the injection site (the abdomen is usually best)

- 🐾 Change the type of short-acting insulin

- 🐾 Check blood sugars before and after exercise to learn the best insulin adjustment for the activity

- 🐾 Wear an ID bracelet or necklace

- 🐾 Try to exercise with a friend who knows about low blood sugar reactions

- 🐾 Make sure coaches know about low blood sugars (see letter at end of this chapter)

- 🐾 Do not exercise if ketones are present

- 🐾 Drink plenty of water, especially in hot weather

- 🐾 If delayed hypoglycemia occurs frequently, extra carbohydrates should be taken with the next meal or snack and the insulin dose decreased

- 🐾 Have fun!! Find an exercise you enjoy and incorporate it into your daily life

NUTRITION FOR EXERCISE

We frequently have adolescents ask us, "Can I take a protein supplement and/or should I take amino acids?" The answer to these questions is "No." Taking extra protein or amino acid supplements will NOT build muscles. The only way to build muscles is to do the physical exercise necessary to expand the muscle mass. The foods to eat are described in Chapters 11 and 12. There is no better food plan for building muscles than the plans described in those chapters.

HYDRATION AND EXERCISE

Proper hydration (drinking fluids) is essential during exercise. Exercising during hot weather requires special attention. Drinking extra fluids should begin an hour or two before starting to exercise. A general rule is to drink 8 oz of fluids for every 30 minutes of vigorous activity. Liquids such as milk, Gatorade and fruit juices help replace water, salts and carbohydrates. Drinking Gatorade (or other sports drinks) at half-hour intervals during strenuous exercise works well for many people. Table 3 recommends suggested fluid amounts for different levels of activity.

AGE AND EXERCISE

Adults are advised to discuss plans to begin a new exercise program with their diabetes care provider first. As with everyone, starting slowly and gradually increasing the amount of exercise is important. Proper stretching (five to ten minutes) **BEFORE**, **DURING** and **AFTER** the exercise will help prevent cramps and stiffness that may otherwise discourage further exercise.

Having a medical check-up before starting a <u>new</u> exercise program is recommended if you:

✔ are over 35 years of age

✔ have had type 1 diabetes more than 15 years

✔ have had type 2 diabetes more than 10 years

✔ have additional risk factors for a heart attack

✔ have eye or kidney complications

✔ have autonomic neuropathy (Chapter 22)

A graded exercise test might also be helpful. The maximum heart rate during exercise should not exceed 220 minus age.

Strenuous activities, including weight lifting and jogging, are discouraged for people who have severe eye changes of diabetes (proliferative retinopathy). This should be discussed with the diabetes eye specialist. Similarly, people with neuropathy should discuss the pros and cons of exercise with their diabetes care provider. When peripheral neuropathy is severe, weight-bearing exercise should be limited. With both severe eye changes and neuropathy, exercises that involve straining, jarring or causing increased pressure on the eyes or feet must be avoided. It is sometimes wise to have a "baseline" electrocardiogram (ECG) done prior to beginning a new exercise program. Other tests are then possible if there are any suggestions of abnormalities. People may ask their diabetes care provider to review with them the ADA guidelines for exercise that were published in January, 2002 (*Diabetes Care* 25, supp.1, p. S64).

SUMMARY

Exercise is important for all people, but especially for a person with diabetes. Exercise can improve the blood lipids, reduce blood pressure and improve cardiovascular fitness. It is very helpful for people with type 2 diabetes to reduce weight. Choose exercises that you enjoy. If possible, the amount of exercise and the time of day should be fairly **CONSISTENT.** You can change the diabetes management to fit the exercise. It is not necessary to change the exercise to fit the diabetes. Suggestions for exercising safely are summarized in Table 4. You can plan the exercise after a meal, reduce the insulin dosage or take extra snacks to help prevent low blood sugars. YOU SHOULD CARRY A SOURCE OF SUGAR AT ALL TIMES AND YOU SHOULD ALWAYS HAVE A LONGER-LASTING SNACK AVAILABLE NEARBY. Remember, it is wise to THINK AHEAD about what the day's schedule will bring and plan accordingly.

DEFINITIONS

Abdomen: The area around the belly button. The fatty tissue of the abdomen can be used as an injection site.

Adrenaline (epinephrine): The excitatory hormone. This normally increases early in exercise and may result in an initial rise in the blood sugar.

Aerobic: A continuous exercise usually lasting 25 minutes or longer.

Buttocks (seat): What a person sits on. The fatty tissue of the buttocks can be used as an injection site.

Delayed hypoglycemia: Low blood sugars occurring 4-12 hours after heavy physical exercise. This usually occurs as sugar leaves the blood to replace depleted muscle sugar stores.

DPP: The **D**iabetes **P**revention **P**rogram. A study of 3,234 people who were overweight and had impaired (not diabetic) oral glucose tolerance tests. Exercise and weight loss (see this chapter) reduced the development of diabetes by 58%.

Glucagon: A hormone (like insulin) which is also made in the islets of the pancreas. It has the opposite effect of insulin and raises the blood sugar.

QUESTIONS (Q) AND ANSWERS (A) FROM NEWSNOTES

Q. My daughter just started swimming practices everyday from 3:30-5:30 p.m. Her pre-dinner blood sugars are over 200 mg/dl (11.1 mmol/L) when she gets home. However, she has awakened at 3:00-4:00 a.m. the past two mornings feeling shaky. Is that possible?

A. Your daughter has the classic symptoms of "delayed hypoglycemia," which is not uncommon. Her blood sugar is high when she gets home from swimming as she has put out adrenaline (epinephrine), the excitatory hormone, during the exercise. All people, with or without diabetes, normally do this. The adrenaline causes breakdown of the stored sugar in liver (glycogen) to help keep the blood sugar up during the exercise. It is a safety mechanism.

At a later time, the sugar goes back into the muscle - often 4-12 hours later. When this happens, the blood sugar falls and she awakens feeling shaky. This is less likely to happen if the evening NPH insulin dose is decreased, and it is often necessary to decrease the dose by as much as two to six units to prevent delayed hypoglycemia.

Q. Our doctor has told us not to reduce the insulin dose on heavy exercise days, but just to eat more food. We were told on one of the Children's Diabetes Foundation's ski days to also reduce the insulin dose. We are now confused.

A. An important part of managing exercise with diabetes is to prevent low blood sugars or "insulin reactions." Planning ahead is very helpful. Some children can just eat more food and will do fine. Many teenage girls are watching their diets, and when told to eat more food, will refuse to do so. Severe reactions can then result. Reduction of insulin dosage is the only way to prevent reactions in such cases. Often a combination of some reduction in insulin dosage and eating extra snacks turns out to be the best solution.

Dear Coach,

This letter is on behalf of _____ who is participating in
_____ this year. Although we do not want to single out people with diabetes,
there are things that you need to be aware of to help _____'s performance and
enjoyment of the sport.

Exercise is very important for children and adolescents with diabetes. The overall effect
of exercise is to lower blood sugar. We hope _____ will take the right amount of
insulin and eat according to the anticipated activity for the day. However, even when
these things are done, there may be times, especially with increased activity, when he/she
may have an "insulin reaction," a low blood sugar, a condition requiring immediate
attention. The symptoms of an insulin reaction include one or more of the following:
shakiness, dizziness, sweating, rapid onset of extreme hunger or tiredness and paleness.
Some people complain of double vision and headaches. You may also notice
_____'s performance to suddenly become very poor, or his/her overall mood
may change to being very crabby or emotional.

If a low blood sugar occurs, a can of fruit juice, 8 oz of Gatorade, or two teaspoons of
sugar followed in five to ten minutes by solid food (fruit, cheese and crackers or a
sandwich) will help correct this condition. He/She should rest for a minimum of ten
minutes to let the blood sugar return to normal. However, some children will still have a
headache and may not feel like continuing. We encourage families to be prepared for
insulin reactions at all times by having the proper foods available.

Many people with diabetes will change their insulin dose on days they anticipate a
practice or game. The scheduling (or cancellation) of these events ahead of time helps
the person (and parents) to be prepared. Again, it is very important for youth with
diabetes to be involved in sports. It helps with their sugar control and allows their insulin
to work more effectively. A person with diabetes should not be and does not want to be
treated differently because of having diabetes.

Please do not hesitate to call if you need more information or have any concerns. Our
phone number is _____.

Sincerely,

(You may copy this letter as often as you wish.)

Chapter 14

TOPIC:
🐾 Monitoring
(Blood Sugars, HbA$_{1c}$)

TEACHING OBJECTIVES:

1. Discuss the four factors associated with good sugar control.

2. Describe the HbA$_{1c}$ test and it's relationship to blood sugar control.

LEARNER OBJECTIVES:

Learner (parents, child, relative or self) will be able to:

1. List two factors that can affect blood sugar control.

2. Explain the HbA$_{1c}$ test, current value and recommended range.

Chapter 14

DIABETES AND BLOOD SUGAR CONTROL

INTRODUCTION

The term "sugar control" is used in diabetes to describe how close the blood sugar is kept to normal limits. "Good sugar control" refers to blood sugar levels that more closely approach the normal sugar levels of someone without diabetes. A person with constant high blood sugar levels is considered "in poor sugar control" and may have side effects such as:

* frequent thirst
* frequent urination
* weight loss
* episodes of acidosis

It is important to have a reliable method to measure "overall" blood sugar control. It is obviously not possible to measure the blood sugar level every second of the day. Advances were made in the late 1970s to make the measurement of "overall" sugar control possible. This is done using the hemoglobin (HbA_{1c}) test. (The glycohemoglobin, glycated hemoglobin or hemoglobin A_1 [HbA_1] tests are names for similar tests.) These tests all reflect how often the blood sugars have been high every second of the day in the past 90 days. This test will be discussed later in this chapter.

THE DIABETES CONTROL AND COMPLICATIONS TRIAL (DCCT)

In 1993, the DCCT proved for people with type 1 diabetes that good sugar control helped to prevent the eye, kidney and nerve complications of diabetes. People receiving **"intensive management"** (insulin pumps or 3-4 shots of insulin per day along with at least four blood sugar levels per day) had better sugar control (lower HbA_{1c} values) than people receiving **"conventional management"** (1-2 shots of insulin per day with 0-2 blood sugars per day). The intensive management group was shown to have a lower chance for the eye, kidney and nerve complications than did the conventional management group.

Similar studies done in the U.K. and Japan showed good sugar control in people with type 2 diabetes also resulted in a reduction in the eye, kidney and nerve complications of diabetes. Some of the studies have also shown a decrease in the risk for heart attacks and strokes with good sugar control.

SUGAR CONTROL

Good blood sugar control for people with type 1 or type 2 diabetes is the result of balancing the following four factors:

1. the correct insulin/oral medicine dosage

2. getting regular exercise

3. having good dietary habits

4. positive ways to cope with stress/developing motivation based on realistic goals

Monitoring blood sugar levels assists in maintaining the proper balance between all four factors. (See diagram in this chapter.) Each of these factors is discussed elsewhere in this book in more detail. For people with type 1 diabetes, perhaps the most important of the four is the correct insulin dosage. Blood sugar control will remain poor if insulin is lacking, even if the other three factors are in balance. It will not help to do extra exercise if the person is not receiving the correct insulin dosage. However, any one of the four factors can result in poor sugar control. For example,

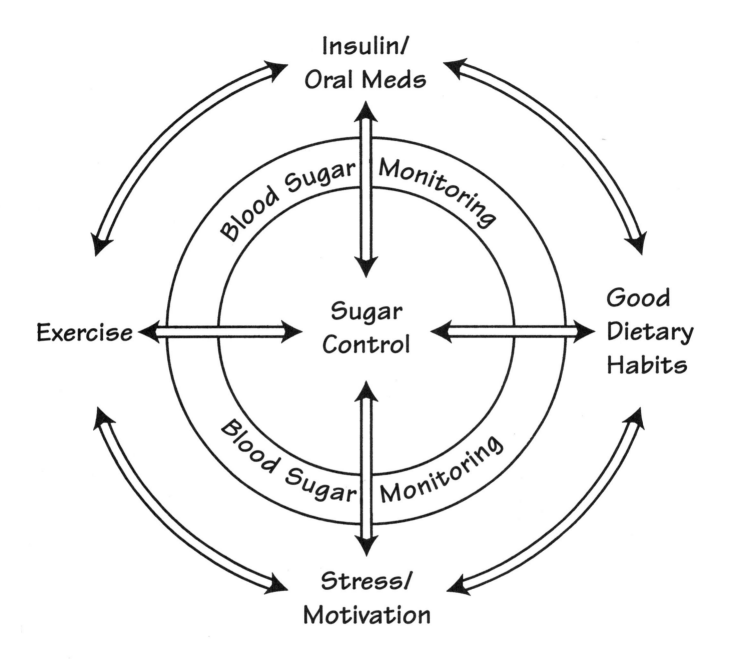

Four of the major influences on blood sugar control.
All four must be in balance for the best sugar control.
Blood sugar control is measured by daily blood sugar
levels and by Hemoglobin A_{1c} (HbA_{1c}) levels done
every three months.

if the other three factors are normally in balance, but the person decides to constantly drink sugar pop (10 tsp of sugar per can), good blood sugar control will likely be lost. Similarly, with a lot of stress, the adrenaline (excitatory hormone) levels will be high and will raise the blood sugar levels. Finally, exercise (Chapter 13) is important both for "burning" extra sugar and for making people more sensitive to insulin. Thus, all four of these factors must be in balance to result in the best sugar control possible for any person.

For type 2 patients, good sugar control results from a combination of exercise, diet, oral medications (or insulin) and motivation. (See the diagram in this chapter.) Little weight will be lost if total food and fat intake are not reduced as an exercise program is initiated. Similarly, following a diet without also exercising is often fruitless. If oral medicines (or insulin) are missed, blood sugars will remain high. If the person does not have realistic goals that result in motivation, they will not succeed. All must be in balance for optimal diabetes control. The regular monitoring of blood sugar levels (Chapter 7) is essential to understand the effects of these four influences.

HOW IS SUGAR CONTROL MEASURED?

It is not always easy to decide whether a person has good or poor blood sugar control. *Some helpful things that reflect sugar control are the following:*

Control of Symptoms of Diabetes

A person who goes to the bathroom very frequently (particularly if a person is getting up two or more times per night), or who is often thirsty has obvious symptoms of high blood and urine sugar. This person usually needs more insulin (or oral medicines), less sugar in the diet or more daily exercise.

Occasionally, blurred vision may occur as a symptom of poor sugar control. High sugar levels in the lens of the eye pull water into the lens. This extra fluid makes it difficult for the shape of the lens to change in order to focus for clear vision. The blurred vision usually stops when blood sugar control improves. People should not be fitted for glasses unless blood sugar levels are stable. If the blurred vision does not improve when blood sugar control improves, the eye doctor should be contacted.

People with diabetes may have numbness, tingling or pain in the feet. This is due to neuropathy (see Chapter 22) which is related to high sugar levels. The sugar and its by-products can collect in the nerves over a period of years.

Vaginal yeast infections are more common in females with diabetes, particularly if the blood sugar levels have been high. This may be because yeast grows well in a high-sugar environment. When antibiotics are taken for bacterial infections, yeast also tends to grow as the bacteria disappear. If vaginal itching or burning is noticed, the primary care provider should be contacted.

Normal Physical and Emotional Growth

Children and adolescents who have poor blood sugar control sometimes have slow gains in height or weight. Even the difference between "fair" and "excellent" control can change the rate of growth in height. One study showed an average growth rate of two inches per year during the adolescent growth spurt when the HbA_{1c} averaged 12.4%, but a gain of 3.3 inches per year when the HbA_{1c} averaged 8.4%. Research reported in 1995 from our Clinic showed final adult height was more likely to be taller if blood sugar control was good during adolescence. Following the height and weight every three months is an important part of the diabetes clinic visit.

Some people just don't feel well when they have high blood sugar levels. They may be constantly tired, have a bad temper or have any of a variety of symptoms. When better sugar control is achieved, they often are surprised to realize how much better they feel. Feeling tired and poorly over a long time does not allow for normal emotional growth.

Blood Glucose (Sugar) Measurements

BLOOD GLUCOSE TESTS ARE THE BEST WAY TO MEASURE SUGAR CONTROL ON A DAY-TO-DAY BASIS and are discussed in detail in Chapter 7. As noted in a previous section, the intensive treatment group in the DCCT tested at least four blood sugar levels each day. All families with someone with diabetes must have a method in the home for measuring blood sugars and must know how to do the tests accurately. Studies have shown that checking blood sugars and using the test results are as important for good sugar control as is the method of giving insulin (two shots per day, an insulin pump or more than two shots per day). The blood sugar levels (fasting, two hours after meals or anytime food has not been eaten for two or more hours) we consider representative of good sugar control vary with the person's age. *Suggested ranges are:*

Age	Desired Range
under 5 years	80-200 mg/dl or (4.4-11.1 mmol/L)
5-11 years	70-180 mg/dl or (3.9-10.0 mmol/L)
12 years and older	70-150 mg/dl or (3.9-8.3 mmol/L)

If good sugar levels are achieved 50-60% of the time, the glucose control is usually good. If more than 50% of values are consistently above the desired range or if more than 10% of values are below these levels, the sugar control is not good. For these problems, the diabetes care provider needs to be contacted. It is important not to be unhappy with a blood test result, but instead to always be pleased that the test was done. Hopefully, the results will be used as information to help attain better sugar control. Blood sugar monitoring was discussed in detail in Chapter 7.

In contrast to blood sugar testing at home, blood sugar measurements in a doctor's office may be of little value. There may be stress associated with the clinic visit, or the drawing of blood through an arm vein may lead to stress. The adrenaline output with stress may cause the blood sugar level to be high in the office.

Hemoglobin A_{1c} (HbA_{1c}), Glycohemoglobin (HbA_1) or Glycosylated (or Glycated) Hemoglobin

These names are used for slightly different forms of the same test. **THIS TEST IS THE MOST VALUABLE WAY TO MONITOR BLOOD SUGAR LEVELS OVER TIME.** Hemoglobin is the protein in the red blood cells that carries oxygen to the various parts of the body. If the blood sugar is high, sugar attaches to the hemoglobin and remains there for the life of the red blood cell (an average of 2-3 months). The sugar doesn't come off if a low blood sugar occurs. For the purposes of this book, we will call hemoglobin with sugar attached hemoglobin A_{1c} or HbA_{1c}. The HbA_{1c} reflects how often the blood sugars have been high for every second of the past three months (for the past 7,776,000 seconds). No one could do that many blood sugars. **The HbA_{1c} represents the forest while the daily blood sugars reflect the trees.** The HbA_{1c} and glycated hemoglobin tests have been used routinely since the late 1970s and have been called the "answer to a prayer" for people with diabetes and their doctors. Previously there was no good test to monitor long-term blood sugar control. No one really knew if they were in good sugar control. The HbA_{1c} test solved that problem.

The HbA_{1c} test can be done at the time of the clinic visit and the person does not have to be fasting. Many clinics now do the test by finger poke and may have the result done in 10 minutes. THE TEST IS NOT ALTERED BY ANYTHING THE PERSON DOES ON THE DAY THAT THE TEST IS DRAWN. Other tests, such as a blood sugar level, can be affected if eating, exercise habits or emotions are changed on the day of the test. The main disadvantage of this test is that an illness may make the level go up quickly by as much as one to two points. After the illness, the HbA_{1c} value comes down much more slowly. (It is a very "unforgiving" test.)

There are now several methods that are used for determining the HbA_{1c}. Unfortunately, normal values and desired ranges for the different methods of doing the test vary from test to test. Three of the more common methods with normal and desired ranges (for different aged people with diabetes) are shown in the Table.

We encourage different ranges for different ages. We want people 12 years old and above, when complications are more likely to develop, to be in better sugar control than younger children. The pre-teens do not have the same risk for complications, so their values do not have to be as low. Finally, low blood sugars are more dangerous for preschoolers, as the brain continues to grow for the first four years after birth. Low blood sugars are dangerous to a growing brain. The blood sugar values of preschoolers should **NOT** be kept as low as those of older children. The lower the HbA_{1c} value, the greater the chance for low blood sugars. After age 20 years, growth has decreased and life (hopefully) starts to become more consistent so that an even lower HbA_{1c} can be a goal (see the Table in this chapter). Some doctors have the suggested HbA_{1c} goal for adults to be below 7.0%. The American Diabetes Association (ADA) Standards of Care (see Chapter 20) recommend this test be done every three months for a person with diabetes. IT IS THE ONLY WAY TO KNOW HOW A PERSON WITH DIABETES IS DOING EVERY SECOND OF THE DAY. We consider it the single best test for measuring long-term diabetes control. The desired ranges shown in the table are achievable and families should continue to strive to reach these goals.

Fructosamine (or Glycosylated Albumin) Test

This test measures the amount of sugar attached to the main serum protein, albumin. It reflects the blood sugars every second of the day for the past 2-3 weeks (whereas the HbA_{1c} reflects the past two or three months). It is often helpful to know how someone is doing more recently (in contrast to the past three months). The test is also helpful for someone who is changing treatment (more shots, an insulin pump, etc.). A commercial meter, the In Charge™, is available and measures either blood sugar or fructosamine in the home setting. This home meter may be particularly helpful to families who are unable to have an HbA_{1c} determined every three months when attending a diabetes clinic.

Blood Cholesterol and Triglyceride Levels

High blood fat (triglyceride or cholesterol) levels in some people with diabetes are related to poor sugar control. Others may have high blood fat levels from eating poorly or it may be because they inherited a tendency to have high blood fat levels. High blood fat levels are sometimes part of the disease process for people with type 2 diabetes. As high blood fat levels can lead to earlier blood vessel aging, this may be a link between high blood sugar levels and later changes in blood vessel walls. We generally recommend that the total cholesterol level (or preferably, a lipid panel including triglyceride, LDL and HDL levels) be measured once a year (if normal). The total cholesterol value should be under 200 mg/dl (5.2 mmol/L). The triglyceride levels vary by age, but fasting levels should be below 130 mg/dl (1.5 mmol/L) for children and young adults. Cholesterol, triglyceride, LDL and HDL levels are also discussed in Chapter 11 (with desired levels given in Table 1; Chapter 11).

Table
NORMAL AND ACCEPTABLE HbA$_{1c}$ AND HbA$_1$ VALUES

		(Hemoglobin A$_{1c}$) HbA$_{1c}$ Values	(Glycated Hemoglobin) HbA$_1$ Values
Normal (Non-diabetic):			
Company:	Miles (DCA 2000)	up to 6.2%	
	Biorad	4.3-6.2%	
	Isolab		4.0-8.0%
Desired ranges for someone with diabetes:			
below five years		7.5-9.3%	10-12%
5-11 years		<8.5%	<11%
12-21 years		<7.8%	<10%
≥21 years		<7.5%	<9.6%

Blood sugar
above 150 mg/dl
(8.3 mmol/L)

Sad red blood cells (rbcs)!
Sugar (glucose) attaches to hemoglobin
(Hb) in the rbcs and forms HbA$_{1c}$

Blood vessel

Blood sugar
below 150 mg/dl
(8.3 mmol/L)

Happy rbcs!
Normal hemoglobin (Hb)
in rbcs

	Hemoglobin: A protein in the red blood cells
	Sugar

DEFINITIONS

Bacteria: Microscopic (only able to be seen with a microscope) agents that cause infections such as "strep throat."

DCCT: The Diabetes Control and Complications Trial. A very large research trial which showed that better sugar control reduced the likelihood of eye, kidney and nerve problems in people over age 13 years with type 1 diabetes.

Emotions: How one feels psychologically (e.g., happy, sad).

Fructosamine: A test that measures the sugar attached to the albumin in the blood. This test reflects how often the blood sugars have been high over the past two or three weeks.

HDL: **H**igh **D**ensity **L**ipoprotein. This is the "good" cholesterol protein which is believed to carry cholesterol from the blood vessel wall. A higher value is good. (See desired values in Table 1, Chapter 11.)

Hemoglobin A_{1c} (HbA_{1c}, glycated or glycosylated hemoglobin): Hemoglobin protein in the red blood cells with sugar attached to it. This is used as a measure of sugar control over the previous three months.

LDL: **L**ow **D**ensity **L**ipoprotein. This is the "bad" cholesterol protein, which is believed to carry cholesterol into the blood vessel wall. The aim is to have to have LDL levels below 130 mg/dl (3.35 mmol/L) for the general population or below 100 mg/dl (2.6 mmol/L) for people with diabetes (see Table 1 in Chapter 11).

Lens: The structure in the front of the eye that changes to allow the eye to focus on near or distant objects (see picture in Chapter 22).

Serum: The clear part of the blood when the blood cells are removed.

Symptoms: The complaints of a person; how they are feeling.

Yeast: A fungus that grows more readily when blood sugar levels are high and can cause an infection.

QUESTIONS (Q) AND ANSWERS (A) FROM NEWSNOTES

Q. Does the hemoglobin A_{1c} really give the average blood sugar over the past three months?

A. No. It reflects how often the blood sugars have been <u>high</u> over the past three months. When the blood sugar is high, the sugar attaches to all body proteins (including the red blood cell hemoglobin) and then stays attached to the hemoglobin (as hemoglobin A_{1c} or HbA_{1c}) until the red blood cell is replaced 2-3 months later. To represent the "average blood sugar," the sugar molecule would also have to detach from the protein when the blood sugar is low. This does not happen. Thus, the test only reflects how often the blood sugar has been high. The test is still far superior to any test in the past which reflects blood sugar control. It should be done on all people with diabetes every three months. In our research, reported in the Journal of *The American Medical Association* in 1989, higher longitudinal HbA_{1c} values correlated with a greater likelihood of developing eye and kidney complications of diabetes. The DCCT confirmed this observation.

Q. Is it possible to get AIDS or other diseases as a result of having a blood test?

A. NO. Only sterile syringes and needles that have not been previously used are utilized in a doctor's office or a hospital setting. Drug users who share the same needle from one person to another without proper sterilization techniques can pass diseases between themselves. However, this is not something that can happen as a result of having blood drawn in a doctor's office.

Q. Our daughter's HbA$_{1c}$ has not reached the desired level. With all the concern from the DCCT on preventing complications, could you please make any suggestions on ways to achieve better control?

A. *I have six suggestions:*

1. This question was addressed in relation to the idea of doing an afternoon blood sugar after school and judging the afternoon snack and/or insulin supplement on the value at that time. This can be helpful in lowering the HbA$_{1c}$.

2. The use of Humalog insulin rather than Regular insulin often results in some improvement.

3. One of the biggest keys to better control, which was reported in the DCCT, was more frequent blood glucose monitoring, along with making good use of the results. All subjects did a **minimum** of four blood glucose levels each day. An unfortunate trend in recent years has been to not record results as they are all recorded in the meter. When this is not done, trends for high and low values are often missed and insulin adjustments may not be made. We prefer using the data sheets for either one or two weeks of values (see Chapter 7). Then fax the results to your diabetes care provider if more than half of the values at anytime of day are "above range" for the age. Be sure to include a fax and/or phone number where you can be reached.

4. Strangely enough, preventing low blood sugars is often important in achieving better control. Low blood sugars often result in excessive eating and sending the blood sugar up to 300 or 400 mg/dl (16.7 or 22.2 mmol/L). Although excessive eating is probably the major cause of the subsequent high blood sugars, output of balancing hormones (rebounding) likely plays a secondary role in some people.

5. I do think that "turning off" the liver's production of glucose (sugar) in the early morning is important in relation to keeping liver glucose production "turned off" all day long. For many people, the human NPH insulin just does not last long enough from pre-dinner to arising the next morning to fulfill this function. It may be necessary to take the evening NPH at bedtime to have it successfully last through the night. An alternative that sometimes works is to use Lantus or Ultralente insulin, as these insulins last longer than NPH insulin.

6. Last but not least, a word must be said about missed insulin shots. One shot missed per week results in upsetting balancing hormone equilibrium and secondarily having very high HbA$_{1c}$ values. It is essential not to miss insulin injections.

Q. How do the following affect blood sugar?

✔ Exercise?

A. This varies according to the duration and difficulty of the exercise, as well as the person. Most people release epinephrine (adrenaline) during exercise which initially makes the blood sugar rise. If the insulin was injected in an exercising extremity, the insulin levels may also increase as more blood flows through the extremity and more insulin is absorbed from the injection site. The more rapid absorption of insulin can lower the blood sugar. Different people release different amounts of epinephrine during exercise to keep the blood sugar higher for varying time periods.

Another important variable is the blood sugar level prior to starting the exercise. If the level is low prior to starting, the person will be more likely to have a reaction during the exercise.

Keep good records the first time the exercise is done so that this information can be used in the future. It should be remembered that the sugar goes back into the muscle in the 2-12 hours following the exercise, and low blood sugars **(delayed hypoglycemia)** can occur at any time in this "after-exercise" period.

✔ Illness?

Blood sugars most frequently increase with illnesses. Remember that ketones must also be checked. Some people who still make some of their own insulin may have a lower blood sugar with illness. Also, if vomiting or diarrhea is a problem, there will be less food in the stomach to maintain the blood sugar and low sugars may be a problem. If there is a question regarding the insulin dose, the diabetes care provider should be phoned.

✔ Alcohol?

Alcohol, or other liquids consumed with alcohol, may initially increase the blood sugar. However, this is temporary and the main effect of alcohol will be to block the release of sugar from the liver and to lower the blood sugar level (up to 12 hours later). It is important to have the carbohydrate/protein bedtime snack even if the blood sugar is high. It is also important to get up at a reasonable time the next morning to get food and insulin into the body.

✔ Stress?

Stress usually results in epinephrine (adrenaline) release and an increase in blood sugar.

✔ Excitement?

Young children react by burning more sugar and lowering the blood sugar. Older children may increase their blood sugar. The reason for the difference in response is unknown.

✔ Good Weather?

Children tend to play outside for longer hours in good weather and the blood sugars are generally lower. The insulin dose may have to be reduced. This is especially true of the evening Humalog/NovoLog or Regular insulin when children are active after supper in the summer months.

✔ Tobacco?

There has been some evidence that nicotine (smoking or chewing) can increase the blood sugar. People report a "buzz" after either, and this may resemble the feelings of low blood sugar. People with (or without) diabetes should not smoke or chew tobacco.

Q. Changes in our daughter's insulin dose have confused my wife and me. Initially she was on a low insulin dose which you increased after reviewing her blood sugars and seeing that her HbA_{1c} was high. She got into good sugar control, but now her dose is coming back down again. This doesn't make sense to us.

A. This is quite common, and follows an old adage that: "**Good control breeds good control; poor control breeds poor control.**" Thus, for someone in poor sugar control, when the liver is making sugar at a very high rate, it takes very little (stress, infection, etc.) to make even more sugar and it may take a lot of insulin to get the liver's sugar production machinery turned off. This may also be the case for a newly-diagnosed person.

However, once the liver's pathways for making sugar are turned off, it may not take as much insulin to keep them turned off. Also, stress and infections will not have as great of an effect in a person in good sugar control. This may be part of the reason for the "honeymoon" period in the newly diagnosed person.

Chapter 15

TOPIC:
❦ Prevent, Detect and Treat Acute Complications (Ketones and Acidosis)

TEACHING OBJECTIVES:

1. Describe causes of ketone production.

2. Present signs and symptoms of having ketones.

3. Discuss treatment plan for preventing or eliminating ketones.

LEARNER OBJECTIVES:

Learner (parents, child, relative or self) will be able to:

1. List two causes of ketones.

2. Describe two symptoms of having ketones.

3. Explain two methods to prevent or eliminate ketones.

Chapter KETONES AND ACIDOSIS

CAUSES OF KETONES AND ACIDOSIS

One "emergency" in diabetes, low blood sugar (hypoglycemia), was discussed in Chapter 6. The other emergency is the build-up of ketones in the blood or urine, which can develop into acidosis. The measurement of urine or blood ketones is very easy and was discussed in Chapter 5.

When people are referred to our Center, the most common knowledge deficits are:

✔ the dangers/meaning of ketone build-up

✔ when to test for ketones

✔ not having the supplies in their home to test for ketones

✔ not knowing what to do when ketones are present

These deficits can result in a serious episode of acidosis.

"Large" urine or blood ketones are usually present for at least four hours before the total body's acidity is increased (acidosis or DKA). Acidosis is very dangerous and people can go into a coma or die from it. It is the cause of 85% of hospitalizations of children with known diabetes. The good news is that it is 98% preventable if people follow the instructions in this chapter. **Acidosis can be prevented in a person who is known to have diabetes.**

Ketones and acidosis are due to not enough insulin being available to meet the body's needs.

The four main causes are:

1. *Illnesses/infections:* extra energy may be needed by the body. This cannot be made unless extra insulin is available to make the extra energy from sugar.

2. *Forgetting to take an insulin shot:* insulin is not available to the body.

3. *A lack of insulin (see Table 1):* this could happen in a person coming out of the "honeymoon" period who has not had insulin dosages increased.

4. *Traumatic stresses on the body (particularly with type 2 diabetes):* people with type 2 diabetes sometimes get ketones during an illness. However, other body stressors such as surgery or a heart attack may result in ketone production.

Remember the statement from Chapter 2:

I MUST TAKE MY INSULIN/ORAL MEDICATION EVERY DAY FROM NOW ON. IF I FORGET MY INSULIN/ORAL MEDICATION, MY DIABETES WILL GET OUT OF CONTROL. THERE IS ABSOLUTELY NO WAY I WILL NOT NEED INSULIN/ORAL MEDICATION EVERY DAY FROM NOW ON.

MAIN CAUSES OF ACIDOSIS

🐾 **Infection**

🐾 **Missed insulin injections**

🐾 **Not enough insulin**

🐾 **Traumatic stress on the body (particularly type 2 diabetes)**

Table 2

MAIN FUNCTIONS OF INSULIN

- **To allow sugar to pass into cells where it can be used for energy**
- **To turn off excess production of sugar in the liver**
- **To turn off fat breakdown**

Insulin is needed to (see Table 2):

1. allow sugar to pass into cells

2. turn off the body's machinery for making sugar

3. turn off fat breakdown which stops ketone production

The blood sugar is usually high with large ketones and acidosis because the second and third functions of insulin are not happening. This is because not enough insulin is available. The stress hormones are also high with illnesses/infections. These hormones act to increase blood sugar and ketone production. The high blood sugar causes sugar to pass into the urine (see Chapter 2) and the person must go to the bathroom a lot **(frequent urination)**. The body may lose too much water and become too dry **(dehydration)**. The tongue may feel dry and furry. Drinking lots of fluids may help prevent this. The main treatment, however, is taking extra insulin to shut off the body's machinery for making sugar and ketones.

It is not high blood sugar that causes ketones or acidosis. In fact, eating sugar does not cause acidosis. Ketones come from the breakdown of body fat (see picture at the end of this chapter). The third role of insulin (see Table 2) is to shut-off fat breakdown. Fat begins to break down because not enough insulin is available and stress hormones are high. The side-product of fat breakdown is ketone production. Ketones are initially passed into the urine (ketonuria). They may start with trace or small levels and gradually build up to moderate and large levels. They also gradually build up in the blood. Once they reach the large level, they may start to build up in the body tissues. They are easier to reverse if treated early. The longer someone has large ketones, the more likely they will build up in the body resulting in acidosis (DKA). Thus, the early detection and reversal

by giving extra insulin is critical.

There are several reasons why fat is broken down:

- Not enough insulin is available to help the cells burn the needed sugar.

- The body needs more energy (e.g., for illness/infections) and the fat is broken down to provide this energy.

- The stress hormones; steroids, adrenaline (epinephrine) and glucagon have been released, causing fat breakdown.

- Sugar is not available due to vomiting or not eating and fat is broken down for the energy needed. Anytime fat is broken down for energy, ketones are formed.

SYMPTOMS OF ACIDOSIS

In any of the above cases, fat is broken down. The ketones are made from the fat. *Acidosis usually comes on slowly, over several hours, and has the following symptoms:*

- Upset stomach and/or stomach pain
- Vomiting
- Sweet (fruity) odor to the breath
- Thirst and frequent urination (if the blood sugar is high)
- Dry mouth
- Drowsiness
- Deep breathing (indicates need to go to emergency room)
- If not treated, coma (loss of consciousness)

On occasion, it may be difficult to know if a person is having difficulty with low blood sugar or with acidosis. Testing the blood sugar and ketones will help identify the correct problem. Table 3 may also be helpful in thinking about the two problems.

THE TWO EMERGENCIES OF DIABETES

	Low Blood Sugar (Hypoglycemia or Insulin Reaction)	Ketoacidosis (Acidosis or DKA)
Due to:	Low blood sugar	Presence of ketones
Time of onset:	Fast – within seconds	Slow – in hours or days
Causes:	Too little food Too much insulin Too much exercise without food Missing or being late for meals/snacks Excitement in young children	Too little insulin Not giving insulin Infections/Illness Traumatic body stress
Blood sugar:	Low (below 60 mg/dl or 3.2 mmol/L)	Usually high (over 240 mg/dl or 13.3 mmol/L)
Ketones:	Usually none in the urine or blood	Usually moderate/large in the urine or blood ketones over 0.6 mmol/L.

	SYMPTOMS	TREATMENT	SYMPTOMS	TREATMENT
Mild:	Hunger, shaky, sweaty, nervous	Give juice or milk. Wait 10 minutes and then give solid food.	Thirst, frequent urination, sweet breath, small or moderate urine ketones or blood ketones less than 0.6 mmol/L.	Call healthcare provider, give lots of fluids and Humalog/NovoLog or Regular insulin every two or three hours. Give Phenergan® medication (suppository or topical cream) if vomiting occurs.
Moderate:	Headache, unexpected behavior changes, impaired or double vision, confusion, drowsiness, weakness or difficulty talking.	Give instant glucose or a fast-acting sugar, juice or sugar pop (4 oz). After 10 minutes, give solid food.	Dry mouth, nausea, stomach cramps, vomiting, moderate or large urine ketones or blood ketones between 0.6 and 1.5 mmol/L.	Continued contact with healthcare provider. Give lots of fluids. Give Humalog/NovoLog or Regular insulin every two to three hours. Give Phenergan medication (suppository or topical cream if vomiting occurs).
Severe:	Loss of consciousness or seizures.	Give 1/2cc (1/2 mg) Glucagon® into muscle (top of thigh) or fat and call healthcare provider. Test blood sugar. If no response in 10 minutes, repeat once. If still no response, call paramedics or go to emergency room. May need intravenous sugar.	Labored deep breathing, extreme weakness, confusion and eventually unconsciousness (coma): large urine ketones or blood ketones above 1.5 mmol/L.	***Go to the emergency room.*** May need intravenous fluids and insulin.

PREVENTION OF ACIDOSIS

Acidosis is the cause of 85% of re-admissions to the hospital for someone with known diabetes. Most of these admissions could be prevented if the problem were treated earlier. The simple rules outlined in Table 4 will prevent most cases of acidosis. It is a good idea to review this chapter every year. Families may forget the importance of checking urine or blood ketones during any illness. Some people with diabetes who still make some of their own insulin, or who are in very good diabetes control, will have the "machinery" (enzymes) for making the ketones remain "turned off." As a result, they may go several years and never have urine or blood ketones with an illness. As they grow older and a few more islet cells are lost, or they outgrow their remaining islets, they may suddenly find ketones present.

The important message is always to remember to check for ketones anytime a person with diabetes is ill. You must also check for ketones anytime the blood sugar is above 240 mg/dl (13.3 mmol/L) fasting or above 300 mg/dl (16.7 mmol/L) during the day.

The prevention of acidosis is based on being able to detect changes early. Knowing when ketones are forming in the urine or blood, but before the ketones build up in the body, is important.

Preventing acidosis - the person with diabetes/or the family:

✔ must have a method in the home to check urine or blood ketones (see Chapter 5)

✔ must remember to check for urine or blood ketones anytime the person is sick (even with vomiting only one time)

✔ needs to check ketones if the blood sugar is high

✔ should call the diabetes care provider immediately (night or day) if moderate or large urine ketones or blood ketones >0.6 mmol/L are present

✔ needs to give extra rapid-acting insulin (Humalog/NovoLog) every two hours or Regular insulin every three hours until the urine or blood ketones have decreased

✔ must drink lots of fluids to wash the ketones out of the body and to prevent dehydration

A low blood sugar can sometimes be present with acidosis, and so urine ketones must be checked with every illness, even if the blood sugar is low. A summary of the instructions is in Table 4.

Extra Insulin

When ketone production becomes total body acidosis, it is usually because the large amount of ketones has been present for 4-12 hours. This can happen because the urine or blood ketones have not been checked or no extra insulin has been given. Insulin shuts off ketone production. Extra insulin must be given if someone has moderate or large urine ketones or blood ketones above 0.6 mmol/L. The dose of extra insulin varies for different people, and the diabetes care provider can help decide on a safe dose.

General Guidelines When Giving Extra Insulin

The blood sugar should be checked before each insulin injection.

👣 Moderate urine ketones or blood ketones (between 0.6 and 1.5 mmol/L):

The extra dose is usually in the range of 5-10% of the total daily dose. The extra dose is given as Humalog/NovoLog every two hours or Regular insulin every three hours.

👣 For large urine ketones or blood ketones above 1.5 mmol/L:

The dose of extra insulin is usually 10-20% of the total daily dose. This extra insulin is given as Humalog/NovoLog every two hours or Regular insulin given every three hours.

Table 5 outlines a possible treatment schedule.

The extra insulin may seem like a large dose, but ketones block the normal sensitivity of the body to insulin. Although every person is different, dosages in these ranges are usually needed.

👣 If the blood sugar drops below 150 mg/dl (8.3 mmol/L), it may be necessary to sip regular sugar pop, juice or other sugared drinks. This is done to bring the blood sugar back up before giving the next insulin injection.

Remember, the extra insulin and fluids are being given to clear the urine or blood ketones.

Extra Fluids

In addition to taking extra insulin, drinking fluids (e.g., water and fruit juices) is important in the prevention of acidosis. These liquids replace the fluid lost in the urine and help prevent dehydration. The juices also replace some of the salts that are lost in the urine. Orange juice and bananas are particularly good for replacing the potassium that is lost. As discussed in the next chapter (Sick-day Management), a medication called Phenergan is sometimes used if vomiting is a problem.

When severe acidosis has been present for many hours, coma (loss of consciousness) can follow. This is dangerous. It is much better to prevent severe acidosis than to have to treat it with IV fluids and a hospital admission. The hospital admission is usually in an intensive care unit, which is scary for everyone. Intravenous lines are usually put in both arms (and sometimes the feet). A constant heart-monitoring machine is attached to the person. The cost is about $10,000.

Preventing acidosis is generally possible when the rules in Table 4 are followed. Ketoacidosis in patients with known diabetes rarely occurs in people who attend clinic regularly. When it does occur, it is usually because the directions in Table 4 were not followed.

PREVENTION OF KETOACIDOSIS

- Remember to check urine or blood ketones with any illness (even an upset stomach or vomiting one time) or anytime the fasting blood sugar is above 240 mg/dl (13.3 mmol/L) or a daytime blood sugar is above 300 mg/dl (16.7 mmol/L).

- Call the diabetes care provider immediately (night or day) if moderate or large urine ketones or blood ketones above 0.6 mmol/L are found.

- Take extra insulin (after checking the blood sugar and urine or blood ketones). Take Humalog/NovoLog every two hours or Regular insulin every three hours until the urine ketones are small or less or the blood ketones are below 0.6 mmol/L.

- If the blood sugar falls below 150 mg/dl (8.3 mmol/L) and urine or blood ketones are still present, drink juice (preferably orange as it replaces potassium), Pedialyte® or sugared pop to keep the blood sugar up so that more insulin can be given to turn off the ketone production.

- Drink lots of fluids to help wash out the ketones.

KETONE LEVELS* IN BLOOD AND URINE WITH THE DOSE OF RAPID-ACTING INSULIN

Urine	Blood (mmol/L)	Dose of Humalog/NovoLog every 2 hours or Dose of Regular every 3 hours
Trace/small	<0.6	per "correction" factor for blood sugar
Moderate - Large	0.6 – 1.5	10% of total daily insulin dose**
Large - Very Large	>1.5	20% of total daily insulin dose**

* The blood and urine ketone results do not agree exactly and are estimates. The blood ketone result reflects the ketone level at the exact time the test is done. If the urine has been in the bladder for some time, then the urine ketone result may not tell the current status.

** The total daily insulin dose is the sum of _all_ insulin taken in a 24 hour period (short-acting plus intermediate-acting plus long-acting).

DEFINITIONS

Acetone: One of the ketones which builds up in the urine, blood and body during acidosis. It is sometimes used (incorrectly) to refer to all ketones.

Acidosis (diabetic ketoacidosis or DKA): What happens in the body when not enough insulin is available. Blood sugar is usually high at this time. Moderate or large ketones are present in the urine or blood and then build up in the body. The ketones make the body fluids more acidic resulting in total body acidosis.

Beta hydroxybutyrate (ß-OH butyrate): The most important of the three main ketones (along with acetone and acetoacetic acid). It is the ketone that is measured in the blood ketone test.

Dehydration: Loss of the body fluids. The tongue and skin are usually very dry and the eyes look sunken. Babies have less than half the usual number of wet diapers.

Ketones: Fat breakdown products that initially spill into the urine and later build up in the blood when there is not enough insulin. Many people can smell a sweet odor on the breath. The fat breakdown products cause acidosis (or ketoacidosis).

Potassium: One of the salts (along with sodium) lost in the urine when ketones are spilled in the urine. Orange juice and bananas contain a lot of potassium and are best to give if urine ketones are present.

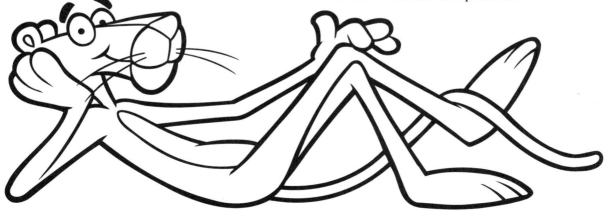

QUESTIONS (Q) AND ANSWERS (A) FROM NEWSNOTES

Q. Please explain what ketoacidosis (acidosis) is and how it can be prevented.

A. Acidosis is one of the two emergency problems of diabetes (low blood sugar being the other). It is the main cause of children with known diabetes being admitted to the hospital. It is responsible for 85% of hospitalizations. Most of these hospitalizations can be prevented with good family education and with following instructions.

Families can check for ketones at home with urine or blood. If using urine Ketostix, use the foil-wrapped strips. The bottles of strips expire six months after they have been opened. Checking for ketones should be done ANY TIME THE PERSON IS FEELING ILL. Also, check ketones if the blood sugar is above 240 mg/dl (13.3 mmol/L) fasting or above 300 mg/dl (16.7 mmol/L) during the day. If moderate/large urine ketones are found or blood ketones are above 0.6 mmol/L, the healthcare provider should be called immediately. Calling the healthcare provider may be necessary every 2-3 hours for dosages of Humalog/NovoLog or Regular insulin. After the ketones have decreased to small amounts or have gone away, the extra injections can be stopped.

On any given day, 5-10 children are being treated for ketonuria by phone by the Barbara Davis Center staff. This happens especially during the flu season. Fortunately, hospital admissions have gone down dramatically as a result of this treatment and are now infrequent.

The cause of ketone production is the body's need for energy. The fat tissue under the skin responds by releasing fats. Some of these fats are made into ketones by the liver. The fat is broken down because there is not enough insulin or sugar available to use sugar for energy. Sometimes, the body needs extra energy (during an illness) and the fat breaks down. As the ketones build up following the fat breakdown, ketoacidosis eventually results. The most frequent symptoms are a stomachache and, eventually, vomiting. Deep breathing is a late sign and indicates a need to go to an emergency room.

Q. Why does someone feel sick when the ketones are moderate or large in the urine or >0.6 mmol/L in the blood?

A. *There are at least three parts to the answer to this question:*

1. The body's acid-base (pH) balance is finely tuned (a bit on the basic side at 7.35-7.45). Acids and bases are difficult to explain. Examples of a base and an acid are: soap is an alkaline (base) material and tomatoes are acidic. Ketones (which are acids) make the body fluids more acidic as they start to build up. As the body becomes more acidic, many of the body's functions can no longer work as they should. If left untreated, death will eventually follow.

2. The second reason a person feels ill is because of a potassium and sodium imbalance. They are important body salts, and are lost with ketones going out in the urine. Potassium is important for the movement of the intestine (moving food through). If too much potassium is lost, this movement decreases or stops. When this happens, an upset stomach and vomiting can occur. We often recommend orange juice (high in potassium) and apple juice in addition to water when someone has urine or blood ketones. Drinking lots of liquids helps to keep good hydration and to flush out the ketones.

3. Poor hydration would be the third reason for feeling ill. Usually frequent urination due to high blood and urine sugar happen together with urine ketones. This can lead to dehydration. Our bodies are 60% water. If even 10% of body weight is lost as water, it is possible to be very sick. Fluids can also be lost in large amounts with the flu (vomiting and diarrhea). If fluid is being lost in large amounts from both the kidneys (frequent urination) **and** from vomiting and/or diarrhea, dehydration can occur even more rapidly. Children under the age of five, can become dehydrated in less than four hours. They are more likely to require IV treatment sooner than older children.

Q. **What is cerebral edema and how does it relate to diabetic ketoacidosis (DKA)?**

A. Cerebral edema refers to swelling of the brain, which is a rare complication of treating DKA. The cause is not fully understood and when it does occur, it is often fatal.

Perhaps we have been lucky. In 21 years since the Center opened, and in my 34 years of working with children with diabetes, I have seen only two or three cases of cerebral edema in children who had been previously diagnosed with diabetes. Part of the reason it is so rare relates to the now relative infrequency of DKA. Our families are asked to check urine or blood ketones with every illness. They are asked to call when urine ketones are moderate or large or the blood ketone level is >0.6 mmol/L. Extra shots of Humalog/NovoLog or Regular insulin are then given to reverse the ketones before DKA occurs. In one period we had only six cases of DKA among 1,200 families in 12 months! Stopping ketone formation early reduces the likelihood of a case of DKA

resulting in cerebral edema. It is better to prevent DKA than to deal with its bad effects. Unfortunately, cerebral edema is more common in newly diagnosed children when the ketones have built up over a longer time period.

Q. **Our son has had diabetes for over two years. Every time he has gotten sick we have checked for urine ketones. The results have always been negative or trace. Can we stop checking now?**

A. **The answer is NO!** This is often the case for someone who still makes some of their own insulin and/or someone who is in excellent sugar control. The machinery (enzymes) for making ketones from fat are so completely turned off that they don't get turned on by the illness. Unfortunately, as your son's insulin production declines or he outgrows his remaining insulin production, he will probably suddenly have moderate or large urine ketones with an illness. One never knows when this will occur. Thus, the only answer is to keep checking the urine ketones at least twice each day with each illness.

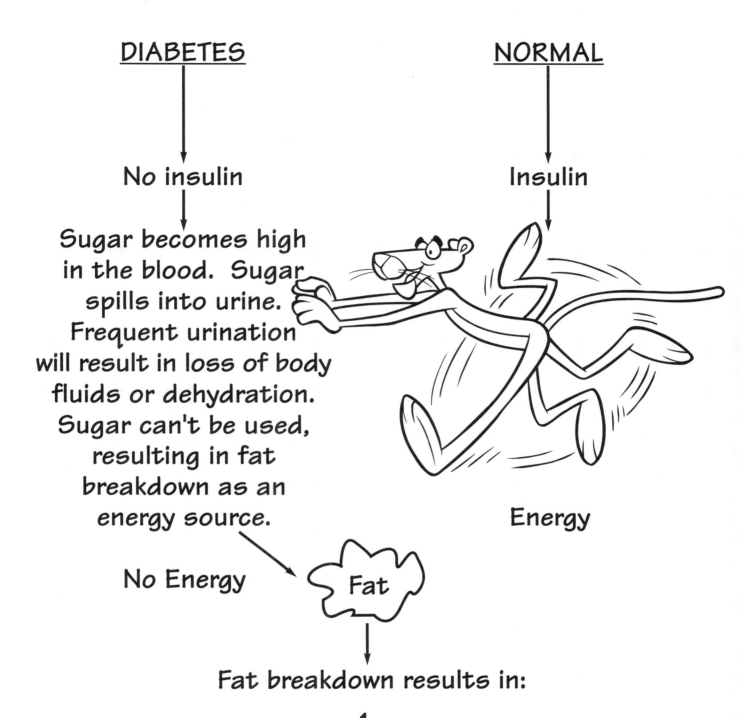

DIABETES	NORMAL
↓	↓
No insulin	Insulin

Sugar becomes high in the blood. Sugar spills into urine. Frequent urination will result in loss of body fluids or dehydration. Sugar can't be used, resulting in fat breakdown as an energy source.

Energy

No Energy → Fat

Fat breakdown results in:

1.
Weight loss
2.
Ketones, which are a breakdown product of fat and appear in the blood and urine
3.
Too many ketones in the body = acidosis

Chapter 16

TOPIC:
❧ Prevention, Detection and Treatment of Acute Complications (with illness)

TEACHING OBJECTIVES:

1. Discuss the information needed when the person with diabetes becomes ill.

2. Distinguish treatment plans for small, moderate and large ketones.

3. Indicate the appropriate time to call a healthcare provider for assistance with illness or planned surgery.

LEARNING OBJECTIVES:

Learners (parents, child, relative or self) will be able to:

1. List three areas of care that must receive special consideration when the person with diabetes is ill.

2. State treatment plans for small, moderate and large ketones.

3. Identify the appropriate time to call the healthcare provider for assistance with illness or planned surgery.

Chapter 16

SICK-DAY AND SURGERY MANAGEMENT

SICK-DAY MANAGEMENT

The person with diabetes can get sick just as any other person does. With proper "thinking ahead" and help from health professionals, the risks from illnesses are not much greater than they are for anyone else. However, there are certain precautions that must be taken. The purpose of this chapter is to review these precautions. If you have a young child with diabetes, just change the "you" to "your child" in your thinking when you read this chapter.

WHAT YOU NEED TO KNOW

When you get sick, the first thing you must do is to get the information you need. This will help you decide if you need assistance from health professionals. They will usually want to know this information. Keep your book open to this page to remind you of the 10 things to report when you phone. They are listed in Table 1 and discussed in the following text.

When calling please give:

- The **name** and **age** of the person with diabetes and who is calling

- About **how long** the person has had diabetes

- **Name of the diabetes doctor**

- **Present problem:** Diarrhea, vomiting, bad headache, cold, cough, earache, sore throat, stomachache or injury. If vomiting or diarrhea is present, note the number of times and when the episodes happen. It is also important to note if there have been any recent illnesses in other family members or close friends. This will help you decide if you have a similar illness.

Fever does not generally occur with diabetes-related problems. Fever is usually a sign of an infection. However, infections can be present without a fever. It is helpful if you are able to take your temperature before calling the diabetes care provider to discuss an illness.

WHEN CALLING, GIVE:

1. Name and age of the person with diabetes
2. About how long the person has had diabetes
3. Name of the diabetes doctor
4. Present problem
5. Blood sugar level
6. Urine or blood ketone result
7. Signs of low blood sugar or of acidosis
8. Intake of foods and liquids
9. Usual insulin dosage, time and amount of last dosage
10. Last body weight (if known)

Sick people usually don't feel like doing much. If you are still active, it is usually a good sign.

🐾 **Blood sugar:** As we noted in the chapter on self blood sugar monitoring, you must do even more blood sugar tests than usual on sick-days. Both parents, spouses and friends should know how to accurately measure blood sugars using test strips or meters in case you are feeling too sick to do the testing. The blood sugar test should always be done before calling your diabetes care provider.

🐾 **Ketones:** DON'T FORGET, URINE OR BLOOD KETONES MUST ALWAYS BE CHECKED AT LEAST TWICE DAILY IF A PERSON DOESN'T FEEL WELL (see Table 2). This is necessary even if the blood sugar is normal! Ketones must always be checked if fasting blood sugars are 240 mg/dl (13.3 mmol/L) or more. During the day, values above 300 mg/dl (16.6 mmol/L) indicate a need to check ketones. However, **with an illness, ketones can be present even when the blood sugar is lower.** It is wise to have some small paper cups in the bathroom. The urine can be left in the cup so that another person can be certain they agree with the reading (and to make sure the test was really done). **Always do the test before calling your diabetes care provider.** If you don't have the foil-wrapped Ketostix (Chapter 5), check to make sure the Ketostix bottle has not been opened for more than six months. They lose sensitivity after six months.

🐾 **Signs of low blood sugar and acidosis:** These were discussed in Chapters 6 and 15, respectively. Deep, labored breathing or continual vomiting can be signs of acidosis. These indicate the person should be seen in an emergency room as soon as possible.

🐾 **Eating and drinking:** It is important to know how well you are taking liquids and/or eating. Use a 1-liter water bottle to help keep track of how much liquid you have had. Often you can look at your tongue in the mirror to see the amount of moisture present. If the tongue starts to become too "dry" (dehydrated), intravenous fluids may be needed. Children five years old and younger can become dehydrated in 4-6 hours. If trips to the bathroom become only 1-2 times per day or if there are half the usual number of diapers, call the healthcare provider immediately.

🐾 **Insulin dosage:** You should know the usual insulin dose and when this was last taken. Were any doses skipped or forgotten? Finally, if you have had a similar illness in the past, it would be helpful for the doctor or nurse to know how much extra Humalog/NovoLog or Regular insulin you took at that time. Did the dose seem to work? If the morning or evening insulin dose has not yet been given and you have moderate or large ketones, **call the diabetes care provider before you give the injection.** Extra short-acting insulin will probably be needed.

🐾 **Oral medications:** If the person is taking Metformin (glucophage) and there is vomiting, diarrhea, difficulty breathing or any serious illness, **the Metformin must be stopped.** Call the healthcare provider **AFTER** checking the blood sugar and ketones.

🐾 **Body weight:** It is helpful to know the last weight from a clinic visit (within three months) and the present weight (if you have a scale). This will help the doctor choose the right amount of insulin and also know how much weight you may have lost.

MOST IMPORTANT

🐾 **Always check ketones with any illness.** Even if the blood sugar is low, check for ketones at least twice daily every day you are sick. Call your healthcare provider if urine ketones are moderate/large or blood ketones are >0.6 mmol/L.

🐾 **Always take some insulin.** Never skip a dose entirely. Call your diabetes care provider if you don't know how much to take.

🐾 It is particularly important to **check ketones if you vomit even ONCE!** Ketones can cause vomiting. If you vomit more than three times, call your diabetes care provider.

CHANGING THE INSULIN DOSAGE FOR ILLNESS

It is important to remember that _SOME INSULIN MUST ALWAYS BE GIVEN EACH DAY (Table 2)_. You cannot skip the injection just because you are sick and/or vomiting. Often the body will require more energy during illness to help fight the infection. Hormones in the body other than insulin (e.g., steroids) increase with illnesses and raise the blood sugar level. More insulin will be needed to allow the body to burn extra sugar for energy when the blood sugar is high. Usually only the Humalog (or NovoLog) insulin is increased. If the blood sugar is low, the short-acting insulin is not increased and may instead be reduced or omitted. Occasionally the blood sugar will be low but ketones will be present. The ketones form because the body needs extra energy and fat is broken down. Ketones are a by-product of fat breakdown for energy. In this case, you should eat and see if the ketones go away.

If **vomiting** is a problem, and the blood sugar is low or normal, sips of regular pop or of another "high-sugar" liquid may help raise the blood sugar. Sometimes sugar popsicles or honey will help. Once the blood sugar is up, you can then give the insulin to help get rid of ketones (if they are still present). Low dose glucagon may also help. Table 3 gives other suggestions for the management of vomiting.

The best way to know how much insulin is needed is to have kept records from a previous similar illness and to know what insulin dose worked then. It is important and helpful to keep good records. If you do not know about previous illnesses, look at the present blood sugar levels. If the blood sugar is high, check for ketones.

Supplemental Short-acting Insulin (Humalog, NovoLog or Regular)

🐾 If ketones are negative (or small) in the urine or <0.6 mmol/L in the blood, extra insulin can be based on the blood sugar level alone. A common formula is to give 1 unit of Humalog/NovoLog for every 50 mg/dl (2.7 mmol/L) above 150 mg/dl (8.3 mmol/L).

🐾 If ketones are moderate or large in the urine or >0.6 mmol/L in the blood, then double the dose calculated above.

🐾 Another way to calculate the dose is to give 10% of the total daily insulin dose for moderate urine ketones (or 0.6-1.5 mmol/L blood ketones). For large urine ketones (or >1.5 mmol/L blood ketones), give 20% of the total daily insulin dose. This is given as Humalog/NovoLog or Regular insulin.

These dosages are in addition to your usual daily dose. When possible, you should call the diabetes specialist to get help with the dose. **You will need to repeat the injections of short-acting insulin every 2-3 hours if moderate or large urine ketones are still present (or blood ketones > 0.6 mmol/L).** We do not generally give extra shots of insulin for elevated blood or urine ketones unless the blood sugar is at least 150 mg/dl (8.3 mmol/L). It may be necessary to first give sips of a high sugar drink, glucose tablets, hard candy, honey or other high sugar containing foods.

GENERAL GUIDELINES: SICK-DAY MANAGEMENT

Generally, the body will require more energy during an illness. More insulin allows more sugar to pass into cells, providing more energy to fight infection. Some insulin is always needed.

Important things to remember are:

🐾 **Ketones:** Always test for ketones if you feel ill. Also check if the blood sugar is over 240 mg/dl (13.3 mmol/L) fasting or over 300 mg/dl (16.6 mmol/L) during the day.

🐾 **Vomiting:** If you are vomiting and have a low blood sugar, an insulin reaction could occur. At the same time, you may still have ketones. Always test for ketones if you are vomiting. Vomiting may be due to an infection or due to ketones. Management of vomiting is outlined in Table 3.

🐾 **Insulin:** Keep a bottle of short-acting (Humalog, NovoLog or Regular) insulin available even if you don't usually use it. You may need to give the extra short-acting insulin during an illness. Be sure it is not outdated.

Blood Sugar Testing: All people must have some method of home blood sugar testing available and be ready to do extra testing on sick-days (usually every 2-4 hours). This has greatly reduced the need for hospitalizations.

Extra Snacks: It is important to take in adequate calories on sick-days or the body will start to break down fat for energy. If this happens, ketones will appear in the urine (see Chapter 15). Regular sugar pop, popsicles and regular JELL-O are good to eat if you do not feel like eating regular food and your blood sugar is below 180 mg/dl (10.0 mmol/L). Much of eating is psychological and we often suggest you eat whatever you feel like eating on sick-days! Also see Table 4.

Past Experience: Base your judgments on past experience. Refer to your record book to see if this illness has occurred before. See what worked or didn't work in the past.

Doctor: Call your pediatrician or family doctor for non-diabetes related problems such as sore throats, earaches, rashes, etc. Unless the diabetes specialist also provides general care, only call him/her if the urine ketones are moderate/large or if the blood ketone level is >0.6 mmol/L. Also call if you need help with an insulin dose, if hypoglycemia is a problem or if you need help with other parts of diabetes management.

FLUID REPLACEMENT

If you have difficulty eating or keeping food down and the blood sugar is below 180 mg/dl (10.0 mmol/L), take sugar-containing liquids (see Table 4). These may include fruit juices, popsicles, slushes, tea with sugar or honey, broth, syrup from canned fruit or even regular pop. Stir pop to get rid of bubbles. If you are vomiting, take a small amount (juice glass size or less) of sugar pop after you vomit. If it stays down 15 minutes, some sugar will be absorbed. If there is no vomiting after 1/2 hour, increase the amount of fluids. If you have ketones and are not vomiting, take at least one cup of liquid every hour. You should have one pint (two cups) to one quart (four cups) of liquid every six hours. The liquids help to prevent dehydration and also to "wash out" the ketones. Specific instructions regarding vomiting are given in Table 3.

MANAGEMENT OF VOMITING
(NEGATIVE KETONES)

🐾 Avoid solid foods until the vomiting has stopped.

🐾 If vomiting is frequent, we recommend giving a Phenergan suppository to reduce vomiting and waiting to give fluids for an hour until the suppository is working. If you do not have suppositories, ask for a prescription for them at the time of your clinic visit. For teens or others who do not like suppositories, Phenergan gel can be applied to the skin. The gel requires composition by a Prescription Compounding Center of America (or equivalent). The usual dose for a teen is 50 mg in 1cc. The gel is rubbed into the skin while wearing a rubber glove, and is then covered with plastic wrap. Preteens usually get 25 mg (1/2cc). The dose can be repeated in four hours. The main side effect of the suppository or gel is sleepiness.

🐾 Sometimes the blood sugar can be low (<60 mg/dl or <3.2 mmol/L) and the person cannot keep any food down. Glucagon can be mixed (Chapter 6) and given just like insulin – using an insulin syringe. The dose is one unit per year of age. If the blood sugar is not higher in 20-30 minutes, the same dose can be repeated.

🐾 Gradually start liquids (sugar pop, juice, Pedialyte, water, etc.) in small amounts. Juices (especially orange) replace the salts that are lost with vomiting or diarrhea. Pedialyte popsicles are also available. Start with a tablespoon of liquid every 10-20 minutes. If the blood sugar is below 100 mg/dl (5.5 mmol/L), sugar pop can be given. For the child five years of age and over, sucking on a piece of hard candy often works well. If the blood sugar is above 180 mg/dl (10.0 mmol/L), do not give pop with sugar in it. If there is no further vomiting, gradually increase the amount of fluid. If vomiting restarts, it may again be necessary to rest the stomach for another hour and then restart the small amounts of fluids. A repeat suppository or topical Phenergan dose can be given after three or four hours. Dairy products should not be used until the person is able to drink fluids and eat crackers and soup without vomiting.

🐾 After a few hours without vomiting, gradually return to a normal diet. Soups are often good to start with and they provide needed nutrients.

SICK-DAY FOODS

Table 4

1. Liquids (In addition to water – particularly if the blood sugar is below 180 mg/dl (10 mmol/L):

✔ Sugar-containing beverages: regular 7-Up, gingerale, orange, cola, PEPSI®, etc.[1]

✔ Pedialyte or Infalyte® (especially for younger children)

✔ Sports drinks: Gatorade®, POWERâDE®, etc. (any flavor)

✔ Tea with honey or sugar[1]

✔ Fruit flavored drinks: regular Kool-Aid, lemonade, Hi-C®[1], etc.

✔ Fruit juice: apple, cranberry, grape, grapefruit, orange, pineapple, etc.

✔ JELL-O: regular (for infants, liquid JELL-O warmed in a bottle) or diet[1]

✔ Popsicles: regular or diet[1]

✔ Broth-type soup: bouillon, chicken noodle soup, Cup-a-Soup®

2. Solids (when ready) – good foods with which to start:

✔ Saltine crackers

✔ Banana (or other fruit)

✔ Applesauce

✔ Bread, toast or tortillas

✔ Graham crackers

✔ Soup

✔ Rice

[1] *Sugar-free may be needed depending on blood sugars (e.g., >180 mg/dl [>10.0 mmol/L])*

LOW DOSE GLUCAGON

Sometimes the blood sugar can be low (< 60 mg/dl [3.2 mmol/L]) and the person cannot keep any food down. Glucagon can be mixed and given just like insulin, using an insulin syringe. The dose is one unit per year of age.

For example:

a 5 year old would get 5 units

a 10 year old would get 10 units

If the blood sugar is not higher in 20-30 minutes, the same dose can be repeated. This treatment has saved many ER visits for our Clinic patients.

FOODS FOR SICK-DAYS

Table 4 suggests carbohydrate-containing foods that might be tried during an illness.

Eating carbohydrates is important to provide energy and to prevent the body from breaking down fats (and thus making ketones). Drinking liquids is important to prevent dehydration. Thus, liquids are usually tried first. A general rule of thumb is to offer whatever you/your child like(s) best. You may want to have a "sick-day kit" on hand which could include items such as sugar-containing 7-UP, sports drinks, regular and diet JELL-O or pudding, apple juice in small cans, regular Kool-Aid mix, Cup-a-Soup, Pedialyte and any other items you would like to have available.

EXERCISE

The person with moderate or large urine ketones should not exercise. Exercise can further increase the ketones.

SICK-DAY MANAGEMENT: WHEN TO CALL FOR EMERGENCY CARE

Table 5

- If you have vomited more than three times and can keep nothing in your stomach, and urine or blood ketones are not elevated, call your primary care physician. If help is needed with an insulin dose, call your diabetes care provider.

- If moderate or large urine ketones or blood ketones (>0.6 mmol/L) are present, call your diabetes care provider.

- If you have difficulty breathing or have "deep breathing," you need to go to an emergency room. This usually indicates severe acidosis (ketoacidosis).

- If there is any unusual behavior such as confusion, slurred speech, double vision, inability to move or talk or jerking, someone should give sugar or instant glucose. (Glucagon [Chapter 6] is given only if the person is unconscious or if a convulsion [seizure] occurs.) The healthcare provider should be contacted if a severe reaction occurs. In case of a convulsion or loss of consciousness, it may be necessary to call the paramedics or to go to an emergency room. Have an emergency number posted by the phone.

CONTACTING YOUR DOCTOR OR NURSE

Keep a card with your doctor's and nurse's phone numbers in a place where you can easily find it. Take the card with you if you are out of town. It is easier to call your own doctor rather than to go to an emergency room and see a new doctor.

Think ahead! You should keep Phenergan or other suppositories on hand in case of vomiting. (Some physicians prefer not to use suppositories.) Before you call the doctor or nurse, be sure you have the necessary information (see the list at the beginning of the chapter). **Always check the blood sugar and urine or blood ketones before calling.** Have the number of your pharmacy available in case the doctor needs it. Table 5 tells when to call or get emergency care. Remember to keep sugar pop, popsicles and soup available for illnesses.

CLINIC OR EMERGENCY ROOM VISITS

If you do decide to go to a clinic or emergency room, remember to take your hospital card if you have one, your diabetes records and your insurance information. Take extra clothes in case you must be admitted to the hospital. A relative or friend going with you will need money for food, telephone numbers of people they might need to call and something to read.

SICK-DAY MEDICATIONS

Our general philosophy is that **if you need a medicine for an illness, take it!** We can handle the problems related to diabetes. The classic example is asthma. With a bad attack, the person will need adrenaline (epinephrine), which raises the blood sugar. Steroids (cortisone) may also be needed which also raise the blood sugar. For the short time that these medicines are needed, extra insulin can be taken to help control the blood sugar. Short-term elevations of blood sugar are not what we worry about in relation to the complications of diabetes.

Over-the-counter medications can be purchased with care. Look at the label to see if sugar is added. Tablets are less likely to have sugar (and alcohol) than are liquids. Again, the small amount of sugar in a medicine taken for a short time is okay. *We do not endorse any products but do suggest these:*

Generic daytime/nighttime cold capsules: Are fine to use in children old enough to swallow the capsules. The capsules are alcohol-free and don't have an after-taste as do liquids. They usually contain pseudoephedrine, which can help reduce any fluid buildup in the middle ear.

Nasal sprays (e.g., Afrin®): Can be used for colds and allergies. A nasal spray is less likely to affect the entire body than pills or liquid medicines. If these do not work, or if long-term use is anticipated (as with seasonal allergies), antihistamine tablets or liquids such as Chlortrimeton® or Triaminic® might be tried next.

Acetaminophen (TYLENOL®) or Ibuprofen: To relieve fever if a flu is going through the community. Do not give aspirin to children or adolescents.

Pepto-Bismol®, Kaopectate® or Imodium AD®: These are fine to use for diarrhea. (Lomotil® should NOT be used in children).

DI-GEL®, MYLANTA®, Gelusil® and Maalox® are all sugar-free antacids.

Cough medications: Use a cold air vaporizer if this relieves the cough. During the day, a cough is often protective to keep material out of the lungs. Thus, we do not give cough medicines. A combined cough and fever means the child should be seen by a physician. If the vaporizer does not stop the cough at night, use sugar-free cough medicines with

less than 15% alcohol. Examples: Colrex Expectorant®, CONTAC Jr.®, Hytuss Tablets®, Queltuss Tablets®, Robitussin CF® liquid, Sorbutuss Syrup®, Supercitin®, Toclonol Expectorant®, Tolu-Sed®, Tolu-Sed DM®, Tussar-SF®.

Sore Throats: A throat culture to rule out a streptococcal (strep) infection should be done because strep can lead to rheumatic fever or other problems. Salt water gargles (1/4 teaspoon salt in one glass water) may help. Chloraseptic Spray® is sugar-free, as are Cepacol®, Cepastat®, Chloraseptic® mouthwashes or lozenges and N'ICE® lozenges.

FOLLOW THE DIRECTIONS ON THE LABEL FOR ANY MEDICINE YOU USE.

FLU SHOTS

The method of preparing the flu vaccine has improved so that side effects are now less likely. The American Academy of Pediatrics recommends flu shots for all children with diabetes, and we agree. Preventing an episode of flu may prevent an episode of ketoacidosis. It is important to get the shots early in the fall so that the flu shot can be working when the flu season begins.

GUIDELINES FOR MANAGEMENT AROUND SURGERY

* Always contact your diabetes care provider if surgery is planned - **AFTER** you find out the time and whether normal food intake will be allowed. You may wish to give the name and phone number of the diabetes care provider to the person doing the surgery.

* Plan to take your own blood sugar and ketone checking equipment.

* Take your own materials to treat low blood sugar (a source of instant glucose and even glucagon).

* Always check the ketones prior to surgery. Then, if they are present at a later time, it will be known that they were negative earlier. If the urine ketones are found to be moderate or large or the blood ketones (>0.6 mmol/L), it may be necessary to cancel the planned procedure. Take the ketone strips with you to the procedure in case vomiting occurs and you need to do a check. It is also wise to check ketones once or twice after the procedure.

* Take your diabetes clinic's phone card so that you may quickly call the diabetes care provider if needed.

SURGERY MANAGEMENT

Some general guidelines for diabetes management around surgery are outlined in Table 6. The insulin dose is almost always changed when a person goes to a dentist or to a hospital for elective surgery. The amount of change is extremely variable depending on the person, the type of surgery that is scheduled and the time of day the surgery is to be done. If possible, surgery should be scheduled early in the morning. In general, it is best to call your diabetes care provider and discuss insulin changes **after** you find out the time of day the procedure is to be done and whether or not food intake will be limited. Sometimes it is also helpful to have the person who is going to do the surgery call the diabetes care provider. This is more likely to be done if the family gives the doctor or dentist a note with the name and phone number of the diabetes specialist. The two of them can then work out the best time for a given person to have elective surgery.

We frequently receive calls from families related to planned dental surgery. Often this can be done under local anesthesia, and sometimes the person can eat regular meals prior to and after the surgery. In this situation it is only necessary to reduce the insulin dose slightly in anticipation of some reduction in food intake due to soreness in the mouth.

If the person is going to have a general anesthetic, eating may be restricted. This is because vomiting can occur while recovering. If vomiting does occur in a person who is still partly under the influence of anesthesia, there is a danger of some of the food getting into the airway. Thus, food restriction is usually necessary if a general anesthetic is to be used. Anytime the amount of food intake is to change, the amount of insulin to be given must also be changed. Different physicians handle the changes in insulin dosage differently. Some physicians reduce the dose of long-acting insulin (often by half) and use short-acting (Humalog/NovoLog or Regular) insulin only if needed. Other physicians give no long-acting insulin, and Humalog/NovoLog or Regular insulin are then given every two or three hours. If the person is going to have a general anesthetic in the hospital, some doctors prefer to give all of the insulin by intravenous infusion. Any of these methods work. **The important thing is the close monitoring of blood sugars! By doing this, low blood sugars can be prevented. It is also wise to check the urine or blood ketones before and after the procedure.** These may increase with changes in the insulin dose and with the stress of surgery. Needless to say, your diabetes care provider must always be notified if the urine ketones are moderate or large or the blood ketones are >0.6 mmol/L following surgery.

Blood sugar monitoring is usually the responsibility of the parent or the patient when procedures are done in the dentist's or doctor's office. If a meter is used for blood sugar monitoring at home, this should be taken along to the dentist's or doctor's office. If the child is being admitted to the hospital, also take the meter along. If the child is to have a general anesthetic, the blood sugar monitoring is the responsibility of the doctor giving the anesthesia or the doctor doing the surgery. The doctor usually orders dextrose, which is glucose (sugar), to be added to the intravenous fluids if the blood sugar is below a certain level (200 mg/dl or 11.1 mmol/L is a safe level to use). Blood sugars are usually measured at regular intervals by the doctor or nurse.

It is also wise to take along urine or blood ketone checking strips. Many doctors or nurses who do not care for people with diabetes on a regular basis may forget the importance of routinely checking for ketones. Also take your diabetes care provider's phone numbers with you. If urine ketones are moderate or large, or the blood ketones are >0.6 mmol/L, you may wish to call your diabetes care provider.

DEFINITIONS

Anesthetic (anesthesia): A medication (such as ether) used to reduce pain or to allow a person to sleep through an otherwise painful procedure.

Dextrose: The name for glucose (sugar) added to an intravenous (IV) feeding to prevent low blood sugar.

Suppository: A medication inserted into the rectum (bottom), usually because liquid, food or medicine cannot be kept down (as with vomiting).

QUESTIONS (Q) AND ANSWERS (A) FROM NEWSNOTES

Q. In the chapter on "Sick-day Management" in the Pink Panther book, you state four times that ketones must always be checked at least twice daily when someone is ill. Is it necessary to be that repetitive?

A. Forgetting to check ketones with an illness is one of the most common errors families make in managing diabetes. As a result, ketones can build up to high levels in the body, which can then be dangerous (and expensive to treat). There is no charge for a few phone calls to a diabetes care provider to receive suggestions for supplemental Humalog/NovoLog or Regular insulin to combat early ketone formation. In contrast, the charge is usually $5,000-$10,000 for one or two nights in an intensive care unit as a result of large ketones building up in the body. As pointed out at the end of Chapter 15 on Acidosis (Ketoacidosis), this charge and the related risk from ketoacidosis can be avoided if families will just check for ketones immediately (and twice daily) when the person with diabetes is ill. The diabetes care provider must then be called when moderate or large ketones are detected, or the blood ketone level is >0.6 mmol/L, and every 2-3 hours thereafter until the ketones are below these levels.

Q. Our son is now a teenager and with a recent episode of vomiting was quite shy about letting us use a rectal suppository. The Phenergan suppository had worked well in the past, and so I was quite disappointed. Do you have any thoughts?

A. Certainly the modesty of teens and young adults must be respected. It is now possible to get Phenergan (promethizine) in a gel which can be applied to the skin. It will be absorbed in about 15 minutes. It can be ordered in a 1 ml syringe. There is 25 mg (one dose) in each 1/2 ml (one syringe has 2 doses). It is available from a pharmacy that is a member of "Prescription Compounding Centers of America". (There are about 1,000 in the U.S.) One such pharmacy noted the cost of one syringe (two doses) was $7.00 which is about the same as suppositories.

Q. Should flu shots be given to children with diabetes?

A. The American Academy of Pediatrics recommends flu shots for all children with diabetes. Flu is a common cause of ketonuria and of acidosis, so the shots may also help prevent ketoacidosis. If you do decide to get them for your child, we would prefer that you go to your primary care physician for this purpose. Call first to make sure the doctor's office has the vaccine. If a young child has not previously received the flu vaccine, it is necessary to get it in two injections, approximately one month apart, and it is best to start during the months of September or October.

Q. Should my child receive the chicken pox vaccination?

A. Yes, if he or she has not had chicken pox! It is recommended by the American Academy of Pediatrics for all children who have not had prior chicken pox infections, and we support that recommendation. There is an additional factor for children with diabetes who still produce some insulin. Chicken pox is probably one of the many infections that stimulate white blood cells in the pancreas to make toxic particles that cause further islet destruction. This is not proven, but we have heard many times of children being diagnosed with diabetes in the month or two after having chicken pox.

The Varivax is a live vaccine. The main side effects are a mild rash (approximately 3%), and/or a temperature elevation (approximately 15%) and/or tenderness at the site (approximately 19%). Ninety-nine percent of people are immune as a result of the vaccination.

17 Chapter

TOPIC:
Psychosocial Adjustment

TEACHING OBJECTIVES:

1. Describe extra stresses which a person/family may experience as a result of diabetes.

2. Provide healthy coping strategies for individual family stress.

WITH SPECIAL THANKS FOR THE SUGGESTIONS OF:

- Ellen Fay-Itzkowitz, MSW, LCSW
- Donna Follansbee, PhD
- Rita Temple-Trujillo, MSW, LCSW, CDE

LEARNER OBJECTIVES:

Learner (parents, child, relative or self) will be able to:

1. Identify the stresses experienced by the person/family with diabetes.

2. Describe a healthy coping strategy for an identified stress.

Chapter 17 FAMILY CONCERNS

WORKING AS A FAMILY

The problems a family may have following the initial diagnosis of diabetes include more demands on their time, money and energy. This is due to the daily routine of the diabetes management and the regular clinic visits. Families must decide how to fairly share these new responsibilities. We encourage **both** the mother and father to share the responsibility for the diabetes care. This should include helping to give the insulin injections. It is important for the parents to support one another in all diabetes related activities. Each parent's interest and investment in care is crucial to the family's adjustment. Both parents should also try to attend all clinic visits.

Diabetes effects the entire family. The family must work together to solve problems and manage the diabetes. Research has shown that the people with the best sugar control are those who had help and support with the tasks of diabetes.

SINGLE-PARENT/BLENDED FAMILIES

Approximately one-fourth of children in the U.S. now live in single-parent families. For parents who live separately, it is important to share vital diabetes information between households.

This information includes:

✔ blood sugar levels

✔ recent low blood sugars

✔ insulin dosages

✔ food intake

✔ exercise

✔ illnesses

✔ other items/events which may effect diabetes management

GOOD COMMUNICATION AND COOPERATION ARE ESSENTIAL

Some suggestions for two households are:

✔ diabetes supplies can be neatly packed in a carrying case to go with the child between households

✔ keep a vial of glucagon and some foil-wrapped urine ketone strips permanently in each household

✔ keep a **current** log book with insulin doses and blood sugars to ensure consistency from household to household

✔ the care of the child should be important enough for parents to put aside any individual differences when dealing with the diabetes and their child(ren)

LEADING A NORMAL LIFE

Diabetes care has changed tremendously over the past 10-15 years. New insulins, blood glucose meters and added flexibility with meal planning and insulin dosing make it easier for children or adults to live normal, healthy lives. It is important for children or adults with diabetes to feel as normal as possible. Though there may be many new worries, it is possible to normalize one's life with diabetes.

For children, leading a normal life means participating in age appropriate activities with their family and peers. There is no question; diabetes can make fun things like sleepovers and birthday parties a little more stressful. But with a little flexibility and creativity, children with diabetes are able to participate in these activities just like their siblings or friends. When in doubt about allowing your child to take part in an activity, ask yourself, "Would I let him/her participate if he/she did not have diabetes?" If the answer is "yes," it should not change because of the diabetes. If you are uncertain, contact your care provider so they can help you create a plan for the activity.

The issue of discipline and diabetes is also an important aspect of leading a normal life. Whether your child has diabetes or not, there will be times when he/she will test limits and act out. Children with diabetes need to be disciplined, too. Sometimes it is hard to tell if your child is being difficult because he/she is a teenager or toddler or because his/her blood sugar is low. When in doubt, check the blood sugar and then deal appropriately with the behavior.

Care providers, parents and children need to strike a balance between good diabetes control and an emotionally healthy lifestyle. It is important for all of us to work as a team so that kids with diabetes can grow and develop physically and emotionally.

CONCERNS OF BROTHERS AND SISTERS

When a child first develops diabetes, it is a crisis for the whole family. Often brothers and sisters feel left out. This is because so much attention is given to the child with diabetes.

Some common concerns may be:

✔ trouble understanding what diabetes is

✔ fearing that their brother or sister will die

✔ thinking they caused the diabetes by having an angry thought against the child with diabetes

✔ fearing that they will be the next to be diagnosed

Important things for the brothers and/or sisters:

✔ to be a part of the beginning education

✔ young children will feel less frightened if they can visit the hospital or clinic

✔ asking the children what they think and understand, even if you think everything has

been thoroughly explained. *One child used the word "diabetes" very literally. When asked why he was so very sad, he said he thought diabetes meant "die of betes."*

✔ discipline should not be different for their brother or sister with diabetes than it is for them

✔ All children in a family should be treated in a similar way. *One sister said she eats a candy bar in front of her brother with diabetes when he gets away with something. She said, "That's how I get even with him."*

✔ it is important to plan individual time and special activities with all children in a family

Some children with diabetes have the opportunity for special activities such as diabetes camp and ski trips. Many brothers and sisters say, "I wish I had diabetes so I could do special things, too." A family can prevent future stress if the members understand some of these problems.

FAMILY STRESS

The diagnosis of any serious condition, especially in children and teens, is stressful for the whole family (including the extended family). Working through the initial shock and grief that comes with the diagnosis is difficult. This can be particularly hard if families have had medical or other serious issues to manage. Parents usually have different coping styles around grief. It is normal that some family members find they are less patient or even irritable with one another for a period after the diagnosis. These feelings usually resolve as everyone adjusts and begins to feel more comfortable managing the diabetes.

When grief or conflict do not resolve, this can obviously be stressful for the relationship and for the whole family.

The crisis of diagnosis can bring up many fears and feelings and:

✔ an individual can become quite anxious or depressed

✔ parents may feel the strain on the relationship with one another. It is particularly important to seek help to try to understand and resolve these feelings.

✔ children and teens can sense tension between parents and may feel responsible for something they can't help

Talking with the psychosocial member of your diabetes team can be helpful in sorting out the problem.

SWEETS IN THE HOME

Perhaps no area of diabetes care is argued more than the one of keeping sweets in the home of a person with diabetes. Those who argue in favor of allowing sweets in the home will say, "They have to learn to avoid sweets when they are with their friends away from home. They should learn to avoid them at home, too."

In our experience, people who say this usually have a sweet tooth themselves and do not want to give up any of their own sweets. Is it fair or reasonable to ask a person with diabetes to do what we are not able to do ourselves?

If sweets such as donuts, cakes, cookies, sugar pop and candy are going to routinely be in the house, they will be eaten by everyone including the person with diabetes. If the person realizes these junk foods are not needed at home, they will not need them outside of the home. Avoiding them when they are in the home can result in more stress and high blood sugar levels. (This is particularly true if resistance weakens and the person is caught and scolded.) Siblings may consciously or unconsciously taunt the child with diabetes. This will raise both the stress and the blood sugar levels, and create conflict at home.

The whole family can be most supportive of the person with diabetes by limiting these foods in the home. They have little nutritional value, and everyone's health will be better. Although current nutritional guidelines do not prohibit eating these foods, they should be eaten in a measured fashion with insulin to cover. People often do not have the will power or discipline to follow this rule. Helping people learn portion/serving sizes can be done by dividing sweets into 15-30 gms sizes and placing in sealed plastic bags. If other family members have a need for these products, they should fill this need when away from the person with diabetes. Better sugar control is usually found

when excesses of sweets are eliminated from the home.

A healthy diet includes foods from all food groups in appropriate amounts. It is permissible to include some sweets as a part of a healthy diet. Fresh fruit and frozen yogurt are good examples of treats that can provide both nutrition and great taste! With or without diabetes, one should not consume sweets and special treats in excess! When diabetes is part of the picture, appropriate insulin must be taken for carbohydrates including sweets that are consumed. Trying to avoid all sweet foods may create undue focus on food restriction. Healthy sweet treats may be allowed as a part of a healthy family diet.

DEALING WITH STRESS AND EXCITEMENT

Emotions and stress may have a big effect on diabetes control. *Many different life events can cause stress such as:*

🐾 family problems

🐾 arguments with parents or between parents

🐾 parent separation or divorce

🐾 death of a relative, friend or pet

🐾 a move to a new home or school

Other kinds of stressful situations include special events such as:

🐾 athletic competitions

🐾 school exams

🐾 holidays like birthdays, Christmas or Hanukkah

Most people will have high sugars following stress, though some young children can have low sugars. For young children, it is important to think ahead and reduce the insulin dose or give extra food. Monitor blood sugars at least four times during the day to prevent low blood sugars on days of excitement.

People with diabetes should lead a normal life and learn to deal with stress in a healthy manner. Stressful situations help them learn to do this. Sometimes, professional assistance in methods of dealing with stress can be helpful. It is possible to learn effective stress-reducing techniques in just a few meetings with a therapist.

The diagram in Chapter 14 on Diabetes and Blood Sugar Control shows how the insulin dose, oral medicine dose, diet, exercise and stress must be in balance for the best sugar control. This is not possible all of the time for anyone.

NEEDLE FEARS

It is now known that needle fear of some degree occurs in about 25% of people with diabetes. It can occur in people of any age group. It is usually obvious from day one, and for many it does not go away. We will often ask people in the clinic, on a scale of 1 to 10 (1 = no pain, 10 = much pain), what level of pain do the shots give you? It is also helpful to know if the pain is greater with the needle going in or with the insulin being injected.

Warning signs of this problem include:

1. high HbA_{1c}

2. a child wanting to do all their own shots - particularly when they want to do the shot in a room by themselves (some shots will probably be missed)

3. lack of site rotation (swelling of the injection site)

4. missed insulin shots

5. excuses for wanting to "put off" the shot

6. parental fear or worry about injections or blood draws

The psychosocial team can be very helpful to children or parents with this problem. Treatment can include behavioral techniques and purposeful distraction. The latter includes TV, music, toys, blowing bubbles and books. Sometimes injection devices help the problem (Inject-Ease, Chapter 9) though they do not cure it. Behavioral techniques include learning to relax, reward programs, systematic desensitization and biofeedback. As fear of shots, blood or injury decreases, the HbA_{1c} usually improves.

PSYCHOLOGICAL DISORDERS

Families need to be aware of two types of psychological disorders that have been described in people with diabetes. The first is **depression** and the second is **eating disorders**.

Depression: Depression, (defined in Definitions at the back of this chapter) is the one psychological disorder that may be more common in older teens and adults with diabetes than in the general population.

Depression:

✔ may lead to poor glycemic control due to not following treatment plans

✔ requires the person or family members to seek help

✔ treatment called cognitive behavioral therapy and/or medication can be highly effective

✔ if left untreated, the consequent poor glycemic control leads to a greater risk for diabetic complications

Eating disorders: The most common types of eating disorders are defined in the Definitions in the back of this chapter.

✔ **Anorexia** is the first and includes limiting food intake and often engaging in excessive exercise.

✔ **Bulimia** is the second which may include self-induced vomiting, use of laxatives and/or excessive exercise.

Both of these conditions result in low blood sugars.

✔ **Missing insulin shots** is an additional problem that is specific to diabetes (but is also a form of an eating disorder).

Effects of missing insulin doses:

• The calories then go out in the urine rather than into the body. Blood sugars are very high.

• If left untreated, chronic complications (Chapter 22) are more likely.

• Blood sugars sometimes become very erratic. This may mean the person is alternating between restricting food (with low sugars) or binging (with high sugars).

✔ **Binge eating** is the third type of eating disorder. It is most frequently associated with type 2 diabetes.

Any of these disorders can be very dangerous for a person with diabetes. They require psychological care from a person with expertise in this area.

CHANGING BEHAVIOR

Sometimes children with diabetes have difficulty with their insulin injections, blood sugar tests at home, the suggested diet, the recommended exercise or other parts of diabetes management. These "problems" can be opportunities to assess what is bothering a child or teenager. At these times it may be very helpful to meet with the clinical social worker or psychologist who specializes in working with families. They can help evaluate problems and suggest ways to effect change. Behavioral change takes time, patience and usually requires help from the whole family. A few visits can often be very helpful to the patient and the family.

SCHOOL/WORK ATTENDANCE

People with diabetes generally shouldn't have more school/work absences for illness. They may have to miss school/work occasionally for routine clinic visits. If a lot of school/work is being missed for diabetes related reasons, it is very important to review this with your medical team. Working together, the underlying cause can be found. With good blood sugar control, there is no reason why people should not participate fully in activities of their choice. However, they may have other concerns that contribute to missing school/work. These concerns should be examined and addressed as soon as possible.

If school/work is missed for a period of time due to illness or hospitalization, the person may be very worried about returning. It is not uncommon for the diabetes to remain in poor control when a person is worried about unfinished work, exams, fellow students, teachers, co-workers or other problems.

If a significant amount of school/work has been missed the following can be helpful:

- Encouraging the person to return to school/work as soon as possible.

- The family may wish to ask members of the diabetes team to help coordinate matters with the school/work. Sometimes a person may fear how peers or co-workers will treat him/her.

- Talking with the school counselor or teacher can help people of school age. They can assist in arranging a schedule and homework after a long absence.

- Arranging for a nurse educator or parent to talk to the class about diabetes can be very helpful for a student. It allows for the development of good peer support and understanding.

DEFINITIONS

Clinical Social Worker: A person with a Master's degree in social work trained to help individuals or families with emotional or behavioral problems, as well as problems with resources.

Depression: A psychological state in which one may show sadness, a lack of energy, inability to do one's normal work or activity or self-depreciation. They may show a lack of interest in enjoyable activities, irritability or withdrawal from friends and family.

Eating disorder: *The three most common types of eating disorders are:*

1. Anorexia: People with a distorted body image who limit their food intake and often exercise in excess to remain very thin.

2. Bulimia: People who eat excessively at times and then vomit (or take medicines such as laxatives) in order to not gain weight.

3. Binge-eating: People who intermittently eat excessively but do not vomit. They may gain excessive weight and develop type 2 diabetes.

Psychologist: A doctor (Ph.D. or Psy D.) trained in helping people with behavior, stress or feelings that are causing problems or discomfort.

Stress: Problems or events that make people feel worried, afraid, excited, upset or scared.

QUESTIONS (Q) AND ANSWERS (A) FROM NEWSNOTES

Q. What are the occupational restrictions for a person with diabetes?

A. Restrictions are based on the idea that all people with diabetes are at a greater risk for hypoglycemia. There are studies which show hypoglycemia does result in an increased risk for accidents. In one study, approximately 10% of the accident reports, in which the accident was due to a medical condition other than alcoholism, were due to an insulin reaction.

My own opinion is that restrictions should not be generic and should be individualized. Some people test their blood sugars frequently and are careful to eat or make sure they are not low before driving a car. Others are less careful. Everyone pays the price from the latter group.

Currently, legal restrictions include working in the military, commercial truck driving and flying a passenger plane. Some state and local governments may also deny employment in the police or fire fighting forces. Most physicians also recommend that people who have frequent low blood sugars do not work at heights, operate heavy equipment or handle toxic substances. Working rotating shifts can also result in more difficulty with blood sugar control. Generally, if the rotations are on a monthly or greater basis, it is possible to alter the insulin dosage to cope. The use of the insulin pump is very effective in providing shift workers the ability to maintain good blood sugar control.

Q. Are psychological problems more or less common in children and adolescents with diabetes compared with people without diabetes?

A. It is a common belief that the presence of any chronic illness increases the likelihood of psychological problems. The presence of pimples or blemishes that make the adolescent feel different from peers can be devastating. We ask youths with diabetes to eat differently than their peers (and not to eat foods generally considered the most tempting), to give two or more insulin shots and do three or more finger pokes for blood sugar every day of their lives. With this, one might expect some psychological problems!

Surprisingly, this is not the case. In the years the Barbara Davis Center has been open, we have had far fewer serious psychological problems (including drug addiction and suicide) than in the general population. Why is this? It is likely related to several factors. One is "preventive counseling" has been available from the day the Center opened. The psychosocial component of the Center has been expensive and is possible only because of financial support from the Children's Diabetes Foundation and its Guild. When families come for their three-month clinic visits, the staff is constantly alert for people who might need some extra help. I often ask teenagers to grade their current stress level from one to ten. An answer of five (or above) usually means the person is asking for help and a visit to the psychologist or social worker might be helpful. I strongly believe the regular clinic visits and the "preventive counseling" have been major reasons for the low incidence of major psychological problems.

Diabetes often results in the entire family focusing on the holistic health of the individual and family, often in ways that might not otherwise have occurred. These often include eating better, getting more exercise and not using tobacco. Factors such as these may also relate to the good mental health of the people seen at our Center.

An added factor in the low incidence of serious problems may be the schedule and seriousness of diabetes care. A number of youths have written in their college applications that having diabetes required them to "grow up" sooner - to learn at an earlier age when they could have fun or when they had to be serious. Good diabetes control and the use of illegal drugs and alcohol do not mix. With the monitoring of diabetes control every three months, any change from good control is quickly detected. Preventive counseling can then be done before the problem becomes too serious.

One parent saw some wonderful, older kids who were in the clinic when her child was diagnosed. Many were in getting check-ups during their winter break from college. She asked how it could be that these kids seemed to be so much more successful than average. She was told, "It's the extra hugs!" All in all, kids with diabetes are special. I have felt very privileged to work with each of them and their families throughout the years.

Chapter 18

TOPICS:
- Psychosocial Adjustment
- Goal Setting and Problem Solving

TEACHING OBJECTIVES:

1. Present the importance of long-term family support and involvement in the diabetes management.

2. Define age-appropriate skills and tasks.

LEARNER OBJECTIVES:

Learner (parents, child, relative or self) will be able to:

1. Outline family support roles for diabetes management.

2. Identify at least one age-appropriate sign of readiness for learning diabetes skills/tasks.

Chapter 18

RESPONSIBILITIES OF CHILDREN AT DIFFERENT AGES

INTRODUCTION

Daily diabetes care has grown more complex in recent years. It is not unusual for families to:

- use insulin "thinking-scales"
- mix 2-4 insulins in one syringe
- give three or more shots each day
- use an insulin pump
- juggle sports and exercise
- count carbohydrates or follow other food plans

Good sugar control requires the active involvement of parents for many years. The myth that children should be encouraged to do all of their own diabetes care at an early age no longer applies. Diabetes is a family disease.

Children of different ages are able to do different tasks and to accept different responsibilities. It is important not to expect more from children than they are able to do. If they are unable to do the tasks, they may develop a sense of failure and later poor self-esteem resulting in poor self-care. Family members need to watch for signs that the child needs more assistance, especially during times of high blood sugars.

The ability to do certain tasks may vary from day-to-day and parents must be available to help as needed. The children should be encouraged to gradually assume care for themselves as they are able. The ability to successfully live independently, both in everyday life and with diabetes care, is the eventual goal for all of our children.

The purpose of this chapter is to review "normal" child development and how it relates to diabetes care. Although parts of this chapter may not be important for each reader,

they may be helpful to some families. It must be remembered that all children develop at different rates (and our own children are always the most advanced).

Age alone, as a guideline, does not tell us when an individual child is ready to assume tasks. There is no such thing as a "magic age" when the diabetes suddenly becomes the responsibility of the child or teenager. Be patient! Independence takes a long time. The suggestions below may vary for any given child or family. Diabetes is a **"family disease"** and the family should work together. Family members need to help each other. Sharing tasks will help prevent the diabetes care from becoming the responsibility of just one person.

CHILD UNDER THREE YEARS

- **Traits and Responsibilities Not Related to Diabetes**

This is a time of rapid development of a small, wondrous creature who eats, sleeps, cries, soils diapers and starts to learn about the world.

Motor and brain development are the most rapid of any time in life:

- ✔ sitting (6-8 months)
- ✔ crawling (6-12 months)
- ✔ walking (12-18 months)
- ✔ language development

These developments open up a whole new world.

Accidents are the infant's major danger. *They must be protected from:*

- ✔ stairs where they might fall
- ✔ poisons and medicines they might swallow (from cupboards, garages and purses)

✔ auto accidents

✔ other dangers (including coffee tables with sharp edges)

All infants with or without diabetes need love. Parents and care providers need to cuddle and hold infants frequently throughout the day. This is particularly true after shots and blood sugar tests, as infants do not understand parents causing pain. Parents must remember that the testing and shots are essential to their infant's life and they must move beyond feelings of guilt (as discussed in Chapter 10). Much of the fussing around blood sugar tests and shots is due to the interruption in the child's activity rather than pain. Infants develop trust during this period and combining the diabetes care with love will help to make the diabetes care a part of normal life. Young adults often look back with appreciation to their parents for the shots and care they gave them when they were young.

🐾 **Responsibilities Related to Diabetes**

Although babies and toddlers are not able to do any of their own self-care, the following are some special suggestions that may help parents.

✔ **Blood sugar testing:**

• Toes are used more frequently as a site for doing the testing.

• The BD Ultrafine lancets are smaller and may hurt less.

More frequent blood sugar testing is usually done (see Chapters 6 and 7) because the babies and toddlers cannot tell if their blood sugars are low.

✔ **Blood sugar levels:**

• The blood sugar level to aim for is also higher (80-200 mg/dl or 4.4-11.1 mmol/L; see Chapter 7) as severe lows may be more dangerous to the infant's rapidly developing brain.

• Low blood sugars can be treated with less carbohydrate than for an older child (usually 5-10 gm due to smaller body size). This amount is found in 1/4 cup of milk, orange or apple juice or 2-3 oz of sugar pop, although the amount needed may vary from infant to infant.

• Infants who suck on a bottle of milk or juice frequently during the day or night will tend to have higher blood sugar levels. Overnight sucking on a bottle can also lead to dental decay.

✔ **Shots:**

• Shots are sometimes given while the infant is sleeping (if he/she tends to get very upset). If the child squirms or awakens at the time of the shot, the dad (or mom) should reassure the child. A statement such as "It is just daddy (or mommy) giving you your insulin" may be all that is needed.

• The bottom (buttock) is used more frequently as a place to give the shot.

• Eating is often variable and parents can wait to give the shot until they see what is eaten. This is important when the rapid-acting Humalog/NovoLog insulin is being used. The dose of insulin can then be reduced if intake is low.

The amount of time taken to eat a meal should be the same for all the children, with or without diabetes. Special treatment can result in eating problems. It is important for the parents to stay in control.

• The amount of Humalog/NovoLog or Regular insulin is kept low due to body size and due to an apparent increased sensitivity to short-acting insulin. With the insulin syringes currently available, it is not usually necessary to dilute insulins. Most parents learn how to judge 1/2 unit dosages using the 0.3cc (30 unit) insulin syringes. The Precision Sure Dose 0.3cc syringes have markings for half-unit measurements (Chapter 9). Similarly, the BD Pen Mini can deliver half unit increments.

It is important for parents of infants with diabetes to incorporate the diabetes into their everyday lives. Children learn through imitation. If parents have adjusted to the diabetes and can view their child with the same positive feelings they had prior to the diagnosis of diabetes, it will help the child to grow up feeling positive and psychologically healthy. A summary of non-diabetes and diabetes traits for each age group is shown in Table 1.

AGE-RELATED RESPONSIBILITIES AND TRAITS

Table 1

	Non-diabetes-related	Diabetes-related
Age below 3 years	• developing gross motor skills • developing speech skills • learning to trust • responding to love	• parents must do all care • acceptance of diabetes care as part of normal life • often give shots after seeing what is eaten
Age 3-7 years	• imaginative/concrete thinkers • cannot think abstractly • self-centered	• parent does all tasks • gradually learns to cooperate for blood sugar tests and insulin shots • inconsistent with food choices - may still need to give shots after meals • gradually learns to recognize hypoglycemia • undeveloped concept of time • adult needs to do all insulin pump management
Age 8-12 years	• concrete thinkers • more logical and understanding • more curious • more social • more responsible	• can learn to test blood sugars • at age 10 or 11, can draw up and give shots on occasion, although they still need supervision • can make own food choices; can learn initial carb-counting • do not appreciate that doing something now (e.g., good diabetes control) helps to prevent later problems (e.g., diabetes complications) • can recognize and treat hypoglycemia • by 11 or 12 years, can be responsible for remembering snacks, but may still need assistance of alarm watches or parent reminders • can do own insulin pump boluses, but needs adult help to remember
Age 13-18 years	• more independent • behavior varies • body image important • away from home more • more responsible • abstract thinking • able to understand the importance of doing something now to prevent problems in the future	• capable of doing the majority of shots or insulin pump management and blood sugar tests, but still needs parental involvement and review to make decisions about dosage • knows which foods to eat; can do carbohydrate counting • gradually recognizes the importance of good sugar control to prevent later complications • may be more willing to inject multiple shots per day

AGES 3-7 YEARS

Traits and Responsibilities Not Related to Diabetes

✔ *They think concretely.*

Concrete thinking means things are either black or white, right or wrong, good or bad. They do not think abstractly. For example, they are unable to realize that "Having a shot of insulin will help me to stay healthy." Instead, a shot may be considered a punishment for doing something wrong. Parents need to repeat over and over that the child hasn't done anything wrong and to try to describe in the child's language why pokes and shots are important.

✔ *They start to see themselves as separate individuals from their parents.*

Children gradually become very curious in this period. They often want to know how things work. They can annoy parents with the simple words "how" and "why."

✔ *Children of this age are very self-centered.*

They may progress from playing with a toy alone to gradually learning to share a toy or to share the love of their parents. Primary attachments are to parents and family. Interest in other relationships, such as school peers, begins at six to seven years of age.

✔ *Age responsibilities in children 5-7 years old begin to increase dramatically.*

They can help pick up their toys, make their bed or put their dirty clothes in the hamper when guided by the parent. They are capable of fixing simple foods, such as cereal or a sandwich, but still do not understand simple dangers such as putting a knife in a toaster or being careful around boiling water. They must have much parental supervision.

✔ *Children 5-7 years old are learning to read, opening a whole new world.*

They are discovering many new things, asking lots of questions and practicing new skills. They feel more independent and, in some ways, they are. Usually they are cooperative and love to be helpful. However, they still require a good deal of adult supervision.

Responsibilities Related to Diabetes

✔ *The parents must do all diabetes related tasks.*

Fine motor coordination (the coordination of the fingers when handling small items) is not yet fully developed. They cannot do tasks such as accurately drawing insulin into a syringe. This is also true when a child of this age is using an insulin pump. The adult must always be available to do all of the pump management.

✔ *They can gradually learn to cooperate with their parents,* (e.g., sitting still for blood sugar tests and insulin shots)

✔ *They can help by choosing or cleaning a finger for a blood test or by choosing the site for the insulin shot.*

✔ *Children as young as 3 or 4 can sometimes recognize low blood sugars.*

They can tell parents when they are hungry. Their complaints may be vague or seem strange to us ("Mommy, my tummy tickles" or "Daddy, I don't feel good.") However, these clues can be very helpful to parents. Helping children verbalize the body sensations of low blood sugars is an important task for family members.

✔ If a shot (e.g., Lantus) is going to be given after the child is asleep, this should be discussed with the child and parents. Some children will say "fine." Others want control and will ask to have the shot given before they go to sleep.

✔ *By age 5-7 years, recognizing low blood sugars is more completely developed, particularly if the parents have encouraged it.*

✔ *Children of ages 4-7 years may have some concept of which foods they can eat.*

They can be taught to ask, "Does it have sugar in it?" or "Do you have a diet pop?" They cannot be expected to always or even very often make the "right" choices over the ones that look or taste good. They will probably choose foods that are similar to what friends or family are eating. They can be expected to have some temper tantrums at being limited in high-sugar food.

There is not much concept of time at this age. An adult will need to make sure that a snack is taken at a specific time. Sometimes a watch that beeps at a set time can be used as a reminder for a snack.

✔ *They usually have no objection to wearing a diabetes ID bracelet or necklace.*

It is good to get children into the habit of wearing the ID when they are young. This may help them to do this as they get older.

It is important for parents of children in this age group (as in all age groups) to keep a positive attitude. Remember the blood sugar tests and insulin shots help to keep the child healthy. Playing games around diabetes chores and gradually getting the child to help (even in little ways) may be beneficial. One fun game is to use quarters or stickers to reward the child for guessing the blood sugar number while the meter counts down. Whoever is closest "wins." It will help the child to learn to tell when they are high or low. Hugs and kisses will reassure the child that the parents' love continues. To be able to keep a positive attitude, parents need their own support for their worries and hard work. Friends, family, diabetes support groups or other sources of support can be extremely helpful.

AGES 8-12 YEARS

❧ Traits and Responsibilities Not Related to Diabetes

✔ *Children of this age continue to think in concrete ways.*

They can gradually think more objectively and understand another person's point of view.

✔ *Fairness and meeting their needs are very important.*

✔ *Children at these ages are more social and peers begin to play a more important role in their lives.*

They usually begin to spend nights at friends' houses. They have more peer activities than do younger children. Becoming involved in some team sports can help them to stay involved as they get older. This is a great age to do classroom education about diabetes. The more peers understand, the less likely they will tease. They can soon become a real support to your child. Peer support is important, especially later during adolescence.

✔ *Children can be helpful by learning to take on increased responsibilities.*

They may help with doing dishes, feeding pets, cleaning their own room and other rooms or taking out the garbage. Special rewards, such as stars on a calendar, may be helpful in encouraging certain activities.

✔ *They are capable of more complex food preparation and can better understand safety and danger issues.*

❧ Responsibilities Related to Diabetes

✔ *Some children begin to do their own blood sugar testing at ages 8-10.*

✔ *At about this age some children wish to begin to give some of their own insulin shots.*

The ability to accurately draw up the insulin is a bit slower in developing, but it is usually present at 10 or 11 years of age. The coordination needed between seeing something and using the fingers to successfully do the job (eye-hand coordination, fine motor skills) develops during this age. This is an exciting time to watch a child develop. Adult supervision is essential for all of these important tasks.

The child can get "burned out" if:

- they begin any of these tasks at too young an age
- they have too much responsibility without the parent being available to take over when needed

They will be more likely to rebel during the teen years by missing shots or not testing blood sugar levels. In addition, they may have difficulty requesting their parents' help when needed if they are expected to perform self-care tasks alone. Parents must stay involved in diabetes management with this age group!

✔ *Children of this age sometimes feel that "life isn't fair," particularly as it pertains to diabetes.*

It is helpful to just listen to them if they express such feelings.

✔ *Children may be able to give their own shots when staying at a friend's house.*

As the children are usually very active when staying at a friend's, we often suggest reducing or omitting the dose of short-acting insulin (Humalog/NovoLog or Regular) and reducing the dose of the evening long-acting insulin by 10-20%. The parent can draw up the shot ahead of time and put it in a small box, toothbrush holder or other container and leave it at the friend's home. They may even place it in the Inject-Ease. They may ask the friend's parent to supervise the shot. It is important to remember to roll the syringe between the hands to re-mix it prior to giving the shot.

It is also essential that the friend's parents be informed about hypoglycemia. The handouts in the school or baby-sitters sections (Chapters 23 and 24) may be helpful.

✔ *Children of this age can eat lunch at school and make choices to avoid high sugar foods.*

Some will begin to learn to count carbohydrates.

✔ *They can gradually learn to recognize and treat their own hypoglycemic reactions.*

✔ *They are also more aware of time and can learn to be responsible for eating a snack at a set time.*

✔ *Insulin pumps are sometimes considered by the family in this age group.*

It is important for the family to meet with all team members (Chapter 26).

This helps to determine who is truly ready to start using the pump.

✔ *Sports can be very important at this age.*

A child who learns to enjoy athletics is starting a healthy pattern for their life as well as for controlling diabetes.

Parents of the child in this age range must be patient in teaching the child about diabetes and how to do diabetes-related tasks. **The parents must still be very involved in supervision of the diabetes care.** They must also be secure enough to let the child begin to assume some responsibilities on his/her road to becoming an independent person.

Diabetes camp, group ski trips, hikes or other events allow the children to receive invaluable support from each other and to realize that they are not the only person in the world with diabetes.

AGES 13-18 YEARS

❧ Traits and Responsibilities Not Related to Diabetes

✔ *Teens gradually develop independence and a sense of their own identity.*

As noted in Chapter 19, Special Challenges of the Teen Years, this age group varies greatly between wanting independence versus needing dependence. Some rebellious behavior may be demonstrated toward parents as teens grow into separate individuals.

✔ *Skills increase greatly in this age group.*

Automobiles can be driven legally and power lawn mowers can (hopefully) be used. Teenagers may take jobs to earn their own money. Activities, in general, are greatly increased.

✔ *Body image becomes a major concern.*

Teenagers worry about how others view them. The slightest pimple may become a catastrophe. Early in this period, friends of the same sex are very important, whereas later, interest in the opposite sex usually begins.

✔ *More time is spent with friends.*

✔ *The older teen is away from the home more and stays out later with friends.*

✔ *Experimentation with alcohol at some point is common.*

❧ Responsibilities Related to Diabetes

✔ *Teens gradually take over more of their diabetes care.*

Parents still need to be available to assist with giving a shot from time to time. They need to take over the diabetes care for a period of time if the youth seems "burned out." Teens generally do better if they get extra help, particularly with insulin dosage.

As noted in Chapter 19, A SUPPORTIVE ADULT CAN BE AN ASSET FOR A PERSON WITH DIABETES REGARDLESS OF AGE. Even parents of older teens still need to help with making sure adequate diabetes supplies are available (and paying for them) and making sure that clinic appointments are made and kept every three months.

Parents should come to the clinic, although the staff may request to see a teen individually to discuss issues that may be difficult to talk about with parents present.

✔ *Many teens dislike the chore of writing blood sugar results in a log book.*

If the parents agree to do this at the end of each day (with the teenagers' OK), it is a way for the parents to keep tabs on the diabetes. Having values written down (and often faxed to the diabetes care provider) is important in looking at trends and knowing when changes in insulin dosages need to be made.

✔ *Experimentation with alcohol will likely upset the diabetes control (see Chapter 11) and can cause severe hypoglycemia.*

✔ *Experimentation with street drugs upsets schedules and diabetes as well. The use of drugs can result in:*

• increased appetite and higher blood sugars

• loss of incentive for good diabetes management

• eating meals irregularly

✔ *Good peer support can help the continuation of:*

• an exercise regimen

• a healthy diet

• a consistent lifestyle

• not using tobacco products (an added risk for diabetic kidney disease and for later heart attacks). Most people who are going to use tobacco will begin prior to age 20 years. Usually, if the peer group does not smoke or chew, the youth will make a similar choice.

Identification with peers is so important in this age group that their support (or lack of it) may greatly affect the teen's diabetes management.

✔ *A belief in God and church, synagogue or mosque activities may help guide the teen.*

✔ *Continued involvement with parents can provide stability, limits, love and support.*

✔ *Grandparents can be a tremendous help at any age (see Chapter 24).*

Again, support from peers (with or without diabetes) is very important in this age group (see Chapter 19, Special Challenges of the Teen Years).

✔ *There is often a feeling of invincibility or "it can't happen to me."*

Regular clinic visits at this age may help the teen realize that diabetes care and responsibility are important. Teens with diabetes are faced with more difficult tasks and more serious life issues than their peers. Teens with diabetes often seem to mature earlier than teens without diabetes. They learn at an earlier age when they have to be serious in life and when they can have fun.

✔ *Insulin pump use is often considered in this age group (Chapter 26).*

Transition to a pump is more successful if this is the teen's choice. If the parents "push" for an insulin pump, but the teen is not ready, there is a lower chance for success. It is important to have the help of the entire diabetes team when making this decision. Readiness for the pump can be assessed together. This age group is often quicker than parents in learning the use of the pump (a mini-computer). Glucose control can improve ONLY if meal boluses are remembered. This activity can often require adult help.

The parents' role for the teenager is to be available to help when either forward or backward steps toward adult maturity are taken. Providing support, stability, limits and love are essential at this difficult age (as at all ages).

Age alone should not be the primary factor in deciding that a person should assume responsibility for diabetes self-management. Parents who offer continued assistance and who share the responsibilities with the teen will generally have a teen in better diabetes control.

The average ages for mastering tasks as recommended by the American Diabetes Association and by a survey of care providers are shown in Table 2.

DEFINITIONS

Eye-hand coordination: The ability to use the hands to finely adjust what is seen with the eyes. This ability usually develops around the age of 10.

Fine motor control: The ability to carefully move the fingers with precision (e.g., drawing insulin to an exact line on a syringe). This ability usually develops around age 10 or 11.

Self-esteem: How a person feels about himself/herself.

QUESTIONS (Q) AND ANSWERS (A) FROM NEWSNOTES

Q. It seems like every time our eight-year-old son stays at his friend's house or has his friend stay overnight at our house he has low blood sugar the next morning. Should we be making changes?

A. "Overnights" are an important social and developmental step in our society. It is important that children with diabetes be able to participate just like any other child. Overnights are also a step in developing independence and are sometimes the first night spent away from the parents. It is important for the child to be safe in relationship to the diabetes. The children usually run and play a bit harder with their friend on overnights. They also stay up a bit later than normal and use more energy. It is generally wise to reduce the insulin dose, both the short-acting (20-50%) and the long-acting (10-20%) insulins, on these nights.

A good bedtime snack is also advisable. Remember the "pizza factor," that pizza tends to keep a blood sugar up better than most other foods. If there is a frozen pizza in the freezer, it may be a good night to use it. It is also wise to awaken the child at a reasonable time in the morning and to get a glass of juice or milk down sooner rather than later.

Do remember that if the child is able to do a shot but is not yet old enough to draw it up, the morning NPH and short acting insulin can be pre-drawn. The syringe can be put into a little box or toothbrush holder and just rolled to mix the next morning. Think about reducing the dose again for the morning shot if it is likely that the two friends will be playing together much of the next day.

AVERAGE AGES FOR DIABETES-RELATED SKILLS
Age of Mastery (in years)

Skill	Recommended by the American Diabetes Association	Survey of Care Providers
A. Hypoglycemia		
1. Recognizes and reports	8-10	4-9
2. Able to treat	10-12	6-10
3. Anticipates/prevents	14-16	9-13
B. Blood glucose testing	8-10	7-11
C. Insulin injection		
1. Gives to self (at least sometimes)		8-11
2. Draws two insulins	12-14	8-12
3. Able to adjust doses	14-16	12-16
D. Diet		
1. Identifies appropriate pre-exercise snack	10-12	10-13
2. States role of diet in care	14-16	9-15
3. Able to alter food in relation to blood glucose level	14-16	10-15

Abstracted from a survey done by Drs. T. Wysocki, P. Meinhold, D.J. Cox and W.L. Clarke at Ohio State University and The University of Virginia (Diabetes Care 11:65-68, 1990).

Chapter 19

TOPICS:
- Psychosocial Adjustment
- Goal Setting and Problem Solving
- Pregnancy

TEACHING OBJECTIVES:

1. Assess the acceptance of diabetes by the teen.

2. Discuss special challenges of teen years, including tobacco use, alcohol, substance abuse, sex, identity issues and life style.

LEARNER OBJECTIVES:

Learner (parents, child, relative or self) will be able to:

1. Discuss plan for sharing diagnosis and diabetes-related needs with peers.

2. Develop action plan with diabetes provider(s) to minimize health risks.

Chapter 19

SPECIAL CHALLENGES OF THE TEEN YEARS

SPECIAL CHALLENGES FOR THE TEENAGER

A. Struggle for independence

B. Growth and body changes

C. Identity

D. Peer relationships, alcohol, drugs, tobacco

E. Sexuality

F. Consistency (exercise, eating, emotions and lifestyle)

G. Driving a car

H. College

I. Changes in psyche

A. STRUGGLE FOR INDEPENDENCE

Parents often despair at the thought of their "angelic" child becoming an adolescent. The teen years have been defined as the period in life when one varies between wanting to be a child and wanting to be an adult. These feelings vary from second-to-second, minute-to-minute, hour-to-hour, day-to-day, week-to-week and year-to-year. The "child" part of the adolescent still wants to be completely dependent on parents and other adults. The emerging "adult" wants to be an entirely independent person. There are many shades between these two extremes that may linger into later life. Hopefully, the variation becomes less with increasing age.

In the past, we believed that children with diabetes should assume their own management at a certain age and that they would suddenly become independent. **We now know that independence is not age specific and is a gradual process.** We think of diabetes as a **family disease**. It requires a

great deal of parent-child partnership to achieve good sugar control and healthy independence.

Parental partnership (involvement) with the teen can be accomplished in a variety of ways:

✔ drawing up and/or giving injections

✔ keeping a log book to record blood sugars and noting trends and problems

✔ helping to fax blood sugars to the diabetes care team (fax sheets are found in Chapter 7)

✔ helping with weekend dosing when teens may want to sleep in and could use some help with shots and a quick breakfast

These not only help the teenager, but also help keep the parent "in the loop" and aware of what is going on with management.

The "child vs. adult" struggle can greatly influence diabetes management during the adolescent years. A teenager may want entire responsibility for the diabetes management at one time - faithfully checking blood sugars, exercising, watching food and sugar intake and taking the responsibility for the injections (or oral medicines for type 2). At another time, blood sugars will not be checked unless the parent is there to help, injections or oral medicines may be forgotten or sugar may be consumed in large quantities. Exercise, which is critical for the person with type 2 diabetes, may be ignored. Parents can lessen the effects of this variable attitude toward the diabetes care by remaining involved and offering to share these responsibilities with their "child-adult." Offering to exercise with the teen makes it more fun and challenging for everyone. **We believe that a supportive adult who is readily available, BUT NOT OVERBEARING OR CONSTANTLY NAGGING, can be a help to any person with diabetes, regardless of age.**

Diabetes care is usually NOT the top priority for a teenager. Their main priorities may be their peers, schoolwork, sports, a car, a job, etc. (in varying orders of importance for different teens). The parents may need to help in keeping a focus on the tasks necessary for good sugar control.

If the teenager's actions (or lack of them) result in possible serious dangers to his/her health, then the parents have no choice but to step back in for a time. This is particularly true when insulin shots or oral medicines (type 2) are being missed. Hopefully, the next attempt at taking on increased responsibilities will be more successful. Sometimes professional counseling is necessary.

However, the majority of teenagers gradually assume adult independence by themselves. In contrast to the parents' worst fears, they do grow up! In fact, the teenager with diabetes may assume adult responsibilities earlier than other teenagers.

The task of how to help children grow to be independent young adults is a challenge for most families. Diabetes complicates that task somewhat. It is normal for parents of children with diabetes to feel anxious about normal separations such as overnights, camp and school trips. Parents worry about injections, low blood sugars and whether the schedule and snacks will be remembered. With good preparation and supervision, these separation experiences are an important part of growing up. They will not only facilitate growing independence, but these experiences are also usually a lot of fun. It is best to start with brief periods of separation, like staying at a relative or friend's house overnight.

🐾 Overnights

Staying at a friend's home, even for one night, can be a big step, as can visiting relatives. We generally suggest a small reduction in insulin dosage (short and intermediate-acting insulins) for overnights (at home or away). They are usually up later and tend to burn more energy. (Then the parents do not need to worry quite as much about low blood sugars while their child is away.)

Julie is a 16-year-old girl who has had diabetes for seven years. She and her family have always prided themselves on Julie's good diabetes control. Julie is a talented dancer and hopes to become a professional dancer some day. She dances on Mondays, Wednesdays and Fridays at 5:30 p.m. At a clinic appointment, it is discovered that her diabetes has become out of control with her HbA_{1c} unexpectedly being over 14%. In talking with Julie, she admits to missing evening injections sometimes when she goes to dance class. She says she just doesn't have time to get her homework, blood test and injection done and still get something to eat before leaving for dance class.

PLAN:

Julie's parents volunteered to help with the blood testing and injections on those nights and to make some dinner for her. Julie was relieved to have her parents take over some of the diabetes care, but admitted it was hard to ask for help after being responsible for her own diabetes care for several years.

NOTE: Another possibility is the missed shots were done on purpose in order to keep her "dancer's figure." If so, this is more serious. More discussion on this topic can be found later in this chapter under the topic "Changes in Psyche" and in Chapter 17 under Eating Disorders.

Summer Camp

Follow these short visits with longer stays at a diabetes or other summer camp. Children learn that they CAN survive without the parents and the parents learn that their children CAN survive without them! (Re-education for these children and their parents is important.)

Clinic Visits

Teenagers can begin seeing diabetes care team members by themselves at diabetes clinic visits. Parents are still needed at these visits to review plans and problems with their teens and the diabetes care team. As noted in Chapter 18, better sugar control usually results if parents stay involved in offering continued assistance and sharing responsibilities with the teenager.

B. GROWTH AND BODY CHANGES

The adolescent growth spurt and the development of adult sexual characteristics result in many body changes - probably more than occur at any other single time in life.

Growth Hormone

The gain in height is a result of increased hormone levels (growth hormone, testosterone and estrogen). Growth hormone partially blocks insulin activity. Insulin requirements increase dramatically and are usually the highest per pound body weight than they will ever be. The insulin requirement usually decreases when growth is completed. If blood sugar control is good during puberty, full growth is usually reached. Research from our Center has shown that better growth (to full adult potential) is more likely with good sugar control.

Sex Hormones

Female sexual development includes breast and hair development, widening of the hips and the onset of menstrual cycles. These pubertal changes may be slightly delayed in girls with diabetes. Blood sugars may increase during menstruation. Many girls will increase their intermediate/long-acting insulin and their Humalog/NovoLog or Regular (short-acting) insulin by one or two units during this time. Some girls, who use an insulin pump, will switch to a different basal rate setting to provide more insulin during the menses.

Males have enlargement of the testes and penis, and facial and other body hair begins to grow. When body odors become noticeable, for males or females, the use of deodorants is desirable. Acne ("zits") or pimples may develop in either sex, making good skin care important. Tetracycline or other antibiotics are fine to use if acne pustules become a problem. Males may be tempted to try steroid drugs to try to make their muscles larger. Use of these steroid drugs can prevent full height attainment, lead to increased blood cholesterol levels and an increased risk for heart attacks later in life. They also may cause aggressive behavior, resulting in problems getting along with others. The drugs reduce insulin sensitivity and cause increased blood sugar levels. Non-prescribed steroid drugs should not be used.

Thyroid Hormone

The thyroid gland (in the neck) must function properly during this time or growth will not progress normally. As part of the regular diabetes check-up visits, the diabetes care provider will monitor the size and function of the teen's thyroid gland. About half of teenagers with diabetes get some thyroid gland enlargement. This is an "autoimmune" disorder, as is diabetes. Antibodies against the thyroid gland can be measured (although expensive and often not paid for by insurance). A simple test called TSH (Thyroid Stimulating Hormone) is usually adequate. Thyroid problems are also discussed in Chapter 22.

Body Image

Teenagers are often very concerned about "body image" (self-consciousness) and a single pimple can be a disaster. Diabetes does not usually result in visible body alterations. Having diabetes may make teens "feel" different from their peers. Wearing an insulin pump (see Chapter 26) is often visible and a constant reminder of having diabetes. This is a reason why pumps should not be "pushed" on a person until they are ready. The refusal to wear an identification (ID) bracelet or necklace, to wear an insulin pump or to refrain from eating high sugar foods may relate to not wanting to feel different from peers. Some teens hide their pumps under baggy clothes. They may choose not to bolus if eating with friends. As they gain confidence and maturity, they will bolus when needed without regard to their peers.

C. IDENTITY

🐾 Who Am I?

Teens are searching for the answer to the question, "Who am I?" It is important to emphasize the positives about who they are at this stage of their lives (e.g., someone who loves a sport, music, mechanics, school plays or other interests), and who secondarily happens to have diabetes. The diabetes should not come first. Positive reinforcement should be given when a good attitude toward living with diabetes is demonstrated. Compliments are important. For example, "Good job on getting your blood tests done even with the stress of finals" (even though the stress and not exercising may have resulted in high sugar values). In contrast, it may be necessary for parents to "bite the bullet" and not respond when stress results in blood sugar testing not being done. A cheerful offer to record results or give injections during busy times can be rewarding for both the teen and the parent.

Warning signs which should alert investigation of behaviors:

✔ withdrawal from the usual routines

✔ change in sleeping pattern (sleeping more/less)

✔ changes in friends

✔ not communicating with family members

🐾 Risk-taking

The in-the-middle age range of teen years (approximately ages 15-17 years) is usually the most difficult time. The teen often sees himself/herself as "invincible." Risk-taking and experimentation tend to occur more frequently.

Some of the experimentation may include:

✔ bright hair colors or styles

✔ unusual clothing

✔ piercings in an unusual place(s)

✔ a tattoo(s)

Some diabetes-related risk behaviors are:

✔ "I don't need to wear a bracelet; I've got an ID card in my wallet."

✔ "I'm not going to carry sugar; I can get something at my friend's house if I need it."

✔ making poor food choices without taking the steps to maintain blood sugar control

✔ not doing blood sugars

✔ missing shots

Regular (or more frequent) clinic visits and HbA_{1c} tests at this time may help the teen. Parents need to let the teen know that they trust their child to act maturely. Patience on the part of the care providers and from the parents is a real virtue at this time.

D. THE PEERS

Peer relationships are very important to teenagers, often more so than relationships with parents. Early in adolescence, close friends are usually of the same sex. In later adolescence this often changes or is "added to" by members of the opposite sex. Being like their peers is very important. Having diabetes and "being different" can be a problem. Some teenagers are comfortable doing blood tests or giving themselves injections in front of their friends. Others will absolutely refuse to let anyone other than the closest friend know that they have diabetes. The willingness or refusal to wear an ID, as well as doing diabetes tasks in front of friends, may reflect the teen's own degree of acceptance of diabetes.

Much of a teen's identity relates to conforming with their peer group. Peer groups can be important in helping the teen make decisions about the use of drugs, alcohol or tobacco. If the peer group rejects or accepts these, the teen with diabetes will probably do likewise.

Effects of the use of the items listed above:

✔ *Tobacco use* (smoking or chewing) affects blood vessels in anyone. Tobacco use by a person with diabetes is particularly harmful as it can lead to possible kidney disease and heart disease later in life.

✔ As in all people, **chewing tobacco** can lead to dental problems and cancer of the mouth.

✔ **Smoking cigarettes** is associated with an increased likelihood of lung cancer and heart disease.

✔ **Alcohol consumption** can result in delayed severe insulin reactions. (This is discussed in more detail at the end of Chapter 11.)

✔ **Drugs** that alter awareness of time have their greatest effects on diabetes by interfering with consistency in eating and insulin injections.

✔ **Chronic drug use** may result in an "I don't care" attitude toward diabetes management with poor health outcomes.

Participation in a support group for teenagers with diabetes can be helpful. A support group can be both a social and a discussion group. It may help the teenagers share their feelings with others who also have diabetes. They soon realize that others have many of the same feelings that they do, and they are quite normal in spite of having diabetes!

Research has shown that the teen with diabetes who involves his/her peers by sharing knowledge about diabetes is more likely to achieve better sugar control. We encourage teens to bring a friend to the clinic visit to continue to learn how they can support their friend with diabetes.

E. SEXUALITY

❧ Teenagers with diabetes run the same risk as non-diabetic teens of contracting diseases such as AIDS, herpes, chlamydia and other sexually transmitted diseases.

❧ *Pregnancy in a woman with diabetes (also see Chapter 27) carries added risks for the baby and the mother:*

✔ If in excellent sugar control PRIOR to becoming pregnant, there will not be an increased risk for miscarriages or birth defects in the baby.

✔ If in poor sugar control, particularly in the early part of pregnancy, the baby will be at increased risk for birth defects.

✔ The pregnancy must be carefully planned and should be undertaken only after the HbA_{1c} has been in the "excellent" range for several months. This is an excellent time to use an insulin pump.

✔ The mother does not generally risk worsening of kidney damage during the pregnancy (in contrast to the Hollywood production of "Steel Magnolias"). This is particularly true if kidney damage is not a problem prior to the pregnancy.

✔ Eye (retinal) changes do sometimes worsen during pregnancy and it is important to see the eye doctor more frequently at this time.

✔ It is wise for a woman with diabetes to consult with a doctor who specializes in diabetic pregnancies before and during her planned pregnancy.

- Research has shown that there is no increased risk for teenage girls with diabetes to use birth control pills compared with non-diabetic teenage girls using birth control pills.

- The only sure way to absolutely prevent a sexually transmitted disease or pregnancy is to abstain from sex. If the teen chooses to have sex, a condom should always be used (even if other methods are already being used). The use of condoms can help prevent sexually transmitted diseases and AIDS, although they do not guarantee absolute protection.

- **If a male or female believes they cannot cause or become pregnant due to diabetes, they are absolutely wrong. People with diabetes can cause a pregnancy or become pregnant just like anyone else.**

- The stress of the teen years may be heightened by conflicts about emerging sexuality.

F. CONSISTENCY (EXERCISE, EATING, EMOTIONS AND LIFESTYLE)

The word CONSISTENCY is in capital letters throughout Chapter 12, "Food Management and Diabetes." If everything could be the same every day, blood glucose control would be much easier. Unfortunately, there is no such thing as consistency in many teenagers' lives. Bedtime may be at 10:00 p.m. on school nights but then at midnight or later on Friday and Saturday nights. Many teens like to sleep late on weekends. We suggest an absolute limit of 9:00 a.m. as the time when the insulin must be taken with at least a glass of juice. The teenager can then go back to sleep for an hour. If the teen sleeps later than 9:00 a.m. without juice or food intake, the insulin taken the previous evening may lead to hypoglycemia. Likewise, taking the insulin later than usual results in overlap with the evening insulin and a greater likelihood of low blood sugar. Once again, supportive adults must be available to make this plan work. For teens using an insulin pump, assuming basals are correctly set (and no alcohol intake), it is possible to sleep in and have more flexibility. The use of Lantus insulin may also be beneficial.

Consistent exercise is often a problem. Seasonal sports, such as football or soccer, call for heavy exercise for a few months, but may be followed by weeks or months of little activity. Blood sugars will vary and the insulin dose and eating plan may need frequent adjustments for changes in activity level. It is good to have a "back-up" activity such as walking, jogging or aerobics so that there is some exercise every day. Daily exercise is also very effective in controlling weight. Some teens who use an insulin pump use one set of basals for exercise days and another set for days without exercise.

Tom is in his last year of high school and was recently diagnosed with diabetes. He feels confident that he can give his own injections and test his blood sugar. His greatest concern is that he enjoys sleeping in on weekends and that he no longer will be able to do this.

PLAN:

Tom's parents are very willing to help Tom with this problem. His dad, the early riser in the family, agrees to draw-up Tom's NPH insulin no later than 9:00 a.m. on weekends and to take the insulin and a glass of orange juice to Tom in bed. Tom can then wake up, take his shot, drink the juice and go back to sleep for another hour. Dad also agrees to wake Tom up at 10:00 a.m. so he can take his rapid-acting insulin and eat his breakfast.

G. DRIVING A CAR

Perhaps no new function in this age group requires more responsibility than the driving of a car. The teen's own life, as well as the lives of friends or total strangers, may be in the balance. The Center's new video* (made in 2001) on hypoglycemia emphasizes safety while driving. If food has not just been eaten, it is essential to do a blood sugar prior to driving. This is particularly true after a sports activity or exercising. It has been shown that driving with a low blood sugar results in greater impairment than driving when drunk. **FRIENDS DO NOT LET A FRIEND DRIVE WHEN LOW!**

If a person does feel low while driving, it is essential to pull over and have a snack. They should never assume they can "make it" home or to the nearest convenience store. The person should not resume driving until the blood sugar is back up. Snacks (a small can of juice, granola bar, etc.) should be kept in the glove compartment.

If an accident does occur as a result of a low blood sugar, most states suspend the driver's license for a year. This points out that teens need to be extra careful not to drive with a low blood sugar.

* The video is available through the Children's Diabetes Foundation (CDF) website shown inside the front cover of this book. The address for CDF is also on the backcover.

H. COLLEGE

Starting college is a challenge for anyone. It is even more so for the person with diabetes. Our Center has offered a "College Workshop" for the past twenty years. Students who have completed one or more years of college are the most helpful in preparing the pre-college students. The Children's Diabetes Foundation website has an educational section about college.

www.childrensdiabetesfdn.com/edu/college.html

Getting all the needed diabetes supplies together in addition to the usual packing is an extra chore.

Other important issues to remember or consider are:

✔ If the college student is to live in a dorm, getting the (meningococcal) meningitis vaccine is important.

✔ The flu shot is also advised.

✔ Hopefully hepatitis shots will have been given by the student's primary care physician.

✔ It is important to take emergency phone numbers.

✔ A copy of this book may be helpful with questions about sick-days or other diabetes-related problems.

✔ This book or the condensed version may also be helpful in educating a roommate about diabetes, especially about hypoglycemia.

✔ Make certain a roommate and/or dorm counselor can recognize and treat low blood sugars.

✔ Be aware of the usual high calorie/high fat cafeteria food, this may help prevent weight gain (often referred to as the "freshman 15").

✔ More frequent testing of blood sugars will help to make the transition safer.

I. CHANGES IN PSYCHE

Much of the above sections of this chapter are about changes in the psyche. However, a few other areas still need to be considered. Rapid mood swings are more common during adolescence. Mood swings may change the blood adrenaline level, affecting blood sugars. Adrenaline (epinephrine) causes the blood sugar to rise. In general, normal adolescent mood changes should not affect overall glucose control significantly. Adolescence is frequently an age when other conditions may emerge. Mood disorders (like clinical depression) and anxiety disorders are common, though they are often unrecognized conditions. If your teenager shows unusual changes which concern you, please talk with your healthcare team. (Also see Chapter 17 for discussions of depression and eating disorders.)

Such changes to watch for include:

✔ frequent irritability or anger

✔ a drop in grades or school performance

✔ loss of interest in activities that were previously enjoyable

✔ suspected substance abuse

✔ changes in sleep habits (unable to go to sleep or sleeping all the time), loss of appetite

✔ "hanging out" with a different group of friends or dropping friends all together

These may be symptomatic of an underlying mood disorder.

Teenagers' eating habits may be affected by their emotions. Teenagers are notorious for rather unusual eating habits and this poses a challenge for teens with diabetes who might not want to see themselves as "different."

Some teenagers develop mild to severe eating disorders:

✔ Anorexia: not eating

✔ Bulimia: binging on food and self-induced vomiting and/or use of laxatives

Parents should be suspicious of eating disorders if their teen overeats or doesn't exercise and still doesn't gain weight. Weight loss without dieting or heavy exercise should also alert the parents to possible missed injections.

More parental supervision and possibly professional help is then necessary. Stress is a normal part of life (e.g., arguments with friends, worrying about grades or concern about making a team). Learning to deal with stress is an important part of adolescence.

It should be apparent that the saying **"DIABETES IS A COMPROMISE"** fits particularly well with the teenage years. Consistency in areas that would benefit diabetes control sometimes needs to be compromised in helping a teenager to develop normally.

SUMMARY

The teen years are stressful for everyone. However, they can be the happiest years of an individual's life. The teen with diabetes has extra stresses, but with a supportive family, these can be managed. Diabetes is a partnership between the parents and the teenager. It is often important for parents to be patient and to remember that they, too, were once an adolescent. Parents must find ways to stay involved in the diabetes management, but not to be overbearing. Parents must be available to help and to be supportive but still let the teenager gain independence. The good news is **they do grow up**!

DEFINITIONS

Adolescence: The term given to the teenage years.

Adrenaline (epinephrine): The stress hormone made in the adrenal gland in the abdomen. It causes blood sugars to rise.

AIDS: Acquired Immune Deficiency Syndrome. This is a serious condition acquired by sexual contact with an infected person or by sharing needles with an infected person. If a mother has AIDS during pregnancy, she can also pass it on to her baby.

Estrogen: Female hormone made in the ovary (located in the abdomen) that causes female body changes.

Growth hormone: A hormone (like insulin) made in the pituitary gland at the base of the brain that is important for growth. It blocks the insulin activity.

Peers: One's group of friends.

Self-consciousness (body image): Concern about how oneself appears to others.

Sexually transmitted diseases (STDs): Diseases contracted through sexual contact, such as herpes, chlamydia, gonorrhea (clap) or syphilis.

Testosterone: A male hormone made in the testes that causes male body changes.

QUESTIONS (Q) AND ANSWERS (A) FROM NEWSNOTES

Q. My son is going to college this fall and has asked if you will write a letter requesting that he has a private room in the dormitory because of his diabetes. Is this a good idea?

A. I have been asked this question many times and have generally replied, "No." First, this is using the diabetes as an excuse when, in reality, the usual reason for wanting the private room has nothing to do with the diabetes. People of all ages should be discouraged from "using" their diabetes.

A second reason for saying "No" is that a roommate can be a very important asset. If a person has a bad reaction and is in a room alone, it may not be discovered as quickly. Likewise, if a person has the flu, the roommate may be the best person to fetch a bowl of soup from the cafeteria across the street, etc.

Finally, if the person is shy about giving shots or doing blood sugars in the presence of another person, it is time to get over that shyness. It is all part of the adjustment to life with diabetes.

Q. Are birth control pills okay to use for a college-aged student with diabetes? Is there an increased risk for cancer if they are used? What are the main side effects?

A. Initial research reported from our Center and published in the *Journal of the American Medical Association* in 1994 (271:1099) did not show any bad effects on the eyes or kidneys of women with diabetes who used oral contraceptives for a mean of 3.4 years (range: 1.0-7.0 years).

Remember that it is important to plan pregnancies very carefully when a woman has diabetes. If a pregnancy occurs when the HbA_{1c} is low (near the non-diabetic normal), the fetus has little or no increase in risk for birth defects from the mother's diabetes. However, if the HbA_{1c} is high, the baby has a high risk for birth defects (abnormalities of the spinal cord, heart, lips and palate and other organs). It is during the first 1-3 months of pregnancy when the vital organs are forming that excellent sugar control is critical to the fetus. Often, women do not even realize they are pregnant during this most crucial time. Therefore, the pill may be very important in allowing careful planning for a married couple who wants to plan the pregnancy around a time of excellent sugar control.

It must be remembered that much of the early research on the pill was done in the 1960s and 1970s when high-dose estrogen and progestin tablets were in use. The current pill has 1/3-1/4 the dose of the earlier pill. Also, women who smoked cigarettes were included in the early studies and it is now realized that smoking was a greater risk for some of the side effects being studied (e.g., blood clots) than was the pill. There is even evidence now to suggest that pill users may have a 20% reduction in risk for heart attacks.

In relation to cancer risk, the Food and Drug Administration (FDA) ruled that after evaluating 29 studies, they found no increased risk for breast cancer among pill users. In fact, epidemiological studies have shown the pill to help prevent ovarian and uterine cancer.

The main reasons women give for discontinuing the pill are acne, weight gain, no menses (amenorrhea) and breakthrough bleeding. In the clinic, we like to follow blood pressure, just to make sure it remains steady.

Q. Is it true that growth is reduced by poor sugar control?

A. Research published from our Center in 1995 (*Diabetic Medicine*, Vol. 12, 129-133) was one of the first studies to use longitudinal HbA_{1c} values to show that optimal growth is not reached if longitudinal HbA_{1c} values are not in a good range. In addition to the growth rate of the person with diabetes, the final adult height was compared to that of siblings, as well as the expected adult height based on the parents' heights. All were reduced in people with increased HbA_{1c} values. In contrast, growth was not altered in people who kept their HbA_{1c} values in a good range.

Q. Our teenage son has had a mildly elevated HbA_{1c} value (9%) over the past year. His physician and his mother and I have warned him about kidney failure and vision problems, but it doesn't seem to do any good. He currently receives Humalog and NPH insulin before breakfast and dinner. What would you suggest?

A. First, it has long been known that scare tactics do not work with teenagers. This is particularly true in the mid-teen period (15-17 years) when they are "invincible," which may in itself lead to risky behavior. If you want your son to change, you and his healthcare providers might start with "planting seeds." It might be suggested that a third shot each day, perhaps of Humalog using the insulin pen, would help at lunch or the afternoon snack. It is also sometimes helpful to switch the evening long-acting insulin (e.g., NPH) to bedtime and to just use the Humalog at dinner. Possibly changing to Lantus insulin would be beneficial. At first, he may resist. Continue to offer education but without the scare tactics. Eventually, he may be willing to try the third shot. Then praise him and offer support. Hopefully, this will help him to continue the positive action he has taken. It helps if he is able to feel a benefit (feeling better, less frequent voiding, etc.). However, he may not feel different. If growth picks up with the lower HbA_{1c} value, point this out to him. The lower HbA_{1c} value should also be a plus and give him positive feedback for this. Hopefully, the sum total will be such that he will want to continue with the new behavior (the third shot). This model for making change has many potential applications, both in diabetes-related change and in other areas.

Chapter 20

TOPICS:
❧ **Goal Setting and Problem Solving**
❧ **Monitoring (clinic visits and laboratory values)**

TEACHING OBJECTIVES:

1. Indicate the importance and frequency of clinic visits as related to positive diabetes outcomes.

2. Present the minimum standards of care for diabetes management.

LEARNER OBJECTIVES:

Learner (parents, child, relative or self) will be able to:

1. State the anticipated clinic visit schedule, relate its importance as well as necessary items to bring (meter, written materials [especially Pink Panther book] labs, etc.).

2. List three expected tasks in good diabetes management.

Chapter 20

OUTPATIENT MANAGEMENT, EDUCATION, SUPPORT GROUPS AND STANDARDS OF CARE

INTRODUCTION

The majority of new-onset treatment is now done in an outpatient setting. Some Health Maintenance Organizations (HMOs) are cooperative in funding outpatient care. Outpatient care is less traumatic for the person with diabetes and the family. It usually saves the HMO money compared with the cost of hospital treatment. It is now relatively rare to hospitalize people with known diabetes in the U.S. to "assess how they are doing." It is possible to have diabetes for over 20 years and never have a diabetes-related hospitalization.

This is a result of many factors, some of which are:

✔ age-appropriate education

✔ good family support

✔ regular clinic visits (every 3 months)

✔ close communication with the diabetes healthcare providers

✔ fulfilling the diabetes standards of care

TELEPHONE MANAGEMENT

Much of diabetes management can be done over the telephone, by fax or the e-mail message system. Some glucose meters can fax or e-mail glucose values. The extra equipment needed can be purchased from the meter company (see Appendix in Chapter 7).

The diabetes care provider should be called:

✔ prior to the next regularly scheduled injection if a severe hypoglycemic reaction has occurred

✔ if more than two mild reactions occurred within a short time

✔ anytime the urine ketones are moderate or large or blood ketones are > 0.6 mmol/L

People with diabetes should have checkups with the health team about every three months. This is the recommendation of the ADA Standards of Care. Some of these Standards of Care are included in this chapter.

At a clinic visit:

✔ the HbA$_{1c}$ can be done (Chapter 14). It reflects the number of high blood sugars for the past three months.

✔ insulin adjustments can be made

FAX MESSAGES

Most families now have access to a fax machine. The two blood sugar record sheets can be found in Chapter 7. They hold either one week or two weeks of blood sugar records. The sheets are an ideal size to send through a fax machine.

We ask that records be faxed anytime the family feels they need some help. We prefer faxes to phone calls to report blood sugar values. The fax saves time and confusion when trying to listen and write down values while on the phone.

If the parents do not have access to a fax machine, most schools (and especially the school nurse) will provide a way to fax in the blood sugars.

Some good reasons for faxing records are:

✔ if over half of blood sugar values at any time of day are **above** the upper level for age (see Chapter 7) and the person/family needs some suggestions

✔ if there are more than two values **below** 60 mg/dl (3.25 mmol/L) in one week

When families fax the records, please remember to:

✔ include the insulin dosages

✔ record the time of any symptomatic low blood sugars (even if it was not possible to do a blood sugar test) and include any relevant information relating to why lows occurred

✔ include the sender's fax and phone number and when that person can best be reached

These same forms can be downloaded from Chapter 7 to use when e-mailing records. The text of the book is on the Center's website. The web address is: http://www.barbaradaviscenter.org

It is only when records are kept that trends can be seen. Calling the healthcare provider **when** values are out of the target range is most helpful. Adjustments can then be made immediately. This prevents delaying any changes until the next clinic appointment.

CLINIC VISITS

When someone is attending our clinic for the first time, the visit usually takes a half to a whole day. Later visits will be shorter. Snacks should be brought to the appointment. Blood sugar records and meters must **ALWAYS** be brought along for the clinic visit. All meters we recommend have memories to store the last 100 to 250 blood sugar values and the ability to download the data upon arrival in the clinic. It is important to analyze this data at the time of the clinic visit.

Having a clinic visit every three months allows:

✔ a review of blood sugars: looking at both highs and lows

✔ changes in insulin dosage

✔ the HbA_{1c} test to be done

✔ growth to be followed

✔ a check for any problems

✔ continued education and introduction of new information/devices

In a clinic, the following people may be seen:

Clinic Nurse, Medical Assistant or Volunteer will:

✔ measure height and weight

✔ check the blood pressure

✔ check a blood sugar

✔ measure the hemoglobin A_{1c} (HbA_{1c})

✔ check for urine ketones and protein

✔ download blood glucose meters

Diabetes Nurse Educator will:

✔ continue the diabetes education

✔ introduce any new information and demonstrate devices available

✔ review diabetes management

The check-in person may wish to check the accuracy of your home meter with a meter in the clinic. The nurse may also wish to review the method for cleaning the meter or to check the control standard with you.

Doctor, Child Health Associate or Nurse Practitioner:

✔ checks to see how the person/family is doing with diabetes care goals

✔ may change insulin or oral medication doses

✔ does a physical examination

✔ coordinates the recommendations of all team members

Dietitian:

✔ reviews food intake and makes suggestions for changes if needed

✔ provides nutrition education and information about snacks and other food needs

Social Worker or Psychologist:

✔ assesses personal, family, school or other problems

✔ provides resource options for the individual or family

✔ monitors current family issues and their effect on diabetes management

It is also helpful to bring this educational book so that it can be used to review knowledge about diabetes.

EDUCATION, SUPPORT AND WORKING GROUPS

Some families gain extra support from meeting with other families who also have a family member with diabetes.

This meeting can happen at:

- the time of the clinic visits
- special group meetings
- special events: sports, picnics or Halloween parties

Additional education courses are important for families who do not live near a specialized diabetes clinic. These courses are important for people who were diagnosed at a young age and have reached an age when they are able to understand material they could not understand earlier.

Some of the additional education courses offered at our Center are:

✔ **Transition to Work and College Bound Workshop:** Offered as people become independent from their parents. A boost in knowledge at this time can be helpful in preventing later problems.

✔ **Grandparent's Workshop:** A one-day course. It is important that children with diabetes have the same relationships with grandparents as do other children (see Chapter 24). This likely involves staying with the grandparents. The workshop may also be useful for aunts and uncles, babysitters or others who are close to the child.

Grandparents wishing to have a child with diabetes stay with them need to know:

1. basic knowledge about drawing up insulin and giving shots

2. how to check blood sugars

3. how to treat hypoglycemia

The grandparents may feel more confident in caring for their grandchild with diabetes as a result of such a course.

✔ **Toddler Workshop (age 5 and under):** Every three months clinic visits are combined with a workshop for the parents of toddlers.

The workshop includes a noon luncheon with an educational presentation. The families have an opportunity to exchange ideas. The families often discover they have many of the same concerns.

STANDARDS OF MEDICAL CARE

Standards of medical care for people with type 1 and type 2 diabetes have been published by the American Diabetes Association. The standards are for both care providers and the people with diabetes.

These standards can be found in:

✔ *Diabetes Care* 25, Supplement 1, s33, Jan 2002

Knowing these standards will allow people with diabetes to:

- assess the quality of medical care they receive
- determine their role in their medical treatment
- compare their treatment outcomes to standard goals

The person and/or family must assume some of the responsibility for meeting the standards of care outlined below.

For example:

▼ if the family member with diabetes has reached puberty and has had diabetes for at least three years, annual eye and kidney evaluations are needed. The family must set up the eye evaluation with an ophthalmologist covered by their HMO.

▼ they need to help the family member do two timed overnight urine collections for the important microalbumin test for the kidneys (directions at end of Chapter 22).

Some of the American Diabetes Association's recommended standards of care with a few modifications are outlined below.

- Insulin-treated people should have clinic visits every three months.
- HbA_{1c} or a similar test should be done at least every three months.
- All people with diabetes must be taught a method of blood glucose testing.

- A comprehensive physical examination, including sexual maturation in adolescents, should be done **annually**.

- Parts of the physical exam affected by diabetes (e.g., height, weight, blood pressure, eyes, thyroid, liver size, deep tendon reflexes, injection sites, feet, etc.) should be checked **every three months**.

- People ≥10 years of age should have a dilated eye examination by an eye doctor within 3-5 years after the onset of diabetes. Screening for diabetic eye disease is NOT necessary before 10 years of age.

- Laboratory tests for microalbuminuria (Chapter 22) should be done annually in postpubertal people who have had diabetes for at least three years. People with type 2 diabetes should be checked initially and then annually.

- The occurrence of severe hypoglycemic episodes (episodes requiring the help of others [when not usually required], seizures or loss of consciousness) are serious and require the help of a diabetes specialist in preventing further episodes.

- The stress of illness frequently affects sugar control and necessitates more frequent monitoring of blood sugar and urine or blood ketones by the family. Medical help must be constantly available when moderate or large urine ketones or blood ketones > 0.6 mmol/L are detected.

- A lipid profile, including cholesterol, triglyceride, LDL and HDL should be performed at least every five years.

- High blood pressure (hypertension) and borderline elevations in blood pressure contribute to the development and progression of the chronic complications of diabetes. Elevations in blood pressure must be treated aggressively to achieve and maintain blood pressure in the normal range.

FOR PEOPLE WITH DIABETIC COMPLICATIONS

- Established diabetic eye disease requires care by an ophthalmologist experienced in the management of people with diabetes.

- The person with abnormal kidney function (proteinuria or elevated serum creatinine) requires heightened attention, control of other risk factors (e.g., hypertension and tobacco use) and consultation with a specialist in diabetic renal disease.

- People with cardiovascular risk factors should be carefully monitored. Evidence of cardiovascular disease (such as angina, decreased pulses and ECG abnormalities) requires efforts aimed at correction of contributing risk factors (e.g., obesity, use of tobacco, hypertension, sedentary lifestyle, hyperlipidemia and poorly regulated diabetes), in addition to specific treatment of the cardiovascular problem.

DEFINITIONS

ADA: American Diabetes Association.

Child Health Associate: A doctor's assistant who is trained to care for children.

Standards of Medical Care:
Recommendations made by an ADA panel for the minimum levels of care for people with type 1 diabetes as included and modified in this chapter.

QUESTIONS (Q) AND ANSWERS (A) FROM NEWSNOTES

Q. Why are regular clinic appointments necessary and how often should these be scheduled?

A. It is our belief that clinic appointments should be scheduled approximately every three months. This is also the recommended interval in the ADA "Standards of Medical Care." The reasons for this are primarily preventive since this is where the emphasis in healthcare now lies. In the early 1900s the emphasis on healthcare was in the treatment of acute problems. This has now switched to a more preventive based healthcare, particularly relating to chronic diseases.

For people with diabetes, the visits every three months allow continued education and increased motivation for doing day-to-day monitoring of the diabetes. It is the experience of our Clinic and of other large diabetes clinics in the U.S. that if regular visits do not occur, diabetes monitoring and knowledge become lax.

In addition, it is very important to check the eyes and perform the remainder of the physical examination at regular intervals. We have seen a case where an eye specialist actually photographed the back of the eye and found normal eye photographs; four months later diffuse eye hemorrhages were present. The earlier such eye problems are detected and treated, the greater the chance for saving vision. In addition, with children, growth should be occurring. Many physicians believe that good diabetes control is one of the best means of assuring good growth. We feel that every three months is a good interval for checking the gain in height and weight. Other parts of the physical exam, such as the thyroid size, liver size and the injection sites are also important to check at regular intervals. The liver can be enlarged if someone is receiving too much insulin (extra sugar is stored) or not enough insulin (extra fat is stored).

In summary, the best management occurs with the family and team working together. Although every three months seems to be an average best time to return to the clinic, there are obviously some situations where more frequent visits are important.

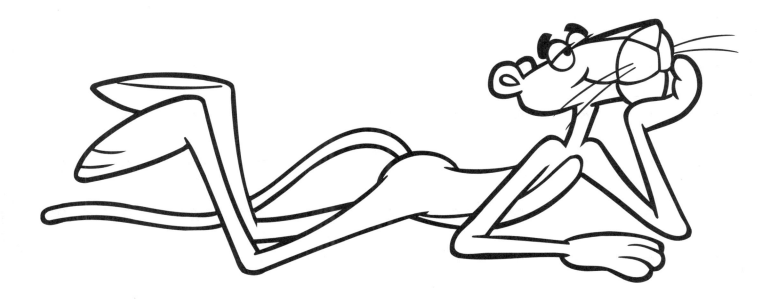

TOPICS:
* Medications
  (Insulin Adjustments)
* Monitoring

TEACHING OBJECTIVES:

1. Discuss when and how to adjust insulin doses.

2. Integrate factors which influence insulin dose into a "thinking" scale.

3. Demonstrate the application of dose adjustment to blood sugar trends.

LEARNING OBJECTIVES:

Learner (parent, child, relative or self) will be able to:

1. Describe when and how to increase or decrease insulin doses.

2. Explain insulin adjustments using blood sugar records.

3. List two factors which effect blood sugars and the appropriate insulin adjustments.

Chapter 21

ADJUSTING THE INSULIN DOSAGE, "THINKING" SCALES AND INSULIN "COCKTAILS"

BLOOD SUGAR GOALS (suggested ranges)

It is our general goal to have blood sugar levels in the ranges listed below (also see Chapter 7). These ranges are when no food has been eaten for at least two hours. They apply to fasting in the morning as well as for two hours after any meal or snack.

Under 5 years of age
= 80-200 mg/dl (4.5-11.1 mmol/L)

5-11 years of age
= 70-180 mg/dl (3.9-10.0 mmol/L)

12 years and above
= 70-150 mg/dl (3.9-8.3 mmol/L)

A person who has difficulty recognizing low blood sugars or who has severe insulin reactions may be asked to keep the blood sugar at a slightly higher level. Families and the diabetes care provider should discuss the desired range. This range should be written down for future reference. It is important to remember that this is a target goal. **If at least 50% of the sugar values are in the target range at each time of day, the HbA$_{1c}$ level will usually be good**. Not all blood sugar values will be in the target range. The exception to this is during the "honeymoon" period shortly after diagnosis. If more than half of the values are in range and the HbA$_{1c}$ is still high, blood sugars at other times of the day should be done. Chapter 7 gives suggestions for other times – including two hours after meals.

After 6-12 months of dealing with diabetes, many families and older teens begin making some of their own insulin adjustments. This should be discussed with the diabetes care provider at a clinic visit. If the decision is mutually agreeable, guidelines for insulin adjustments should be discussed.

ADJUSTING THE INSULIN DOSAGE

The first step in learning to adjust insulin is to know the times of action of the insulins used. Refer to the figures in Chapter 8 and Table 1 in this chapter to review the times of action of various insulins.

Changes in insulin dosage are best considered under four categories:

A. Reducing the Insulin Dose

B. Increasing the Insulin Dose

C. Insulin Adjustments for Food and Correction Factor

D. Insulin Adjustments for People Receiving Lantus Insulin

A. <u>Reducing the Insulin Dose</u> (TO PREVENT LOW BLOOD SUGARS)

❦ **Responding to trends in the blood sugar levels**

Reducing a specific insulin dose should be done if:

✔ blood sugars are below the suggested ranges two or more days in a row at the same time of day (see Table 1)

✔ blood sugar values are below 60 mg/dl (3.3 mmol/L), which we consider is the level of true hypoglycemia, or below 70 mg/dl (3.9 mmol/L) in a preschooler

✔ all blood sugars in a day are below the desired lower limit. The insulin dose should be reduced with the next injection.

We do not know why blood sugars will suddenly be low for a day or longer in a person who has been stable. Most often this is due to increased physical activity, eating less food or opening new bottles of insulin. Also, current

THE FOUR TIME PERIODS OF INSULIN ACTIVITY FOR PEOPLE RECEIVING TWO SHOTS PER DAY

Period **1**: a.m.   Humalog/NovoLog and/or Regular   Works primarily from breakfast (**B**) to lunch (**L**)

Period **2**: a.m.   NPH or Lente   Works primarily from lunch to dinner (**D**)

Period **3**: p.m.   Humalog/NovoLog and/or Regular   Works primarily from dinner to bedtime (**BT**)

Period **4**: p.m.   NPH, Ultralente, Lantus   Works primarily from bedtime to the following morning (or longer)

Period:

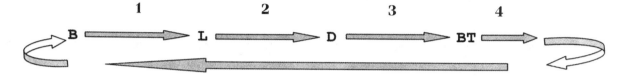

intermediate-acting insulins such as NPH, Lente and Ultralente have variable absorption from day-to-day.

How much the insulin is reduced depends on the age and size of the person and the dose being given. Sometimes all that is needed is to omit or reduce the short-acting (Humalog/NovoLog or Regular) insulin for a few days.

When are the low values occurring?

✔ If the low values occur before dinner, the morning NPH or Lente insulin can be reduced by one or two units.

✔ If the reactions are in the early morning hours, the evening NPH, Lente, Ultralente or Lantus can be reduced by one or two units.

✔ If the values are still low the next day, reduce the insulin again.

Think about what time of the day the reactions are occurring and which insulin is having its main action at that time of day. Reduce the insulin that is working at that time by one or two units.

Sometimes the values are high the day after the insulin dose is reduced. This is because the insulin-balancing hormones may require a day or two to adjust. It is important to be

patient when a dose is reduced, and **DO NOT GO BACK UP ON THE DOSE** just because blood sugars are a bit higher. Wait a few days to let the balancing hormones re-adjust before deciding to go back up on the dose. Remember that even though we suggest waiting a few days to make further changes if the blood sugar is high, this is NOT necessary if it is low. **It is OK to make a further reduction the next day if values are still low.**

Thinking ahead to prevent lows (reactions)

Although discussed in more detail in Chapter 6, families need to **"think ahead" to prevent lows.** Consider reducing the insulin dosage during days of high excitement and activity or when eating less. **When children stay overnight at a friend's house (or have a friend spend the night)** there is often an increase in activity and less sleep. More energy is expended, and it is wise to reduce the p.m. insulin dose.

The following can all lead to low blood sugars:

✔ school trips and field days

✔ family picnics and playing with cousins

✔ long hikes or bike trips

✔ spending the night with a friend

✔ vacations to places like Disneyland® or the beach

✔ deciding to begin a diet

✔ when school is out and the weather is nice, children will play outside after dinner. The evening Humalog/NovoLog and/or Regular insulins almost always have to be reduced.

✔ getting cold when playing outside in cold weather (not wearing enough warm clothing)

Temporary reductions in dosage of insulins acting at the time of activity or excitement can help to prevent problems. If there are questions about reducing the insulin dosage, call the diabetes care provider during office phone hours. (Save home calls and pager calls for emergencies.) **Remember it is generally best to err on the safe side.** Alterations in the insulin dose for sick-day and surgery management are discussed in Chapter 16, Sick-day and Surgery Management.

Responding to severe insulin reactions

If a severe insulin reaction occurs, it is important to call the diabetes healthcare provider before giving the next scheduled insulin shot. The stores of balancing hormones (e.g., adrenaline) are reduced with a severe reaction and there is a greater risk for more reactions. The insulin dose should be reduced temporarily. It is important to prevent a severe reaction from occurring again. Sometimes it is helpful to schedule a clinic appointment to discuss this.

B. Increasing the Insulin Dose (TO TREAT HIGH BLOOD SUGARS)

Understanding why more insulin is required

An insulin dose may need to be increased:

✔ if the blood sugars have been above the desired range for three or four days in a row and there is not an obvious illness or stress that will soon go away

✔ when children grow, their insulin needs generally increase by one unit for every two pounds gained. Also, when growth hormone levels increase, insulin activity is blocked.

✔ because in some people their own pancreas gradually makes less insulin

✔ in the winter when many people exercise less and their insulin needs increase

✔ during times of high stress or during menses (menstrual period)

✔ if HbA_{1c} values are high (reflecting blood sugars over the past three months)

✔ during an illness, there may be a temporary need for more insulin (especially if ketones are present). This is discussed in Chapter 16, Sick-day and Surgery Management.

Resistance to increasing the insulin dose

Some people resist increasing the insulin dose. When blood sugars have been running high, the person's body becomes accustomed to higher levels. They may feel uncomfortable at lower blood sugar levels. This unpleasant feeling lasts for a short period and will gradually disappear. Also, the most frequent fear of people with diabetes (and their family members) is of low blood sugars. This is particularly true if severe reactions have occurred. People may resist (sometimes subconsciously) increasing the dose and lowering the blood sugars. An increase in the dose may mean a loss of further insulin production in the eyes of some families. This can seem like a time of additional loss. Working with a counselor may help some families.

Knowing which insulin to increase

It is essential to know the times of action of the insulins and the desired ranges for the blood sugars. The four time periods of insulin activity shown in Table 1 are obviously the same when increasing the dose. *Thus, when the blood sugars are above the desired range for three to seven days with no obvious cause, insulin is increased if:*

✔ the sugars are high before lunch, increase the morning Humalog/NovoLog and/or Regular insulin

✔ the sugars are high before dinner, increase the morning NPH and/or Lente

✔ the sugars are high before the bedtime snack, increase the dinner Humalog/NovoLog and/or Regular insulin

✔ the sugars are high before breakfast, increase the dinner (or bedtime) NPH, Lente, Ultralente or Lantus (see Table 2)

The increases are usually by a half unit for a preschooler or by a unit for an older child or adult. The blood sugars will tend to run lower on the first day of increased insulin. It may be helpful for the family and care provider to fill out Table 2 together.

The dose may need to be increased again as the balancing hormones adjust. Extra snacks on the first day of an increased dose are often wise. We often suggest a slice of pizza at bedtime on the first night if increasing the insulin working during the night. If the blood sugars are still above the desired range after three to seven days, repeat the increase again. **Continue this program until at least half of the blood sugars at the time of day being worked on are in the desired range.** A general rule is to increase the dosage slowly. If you are not sure whether to make further increases in the insulin dose, fax or mail the blood sugars. You can also call to discuss changes with your diabetes care provider. Faxing or mailing in the blood sugar values allows the diabetes care provider time to review and think about recommendations. It saves the need for copying values over the phone. Sample fax sheets are included in Chapter 7. This reporting should be done during office phone hours. Save home calls and pager calls for emergencies.

ADJUSTING INSULIN DOSES

Desired range for blood sugars _____ *to* _____ .

PATTERN TO FOLLOW FOR CHANGING INSULIN DOSE

Blood sugar levels

If *HIGH* for 3-5 days

Time of Day	Insulin to Increase	How Much
• before breakfast	dinner or bedtime NPH, Lente, Ultralente, Lantus	by _____ unit(s)
• before lunch	morning Humalog/NovoLog or Regular	by _____ unit(s)
• before dinner	morning NPH, Lente, Ultralente, Lantus	by _____ unit(s)
• before bedtime	dinner Humalog/NovoLog or Regular	by _____ unit(s)

NOTE: Most people wait 3 days between increases in doses.

- -

If *LOW* for 1 or 2 days

Time of Day	Insulin to Decrease	How Much
• before breakfast	dinner or bedtime NPH, Lente, Ultralente, Lantus	by _____ unit(s)
• before lunch	morning Humalog/NovoLog or Regular	by _____ unit(s)
• before dinner	morning NPH, Lente, Ultralente, Lantus	by _____ unit(s)
• before bedtime	dinner Humalog/NovoLog or Regular	by _____ unit(s)

NOTE: If still low after decreasing the dose, making another decrease the next day is fine.

C. Insulin Adjustments for Food and Correction Factor

When choosing a dose of short-acting insulin, thinking about the blood sugar level and the food to be eaten is always important. To make dose decisions a bit easier, many families and care providers choose a **correction factor** which can be added to the insulin dose to cover carbohydrate eaten (if they are carb-counting). The **correction factor** refers to the units of insulin needed to correct a blood sugar level. The goal is to return the blood sugar level into the desired range. A correction factor is generally used when Humalog/NovoLog has not been given within the previous two hours. The most common correction dose is one unit of Humalog/NovoLog per 50 mg/dl (2.7 mmol/L) of glucose above 150 mg/dl (8.3 mmol/L). However, every person is different. A preschooler may do better with one unit per 100 mg/dl (5.5 mmol/L) above 200 mg/dl (11.1 mmol/L). The person or family will need to find out what works. It is a helpful way to get the blood sugar back on track.

If food is to be eaten at the time of doing the correction (e.g., time for lunch or afternoon snack), the insulin to cover the food can be added to the correction dose. For example in Table 3, if a person planned to eat three carb choices (45 gms of carbohydrate), the dose of short-acting insulin would be 3 units. If their blood sugar was 250 mg/dl (13.9 mmol/L), the correction factor would be 2 units. The total dose to be taken would be 5 units (3 units + 2 units). If no food were to be eaten, then the dose to be taken would just be the 2 unit correction factor.

If the correction dose is to be given after an exercise induced high sugar, it should be reduced by half. (Delayed hypoglycemia may follow as adrenaline levels decrease and sugar goes back into muscle – see Chapter 13.) Also, if a correction is to be done at bedtime, many people use half of the usual dose. Prevention of lows during the night is important.

EXAMPLE OF INSULIN ADJUSTMENTS

Blood Sugar mg/dl	mmol/L	Correction Factor* Units of Insulin	Carb Choices** (15 gm carb)	Total Units of Insulin
≤ 150	8.3	0	1	1
200	11.1	1	2	3
250	13.9	2	3	5
300	16.7	3	4	7
350	19.4	4	5	9

* Assuming a correction factor of 1 unit of short-acting insulin per 50 mg (2.8 mmol/L) above 150 mg/dl (8.3 mmol/L).

** One Carb choice = 15 gm carbohydrate. In this example, 1 unit of insulin is given for each 15 gm carb choice.

D. Insulin Adjustments for Lantus Insulin

In **Chapter 8** you can find:

✔ The four most common ways we currently use Lantus insulin.

✔ A method to determine the starting Lantus dose.

✔ An example for Lantus given at dinner or in the evening (Figure 1). The dose of Lantus is increased or decreased until most of the morning blood sugars are in the desired ranges.

These ranges are:

Under 5 years of age
    = 80-200 mg/dl (4.5-11.1 mmol/L)

5-11 years of age
    = 70-180 mg/dl (3.9-10.0 mmol/L)

12 years and above
    = 70-150 mg/dl (3.9-8.3 mmol/L)

Most people will adjust up or down by one or two units of Lantus insulin (or one-half unit for toddlers) every two or three days until morning values are in the ranges listed above.

As stated in Chapter 8, Figure 1, we often use a mixture of Humalog/NovoLog and NPH in the morning. The Humalog/NovoLog dose may be the same dose as previously used. The NPH dose is about one-third the previous intermediate-acting insulin dose that had been given in the morning. The amount of NPH is adjusted up or down until the sugar levels at dinnertime are mostly within the ranges listed above. Table 4 provides an algorithm that may be helpful in adjusting insulin dosages.

Humalog/NovoLog dosages for meals are best adjusted by measuring blood sugar levels two hours after the meal. The same sugar levels given above can also apply for the desired values two hours after eating. If the values are not in the desired range for age group, two hours after eating, the "thinking scale" or the Insulin to Carbohydrate (**I/C**) ratio will need to be changed. If the blood sugar value is high, the grams of carbohydrate in the **I/C** ratio will need to be lowered. An example would be to change from 1:15 (1 unit/15 gm carbohydrate) to 1:10 (1 unit/10 gm carbohydrate). If the sugar level is below the lower limit, a higher amount of carbohydrate is needed. An

example would be to change from a ratio of 1:15 (1 unit/15 gm carbohydrate) to 1:30 (1 unit/30 gm carbohydrate). Call your healthcare provider if you need help.

Snacks are often not necessary with Lantus insulin. However, if the blood sugar is below 150 mg/dl (8.3 mmol/L) at bedtime, it is usually wise to have a bedtime snack. When having more than 15 gm of carbohydrate at bedtime, Humlog/NovoLog may be necessary.

"THINKING" SCALES (AND REPLACING THE TERM "SLIDING" SCALES)

It is important to emphasize that "sliding" scales are really "thinking" scales. They give the person or family ranges of Humalog/NovoLog and/or Regular insulin to "think about." **The blood sugar level SHOULD NEVER be the only factor considered. Food intake and both recent and expected exercise also need to be considered with every shot.** An example would be a five-year-old going out to play with friends after dinner in the summer. Even if the blood sugar was 200 mg/dl (11.1 mmol/L) before dinner, it would be wise to reduce (or omit) the evening dose of short-acting insulin. This would also apply if mom (or dad) were making tuna noodle casserole for dinner, and they knew that the five-year-old disliked tuna noodle casserole. **Sliding scales require careful thinking prior to giving each insulin shot, and it is better to call them "thinking" scales.** Thinking scales for different aged children are often based on whether they are still quite sensitive to short-acting insulin or not as sensitive. Possible scales should be discussed with your diabetes care provider.

Many families adjust Humalog/NovoLog and/or Regular (not NPH or Lente) insulin dosages with every injection. *They use a thinking scale in which the amount of short-acting insulin given is based on:*

1. **the blood sugar level**

2. **the expected food intake**

3. **both recent and expected exercise**

ALGORITHM FOR ADJUSTING LANTUS INSULIN REGIMENS

Table 4

1. Lantus dose:

When using <u>only</u> Lantus insulin, determine the dose based on the pre-breakfast blood sugar (examples 1-3, page 67 and example 4 for the p.m. Lantus dose)

*(morning blood sugar goal = 70-180 mg/dl [3.9-10 mmol/L]) ***

If morning blood sugar value is:
- 60-70 mg/dl (3.3-3.9 mmol/L) = decrease the dose by one unit ⎫ daily changes
- <60 mg/dl (<3.3 mmol/L) = decrease the dose by two units ⎭ can be made

- 180-240 mg/dl (10-13.3 mmol/L) = increase the dose by one unit ⎫ wait 2-3 days
- >240 mg/dl (>13.3 mmol/L) = increase the dose by two units ⎭ between changes

2. Using an **a.m. NPH** dose as in example 2, page 67

(afternoon or dinner blood sugar goal = 70-180 mg/dl [3.9-10 mmol/L])

If afternoon blood sugar value is:
- 60-70 mg/dl (3.3-3.9 mmol/L) = decrease **a.m.** NPH dose by one unit ⎫ daily changes
- <60 mg/dl (<3.3 mmol/L) = decrease **a.m.** NPH dose by two units ⎭ can be made

- 180-240 mg/dl (10-13.3 mmol/L) = increase **a.m.** NPH dose by one unit ⎫ wait 2-3 days
- >240 mg/dl (>13.3 mmol/L) = increase **a.m.** NPH dose by two units ⎭ between changes

3. Humalog or **NovoLog**

(2 hours after a meal blood sugar goal = 70-180 mg/dl [3.9-10 mmol/L])

If blood sugar value 2 hours after the meal is:
- 60-70 mg/dl (3.3-3.9 mmol/L) = decrease the insulin dose <u>prior</u> to the meal by at least one unit **
- <60 mg/dl (<3.3 mmol/L) = decrease the insulin dose <u>prior</u> to the meal by at least two units **
    Daily changes can be made for the two blood sugar levels listed above.

- 180-240 mg/dl (10-13.3 mmol/L) = increase the insulin dose prior to the meal by one unit
- >240 mg/dl (>13.3 mmol/L) = increase the insulin dose prior to the meal by two units
    Wait 2-3 days between changes for these high blood sugar levels.

*For teens and adults, the healthcare provider may wish the blood sugar goal to be 70-150 mg/dl (3.9-8.3 mmol/L) rather than 70-180 mg/dl (3.9-10 mmol/L).

**If carb counting, subtract or add these amounts, but it may be necessary to talk with the dietitian to change the I/C ratio.

Call your health care provider if you have questions.

The range of insulin is usually preset by the family and the diabetes care provider working together. The insulin scale can be written down in Table 5. Thinking scales are particularly helpful when parents alternate giving injections and desire a pattern that both can follow. If the blood sugar is low, the amount is decreased. In contrast, the dose is increased for higher blood sugars, if less exercise is expected or if a large meal is to be eaten. Smaller children obviously have lower dosages than larger children. Children in the first year after diagnosis (who make more of their own insulin) are usually more sensitive to short-acting insulins and will have lower dosages.

Many families now use **carbohydrate counting** (see Chapter 12) as the method to determine insulin dosage for food to be eaten. They must still consider the blood sugar level.

Examples are:

✔ subtracting one or two units if the value is below 70 mg/dl (3.9 mmol/L)

✔ adding one or two units if the value is above 180 mg/dl (10.0 mmol/L)

✔ giving the insulin after the meal, allowing the insulin dose to be based on the carbs actually eaten

Additional short-acting insulin can be added to this meal dose. The amount added should take into consideration the current blood sugar and any planned activity. If gym occurs one to two hours after the morning shot, one or two units of short-acting insulin might be subtracted. If it is raining on a summer evening and exercise is to be less, one or two extra units of the short-acting insulin might be given. Even if a family is using carbohydrate counting to determine insulin for food intake, they must use thinking scales. Giving insulin after the meal provides a more accurate way to choose an insulin dose based on actual food eaten.

One advantage of thinking scales is that the blood sugar level must always be measured if the scale is to be used. Sometimes one scale is used for the morning and a different scale for the evening. As indicated in Table 5, it may even be necessary to use one scale for an active day and a different scale for a quiet day.

It is important to remember that thinking scales are not "written in stone." A scale that works fine for a few months may have to be altered if the blood sugars are not in the desired range. Always bring the scale along to clinic visits so the dose can be reviewed with the diabetes care provider. Also, write down the dose of insulin given in each shot on the blood sugar record sheet (see Chapter 7). This makes it possible for you and the diabetes care provider to more easily review dosages and how the scales being used are working.

 ## SUGGESTED "THINKING" SCALE FOR HUMALOG/NOVOLOG (H/NL) OR REGULAR (R) INSULIN DOSAGE

| Blood Sugar Level | Morning H/NL/R | | Afternoon H/NL/R | | Dinner H/NL/R | |
	Active (or not eating much)	Not active (eating normally)	Active (or not eating much)	Not active (eating normally)	Active (or not eating much)	Not active (eating normally)
___ =	___	___	___	___	___	___
___ =	___	___	___	___	___	___
___ =	___	___	___	___	___	___
___ =	___	___	___	___	___	___
___ =	___	___	___	___	___	___
___ =	___	___	___	___	___	___

NOTE: *This table does not apply to sick-day management (See Chapter 16). Call your diabetes care provider AFTER CHECKING THE BLOOD SUGAR AND KETONES if you have questions. Scales may also be used for short-acting insulin dosages given at other times during the day. Copy this table as often as you wish.*

INSULIN "COCKTAILS"

This is a term applied to mixtures of three or more insulins in the same syringe. A cocktail is often Humalog/NovoLog and Regular insulins and an intermediate-acting insulin (NPH, Lente or Ultralente). As noted in Chapter 8, it is fine to mix the Humalog/NovoLog and the Regular insulins. Either can be drawn into the syringe first. Both should be in the syringe prior to drawing the intermediate-acting insulin into the syringe. It should be remembered that the NPH insulin delays the activity of Humalog/NovoLog slightly (but not of Regular). Lente and Ultralente delay the action of Regular insulin slightly (but not of Humalog/NovoLog). The advantage of using a mixture of Humalog/NovoLog and Regular is there is an immediate effect from the Humalog/NovoLog. This is especially good when eating right after the shot or if the blood sugar is high. There is also a later effect from the Regular. This is often important for school children in the morning to cover lunch as Humalog/NovoLog activity is mostly gone after four hours.

The adjustments in the insulin cocktails require extra "thinking." *For example, a lower dose of Humalog/NovoLog and more Regular insulin should be used if:*

🐾 the blood sugar level is on the low side

🐾 not much is going to be eaten or was eaten (e.g., a teenager rushing to school in the a.m.)

🐾 there is to be heavy exercise in the hour after the meal

In contrast, a higher dose of Humalog/NovoLog and a lower dose of Regular might be used if:

🐾 the blood sugar level is high

🐾 there is to be exercise in three or four hours (but not in 1-2 hours)

🐾 a big meal is to be eaten

This really does require "thinking." Remember that two heads are better than one - particularly early in the morning. An example of an "insulin cocktail" for a 15-year-old boy receiving 6-8 units of short-acting insulin is shown in Table 6. Note that when the blood sugar is low (less than 60 mg/dl [3.25 mmol/L] for some, or less than 100 mg/dl [5.5 mmol/L] for others), it might be better to wait to give the shot **after the meal** if Humalog/NovoLog is to be given.

INSULIN COCKTAILS (COMBINING 2 SHORT-ACTING INSULINS)

Units of Humalog/NovoLog (H/NL) and of Regular (R) Insulins

Blood Sugar		Not eating much or exercising in next hour		Eating now and not exercising in next hour	
mg/dl	mmol/L	H/NL	R	H/NL	R
<100	<5.5	0	6	2*	2
100-200	5.5-11.1	2	4	4	4
>200	>11.1	4	4	6	2

* Might best be given after eating

We encourage families to try to think about food intake and exercise (as in the example above). As Humalog/NovoLog peaks earlier than Regular insulin, different ratios may work better for different days.

The mixing of three or more insulins (an insulin "cocktail") can also refer to the mixing of a short-acting insulin with two long-acting insulins in the same syringe.

Two examples are:

- A child who receives Humalog/NovoLog and NPH insulins in the morning, and whose parent arrives home late (so that supper will be delayed), may need to add Ultralente (a longer-acting insulin) to the morning NPH insulin.

- When puberty comes and growth hormone levels are high from 4-9 a.m. (the "dawn phenomenon"), a child who was previously well controlled on Humalog/NovoLog and Ultralente insulin at dinner may now do better with adding a bit of NPH insulin to the evening Humalog/NovoLog and Ultralente insulins.

The current "extreme cocktail" is one in which four insulins are mixed in the same syringe. This might be Humalog/NovoLog, Regular, NPH and Ultralente insulins. Obviously, keeping the dosages and insulins accurate is essential and, once again, "two heads are better than one."

SUMMARY

In summary, it is important for families to consistently look at blood sugar levels. They then need to make insulin adjustments to obtain or maintain optimal diabetes control. **Keeping a blood sugar and insulin dose log (record) will allow the family to see patterns to make the insulin adjustments.** It is most frustrating when high blood sugars are obtained week after week and no adjustments are made. If a family is uncertain whether changes in insulin need to be made, fax or mail the blood sugar values and insulin dosages to the diabetes care provider to get help. Remember to bring your log book to the clinic visit. We have heard every possible excuse ("My dog ate them," "I left it at home"). Needless to say, we don't believe any of them. As a compromise, consider using the log book for 1-2 weeks out of the month. Another helpful time would be if exercise or schedules change. This will help you know when you need assistance with insulin adjustments.

DEFINITIONS

Correction factor: Use of a set amount of insulin to correct the blood sugar into the desired range. The most common example is giving one unit of Humalog/NovoLog insulin for every 50 mg/dl (2.7 mmol/L) above 150 mg/dl (8.3 mmol/L) blood sugar level.

Extreme cocktail: The mixing of four or more insulins in the same syringe.

Insulin cocktail: The mixing of three or more insulins in the same syringe.

Sliding scale: Altering the insulin dose based on the blood sugar levels.

Thinking scale: Altering the insulin dose considering factors other than just blood sugar levels. The other factors might include: food amount, exercise, stress, illness and menses.

QUESTIONS (Q) AND ANSWERS (A) FROM NEWSNOTES

Q. What is meant by "sliding" scales for insulin adjustments and who should use them?

A. "Sliding" scales generally refer to giving different dosages of Humalog/NovoLog or Regular insulin depending on the level of blood sugar. They should not be used for the intermediate-acting or long-acting insulins (usually NPH, Ultralente, Lente or Lantus). We prefer the term **"thinking"** **scale** to emphasize that the blood sugar level, food intake and exercise must all be considered before each insulin dose is chosen. On some occasions, illness, stress and menses must also be considered. The diabetes care provider should discuss the "thinking" scale for the dose of short-acting insulin individually for each person. Some people are still making their own insulin and will need less short-acting insulin, particularly at younger ages; see below.

Both of these scales would then need to be adjusted after "thinking" about food intake, exercise, stress, illness or other factors. Some people even need a different scale for their morning compared with their evening dosage of short-acting insulin. It should always be remembered that the scale may have to be reduced if heavy exercise has just been done or is about to be done. There is no good substitute for thinking and reasoning! If you do at least three blood sugar tests per day and want to try a thinking scale, you should discuss this with your diabetes care provider.

Q. Do the needs for insulin change with the seasons?

A. The short answer is "yes." To illustrate this, think of summer camp. Nearly every person going to camp has their routine dose of insulin substantially reduced because of all the extra activity. To a lesser degree this happens in spring - over a week or two the snow suddenly disappears, the sunshine appears and children are out playing, bicycling, etc. With the increased activity, low blood sugars are more likely. Snacks may have to be adjusted and/or insulin doses may need to be lowered.

In contrast, the opposite happens with going back to school in the fall, especially for those going to new schools. This may be a time of extra stress as well as reduced activity. Activity is decreased with the evening homework. Blood sugars may go up and insulin doses may need to be raised.

A four-year-old diagnosed at age three might do fine with a thinking scale of:

Blood Sugar mg/dl	mmol/L	Units of Humalog/NovoLog or Regular Insulin
<100	<5.5	0
100-200	5.5-11.1	1
201-300	11.2-16	2
>300	>16.6	3

A 16 year-old who developed diabetes at age three might have an entirely different scale:

Blood Sugar mg/dl	mmol/L	Units of Humalog/NovoLog or Regular Insulin
<70	<3.9	2
70-150	3.9-8.3	4
151-200	8.4-11.1	6
>200	>11.1	8

Chapter 22

TOPICS:
- Prevent, Detect and Treat Chronic Complications Through Risk Reduction
- Monitoring (Complications and Associated Diseases)

TEACHING OBJECTIVES:

1. Discuss the relationship between glucose control and diabetic complications (eye, kidney, nerve).

2. Summarize the tests, which monitor eye and kidney complications.

3. Present associated autoimmune diseases (e.g., thyroid and celiac).

LEARNER OBJECTIVES:

Learner (parents, child, relative or self) will be able to:

1. Describe the relationship between glucose control and complications.

2. Identify routine tests used to monitor the eyes and kidneys.

3. List one symptom associated with each disease (thyroid and celiac).

Chapter 22

LONG-TERM COMPLICATIONS OF DIABETES

INTRODUCTION

In addition to the acute complications of diabetes, insulin reactions and acidosis, there are also problems known as "long-term" complications. Generally, the long-term complications occur in people who have had diabetes and high blood sugar levels for many years.

About this chapter:

🐾 Many families may prefer to read this chapter when they are ready to deal with the subject.

🐾 Teenagers may be able to understand the material better than pre-teens.

🐾 Many new and difficult words are used in this chapter. They are introduced and defined in the back. If your diabetes care provider uses them you will have a place to find their meaning.

The three most common parts of the body to be effected by high sugar levels are:

1. **Eyes (retinopathy)**

2. **Kidneys (nephropathy)**

3. **Nerves (neuropathy)**

Two other areas, which can be effected by high sugar levels are:

4. **Joints (finger curvatures)**

5. **Children born to mothers with poorly controlled diabetes (birth defects)**

THE DCCT

The Diabetes Control and Complications Trial (DCCT) has been mentioned previously in this book (Chapter 14). The results of this study became available in 1993 and proved without question that **the eye, kidney and nerve problems of type 1 diabetes were**

decreased in people ages 13-39 years whose blood sugars were kept closer to normal.

For people with type 2 diabetes, studies in the U.K. and Japan showed the risks for eye, kidney and nerve complication were reduced as a result of better sugar control.

Some important factors which effect the complications:

✔ **good blood sugar control:** Although this is one important factor in relation to these three complications, **IT IS NOT THE ONLY FACTOR**

✔ **blood pressure** is important in relation to both the eye and the kidney complications

✔ **tobacco use** adds to the risk for kidney and eye damage

✔ **increased blood clotting** is also a possible risk factor

✔ **other unknown factors**

Some facts about the occurrence of complications:

✔ Most of the long-term complications do not occur in young children.

✔ The years of greatest risk for complications seem to start after puberty. Research has shown that in people with diabetes, the small blood vessels show no changes before puberty, whether good sugar control was present or not.

✔ After puberty, the blood vessels usually remain normal in people with good sugar control, but changes may appear in people with poor sugar control.

✔ Around the time of puberty, levels of growth hormone, sex hormones and other hormones increase greatly.

✔ The risk of complications after puberty may increase because of the changes in hormone levels, because of poor sugar control caused by the changes in hormone levels or possibly due to both.

We do not know how the high blood sugar levels cause the complications.

Sugar does attach to parts of the body:

▼ the protein (hemoglobin) in the red blood cells to form hemoglobin A$_{1c}$ or HbA$_{1c}$ (see Chapter 14)

▼ to the skin proteins in people who have curvatures of several fingers (see "Finger Curvatures" in this chapter)

▼ it may attach to proteins in the blood vessels or other parts of the body when the blood sugar levels are very high

Once the sugar attaches to any body protein, the protein may not work as well as when sugar is not attached.

Even though the actual complications are not usually seen until puberty, it is important to work for good sugar control in the pre-pubertal years. There are some side effects of poor sugar control that can occur at any time (see Chapter 14 on Diabetes and Blood Sugar Control). Also, the habits for the future are formed when the person is young.

COMPLICATIONS IN PEOPLE WITH DIABETES

We have divided complications into two groups: Complications related at least in part to blood sugar control and complications not related to blood sugar control.

Complications related, at least in part, to blood sugar control:

1. Eye Problems

✔ **Cataracts**

Cataracts are small thickenings in the lens (which is located at the front of the eye; see picture on the following page).

• The damage to the lens is believed to be caused by sorbitol, a compound made in the lens from glucose.

• Sorbitol damage occurs when blood glucose (sugar) levels have been very high in the body for a long time.

• Sorbitol in foods is changed by the body (liver) and *does not* cause this damage.

• Damage to the lens can happen at any age.

• Cataracts can be present at the onset of diabetes if sugar levels have been high for a long time before insulin is started.

• They may show some improvement with good sugar control.

• These lens changes *are not* the same as the more severe retinal complications in the back of the eye that are discussed next.

• The eye doctor (ophthalmologist) will do a detailed exam for cataracts in the yearly eye exam.

• If cataracts interfere with vision they can be removed surgically by the eye doctor.

✔ Retinal Changes or Retinopathy

The word retinopathy refers to changes of the retina, which is the layers of tissue at the back of the eye. This part of the eye has many small blood vessels similar to those found in the kidney.

A. *Retinopathy facts:*

Retinopathy is a change in the small blood vessels found in the back of the eye (retina), which occurs mainly after puberty.

These changes depend on various factors:

▼ the duration of diabetes after puberty

▼ the degree of blood sugar control

The DCCT showed that in people without eye changes from diabetes, lower blood sugars delayed development of retinopathy by 76%. The DCCT also showed that intensive therapy slowed the progression of retinopathy by 54% and reduced the incidence of severe retinopathy by 47% in people with known early eye changes from diabetes.

▼ increased blood pressure results in a greater risk for retinal changes

▼ tobacco use makes these changes progress more rapidly

Retina (back of eye)

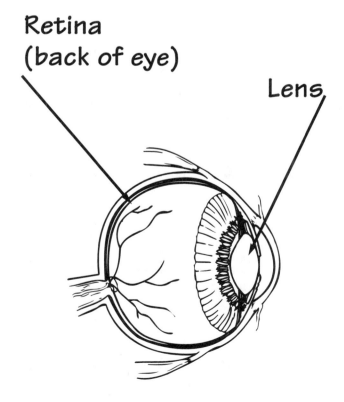

Lens

We do not understand all of the causes of the eye changes of diabetes. There is a small group of people for whom the presence or absence of eye changes show no relation to sugar control.

B. *Early detection:*

✔ is very important and is one clear argument for having diabetes check-ups every three months.

✔ the diabetes care provider doing the physical exam should be able to detect eye changes and make appropriate referrals to an eye doctor (ophthalmologist) who specializes in diabetic changes (retinal specialist).

✔ **The ADA does not suggest seeing an eye doctor for diabetic reasons before the age 10. We usually wait until the person with type 1 diabetes has had diabetes three years and is ≥ 10 years old. How long someone has had type 2 diabetes before diagnosis is often not known. For this reason, people with type 2 diabetes should see the eye doctor soon after diagnosis (if ≥ 10 years old).**

✔ Thereafter, if there are no diabetic eye changes, or if the changes are minor, yearly visits to the diabetes eye specialist are adequate.

✔ Minor eye changes include a ballooning of the small retinal blood vessels; these changes are reversible and are called **"microaneurysms."** Some people can have these minor changes for many years and not develop more severe eye disease. Careful blood sugar control is particularly important when any changes are detected. If more severe eye changes occur, then more frequent visits to the diabetes eye specialist are needed.

C. *More severe eye disease:*

✔ **"pre-proliferative"** and **"proliferative" retinopathy:**

- Usually involve formation of new (proliferative) and fragile retinal blood vessels, which are at a greater risk for breaking (hemorrhaging).

- The more severe changes are referred for **laser treatment**. This involves the use of a very bright light. It was begun in the 1970s as a way to save vision in people with diabetes who have severe eye changes.

- Laser treatment destroys the fragile (proliferative) new blood vessels and has been very effective in preventing loss of vision.

- The most important factor is to have close follow-up once the more severe changes appear. Laser treatment can then be done at the proper time to prevent loss of vision.

- The biggest danger is a hemorrhage. It could damage the retina or send blood into the vitreous fluid between the lens and retina **(vitreous hemorrhage)** or cause the retina to separate from the other layers in the back of the eye **(retinal detachment)**.

2. Kidney Disease or Diabetic Nephropathy

A. *The job of the kidneys in the body:*

✔ They normally filter wastes and water from our blood and make urine (Chapter 2).

✔ When blood sugar levels are high, sugar is passed into the urine. When this happens, the pressures are higher in the kidney filtering system (the glomerulus) and changes in the small blood vessels of the kidney can occur. This increased pressure causes damage to the filtering system so that some proteins start leaking through the filter and appear in the urine.

B. *Kidney disease is one of the most feared of the complications of diabetes and is spoken of as "nephropathy." Nephropathy is more likely to occur in people:*

✔ after puberty

✔ who have had diabetes for a long time

✔ with poor sugar control

✔ with elevated blood pressure

✔ who smoke or chew tobacco

It occurs in about one in three people with type 1 (insulin-dependent) diabetes, and in about one in four people with type 2 (adult onset) diabetes.

C. *Signs of kidney disease may include:*

▼ increased blood pressure

▼ ankle swelling, also known as edema (due to fluid collection)

▼ excessive urine protein spillage

▼ elevation of the waste materials in the blood (increased blood creatinine and urea nitrogen or BUN)

D. *The Microalbumin Test*

About the Microalbumin test:

- Detects diabetic kidney damage at an early stage when it might still be reversible.

- It is usually done on a timed overnight or on a 24-hour urine sample.

- Essential for people and those who have had type 1 diabetes for three or more years and are at least 10 years of age.

- For people with type 2 diabetes, the tests should be done soon after diagnosis.

- It should then be done once yearly so that the interval is not missed when the early damage is still reversible.

- The method for collecting the overnight sample is included at the end of this chapter.

If there is an increased level of microalbumin in the urine:

▼ WITH A LEVEL ABOVE 20 MICROGRAMS (µg) PER MINUTE, IT IS NOW ACCEPTED THAT THERE IS A 95% RISK FOR DEVELOPING NEPHROPATHY AND KIDNEY FAILURE IF NOTHING IS DONE.

▼ A "borderline microalbumin level" for timed overnight urine collections is a value between 7.6 µg/minute and 20 µg/minute. This "borderline" range represents a time period when good sugar and/or blood pressure control will help to lower the value or keep it from going higher.

▼ Medications are not usually given for a "borderline" level, as it may still be possible to return the value to normal by lowering the HbA_{1c}.

▼ If the urine microalbumin value is between 20 and 200 µg/minute, it is called **"microalbuminuria"** and may still be reversible with good sugar and blood pressure control and medications (ACE-inhibitor, see part E).

▼ Smoking cigarettes and chewing tobacco lead to a greater risk for kidney damage and must be avoided by people with diabetes.

▼ A decrease in protein intake is recommended (to lessen the load on the kidneys) for anyone who has microalbumin levels above 20 µg/minute, but particularly for those who have levels above 300 µg/minute (nephropathy or **macroalbuminuria**).

▼ The DCCT showed that improved glucose control reduced the occurrence of microalbuminuria by 39%. Gross kidney damage (nephropathy or albuminuria) was reduced by 54%. It must once again be remembered that glucose control is NOT the only cause of diabetic kidney damage.

E. *The 1980s and the 1990s have brought significant advances in the prevention, detection and treatment of diabetic kidney damage.*

✔ It is up to the family and the physician to make sure that the urine tests to detect kidney changes are done at the recommended times.

✔ If the tests are not done, the "window" during which changes may be reversible could be missed.

✔ If the microalbumin levels are high on the overnight or 24-hour urine test, medicines may be effective in reversing or slowing the kidney damage.

• The usual medicine that is tried first is an **ACE-inhibitor (ACE = A**ngiotensin-**C**onverting **E**nzyme). This medication prevents formation of angiotensin II, which is a very potent constrictor of blood vessels. The result is less pressure buildup in the kidneys. There are several varieties of ACE-inhibitors, all of which are probably effective if given in adequate dosage.

• Early kidney damage is detectable and methods to reverse or slow down kidney damage are available. This has now resulted in a decline in the cases of renal failure from diabetes.

3. Neuropathy (nerve damage)

Diabetic neuropathy, or "damage to the nerves", is a condition seen after puberty, usually in people who have had very high sugar levels for a long time.

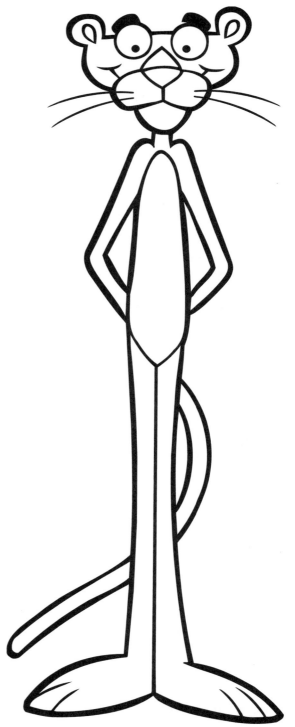

About neuropathy:

✔ It is a complex condition that we still do not completely understand.

✔ The DCCT found that the incidence of neuropathy was 60% less in the group with the lower blood sugar levels.

✔ As with cataracts, neuropathy is believed to be related, at least in part, to increased sorbitol levels deposited in the nerves. The sorbitol is made from sugar.

✔ There is also a decrease in another compound (myoinositol) which is important for the nerves.

✔ Some people with type 2 diabetes have neuropathy when they are diagnosed with diabetes.

✔ *The neuropathy usually makes itself known with*:

▼ numbness, tingling, sharp pains in the lower legs or feet

▼ changes in other parts of the body: e.g., the rate at which food moves through the intestines may change (gastroparesis)

Much research is being done to find new and better medications for the treatment of neuropathy.

4. Joint Contractures

Some facts:

✔ Some people cannot touch the knuckles of the second joint in their fifth fingers (little fingers) when their hands are in a "praying" position.

✔ The joints of the other fingers or other joints in the body can also be involved.

✔ When other joints or fingers other than just the fifth finger are involved, there has usually been a period of very high sugar levels and sugar has attached to the proteins in the skin over the joints.

✔ No pain or other problems are usually related to these changes.

✔ Some doctors believe the curvatures of the fifth fingers may be partly inherited.

✔ Parents and siblings of people with diabetes often have curvatures of the fifth fingers even though they don't have diabetes.

✔ It is not yet known if the more severe curvatures will disappear as blood sugar control improves.

5. Birth Defects (discussed in more detail in Chapter 27)

This complication is primarily important to a woman who might get pregnant.

Some facts:

✔ IT IS VERY IMPORTANT TO TALK TO YOUR DIABETES PHYSICIAN BEFORE GETTING PREGNANT.

✔ Insulin pumps and intensive diabetes management must be considered PRIOR TO THE PREGNANCY.

✔ If diabetes is not well controlled (e.g., high HbA_{1c}), a pregnant woman with diabetes is more likely to have a baby with one or more birth problems or defects.

✔ The first few months of pregnancy are the most important in preventing defects.

✔ A woman should not stop using birth control or decide to get pregnant until her diabetes is well controlled.

✔ If the HbA_{1c}, blood pressure and kidney tests are normal or low prior to the pregnancy, the likelihood of kidney deterioration during pregnancy is minimized.

✔ Diabetic eye changes do sometimes worsen during pregnancy and it is wise to be followed more closely by one's retinal specialist during this time.

COMPLICATIONS NOT PRIMARILY RELATED TO SUGAR CONTROL

🐾 Macrovascular (large blood vessel) Problems

The "large" blood vessels are in contrast to the very small (sometimes microscopic) ones found in our eyes and kidneys. The large ones include the heart blood vessels that provide blood (and thus nutrition and oxygen) to our heart. When a heart blood vessel is blocked, a "heart attack" can result.

People with diabetes have a greater risk for heart attacks. Heart attacks have many causes, but *high risk factors include:*

▼ **increased blood pressure**

▼ **family history** of relatives who had heart attacks before age 50

▼ **smoking**

▼ **elevated LDL (low-density lipoprotein) cholesterol, reduced HDL** (high-density lipoprotein), which is the "good" cholesterol

▼ **elevated <u>total</u> blood cholesterol levels**

Some causes of high cholesterol levels:

✔ Until a few years ago, diets that contained 40% of calories from fat were routinely recommended. Most dietitians now recommend that no more than 30% of calories be from fat sources (see Chapters 11 and 12).

✔ Heredity and poor sugar control also can be causes of high cholesterol levels.

✔ It will be many years before we know if the reduced fat intake and better sugar control lower the likelihood of heart attacks in people with diabetes.

Recommendations:

• Blood cholesterol levels should be checked each year. Desired levels are given in Table 1 of Chapter 11.

• Medications (the "statins") that block our body's cholesterol synthesis are available for people who have very high cholesterol or LDL levels. The statins have been shown to decrease the risk for heart attacks.

• The blood pressure should be checked at regular clinic visits. Increases in blood pressure should be treated early.

• People with diabetes should not use tobacco!

🐾 Foot Problems

Some facts:

✔ Foot problems due to poor or decreased blood flow and neuropathy do not occur in children. Some families who are educated by diabetes care providers who care mainly for adults with diabetes will be told that children must "wash their feet daily" or "never go barefoot." Although it is nice to have clean feet for clinic visits, these precautions are NOT necessary for children.

✔ Foot problems usually occur in older adults and may be related to the blood fat levels and poor circulation or to neuropathy.

✔ There is research suggesting that regular exercise may help to maintain normal foot circulation later in life (see Chapter 13).

✔ It is important for diabetes care providers to do careful examinations of feet in post-pubertal patients.

✔ It is also important for a person to know to call the doctor if a foot sore does not heal well or if there is any sign of an infection (redness, warmth or pus) or ulcer.

✔ Ingrown toenails (an infection) occur with similar frequency in children with or without diabetes.

✔ The ingrown toenails are usually caused by toenails that are cut too short at the corners.

✔ The toenails should be cut straight across with a straight nail clipper and the length should be even with the end of the toe. Good prevention is much easier than treatment.

✔ Ingrown toenails are more of a problem in people with diabetes as infections cause high sugar levels. The high sugar levels, in turn, support the infection.

✔ Warts are not more common in people with diabetes. The best way to remove them is with the use of liquid nitrogen.

Other Autoimmune (self-allergy) Diseases Associated with Type 1 Diabetes

🐾 Thyroid Disorders

Some facts:

✔ Some thyroid enlargement occurs in about half of people with type 1 diabetes, although only about one in 20 ever needs treatment. The reason for this is believed to be a similar "self-allergy" (autoimmune) type of reaction that causes both diabetes and the related thyroid enlargement.

✔ People who get diabetes often have an antibody (allergic reaction) in their blood against their pancreas (specifically, the islet cells in the pancreas as discussed in Chapter 3). Likewise, people with diabetes who get thyroid problems usually have an antibody (allergic reaction) in their blood against the thyroid gland.

✔ Thyroid antibody tests can be done, but are usually not done as they are expensive and are often not paid for by insurance.

✔ It is important for the diabetes care provider to always check the size of the thyroid gland at the time of clinic visits.

✔ If the thyroid is not functioning normally, body growth may be slowed.

✔ The person may feel tired all the time.

✔ If the gland is enlarged, specialized blood tests should be done (**particularly a TSH test,** as this is almost always the first test to become abnormal). If thyroid problems are suspected, a TSH (± free T_4) test should be done.

✔ If the thyroid tests are abnormal, a thyroid tablet can then be taken once daily. Thyroid problems are not serious unless unrecognized or untreated. The treatment is excellent, easy, inexpensive and involves taking pills (not shots).

✔ Sometimes the tablets can be discontinued (under a doctor's supervision) when the person is finished growing.

✔ Thyroid problems are common even in people who do not have diabetes (about one in 50 adults).

Adrenal Disorders (autoimmune adrenal insufficiency, Addison's Disease)

Some facts:

✔ Autoimmunity against the adrenal gland can also occur.

✔ It is quite rare (about one in 500 people with type 1 diabetes), but it is important to diagnose and treat, as it can result in death if untreated. President Kennedy is an example of a famous person who had autoimmune adrenal insufficiency.

✔ *Some early signs for someone with diabetes may be:*

- an increased frequency of severe low blood sugars

- episodes of feeling weak or faint (with normal blood sugars - but sometimes low blood pressure)

- two electrolytes in the blood, sodium (Na+) and potassium (K+), may be low and high, respectively

- later, darker skin coloring over the back of the hands (or knuckles or elbows) may occur

✔ Initial screening may be for an antibody against the adrenal gland.

✔ Eventually, a morning ACTH and cortisol (cortisone) blood levels (± an ACTH stimulation test) should be obtained.

✔ The treatment (as with thyroid disease) is with tablets. Treatment includes training the person (or family) to increase the tablets during periods of stress (as with an infection or with surgery).

Celiac Disease

Some facts:

✔ Celiac disease (Sprue, Gluten-enteropathy) is carried on one of the genes (DR types, DR3) that is also related to being at high risk for type 1 diabetes (see Chapter 3).

✔ Approximately one in 20 people with diabetes also has celiac disease.

✔ As other family members who do not have diabetes may also have the DR3 genetic type, they are also more likely to have celiac disease (even though they do not have diabetes).

✔ Celiac disease is an allergy to the protein, gluten.

✔ It can be diagnosed using a blood antibody test (transglutaminase and/or anti-endomysial antibodies). At present, an intestinal biopsy is usually also done to confirm the diagnosis.

✔ Some people with celiac disease have symptoms, whereas others may not have any symptoms at all.

Symptoms may include:

- stomach pain

- gas

- diarrhea

- in children, decreased height or weight gain

✔ The symptoms, the abnormal blood tests and the intestinal biopsy changes may return to normal within a few months after treatment is begun.

✔ *The treatment involves:*

- removing all wheat, rye and barley products from the diet (rice, corn, oat products, and all foods, except those containing gluten, can still be eaten)

- working with a dietitian to learn which foods contain the protein, gluten

✔ Adults who have no symptoms may not wish to restrict all gluten from their diet. The main argument for doing so is that in a few case reports of adults dying with a cancer (lymphoma) of the intestine, celiac disease has been found present (and a possible causative factor).

INGREDIENT CONTENT GUIDELINE

Table 1

Acceptable	Use with Caution	Not Acceptable
Corn	Oats	White flour
Rice	Flax	Wheat, whole wheat
Soy and other beans		Rye
Tapioca		Barley
Potato		Durum
Hominy		Semolina
• Amaranth		Spelt
• Buckwheat		Kamut
• Millet		Triticale
• Quinoa		Graham
• Teff		Bulgar
		Bran
		Wheat germ

There is a series of cookbooks called *The Gluten Free Gourmet*, which can be ordered from any of the on-line bookstores such as Amazon.com and there are also several good bread mixes now. It is easier if the entire family eats as "gluten free" as possible. In the U.S., products are available in most health food stores. *The following are some other places you can shop/links:*

http://www.glutenfree.com

http://www.glutenfreemall.com

http://www.causeyourespecial.com/index_nn4.html (favorite bread mix is #10 Favorite Sandwich Bread Mix)

There is much that we still do not know about this disease. Some people may have a secondary deficiency of vitamin B12. This deficiency can cause symptoms similar to those of neuropathy or multiple sclerosis (MS).

❧ Skin Problems

Some facts:

✔ Yellow fatty deposits **(necrobiosis)** can collect in the skin over the front of the lower legs. No one knows what causes these fat deposits.

✔ A rare condition called **dermatitis herpetiformis** is also related to a sensitivity to the protein, gluten (see celiac disease). It is characterized by blisters on the elbows, buttocks and knees. Like celiac disease, it responds to a gluten-free diet.

❧ Sexual Function

✔ Some males with diabetes have problems with penile erections. The cause of this problem is unknown. The medicine Viagra® may be helpful to some men with diabetes who have this problem.

✔ There is no evidence that women with diabetes have problems with sexuality related to diabetes.

SUMMARY

In summary, much is still unknown about the long-term complications of diabetes. However, recent research suggests that good sugar control, normal blood pressure and not using tobacco can help prevent some of these complications.

DEFINITIONS

Adrenal gland: A hormone-producing gland located above each kidney, which has the function of making cortisone, salt-retaining hormones and other hormones.

Autoimmunity (self-allergy): As defined in Chapter 3, this involves forming an allergic reaction against ones own tissues. This happens in type 1 diabetes and can happen in thyroid disorders and, more rarely, with the adrenal gland.

Blood pressure: The blood pressure consists of a higher (systolic) pressure that reflects the pumping or working pressure of the heart and a lower (diastolic) pressure which reflects the resting pressure of the heart between beats. It is important to have the blood pressure checked regularly.

Blood Urea Nitrogen (BUN): A material in the blood normally cleared by the kidneys. It is elevated in advanced kidney disease as well as with dehydration.

Cataract: A density (clouding) in the lens that may cause spots, blurred or reduced vision.

Celiac disease (Sprue, Gluten-enteropathy): An allergy to the protein, gluten.

Creatinine: A material in the blood normally cleared by the kidneys. The test to measure its clearance from the blood is called a creatinine clearance test.

DCCT: Diabetes Control and Complications Trial. A very large trial of people ages 13-39 years old, which showed that lower HbA_{1c} values resulted in a lower risk for diabetic eye, kidney and nerve problems. The trial ended in June, 1993.

Edema: Collection of fluid (swelling) under the skin.

Filter: To separate out or remove. The kidneys filter wastes from our blood.

Gastroparesis: Neuropathy involving the stomach and/or intestine.

Glomerulus: Small groups of blood vessels in the kidneys that filter the blood to remove wastes and water to make urine.

Hemorrhage: The breaking of a blood vessel. In the eye, this can occur in the retinal layer or, in more advanced cases, in the fluid (vitreous) in front of the retina (vitreous hemorrhage).

Laser treatment: Using a very bright beam of light to destroy the new (proliferative) blood vessels in the retina, which are at high risk for hemorrhaging and causing a loss of vision.

Lens (see picture of eye): The oval structure in the front of the eye that changes shape to allow the eye to focus on near or distant objects.

Microalbumin: A test that can measure small amounts of a protein (albumin) in the urine to detect kidney damage from diabetes at a stage in which it might still be reversible.

Microaneurysm: A small dilatation of a blood vessel, which is a minor change caused by diabetes that can be reversible.

Myoinositol: A compound, which is reduced in nerves when sorbitol levels are elevated (in neuropathy).

Necrobiosis: The name for yellow fatty deposits that can occur over the lower legs in people with diabetes.

Nephropathy: A generic name for kidney disease. It is usually used to indicate a more advanced stage of kidney involvement.

Neuropathy: A disease of the nerves. This is believed to happen in people with diabetes due to accumulation of sorbitol (formed from blood glucose), or possibly due to deficiency of another metabolite, myoinositol.

Ophthalmologist: The name for a doctor (MD) who specializes in eye diseases. The ophthalmologist may further specialize in the retinal layer in the back of the eye, which is affected by diabetes. The doctor is then called a "retinal specialist."

Optometrist: A person who is primarily trained to check for the need for glasses. An optometrist is not an MD (although they are still important care providers).

Podiatrist: A person who is specially trained in the care of the feet. They are not MDs (although they are still important care providers).

Pre-proliferative or proliferative retinopathy: Terms for more advanced stages of eye involvement from diabetes (when a diabetes eye specialist needs to be seen more frequently).

Puberty: The time in a teen's life when adult sexual changes start to occur.

Retina: The layers of small blood vessels and nerves in the back of the eye that are very important for vision.

Retinal detachment: Separation of the retinal layer in the back of the eye from other layers in the eye.

Retinopathy: Changes in the retinal (small blood vessel) layer in the back of the eye from diabetes. These are more likely to occur after puberty in people who have had diabetes for a long time and who have been in poor sugar control.

Sorbitol: A compound derived from glucose, which collects in the lens and nerves when blood sugars are high and is believed to cause cataracts and neuropathy.

Thyroid: A hormone-producing gland in the lower front of the neck on each side of the windpipe (trachea). The hormone is called thyroid hormone.

Vitreous fluid: The fluid between the lens and the retina. When retinal blood vessels break, they can bleed into the vitreous fluid (vitreous hemorrhage).

QUESTIONS (Q) AND ANSWERS (A) FROM NEWSNOTES

Q. What is the best way to screen for early microvascular (small vessel) disease of the kidneys and the eyes in people with diabetes and when should it be done?

A. The microalbumin urine test is the best way to currently diagnose early kidney involvement in people with diabetes. The test is done by measuring the microalbumin in a timed overnight or 24-hour urine. It is very important to repeat the two overnight (or 24-hour) urine collections every year. If a person has begun pubertal changes (usually ages 11-13 years) and has had diabetes for at least three years, we recommend doing the two overnight urine collections for microalbumin and having an eye exam by an ophthalmologist once yearly. Directions for the urine collections are in the back of this chapter.

Q. Why is it necessary to reduce my protein intake as I lose protein in my urine? Shouldn't I eat more protein?

A. The protein (albumin, microalbumin) loss in the urine is most likely due to kidney damage from diabetes. This is a result of HbA_{1c} levels being too high, the blood pressure being too high (hypertension) or as a result of using tobacco. There are probably other causes as well that we do not yet understand. When someone gets kidney damage from any cause (diabetes, hypertension, nephritis, lupus, etc.), it generally helps to slow down the process by eating less protein. The protein seems to be an extra load for the kidney to handle, and reducing the protein will make less work for the damaged kidneys. It is wise to meet with the dietitian at this stage to discuss what the correct amount of protein should be.

Q. What level of glucose control is necessary to prevent the eye and kidney complications of diabetes?

A. Our longitudinal study reported in the *Journal of the American Medical Association* in 1989 correlated glycohemoglobin (hemoglobin A_1) values with complications and showed that blood sugar control (HbA_1 levels) were definitely related to the eye and kidney complications. No person who had kept their HbA_1 (reflecting frequency of high blood sugars over the previous three months) below 9% by the affinity column method (normal to 8.0 %) or below 6.8% for the DCA 2000 method (normal to 6.2%) had evidence of eye or kidney changes. Likewise, no person who had kept their HbA_1 below 9.8% for the column method (7.4% for the DCA 2000 method) had kidney changes, and only two of 230 had serious eye changes. This is in contrast to people who had a mean HbA_1 above 12.3% for the column method, or above 9.3% for the DCA 2000 method, where 41% of people had more severe eye changes and 28% had evidence of kidney damage.

The extra effort to stay in good blood sugar control may indeed save much work later in life in dealing with the eye and kidney complications of diabetes.

Q. Is cigarette smoking bad for someone with diabetes?

A. Yes. It is linked to lung cancer, high blood pressure and heart attacks in ALL people and is thus a poor choice for everyone. In addition, data from our Center has shown that smoking results in about a three-fold greater likelihood of diabetic kidney complications. Smoking also causes diabetic eye disease to progress more rapidly. The mechanism by which smoking does this is unknown, but as people who chew tobacco seem to have the same consequences, it may be from the absorption of nicotine into the body. Glycohemoglobin (HbA_{1c}) levels are often high in smokers with diabetes. Therefore, these effects had to be removed before a conclusion about smoking could be reached. Smoking results in higher HbA_{1c} levels by increasing levels of other hormones, such as adrenaline, which raise the blood sugar. The heart rate and blood pressure also increase and this may be related to the increased eye and kidney problems.

Q. Our son has been chewing tobacco. Is this really bad? Should we be bothered by it or just be glad he is not smoking cigarettes?

A. The use of "smokeless" tobacco is increasing greatly in teenagers and should be actively discouraged. One study of Denver high school students (mean age = 16 years) showed that more than 10% used smokeless tobacco.

The tobacco contains dangerous components that could be cancer-causing. In addition to the increased risk for cancer of the mouth, the nicotine is absorbed from the tobacco and can cause any of the following: stimulation, increased muscle tone and aggression, increase in heart rate and blood pressure, dizziness, nausea and shakiness of the extremities. **The latter three symptoms may be confused with the symptoms of low blood sugar.** Reduced taste is common and increased use of salt (and sugar) often occurs. Dentists note that users typically have discolored teeth, receding gums, periodontal destruction and excessive wear of the teeth due to abrasives in the tobacco. Withdrawal symptoms of irritability and decreased cognitive functions are frequently found between doses.

Fortunately, the Comprehensive Smokeless Tobacco Health Education Act, which bans radio and TV advertisements, was signed into law during the Reagan Administration. As a result, famous sports and movie stars are no longer seen promoting chewing tobacco on TV. Needless to say, it is well worthwhile for responsible people (including parents) to take a strong stand against chewing (or smoking) tobacco!

Q. Do children with diabetes have to take special care of their feet?

A. Much is written about diabetes and foot care, and this was one of the initial stimuli to write this educational book. All of the books available at the time talked about washing the feet daily and taking special care of the feet. Although it is nice to have clean feet (especially when coming for clinic check-ups), children with diabetes do not have any more problems with their feet than do other children. *Foot problems for people with diabetes occur in older age, particularly in relation to two problems:*

i. Neuropathy: People in poor glucose control accumulate sorbitol in their nerve fibers and develop neuropathy and a loss of normal feeling. It may then not be possible to feel hot or cold normally, thus the need to be careful when getting into hot bath water, etc.

ii. Atherosclerosis: If blood vessels age and the walls thicken, less blood flow will go to the feet. This happens only in later years - and one precaution we take in the clinic is the yearly check of blood cholesterol levels. High cholesterol levels, high blood pressure and smoking are all believed to hasten the aging of blood vessels.

One problem with the feet which is no more common in children with diabetes than in other children, but which is more difficult to cure in children with diabetes, is INGROWN TOENAILS. These usually occur because toenails (especially the large nails) are cut too short and the surrounding skin then grows over the nail. The nail then grows into the skin and an infection is set up. The infection can cause high sugars - and the high sugars can help the infection grow. The result is often a chronic problem cured only by removal of the toenail. A better solution is PREVENTION. Cut the toenails straight across, preferably with a straight toenail clipper and not a rounded fingernail clipper. The length should be out to the end of the toe. Ingrown toenails are rare when nails are properly cut!

Q. Are thyroid problems more common in children with diabetes, and if so, why?

A. Yes, thyroid problems are more common in children with diabetes. They are caused by an "autoimmune" or allergic-type reaction that is very similar to the allergic-type reaction that is believed to be important in causing diabetes. Thus, most people with new-onset diabetes have islet cell antibodies (an allergic reaction against the islet cells that make the insulin) at the time of diagnosis of type 1 (but not type 2) diabetes. Likewise, the people with diabetes who develop thyroid problems have an antibody in their blood against the thyroid gland. Both the pancreas and the thyroid are endocrine glands that make the hormones insulin and thyroid hormone, respectively. Thus, the two glands have much in common. Some physicians recommend thyroid blood tests yearly in children with diabetes. The practice in our Clinic is to do the tests if the thyroid gland is large or if there is a special indication, such as a fall-off in height. Fortunately, when low thyroid function is detected, it can be treated with a tablet. Also, the pills can sometimes be discontinued after a few years. Thus, most people handle the problem easily.

Q. How common is kidney disease in association with diabetes, and can it be prevented?

A. Kidney problems occur in up to 30% of people with type 1 diabetes, usually when the person reaches their 30s or 40s. There are things that we can do now to help reduce the likelihood of kidney problems.

These include:

Good sugar control

There is evidence to suggest that the kidney problems may result from the increased sugar load the kidney constantly has to handle. Gradually, the tissue starts to thicken due to increased pressure resulting from this increased sugar load. The closer to normal the blood sugars are kept, the less likely the kidney has to handle an excessive load. Thus, good sugar control may be the most important parameter in preventing kidney disease.

Blood pressure

It is important to have the blood pressure monitored at regular intervals to make sure the systolic and the diastolic pressures are not above the 90th percentile for age. If blood pressure elevations are found, early treatment is important in preventing kidney disease. It is also advisable to avoid adding extra salt to foods, which can increase blood pressure in some people.

Prompt treatment of urinary tract infections

It is important to treat infections that might get to the kidneys and cause damage. Problems with infections are more common in women than in men. It is important to repeat urine cultures after the antibiotic treatment to make sure the infection has really gone away.

Dietary protein

There is evidence that a high protein diet adds to the material that must be filtered by the kidneys and the likelihood of kidney problems from diabetes. Most Americans eat much more protein than is needed and it would be wise to reduce the quantity of protein. This can be discussed with the dietitian at the time of clinic visits.

Avoid medicines that list kidney damage as a possible side effect

When your physician chooses a medicine (e.g., an antibiotic to treat an infection), make sure that he/she is aware you have diabetes and that he/she is using a medicine that does not have possible side effects of damaging the kidneys. There is often an alternative medicine, which may be used that does not have this potential side effect.

Smoking

Data from our Clinic has clearly shown that smoking adds to the likelihood of diabetic kidney damage. Smoking must be avoided in people who have diabetes.

Regular check-ups

Protein is evaluated in the urine with every three-month check-up at the clinic because it may indicate kidney problems. Having the microalbumin tests done yearly is the best way to detect early problems.

Preventive medicines

Recent studies have shown that at least one type of blood pressure medicine (an ACE-inhibitor) also has an effect of reducing kidney filtration pressure. Eventually, it may be possible to give medications to specifically prevent kidney problems from diabetes.

Q. Are contact lenses OK for a person with diabetes to use?

A. Yes, people with diabetes can wear contact lenses, but there are some extra precautions. The contact lens fits over the superficial layer of the eye called the cornea. The cornea needs a constant supply of oxygen and tears to keep it healthy. Thus, the contact lens must fit properly so that the cornea is not injured and the tears are able to continue to flow. A qualified (experienced) eye doctor should fit the lenses - probably in a contact lens clinic.

It is even more important for people with diabetes to follow the instructions for care and cleaning of the contact lenses than it is for other people. The corneas of people with diabetes are sometimes less sensitive to pain or irritation, so people may be less likely to feel discomfort when their contacts are causing problems. Infections may also not clear as quickly if they do occur. Thus, use the solutions and disinfectants exactly as your eye doctor recommends. Don't get lazy in cleaning or try to cut corners. Don't leave the contacts in any longer than recommended. Don't mix cleaning solutions. Finally, it is probably better not to get the extended wear lenses.

MICROALBUMINS

Doctor: _____   Your Name: _____

A. INSTRUCTIONS FOR DOING THE OVERNIGHT URINE COLLECTIONS

COLLECTION #1   DATE: _____

1. Empty your bladder at bedtime and discard this sample.

                                                        TIME: _____

2. Save **EVERY DROP** of urine during the night.

3. Save **EVERY DROP** of the first morning sample. **ALL** urine from collection #1 should be placed in the same container.

                                                        TIME: _____

4. Measure the volume of the urine sample.   TOTAL VOLUME: _____

COLLECTION #2   DATE: _____

1. Empty your bladder at bedtime and discard this sample.

                                                        TIME: _____

2. Save **EVERY DROP** of urine during the night.

3. Save **EVERY DROP** of the first morning sample. **ALL** urine from collection #2 should be placed in the same container.

                                                        TIME: _____

4. Measure the volume of the urine sample.   TOTAL VOLUME: _____

B. IMPORTANT INFORMATION ABOUT YOUR COLLECTIONS

1. Label each container with your name and #1 or #2.

2. You may use any CLEAN container you have at home that will not leak to collect the sample. We do not provide containers.

3. Store urine aliquots in refrigerator until your visit (samples are good for one week if kept **cold**).

4. <u>DO NOT</u> mix collections #1 and #2 together in the same container.

5. <u>DO NOT</u> drink caffeinated or alcoholic beverages or use tobacco after 10 p.m. the evening of the collections.

6. <u>DO NOT</u> exercise strenuously for the four hours prior to bedtime.

7. <u>DO NOT</u> collect specimens during a menstrual period.

8. Failure to follow directions exactly may cause incorrect results.

9. If you have any questions, please call your healthcare provider.

C. DIRECTIONS FOR MEASURING THE VOLUME

1. Have a measuring cup or (better) a cylinder - preferably marked in cc (mL). One cup is 240cc. Urine is sterile and it is ok to use cooking measuring cups (just wash prior to next use for cooking).

2. Measure the total cc of each overnight sample and put the amounts in the blanks for step 4 for collections #1 and #2.

3. Put a sample of each urine collection in a clean tube. Any clean red top tube from a doctor's office, clinic or hospital lab will work. Label which sample (#1 or #2) it is, put your name on the tube, and put the tube in a cup in the refrigerator until you get to your clinic. Bring this sheet with the times and total volumes with you.

23 Chapter

TOPICS:

- Monitoring (checking blood sugars/ketones, giving insulin)
- Prevent, Detect and Treat Acute Complications
- Psychosocial Adjustment

TEACHING OBJECTIVES:

1. Assess who will educate school/work personnel about diabetes.

2. Identify supplies needed to prevent acute complications at school/work.

3. Develop a health action plan for school/work.

LEARNER OBJECTIVES:

Learner (parents, child, relative or self) will be able to:

1. Define who will educate school/work personnel about diabetes.

2. List all supplies needed at school/work to prevent acute complications.

3. Design a health action plan for school/work with healthcare provider(s).

WITH SPECIAL THANKS FOR THE SUGGGESTIONS OF:

- Susie Owen, RN, CDE.
- In addition, appreciation is expressed to Jan Murayama, RN and the Jefferson County School District for the School Nurse Health Care Plan Checklist and the Colorado School Task Force for the use of their School Intake Interview and Individualized School Health Care Plan.
- Fran Kaufman, MD and Georgeanna Klingensmith, MD, for reviewing the final draft of this chapter and giving suggestions.

Chapter 23

THE SCHOOL/WORK AND DIABETES

INTRODUCTION

The first and main job of parents in relation to school is to educate those who will be working with the child at school about diabetes. Parents want to feel that their child is in safe hands while at school (often the place where the majority of the child's waking hours are spent). Parents also want to make sure their child is not treated differently because of having diabetes. The next few pages are meant to be cut out or copied (permission is granted to copy as often as wished) for the school. It is wise for the parent to phone the school nurse, teacher or principal to discuss the best way to inform all of the necessary people. The week before classes start is usually the best time. A checklist is provided in Table 1 to remind parents of their responsibilities. The school may want a School Intake Interview (Table 2). There is also a letter at the back of this chapter that may be helpful.

Some parents in our area will buy or borrow a copy of one of the videos (see Resources at the end of this chapter) on diabetes and the school or on hypoglycemia and take it to show the nurse, health aide, teachers and others likely to be involved with their child. It can be a good starting place for a discussion about hypoglycemia, the most likely emergency to occur at school.

It is essential for the family to educate the:

▼ teacher(s)

▼ school nurse

▼ health aid

▼ bus driver

▼ gym teacher

▼ lunchroom workers

▼ playground aides

▼ others involved with their child at school

Sometimes the school nurse or the teacher will help educate other staff. It is also important that when a substitute teacher is at school, the substitute knows that a child in the classroom has diabetes. A copy of your child's school care plan should be placed in the "substitute" folder and in the teacher's attendance book. Attach a recent photo of your child to the plan. **It is important NOT to leave it up to the child to inform and educate the school.** They may be self conscious or embarrassed and not get the job done.

A second job of parents is to keep an adequate supply of items at school for the treatment of low blood sugars.

Such as:

✔ instant glucose

✔ small cans of juice or juice boxes

✔ Gatorade or a can of sugar pop

✔ peanut butter or cheese and crackers and/or graham crackers

✔ quarters so the school staff can purchase these items.

These should be kept in a container in the teacher's, principal's or nurse's drawer. The container should be clearly labeled with the child's name and a set of instructions (with contact phone numbers).

There is often a special anxiety about a young child starting preschool.

This anxiety is due to a young child who:

• may not yet be able to recognize low blood sugars

• may not be mature enough to help remember snacks. The teacher will need to remind the child or the child may wear a watch with a preset alarm.

- might not have been away from the care of the parents for any significant period of time prior to starting preschool

Separation may be difficult for the parents and the child. And yet, preschool may be important for the child in learning social and other skills. It is important to allow participation just as one would if the child did not have diabetes. The information at the end of this chapter may be given to the preschool teacher just as it is to regular schoolteachers.

SCHOOL HEALTH PLAN

Schools in most states now require a School Health Plan. We have included a possible plan in this chapter (Table 3). It would be appropriate for all children and schools. You have our permission to copy the form as often as you wish. There is also a generic school letter at the end of this chapter that may be of help in introducing your child's diabetes to the school. Also note that there is a letter for sports coaches at the end of Chapter 13. Either of these letters may be copied as often as desired.

BLOOD SUGAR TESTING IN THE SCHOOL

All children must have at school:

▼ a blood sugar (glucose) meter; it should NOT be kept in the child's locker

▼ strips for the meter

▼ a lancing device (finger poker)

At a minimum, a test must be done whenever the child is feeling low. Some physicians and parents ask that a test be done routinely prior to lunch. Often children carry their own meter in their backpack. This should then be noted in the School Health Plan.

We prefer that the child be allowed to test in the classroom. Less school is missed when this is allowed. If the child is testing in the classroom, an adult may need to look at the result. The adult can determine if a low blood sugar has occurred. The biggest disadvantage of testing in the classroom is that the hands cannot be washed first if there isn't a sink. A trace of sugar on the finger can cause a high reading. If alcohol is used to clean the finger, be sure to let it dry completely before lancing.

It should be noted, if the child feels low and no blood sugar equipment is available, **TREAT the low with a source of carbohydrate**.

INSULIN IN THE SCHOOL

If insulin is to be given at school, the parent and the child's physician must sign a school medication form. It must specify when the insulin is to be given and the dose. The school nurse may not always be available to give or supervise this injection. Under some circumstances, the child may give his/her own shot. Sometimes the nurse will train another staff person who is always available. If a child is drawing up the insulin and giving their own dose, it is a good idea to have an adult check the amount. On other occasions the parent may need to come in and give the injection. Insulin pens are very convenient, more accurate and leave less room for error when drawing up the dose at school.

GLUCAGON IN THE SCHOOL

As discussed in Chapter 6, glucagon is a hormone with the opposite effect of insulin. It raises the blood sugar, but *it is not sugar*. Glucagon is used for emergencies when a person becomes unconscious, has a seizure or is unable to safely drink a liquid carbohydrate due to a low blood sugar. The use of glucagon in the school can be found in the Emergency Response Plan (Table 4). Unfortunately, it must be mixed and then injected just like insulin. It can be injected under the skin into the subcutaneous fat (like insulin) or deeper into muscle. It works just as well either way. Some physicians, schools and families work out a way that the glucagon can be given at the school in case of an emergency. (The physician must give orders for dose and when to give it.) If the family lives in a rural area, where emergency personnel are not immediately available (we have heard of responses taking as long as 40 minutes), glucagon should be kept in the school. It may have to be administered by a layperson, but most parents are lay people. The school nurse must arrange for routine recertification of these skills for the school staff member assigned to do this task. The instructions from Chapter 6 should be taped to the box. Our 2001 video on hypoglycemia (see Resources at the end of this chapter) also teaches how to give glucagon.

LOW BLOOD SUGAR ("Insulin Reaction" or "Hypoglycemia")

See the Emergency Response Plan (Table 4) for the specific care for a given child.

This is the only emergency likely to occur at school.

A. Onset: SUDDEN and, if not treated promptly, can be an emergency.

B. Signs: Variable, but may be **any** of the following:

- hungry
- sweating, shaking
- pale or flushed face
- headaches
- weak, irritable or confused
- speech and coordination changes
- eyes appear glassy, dilated or "big" pupils
- personality changes such as crying or stubbornness
- inattention, drowsiness or sleepiness at unusual times
- if not treated, loss of consciousness and/or seizure

C. Most likely times to occur: Before lunch or after gym class.

D. Causes: Too much insulin, extra exercise, a missed snack or less food at a meal than is usually eaten. Field days or field trips with extra exercise and excitement may result in reactions. The parents should be aware of all field days or trips so that the insulin dose can be reduced and/or extra snacks can be provided.

E. IF YOUR CHILD IS SENT TO THE OFFICE, THEY MUST ALWAYS HAVE SOMEONE ACCOMPANY HIM/HER. The child may become confused and not make it to the office if he/she is alone.

F. Treatment: This depends on the severity of the reaction:

1. Mild Reaction (also see Table 4: Emergency Response Plan)

Symptoms: Hunger, shaking, personality changes, drowsiness, headache, paleness, confusion or sweating.

Blood sugar: If equipment is available to do a blood sugar test, this is ideal to do even if juice has been taken. We prefer this to be done by the student (if old enough) in the classroom so that extra energy is not spent going elsewhere. However, we realize that for some schools this is not possible. It takes 10 minutes for the blood sugar to rise after the juice has been given. Doing the blood sugar tests will help to tell if the blood sugar was truly low and how low. A rapid fall in blood sugar, even though the blood sugar is in a normal range, may cause symptoms of being low and require a solid food snack to stop the symptoms.

Treatment: Give three or four sugar packets, cubes or tablets, or 4-6 oz or 1/2 cup of juice, or any sugar containing food or drink. Liquids are absorbed in the stomach more rapidly than are solid foods. However, **INSULIN REACTIONS TREATED WITH LIQUIDS INITIALLY SHOULD BE FOLLOWED IN 10 MINUTES WITH MORE SUBSTANTIAL FOOD** (e.g., cheese and crackers or 1/2 sandwich, etc.).

2. Moderate Reaction

Symptoms: Combative behavior, disorientation, lethargy.

Blood sugar: Do the same as in a Mild Reaction (see above).

Treatment: Always check for the risk of choking **before** treating. Give instant glucose immediately, and then give sugar or juice when the person is more alert. After the person is feeling better (10 minutes), give solid food as above.

3. *Severe Reaction*

Symptoms: Seizure or unconsciousness

Treatment: CALL 911 IMMEDIATELY

Give glucagon subcutaneously or intramuscularly if a nurse or a trained person is available to administer. Check the School Health Plan for the dose.

A checklist for the school nurse to follow in developing the Individualized Health Care Plan is shown in Table 5.

HIGH BLOOD SUGAR/KETONES

People with diabetes may have high blood sugars and spill extra sugar into the urine on some occasions. These occasions include periods of stress, illness, overeating and/or lack of exercise. High sugars are generally NOT an emergency (unless accompanied by vomiting). When the blood sugar is above 300 mg/dl (16.65 mmol/L), urine or blood ketones also need to be checked. When the sugar is high, the child will have to drink more and urinate more frequently. **It is essential to make bathroom privileges readily available.** If the teacher notes that the child is going to the bathroom frequently over a period of several days, a parent should be notified. The diabetes care provider can then adjust the insulin dose.

The student may also occasionally need to check ketones at school. This may be because ketones were present earlier at home, because the blood sugar is above 300 mg/dl (16.65 mmol/L) or because the child is not feeling well. The parents should be notified if moderate or large urine ketones (or a blood ketone test shows > 0.6 mmol/L) are present, as extra insulin will be needed. When a child has moderate or large ketones, we recommend that the child be treated by adults who can provide constant supervision, usually at home.

CLASS PARTIES

If the class is having a special snack, the child with diabetes should also be given a snack. Parents should be notified ahead of time so that they can decide whether the child may eat the same snack as the other students, or they may want to provide an alternate food.

If an alternate snack is not available, the student should be given the same snack as the other children.

BUS TRAVEL

It is important for the child with diabetes to take some food with him/her on the bus. If the child feels low, he/she must be allowed to eat the food. At times, bus rides take longer than usual due to bad weather or delays, and **the child needs to have a snack available and permission from the bus driver to eat it if necessary.**

SUBSTITUTE TEACHERS

Ask to have a copy of the School Health Plan (Table 3) placed in the substitute teacher's folder and the attendance register so that a substitute would know:

1. which child in the class has diabetes (attach a photo)

2. when he/she usually eats a snack

3. symptoms and treatment of an insulin reaction

4. where the treatment supplies are kept

GYM (PHYSICAL EDUCATION) TEACHERS AND COACHES

It is particularly important for the gym teacher or coach to also have a copy of the School Health Plan. Low blood sugars may occur during exercise and a source of instant sugar should be close. Often a snack is recommended before gym. The child should get the snack early enough to help them be on time. Exercise is even more important for children with diabetes than for other children. They should not be excluded from gym or sports activities.

AFTER SCHOOL DETENTION

Children with diabetes should not be singled out or treated differently from the rest of the class. However, if required to remain after school (at noon or in the afternoon) for a longer time than usual, the teacher should be asked to give an extra snack. Most parents will have packets of cheese and crackers, peanut butter and crackers or some such snack for the teacher to keep in the drawer. This is a common time of the day for the morning or afternoon insulins to be peaking. If a snack is not taken, an insulin reaction is likely to occur.

SPECIAL DAYS (FIELD TRIPS, FIELD DAYS)

Field trips or field days usually involve extra excitement and exercise. Both of these can result in an increased chance of low blood sugars. The parents should ask to be notified beforehand so that they can reduce the dose of insulin. They may also wish to send extra snacks (granola bars, fruit roll ups, etc).

INSULIN PUMPS IN THE SCHOOL

More and more children are now using insulin pumps. The pumps allow sugar control to be more like that of a person who does not have diabetes. Table 6 lists some of the special issues of insulin pump use in the school. If more information is desired, Chapter 26 deals with insulin pumps.

LEGAL RIGHTS

Section 504 of the Rehabilitation Act of 1973 prohibits recipients of federal funds from discriminating against people on the basis of a disability (including diabetes). In our experience, the parents and school staff are usually able to agree on a School Health Care Plan (Table 2). Formalizing the care through a 504 plan is then not necessary. However, in the rare case where it is necessary, additional resources are provided below. A child with diabetes has the right to a free and appropriate public education including accommodations to manage their diabetes at school. You can review these rights on the ADA website, http://www.diabetes.org. The ADA also has a brochure called *Your School and Your Rights*.

Additional resources for parents who wish to formalize the health care plan through a Section 504 are listed here:

1. The Law, Schools and Your Child with Diabetes at: http://www.childrenwithdiabetes.com/d_0q_000.htm

This website allows access to:

- *Your School and Your Rights*, from the American Diabetes Association, discusses the legal obligations of school systems under Section 504 of the Rehabilitation Act of 1973 and the Education for All Handicapped Children Act of 1975, amended in 1991.

- *The National Information Center for Children and Youth with Disabilities* (NICHCY) is a U.S. Government sponsored clearinghouse that provides information about disabilities, including information about obtaining assistance at school. Important information on their web site includes:

2. The US Department of Education website (http://www.ed.gov/index.jsp) includes:

The *Individuals with Disabilities Education Act,* with detailed information about IDEA.

IDEA: The Law contains links to downloadable versions of the law.

3. *What a Child's Health Care Team Needs to Know About Federal Disability Law.* Kaufman, F. R. Diabetes at School. Diabetes Spectrum 15:63-64, 2002.

4. *How to Write an I.E.P.* is a book designed to help parents who have children with disabilities succeed in school. Many parents of children with diabetes use an IEP to ensure that their children can care for their diabetes in school.

QUESTIONS (Q) AND ANSWERS (A) FROM NEWSNOTES

Q. My son recently had a cold and small urine ketones when he woke up. He felt good enough to go to school and wanted to go. Was I wrong in letting him do this?

A. As long as he felt well enough and wanted to go, I think it was good that you let him do so. At least he wanted to go and must like school! You might have sent one of the large plastic drinking cups with a straw so that he would remember to drink fluids to help wash away the ketones. Probably a special note to the teacher explaining the situation and the possible need for extra bathroom privileges would be wise. Finally, it would be important for a parent (or the child, if old enough) or the school nurse to make sure the urine ketones were checked again at lunchtime to make sure they went away and did not increase to the moderate or large level. Children with moderate or large urine ketones or blood ketones > 0.6 mmol/L need to stay home with adult supervision until the ketones have gone down.

SCHOOL DIABETES MANAGEMENT CHECKLIST FOR PARENTS:

_____ Discuss specific care of your child with the teachers, school nurse and other staff who will be involved.

_____ Complete the individualized school health care plan with the help of school staff and your diabetes care staff (see two examples in this chapter).

_____ Make sure your child understands the details of who will help him/her with testing, shots and treatment of high or low blood sugars at school and where supplies will be kept. Supplies should be kept in a place where they are always available if needed.

_____ Keep current phone numbers where you can be reached. Collect equipment for school: meter, strips and finger-poker, lancets, insulin, insulin syringes, biohazard container, log book or a copy of testing record form (make arrangements to have blood sugars sent home routinely), extra insulin pump supplies, ketone testing strips, photo for substitute teacher's folder.

_____ Food and drinks; parents need to check intermittently to make sure supplies are not used up:

▼ juice cans or boxes (approximately 15 grams of carb each)

▼ glucose tablets

▼ instant glucose or cake decorating gel

▼ crackers(± peanut butter and/or cheese)

▼ quarters to buy sugar pop if needed

▼ Fruit-Roll Ups

▼ dried fruit

▼ raisins or other snacks

_____ box with the child's name to store these food and drink items

Table 2   <u>SCHOOL INTAKE INTERVIEW - DIABETES</u>

Student _____ Date of birth _____

School _____ Grade _____ Homeroom Teacher _____

Parent(s)/Guardian(s) _____

Phone (H) _____ (W) _____ (Other) _____

Emergency contact (other than parent /guardian) _____ Phone _____

Physician name _____ Office Phone _____ Fax _____

Diabetes Nurse Educator's name _____ Office Phone _____

Medical release of information signed? Yes ___ No ___

Mode of transportation to and from school? _____ Bus driver notified of diabetes? Yes ___ No ___

Does child participate in after school activities? Yes ___ No ___   Before ___ or after ___ care?

Explain _____

Adult leader notified of diabetes? Yes ___ No ___

Field trip recommendations: _____

Blood Sugar Monitoring:

    Test will be performed in _____ (location).

    Needs assistance with testing? Yes ___No ___ Explain _____

    Required test times _____

    Call parent if blood sugar below _____ or above _____

    Staff to record values and report to parents daily ____ weekly ____

Comments: _____

Meds: **<u>Insulin:</u>** Can child give own injections? Yes ___ No ___ Explain _____

          Order for insulin on file? Yes ___ No___

          Time(s) insulin is to be administered at school: _____

          Type/Dosages: _____

          Form of administration: _____

                   (Injection, Pen, Pump)

          <u>Oral medications</u>: Type _____ Times _____ Dose _____

Comments: _____

Diet: **Assigned** student lunch time(s)? _____

          Is child following a prescribed meal plan? Yes____ No____ Assistance required? Yes ___ No ___

          Explain_____

          _____

          Snack time(s)? _____ Assistance required? Yes ___ No ___

          Explain_____

          Snack will be eaten in _____ (location)

          Snacks will be stored in _____ (location)

          Recommended snacks_____

          Parent wishes to be notified in advance of class parties? Yes ___ No ___

          Child may partake in class treats? Yes___ No ___ Explain _____

Comments: _____

Physical Education:

    Scheduled at:_____

    Is snack necessary before physical education?   Yes ___ No ___

    Does child participate in after school sports?   Yes ___ No ___

    P.E. Teacher/Coach aware of child's diabetes?   Yes ___ No ___

Comments: _____

Table 2   <u>INTERVENTIONS FOR EMERGENCY SITUATIONS</u>
(continued)
INTERVENTIONS FOR LOW BLOOD SUGAR

Hypoglycemia (<u>Low</u> blood sugar) – Insulin Reaction **(Must be accompanied to Health Office)**:
(Any blood sugar level below _____ constitutes a <u>low</u> blood sugar.)
If blood sugar cannot be obtained, treat based on symptoms? Yes ____ No ____

<u>Mild reaction</u> signs person might exhibit are:

    hunger   irritability   shakiness   sleepiness   sweating   pallor

    other _____

Person <u>usually</u> recognizes the symptoms? Yes _____ No _____

    Time reactions most frequently occur? _____

✔ **Treat mild** low blood sugar as follows:

    ____ glucose tabs   ____ cup juice   ____ cup regular pop

    other: _____

Follow initial treatment with a snack of _____ in _____ minutes

---

<u>Moderate reaction</u> signs person might exhibit are:

    confusion   slurred speech   disoriented   sleepiness   change in personality

    other _____

✔ **Treat <u>moderate low</u>** blood sugars as follows:

    ___ tube glucose gel   ___ tube cake decorating gel   ___ cup juice

    other: _____

Person should _____ should not _____ follow with a snack of _____ in____ minutes
or once symptoms subside.

<u>Severe reaction</u> signs person might exhibit are:

    unconscious episode   seizure   unable/unwilling to take gel or juice

✔ For **<u>severe low</u>** blood sugar, **treat** as follows:
    ___ cc. Glucagon injection (____ units)   Call 911   Notify parents

    Order for Glucagon on file? Yes____ No____

Call parent in the event_____

INTERVENTIONS FOR HIGH BLOOD SUGAR:

<u>Hyperglycemia</u>:
    A blood sugar above _____ will____ may ____ require an insulin administration (see insulin dosages).
    If blood sugar is greater than_____, test blood ketones ___ urine ketones___ .
    Child will____ will not ____ need supervision in testing ketones.
Notify parent if blood glucose is above _____ or when ketones are _____

<u>Comments</u>: _____
_____

Table 3 INDIVIDUALIZED SCHOOL HEALTH CARE PLAN: DIABETES

Date: _____ (Also see Emergency Response Plan on Opposite Side)

Student _____ Date of birth _____
School _____ Grade _____ Teacher _____
Parent(s)/Guardian(s) _____
Phone (H) _____ (W) _____ (Other) _____
Additional emergency contact information _____
Diabetes Care Provider _____ Phone _____ Fax _____
Diabetes Nurse Educator _____ Phone _____ Fax _____
Hospital of choice _____
ROUTINE MANAGEMENT Target Blood Sugar Range _____ to _____

Required blood sugar testing at school:
❏ Trained personnel must perform blood sugar test
❏ Trained personnel must supervise blood sugar test
❏ Student can perform testing independently

Times to do blood sugar:
❏ Before lunch
❏ After lunch
❏ Before P.E.
❏ After P.E.
❏ As needed for signs/symptoms of low or high blood sugar

❏ Call parent if values are below _____ or above _____

Medications to be given during school hours:
❏ Oral diabetes medication(s)/dose _____ Time to be administered:_____.
❏ Sliding scale:

To be administered immediately:

Insulin (subcutaneous injection) using Humalog / NovoLog / Regular (circle type)

		Before lunch	After lunch
____ Unit(s) if lunch blood sugar is between ____ and ____		❏	❏
____ Unit(s) if lunch blood sugar is between ____ and ____		❏	❏
____ Unit(s) if lunch blood sugar is between ____ and ____		❏	❏
____ Unit(s) if lunch blood sugar is between ____ and ____		❏	❏

❏ Insulin/Carb Ratio ____ Unit for every ____ grams of carbohydrate eaten,
   plus ____ unit(s) for every ____ mg/dl points above ____ mg/dl
❏ Student can draw up and inject own insulin   ❏ Student cannot draw up own insulin but can give own injection
❏ Trained adult will draw up and administer injection   ❏ Student can draw up but needs adult to inject insulin
❏ Student is on pump (attach Table 6 to these instructions) ❏ Student needs assistance checking insulin dosage
❏ Glucagon (subcutaneous injection) dosage (see Table 2 in in this chapter); dosage = ____ cc

---

Diet:
Lunch time _____ Scheduled P.E. time _____ Recess time _____
Snack time(s) ____ a.m. ____ p.m.   Location that snacks are kept _____ Location eaten _____

❏ Child needs assistance with prescribed meal plan (see attached) . Parents/Guardian and student are
responsible for maintaining necessary supplies, snacks, testing kit, medications and equipment.

Field trip information:
1. Notify parent and school nurse in advance so proper training can be accomplished.
2. Adult staff must be trained and responsible for student's needs on field trip.
3. Extra snacks, glucose monitoring kit, copy of health plan, glucose gel or other emergency supplies must
   accompany student on field trip.
4. Adults accompanying student on a field trip will be notified on a need to know basis.

People trained for blood testing and response:
Name _____ Date _____
Name _____ Date _____

Permission signatures:
As parent/guardian of the above named student, I give permission for use of this health plan in my student's
school and for the school nurse to contact the below providers regarding the above condition. Orders are
valid through the end of the current school year.

Parent Signature _____ Date _____
Nurse Signature _____ Date _____
Physician Signature _____ Date _____

Table 4 — EMERGENCY RESPONSE PLAN

Student Name _____ Grade/Teacher _____ Date _____

Mild Low Blood Sugar: (Student to be treated when blood sugar is below _____.)

Symptoms could include (please circle all that apply): hunger, irritability, shakiness, sleepiness, sweating, pallor, uncooperative, crying or other behavioral changes. Additional student symptoms: _____

Treatment of Mild Low Blood Sugar: With any level of low blood sugar **never** leave the student unattended. If treated outside the classroom, **a responsible person should accompany to the health clinic or office** for further assistance.

❑ Test blood sugar. <u>If kit is not available</u>, treat child immediately for low blood sugar.
❑ If blood sugar is between _____ and _____ and lunch is available, <u>escort</u> to lunch and have child eat **immediately!**
   If lunch is unavailable, treat immediately as listed below.
❑ If blood sugar is below _____, give <u>4 oz</u> of juice or <u>6 oz</u> (1/2 can) of regular sugar pop or 2-3 glucose tablets.
❑ Wait 10 minutes. Recheck blood sugar. Re-treat as above if still below _____.
❑ Follow with snack or lunch when blood sugar rises above _____ or when symptoms improve.
❑ Notify _____ school nurse _____ and parent.
Comments: _____

Moderate Low Blood Sugar:

Symptoms: In addition to those listed above for a mild low blood sugar, student may be **combative, disoriented or incoherent.**

Treatment of Moderate Low Blood Sugar:

If student is conscious yet <u>unable</u> to effectively drink the fluids offered:

✔ Administer 3/4 to 1 tube (3 tsp) of glucose gel, or 3/4 to 1 tube of cake decorating gel.
✔ Place between cheek and gum with head elevated. Encourage student to swallow. May be uncooperative.
✔ Call _____ parent and _____ school nurse.
✔ Retest in 10 minutes. If still below _____, retreat as above.
✔ Give regular snack after 10 minutes, when blood sugar rises above _____ or when symptoms improve.
Comments: _____

Severe Low Blood Sugar:

Student symptoms include: **<u>Seizures or loss of consciousness, unable/unwilling to take gel or juice</u>**

✔ **Stay with student**	✔ **Roll student on side**	✔ **Do not put anything in mouth**
✔ **Appoint someone to call 911**	✔ **Protect from injury**	

❑ Give Glucagon subcutaneously (if ordered and if an nurse or other delegated person is available); dose = _____ cc (can use an insulin syringe to mix and administer if needed: number of units of glucagon = _____ units)
Comments: _____

High Blood Sugar: This student needs to be treated when blood sugar is above _____. Call parent or guardian when blood sugar is greater than _____.
Symptoms could include (circle all that apply): extreme thirst, headache, abdominal pain, nausea, increased urination
Additional student symptoms: _____

Treatment of High Blood Sugar:

❑ Drink 8-16 oz of water or DIET pop <u>every hour</u>.   ❑ Be allowed to carry water bottle with them
❑ Use restroom as often as needed

❑ Check urine ketones _____ or blood ketones _____ if sugar is greater than _____ or when ill. If urine ketones are moderate to large, or if blood ketones are greater than 0.6 mmol/L, **call parent immediately!**
   Do not allow exercise.
❑ Administer insulin if ordered. If student is on an insulin pump, see pump addendum.

If student exhibits nausea, vomiting, stomachache or is lethargic, notify ___ school nurse and ___ parent contact ASAP. Send student back to class if none of the above physical symptoms are present.

Signatures:
Parent: _____ Physician: _____
Nurse: _____ School Principal: _____
Phone: _____ Fax: _____

Table 5   INDIVIDUALIZED HEALTH CARE PLAN CHECK LIST
FOR THE SCHOOL NURSE

STUDENT: _____ D.O.B.: _____

STUDENT #: _____ SCHOOL: _____ DATE: _____

> 1. Enter completion date and initial each step listed below.
> 2. File completed checklist in the student's health file.

Date and Initial

_____ 1. Health Care Plan developed with _____ and _____
                                                        parent or guardian   area nurse consultant

_____ 2. Physician signature needed: _____ is not needed: _____

_____ 3. Send home original Health Care Plan and memo from nurse consultant:
with student: _____ by mail: _____ by email: _____ for parent signature

_____ 4. School staff information and copy of Health Care Plan to the following:

Clinic aide	_____	Secretaries	_____	Classroom teacher	_____
EA	_____	P.E.	_____	Art	_____
Music	_____	Cafeteria	_____	Transportation	_____

Others: _____
                                             List Names

_____ 5. Copies of signed plan in   _____ Clinic Health Care Plan Book
                                           _____ Substitute Folder
                                           _____ With student information/emergency page

_____ 6. Original plan with signatures in health file

_____ 7. Classroom presentation requested: ___ No ___ Yes ___ Who requested: _____

_____ 8. Inservice: ___ No ___ Yes Who requested: _____

_____ 9. Training/delegation needed: ___ No ___ Yes ___

Procedure: #1_____

Staff: Name: _____ Position: _____ Date: _____

Staff: Name: _____ Position: _____ Date: _____

Staff: Name: _____ Position: _____ Date: _____

Procedure: #2_____

Staff: Name: _____ Position: _____ Date: _____

Staff: Name: _____ Position: _____ Date: _____

Staff: Name: _____ Position: _____ Date: _____

> **ALL HEALTH CARE PLANS ARE CONFIDENTIAL**
> **(Information to be shared on a need to know basis only!)**

Table 6 INSULIN PUMPS IN THE SCHOOL SETTING

_____ is a student in your school who has diabetes and is wearing an insulin pump. An insulin pump is a device that provides small amounts of fast-acting insulin **(basal)** every few minutes through a small catheter under the skin. The student then takes an additional amount of insulin doses **(boluses)** through the pump for meals and snacks. We would like to emphasize that problems and complications with insulin pumps are seldom seen. For the most part, you will not be aware that the student is using the pump, although you may hear an occasional quiet beep when insulin is taken for a meal or a snack. The following information may assist you in helping the student wearing an insulin pump.

LOW AND HIGH BLOOD SUGARS

These occur with the students receiving insulin pump therapy just as they do with children receiving insulin shots. They are handled similarly, and this should be outlined in the specific student's Emergency Response Plan (Table 3). If a severe low did occur in a person using a pump, it is important for the school personnel to know how to disconnect the plastic tube from the pump to the person's insertion under the skin.

High blood sugars with moderate to large urine or blood ketones (levels > 0.6) will necessitate administration of an injection of fast-acting insulin with a syringe immediately. The student may need to perform a change of infusion set at school.

BASAL AND BOLUS INSULIN PUMP DOSAGES

Insulin pumps give a constant basal dose of insulin that is set by the doctor and family. The school personnel will not be involved with the basal settings. A bolus insulin dose is given before or after food intake. It may require assistance from the school staff to help to calculate the bolus dose. **Some children need help from the school staff in remembering to administer their bolus**

dose, particularly at lunch. Missing bolus dosages of insulin is the main reason for poor diabetes control (high blood sugars) in people who use pumps.

CALCULATING THE BOLUS DOSE

This is usually done by counting grams of carbohydrate and giving a unit of insulin for a certain number of grams of carbohydrate (carb). One unit per 15 grams of carb is most common, but everyone is different. The ratio used by our child is: ____unit per ____grams of carbohydrate.

In addition, a correction bolus to bring the blood sugar into the desired range (70-150) is often added to the above dose. The most common dose is one unit per 50 mg glucose above 150. Thus, using these two "most common" doses, a person eating 45 grams of carbs would take three units. If their blood sugar was 250 mg/dl, they would also take a correction dose of two units (two 50 mg amounts above 150). Their total bolus in this case would be five units.

EXERCISE

During times of vigorous exercise, the student may need to disconnect the pump. For this, the student needs to place the pump in a safe place where it will not be damaged. During prolonged exercise, many students reconnect the pump periodically and take insulin. Some students wear their pump during exercise and use a special case to protect it.

ALARMS

Pumps are programmed to alarm under various circumstances, e.g., low battery, no insulin delivery, out of insulin, etc. This is discussed in detail in Chapter 26. There is also a 1-800 number on the back of all pumps to call for assistance.

There is an entire chapter (Chapter 26) in this book about insulin pumps. This may be helpful for school personnel wanting more information.

RESOURCES

Three videos parents often take to show the school personnel are:

1. "Managing and Preventing Diabetic Hypoglycemia." This video, made in 2001, is available from the Children's Diabetes Foundation. Call for prices at 303-863-1200 or 1-800-695-2873. Credit cards may be taken by phone. Their address is: Children's Diabetes Foundation at Denver, 777 Grant Street, Suite 302, Denver, CO 80203.

2. "The Care of Children With Diabetes in Child Care and School Settings". (This comes as two tapes with the skills part sold separately for approximately $198.00 or both tapes for $279.00.) The address is: Managed Designs, Inc. P.O. Box 3067, Lawrence, KS 66046, Phone: 785-842-9088, Fax: 785-842-6881.

3. "Living With Diabetes: Tips for Teachers" is a 19 minute video tape available from Maxishare. Call for prices. Their address is: Maxishare, P.O. Box 2041, Milwaukee, WI 53201. Phone: 1-800-444-7747, Fax: 414-266-3443. A customer service representative for Maxishare can be contacted at 414-266-3428. Hospitals can pay for this video with purchase orders and individuals can pre-pay with a check or credit card. Some clinics have copies of these videos that can be loaned to parents to take to their school.

Attention: Principal   *Date: _____*

Attention: School Nurse

Dear Principal and School Nurse,

_____ is a _____ year old with type 1/type 2 diabetes who will be attending school at _____ this year. Children with diabetes may need to test their blood sugars 2-4 times per day by poking a finger and placing the blood on a strip in a meter that then gives a number. The blood sugar tests are often done at school prior to lunch and must be done if the child is having a possible low blood sugar. These children may take insulin by injection, by an insulin pump or may take oral diabetes medication (type 2 diabetes) to control their blood sugar.

Children with diabetes can participate in all activities without restrictions, but they may need extra snacks to prevent low blood sugars before or during P.E. or other activities.

Children with diabetes may not feel well if they have low or high blood sugar. A child with a high blood sugar may require increased water intake and access to restroom facilities <u>without embarrassing restrictions</u>. Please refer to the school health care plan for details.

If you or your staff have any questions, you may contact one of our nursing staff at _____.

Sincerely,

_____   *_____*

Physician   *Nursing Case Manager*

_____

Parent

SCHOOL BLOOD SUGAR RECORD SHEET

Student:_____ Date of Doctor's Order: _____

School year: _____ School: _____ Grade: _____ Teacher: _____

Medication: Insulin, _____ Dosage: _____

Special instructions: _____

Initials and signatures of persons giving medication   Abbreviations:

_____ _____   A = Absent   NS = No show

_____ _____   C = Comment on back

_____ _____   PN = Parent Notified   FT = Field trip

Please note time and result of each blood sugar

Aug./Sept.

M	T	W	Th	F

Oct.

M	T	W	Th	F

Nov.

M	T	W	Th	F

Dec.

M	T	W	Th	F

Jan.

M	T	W	Th	F

Feb.

M	T	W	Th	F

March

M	T	W	Th	F

April

M	T	W	Th	F

May/June

M	T	W	Th	F

Chapter 24

TOPICS:
- 🐾 Prevent, Detect and Treat Acute Complications
- 🐾 Monitoring (blood sugars, ketones)
- 🐾 Psychosocial Adjustment

TEACHING OBJECTIVES:

1. Present the signs, symptoms and treatment of hypoglycemia to caregivers.

2. Instruct caregivers about essential information for the care of the child (e.g., meals and activity).

3. Teach the skills needed for the care of the child (injections, blood and ketone checking, etc.).

4. Encourage the utilization of babysitters and grandparents for maintaining parental and child sanity.

LEARNER OBJECTIVES:

Learner (parents, child, relative or self) will be able to:

1. Describe three signs and symptoms of hypoglycemia with the appropriate treatment.

2. Define two factors important in the management of diabetes.

3. Demonstrate the necessary skills for the care of the child.

4. Formulate a sanity plan for the family.

WITH SPECIAL THANKS FOR THE SUGGGESTIONS OF:

- Carolyn Banion, RN, MN, PNP, CDE for reviewing this chapter.

Chapter 24

BABY-SITTERS, GRANDPARENTS AND DIABETES

INTRODUCTION

Cut out these pages and/or make copies of them to have available for baby-sitters or grandparents. The time required to instruct a sitter or grandparent will depend on how long he/she will be with your child. A person helping for a few hours will generally do fine after you teach him/her the basics in this handout. A person staying with a child for a longer time or day-sitting for many weeks, will require more time to learn to give shots and to gain other knowledge. You are welcome to bring the sitter or grandparent along to diabetes clinic visits. In some cities, baby-sitting courses are offered to teach people diabetes-related skills.

Our Center offers a one-day course several times each year for grandparents and other caregivers of children with diabetes. It is important for grandparents to have a normal relationship with their grandchildren. This includes having the children for a day or, when parents are away, caring for them for a longer period. This requires having some knowledge and skills in many areas of diabetes management. Certainly recognizing low blood sugars and knowing how to treat them is essential. Checking blood sugars (Chapter 7) and if the child is going to spend more than the day, knowing how to draw and give insulin (Chapter 9) also becomes essential. Grandparents do not usually need to know how to manage illness or how to adjust insulin doses. They should be in contact with the parents or health care team if the child is ill or has high blood sugars for other reasons. Grandparents who take the time to learn about diabetes are showing love and support for their children and their grandchildren. Aunts, uncles, Godparents and others close to the child are encouraged and welcome to attend if they will have the opportunity to care for the child.

INFORMATION FOR THE SITTER OR GRANDPARENT

Our child, _____, has diabetes.

Children with diabetes are generally normal and healthy. In a child who has diabetes, sugar cannot be used by the body because the pancreas no longer makes the hormone insulin. Because of this, daily insulin injections are needed. Diabetes is not contagious. Caring for a child with diabetes is not very difficult, but it does require a small amount of extra knowledge.

Low Blood Sugar

The only emergency that could come on quickly is **LOW BLOOD SUGAR** (otherwise known as "hypoglycemia" or an "insulin reaction"). This can occur if the child gets more exercise than usual or does not eat as much as usual. *The warning signs of low blood sugar vary but include any of the following:* (They are discussed in greater detail in Chapter 6.)

1. Hunger

2. Paleness, sweating, shaking

3. Eyes appear glassy, dilated or "big" pupils

4. Pale or flushed face

5. Personality changes such as crying or stubbornness

6. Headaches

7. Inattention, drowsiness, sleepiness at an unusual time

8. Weakness, irritability, confusion

9. Speech and coordination changes

10. If not treated, loss of consciousness and/or seizure

The signs our child usually has are: _____

_____

_____

BLOOD SUGAR: It is ideal to check the blood sugar if this is possible. It takes 10 minutes for the blood sugar to increase after taking liquids with sugar. Thus, the blood sugar can even be done after taking sugar. If it is not convenient to check the blood sugar, go ahead with treatment anyway.

TREATMENT: Give SUGAR (preferably in a liquid form) to help the blood sugar rise.

You may give any of the following:

1. Soft drink that contains sugar (1/2 cup) - **NOT a diet pop**

2. Three or four glucose tablets, sugar packets or cubes or a teaspoon of honey

3. Fruit juice (1/2 cup)

4. LIFE-SAVERS candy (FIVE or SIX) if over three years of age

5. One-half tube of Insta-Glucose or cake decorating gel (see below)

We usually treat reactions with: _____

If the child is having an insulin reaction and he/she refuses to eat or has difficulty eating, give Insta-Glucose, cake decorating gel (1/2 tube) or other sugar (honey or syrup). Put the Insta-Glucose, a little bit at a time, between the cheeks (lips) and the gums and tell the child to swallow. If he/she can't swallow, lay the child down and turn the head to the side so the sugar or glucose doesn't cause choking. You can help the sugar solution absorb by massaging the child's cheek.

If a low blood sugar (insulin reaction) or other problems occur, please call (in order):

1. Parent: _____ at: _____

2. Physician: _____ at: _____

3. Other person: _____ at: _____

❖ Meals and Snacks

The child must have meals and snacks on time. The schedule is as follows:

	Time	**Food to Give**
Breakfast	_____	_____
Snack	_____	_____
Lunch	_____	_____
Snack	_____	_____
Supper	_____	_____
Snack	_____	_____

Sometimes young children will not eat meals and snacks at exactly the time suggested. If this happens, DON'T PANIC! Set the food within the child's reach (in front of the TV set often works) and leave him/her alone. If the food hasn't been eaten in 10 minutes, give a friendly reminder. Allow about 30 minutes for meals.

❖ Blood Sugars

It may be necessary to check the blood sugar (Chapter 7) or ketones (Chapter 5).

The test supplies we use are: _____

The supplies are kept: _____

Please record the results of any blood or urine tests in the log book.

Time: _____ Result: _____

❖ Side Trips

Please be sure that if the child is away from home, with you or with friends, extra snacks and a source of sugar are taken along.

❖ Other Concerns: *Concerns that we have are:*

_____

_____

_____

_____

_____

_____

If there are any questions or if our child does not feel good or vomits, please call us or the other people listed above.

Thank you.

QUESTIONS (Q) AND ANSWERS (A) FROM NEWSNOTES

Q. What is the Grandparents' Workshop and why does the Center have this?

A. The Center has the Grandparents' Workshop (usually two to four times per year based on need) so that grandparents can care for grandchildren and grandchildren can stay with grandparents. Both are very important to each other! I recently had a family tell me that when their five-year-old was diagnosed with diabetes, one set of grandparents jumped in and learned about diabetes including how to check blood sugars, give insulin shots and the whole "ball of wax." The other set of grandparents were scared of the diabetes and never learned any of the needed diabetes skills. Needless to say, the first set of grandparents gained a grandchild while the second set lost a grandchild (and the grandchild lost the opportunity for a close relationship with the second set of grandparents).

For most grandparents, attending the one-day workshop and possibly reading the Center's detailed educational book or the shorter more basic book, results in enough skills to be able to have the child spend a night or a week with them like any other grandchild. Perhaps even more importantly, attending the workshop helps lessen the fears of diabetes, particularly involving hypoglycemia and giving shots.

The child must not feel different or be punished because of having diabetes (particularly if siblings get to stay with the grandparents). It is also a chance for the child (and parents) to break inter-dependencies.

Finally, all parents need a break and an occasional vacation without the children. Grandparents are often the best possible solution and can sometimes be the only option. The chance to get to know one's grandparents better and to have memories of staying with them, is something that is valued for many years to come.

Chapter 25

TOPICS:
❦ Psychosocial Adjustment
❦ Physical Activity

TEACHING OBJECTIVES:

1. Explain the benefits of camps and vacations.

2. Discuss the value of developing independent knowledge and skills.

LEARNER OBJECTIVES:

Learner (parents, child, relative or self) will be able to:

1. List three benefits of attending camps or having vacations.

2. Identify one area of additional knowledge and/or one skill and/or one more area of personal growth needed for the person with diabetes.

Chapter VACATIONS AND CAMP

VACATIONS

Diabetes should not interfere with vacations, which are a normal part of life. Some extra "planning ahead" should help prevent problems related to the diabetes.

Planning may include:

✔ a clinic visit two weeks before leaving

✔ sharing with the healthcare team if your travel will be overseas

The information should include:

▼ both departure and arrival times - going and returning

▼ the number of hours traveling

✔ a review of sick-day management and the need to have a way to check for ketones

✔ buying Kaopectate© and Imodium AD if going to areas where the risk for diarrhea is high

✔ taking along your doctor's/nurse's phone numbers

✔ preparing for the new security measures (see below)

SECURITY MEASURES

The new security measures since 9/11/01 for flying in the U.S. are as follows:

1. Passengers may board with syringes or insulin pumps only if they can show a vial of insulin with a professional pre-printed label which clearly shows the medication. No exceptions will be made. Since the prescription label is on the outside of the box of the vial of insulin, the FAA recommends that passengers come with their vial of insulin in its original labeled box.

2. For passengers who have diabetes and must test their blood sugar levels but who do not need insulin, bringing their lancets is all right as long as the lancets are capped. The lancets must be with the glucose meter that has the manufacturer's name on the meter (e.g., One Touch meters say "One Touch," Accucheck meters say "Accucheck", etc.).

3. People who are traveling with a glucagon kit should keep it in its original pre-printed labeled container.

4. Because of forgery concerns, prescriptions and letters of medical necessity will not be accepted.

There have been no problems with taking insulin or other diabetes supplies (including meters and insulin pumps) through X-ray security. Remember to take extra batteries for meters and insulin pumps.

FOOD

Concerns regarding food should include:

✔ meals will probably not be served on time

✔ have a good supply of snacks (e.g., cheese or peanut butter crackers)

✔ have sources of sugar always available (glucose tablets, fruit roll-ups or whatever works best)

EXERCISE

Concerns regarding exercise include:

✔ if traveling in a car, plan regular stops to get some exercise

✔ when traveling in a car, **MORE** insulin will probably be needed due to less physical activity

✔ on active days (e.g., at beach or at Disney World) **LESS** insulin will probably be needed (THINK AHEAD)

✔ the best way to know the effects of increased or less activity is to do more frequent blood sugar checks

INSULIN

A few points to remember:

▼ Pack enough insulin to last the entire trip. Supplies may not be available at your vacation area.

▼ If going on a plane, carry **insulin, glucose strips and glucagon** on board (if put in checked luggage they can freeze and spoil or be lost if luggage doesn't arrive).

▼ If going by car, keep all three items listed above in plastic bags in a cooler (so they do not get too hot and spoil).

▼ If using an insulin pump, see the list of supplies to take in the Q and A section in the back of Chapter 26.

Make a **check list** ahead of time of things to take. Double check this list at the last minute. If using an insulin pump, take intermediate-acting insulin and syringes in case the pump breaks down and you need to return to shots. It is helpful to know the dosages you were on before starting the pump. Remember you can always take the pump insulin (Humalog/NovoLog) every three to four hours until you can get other insulins.

Some "Generic Reminders" are:

✔ **ALWAYS** carry a form of **sugar** with you to treat reactions.

✔ Have enough **snacks** available in case meals are not served on time.

✔ Always wear a diabetes **identification tag**.

✔ Get the name of a **doctor** in your vacation area so you can call him/her if necessary. Take your own doctor's and nurse's phone number, too. He/she knows your case best, and it may be comforting to make a long distance phone call when help is needed.

✔ Visit your doctor **two weeks before** you leave so you have time to work out any problems. Remember to take his/her list of suggestions with you.

✔ If you expect to be **more active** on the vacation (hiking, camping, skiing, etc.), you may need to reduce the insulin dose. Discuss this with your doctor or nurse.

✔ For **international travel**, remember to check far enough ahead of time to see if you need special immunizations. State health departments can usually give this information.

✔ If **international travel** is planned, it is wise to carry a letter from the doctor explaining why insulin syringes and other supplies are being taken through customs. As stated earlier, it is necessary to have prescription labels on the insulin and any other supplies to be carried on board. Check to see if your health insurance covers you in other countries, or if you need supplemental insurance.

✔ The most important advice is to **HAVE FUN!**

CAMP

Children with diabetes are very dependent on their parents for:

✔ blood sugar tests

✔ injections

✔ proper nutrition

✔ help with preventing and treating potentially dangerous low blood sugars

These are in addition to their non-diabetic needs. The diabetes care for their child can become one of the main functions in life for a parent. As a result, children with diabetes may become too dependent on their parents.

Advantages of Attending Camp

✔ Diabetes camp often offers the first chance to alter these dependent relationships.

✔ Most diabetes camps have doctors and nurses at the camp so the parents can feel their children will be safe.

✔ Camp food is monitored and amounts calculated by a dietitian. This helps to have the correct content and amounts available for the increased activity.

✔ Adequate snacks are routinely available and provided.

✔ It is often a major help for children to meet other friends who take shots and do tests just like they do.

✔ It is also a chance for a child to realize that he/she is not the only person in the world who has diabetes.

✔ Children who are old enough and who do not give their own shots or do their own blood sugar levels may try doing these tasks at camp.

✔ The children also understand that with proper planning, they can do the same hiking, overnights and other activities that other children do.

✔ Older teens with diabetes may serve as junior counselors and find that they must take good care of themselves in order to set a good example for younger campers.

It is important for parents not to be upset if they receive the "typical" camp letter from their child asking the parents to come and get them immediately. This type of letter is not unusual and should not cause concern. Most campers are having a wonderful time. If you are overly concerned, call the camp coordinator for support. Whatever you do, don't upset the child by trying to call them at camp, and don't suddenly appear at camp ready to take the child home.

Most diabetes camps also have some educational programs. *These may be:*

✔ "rap-sessions"

✔ problem-solving sessions

✔ games to help learning (e.g., carb-counting "guesstimates")

The major goal of the camp, however, should be to have fun and to make new friends. It is not unusual for pen pals to develop who can't wait until the next summer at camp when they can meet again.

Scholarship programs are offered at most diabetes camps. If finances are a problem, a request for financial help should be made. Sometimes children can earn part of their own expenses.

After having been at a diabetes camp, the child may decide to try other camps. *When this happens, the parents will need to:*

✔ discuss insulin dose changes with their diabetes care provider

✔ be in touch with the nurse at the other camp

✔ provide all of the needed diabetes supplies for the period at camp

✔ give telephone numbers for emergencies

✔ work out an emergency treatment plan as in the school chapter

✔ work out a way to have the blood sugars faxed to the family or healthcare provider

Attending a diabetes camp or another camp is often the first step toward independence for the child with diabetes. Encouraging camp attendance can result in a healthy parent-child relationship.

Updated camp information for camps throughout the world can be found at: http://www.childrenwithdiabetes.com/camps/

QUESTIONS (Q) AND ANSWERS (A) FROM NEWSNOTES

Q. **Should my child go to diabetes camp?**

A. We are often asked this question. The lower age limit for the Colorado camp is eight years, although not all eight-year-olds are mature enough to be away from home. Some camps (Texas) take children at even younger ages. This question was directed to me specifically as it relates to a 10-year-old and I replied without hesitation, "Yes, your child should go to camp."

Camp offers many benefits:

✔ fun (our major emphasis!)

✔ getting to know and live in a cabin with other children the same age who also have diabetes

✔ a great help for children to learn that they are not the only persons their age in the world with diabetes

✔ ten others in the cabin also have to take shots and do blood sugars

✔ the first chance to break the inter-dependencies (child on parents and parents on child) which can develop when diabetes is diagnosed at a young age

✔ a good time for parents to also have a break!

"Horse Camp"

Q. Our family is going on a two-week vacation this summer. Are there any special concerns regarding the insulin and supplies?

A. The means of travel and the type of vacation are important. *If you are traveling by plane:*

✔ Make sure the insulin is carried with you and not in the luggage. Freezing or pressure changes in the baggage compartments may change the insulin, blood test strips and glucagon. If your luggage is lost, all of your supplies would be as well.

✔ You will need a pharmacy label on the insulin (and any other supplies needed) you will be carrying on board.

✔ Have two vials of each insulin in case one is broken (many foreign countries do not have all of the insulin types [particularly Lantus]).

✔ Do not forget that meals on airplanes are never served on time, so extra snacks are essential.

✔ If time changes during travel to foreign countries are known, sharing these with your nurse or physician is important so the insulin dose can be adjusted.

For long trips in a car:

✔ Tips for avoiding high blood sugars which result in frequent urination:

▼ stopping for regular exercise at two-hour intervals

▼ eating less

▼ taking extra Humalog/NovoLog and or Regular insulin

✔ Remember that insulin does lose activity at temperatures above 90°. Insulin, glucagon and blood sugar test strips must always be kept in the thermos or cooler with ice. The strips should be brought to room temperature before use.

✔ Do not forget to take your ketone testing strips and a card with your doctor's phone number(s).

It is often better to call your doctor long-distance when you have questions than to get advice from someone who may be unfamiliar with your diabetes. Routines are often broken during vacations. Sleeping late or eating snacks or meals late can result in insulin reactions. Be aware of possible inconsistencies and try to prevent problems. Thinking ahead can help prevent problems and result in more fun!

Q. We are going to the East Coast on vacation this summer. Will times for giving shots need to be adjusted?

A. No. A change of one or two hours does not usually make a difference; simply adjust to their time zone.

This is not the case when traveling to Europe, the Far East or even Hawaii. *When greater time changes happen, call your diabetes care provider with the:*

✔ time of leaving home and/or the U.S.

✔ number of hours you will be traveling

✔ time of planned arrival (a.m. or p.m.)

✔ same information for your return trip

✔ scheduled meals on planes

Your diabetes care provider can then help you with the insulin adjustments.

Swimming is good and fun

Chapter 26

TOPICS:
- Medications (Insulin Delivery Systems)
- Prevent, Detect and Treat Chronic Complications Through Risk Reduction

TEACHING OBJECTIVES:

1. Introduce basic pump concepts including basal and bolus insulin dosing.

2. Discuss advantages and disadvantages of insulin pump therapy.

3. Review risk factors resulting in hypo/hyperglycemia in pump users.

4. Explain pump options during exercise (disconnect, reduce basal/boluses).

LEARNING OBJECTIVES:

Learner (Parents, child, relative or self) will be able to:

1. Differentiate between basal and bolus insulin doses.

2. Cite two advantages and two disadvantages of insulin pump therapy.

3. Identify two causes of low and high blood sugars in pump users.

4. Summarize two options for pump therapy during exercise.

WITH SPECIAL THANKS FOR THE SUGGGESTIONS OF:

- Susie Owen, RN, CDE

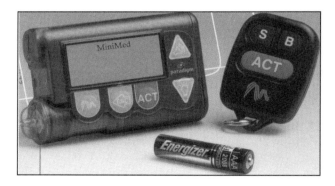

The new Medtronic MiniMed Paradigm insulin pump

Chapter 26 INSULIN PUMPS

INTRODUCTION

This chapter is not meant to teach everything one needs to know about insulin pumps. There are entire books (see end of the chapter) written about pump therapy, and this chapter is only meant to provide an overview. An insulin pump is a microcomputer (the size of a pager) that constantly provides insulin. When an insulin pump is used, insulin is first put into a special syringe which is then placed within the pump case. A small plastic tube called a cannula has a needle placed in the middle to introduce the set into the body just under the skin (the needle is then removed, leaving the plastic tube in place). Insulin is infused through the small plastic cannula to an area under the skin (most commonly the abdomen or buttock). Tape is placed over the cannula set to keep it in place for up to three days.

Pump management involves a high level of diabetes care. It requires a commitment by the entire family to help with the daily management. No matter what age a person begins pump treatment, they will need assistance that ensures safety and a positive outcome. Pump management needs to begin during a time when the family can focus on developing new knowledge and skills.

It is important to realize that the current insulin pumps do not "know" the blood sugar level. The pump is programmed to give a pre-set amount of insulin at regular intervals (called the **"basal"** rate). It doesn't consider the blood sugar level at any time. Each time the person eats, buttons on the pump must be pushed to give a **"bolus"** insulin dose. There is not a "closed-loop" pump at this time that measures blood sugars and turns off the basal insulin if the blood sugar is low or gives more insulin if the blood sugar is high. This will

likely become possible at some time in the future.

Pump therapy is usually begun after establishing regular care with the healthcare team over a six month period or more. Four visits are generally required to begin treatment with an insulin pump. A nurse educator, social worker, dietitian and physician usually spend 4-6 hours with the person and family in the two pre-pump visits, another 4-6 hours at the time of starting the pump and then another 3-4 hours at the first follow-up visit.

There is not a "best age" to begin using an insulin pump. The time is right when the person with diabetes is ready and willing. It must not be the parents who want and are pushing for the pump. The ability to count carbohydrates and to reliably calculate and give an insulin dose is an obvious need. Younger children who cannot count carbohydrates or reliably give a bolus insulin dose must be considered on an individual basis. The availability of a parent becomes a major factor when putting younger children on a pump. No matter at what age a person begins pump treatment, assistance will be needed when the person is ill, depressed or shows a lack of consistent follow-through with daily tasks.

ADVANTAGES OF INSULIN PUMPS

❣ Improved Glucose Control

The Diabetes Control and Complications Trial (DCCT), as discussed in Chapter 14, showed that improved glucose control lessened the likelihood of the eye, kidney and nerve complications of type 1 diabetes. Glucose control is measured by doing a HbA$_{1c}$ test (see Chapter 14) every three months. Most people who use pump therapy have some decrease in their HbA$_{1c}$ values and thus some decrease in their risk for complications. People who are not able to have good sugar control on multiple daily injections of insulin may benefit from insulin pump therapy.

 Insulin Delivery (and availability)

One of the big advantages of using a pump is that the insulin is readily available. The pump is attached to the person so if they are with friends and are going to share a meal, the insulin is available. It is relatively easy to push a few buttons to take extra insulin. *The insulin pump is designed to deliver insulin in two ways:*

1. A programmed **basal rate** (delivered in small amounts every few minutes)

2. A user-initiated **bolus dose** (a quick burst) of insulin with meals or with high blood sugars

This is similar to the insulin output by the normal human pancreas, with a constant (basal) output of insulin and boluses of insulin with meals. The pump has advantages over multiple daily shots in that the absorption of the insulin is more consistent and is thus very predictable. Only short-acting insulin is used in the pump (usually Humalog/NovoLog). Long-acting insulins (such as NPH or Lente), which vary in their absorption in the same person from day-to-day, are NOT used in a pump.

 Hypoglycemia

Severe low blood sugars were three times more common in pump users or in people taking three or more shots per day (all using Regular insulin) compared with people receiving one or two shots of insulin per day in the DCCT (see Chapter 14). The use of Humalog/NovoLog with more timely absorption, action and disappearance has now made pumps safer in relation to hypoglycemia. Data from our clinic suggests severe lows are LESS common for "pumpers" than for people receiving three or more shots per day.

Flexibility and Freedom

For some people, the use of a pump provides a greater opportunity for flexibility and freedom.

Some of the ways in which this happens are:

✔ being able to sleep late in the morning

✔ the ability to alter the time or size of meals or exercise

✔ the ability to take extra insulin when the blood sugar is high or with illnesses (and having the insulin readily available)

✔ Being able to easily remove the pump for baths, showers, heavy exercise, etc. The Medtronic MiniMed Paradigm pump can be worn in the bathtub or shower if desired.

✔ The long plastic tubing permits placement of the pump on the bedstand while sleeping at night. Several special holders are available for the pump.

Miss America (1998), Nicole Johnson, wore her pump strapped to her leg during the evening gown competition. She disconnected it for the swim suit competition.

 Reduction of Blood Sugars After Meals or Whenever High

With the quick-acting Humalog/NovoLog insulin, the high blood sugars that occur after meals can be reduced using boluses at mealtime. In addition, extra doses of insulin are easy to take if a high blood sugar is found between meals. This is discussed later under Correction Insulin Dosages. The Humalog/NovoLog insulin in the pump works just like when it is given in shots. It starts to work in 10 minutes, peaks in 30-90 minutes and is gone in four hours. Special bolus settings (square-wave, dual-wave) are available to help with the delayed absorption found with high fat, high carb meals (e.g., pizza).

Decrease in Total Insulin Dose and Absorption Rate Variability

The total daily insulin dose is usually decreased (by about 30%) when changing from multiple shots of insulin to an insulin pump due to more efficient delivery and use of insulin. Some people think the lower total insulin dose may be important in helping to prevent hardening of the arteries or elevated blood pressure, but this has not been proven.

DISADVANTAGES OF INSULIN PUMPS

☙ Remembering to Bolus

Giving an insulin bolus with each meal is difficult for some people to remember. HbA_{1c} values will not improve if boluses are forgotten and in fact they may rise. The basal dose turns off "internal" sugar production (Chapter 2). It does not cover food eaten. There is no intermediate-acting insulin (e.g., NPH) to peak at a mealtime. If the bolus is forgotten, the blood sugar will rise quite high. In our experience, forgetting bolus doses is the major reason for people not improving glucose control when on a pump. It is our current "guesstimate" that the HbA_{1c} increases one-half point if one meal bolus per week is missed for three months. The increase will be by one HbA_{1c} point if two meal boluses per week are missed for three months. Alarm watches can help some people. Receiving a reminder from another person can also be helpful. It is also useful to download bolus dosages given at the time of the clinic visit.

☙ Ketonuria or Ketoacidosis

When problems occur with insulin delivery, there is no long-acting insulin in the body. Ketones will start to form in four hours (the duration of the last Humalog/NovoLog infused). The alarm on a pump will sound if a line or catheter is plugged, or if very little insulin is left in the pump. However, it is possible to have a kinked tube that will deliver less insulin but won't set off an alarm. If more frequent urination or thirst are noted, people must do an immediate blood sugar, a ketone test and a pump and site inspection (particularly to check for leaks, plugged line or a catheter that may have come out). Insulin has a scent that may be detected. In these cases, the infusion set must be changed and a correction insulin dose given by a shot until the blood sugar level comes down.

If sugar control has been good for a period of time, ketones will generally not form as rapidly and/or can be cleared more easily. In contrast, if glucose control has been poor, the ketones will develop more rapidly and build up more easily. In our experience, most pump users have times when their catheter comes out or plugs. Insulin and syringes must be kept available in case they are needed for individual shots. Urine or blood ketone test strips (see Chapter 5) must always be readily available.

☙ Psychological Factors

Wearing a pump, even though it is not much bigger than a pager, is difficult for some people. We have heard the comment that "Starting the insulin pump was like getting diabetes all over again. People who had not known that I had diabetes now ask me what the pump is." A considerable amount of learning about the pump is necessary, which is not that much different from the amount required when diabetes was first diagnosed. There are other feelings expressed such as "constantly being hooked to an instrument." (In contrast, as discussed earlier, some people always like having insulin with them.)

☙ Expense

Pumps are expensive but most insurance companies will now pay for at least a portion of the expense. Initial expenses include buying the pump (approximately $5,500 U.S.), starting the pump ($1,500-$10,000, depending on whether the pump start is done as an outpatient or in the hospital) and yearly pump supplies (about $2,000). Although this may seem like a lot, the cost savings in the prevention of the eye, kidney and nerve complications of diabetes more than offsets these expenses.

☙ Weight Gain

Some people using insulin pumps who now have better glucose control may gain weight. The sugar is used rather than going out in the urine. The weight gain can happen in any person who improves their sugar control. Working with a dietitian before and after starting the pump can help to prevent this gain. It may be less of a problem with the pump in comparison with multiple injections as it is not necessary to eat to keep up with insulin previously injected. In our clinic, excessive weight gain for people using insulin pumps has not been a problem.

Skin Infections

Infections can occur at the infusion sites, particularly if the infusion sets are left in for longer than three days. However, if proper cleaning techniques are followed, this is a minimal risk. If redness and pus are noted, the physician should be called to get a prescription for antibiotics. Such an area should not be used as an infusion site until it has healed.

Insulin Availability

One must remember to routinely fill the insulin reservoir (syringe) in the pump so that the pump does not run out of insulin at an awkward time. Also, remember that insulin spoils if it freezes (unlikely next to the body) or reaches temperatures above 90°. One of our patients "cooked" her insulin by wearing her waterproof pump in a hot tub. Others have frozen insulin by exposing tubing while skiing. This can be prevented by keeping the tubing close to the body.

CLINIC VISITS

Pre-pump Visits

Insulin pumps are not for everyone. The person with diabetes (not just other family members) must be ready for the insulin pump, want the pump and be fully committed to using the pump. Our greatest success has been with people 13 years old and older.

Initial pre-pump visit

✔ The person with diabetes and their family meet with the physician, nurse, dietitian and social worker to discuss the basics and the advantages and disadvantages of pump therapy.

✔ We request four or five blood sugars be done per day, recorded and faxed to us weekly (often for one-month). This gives us an idea of the commitment of the person and the family, as well as their reliability.

✔ If the person is not already counting carbohydrates, the dietitian will give instructions in this area. We usually ask that potential pump users (or their parents) be able to count carbohydrates. We also ask that they bring or send completed blood sugar and food records, as well as insulin doses, to the dietitian.

✔ A video on the pump and other information is sent home with the family for review. Either the person or an adult must be able to reliably give bolus dosages, and must be able to deal in tenths of units of insuln.

People who are ready for a pump:

- are willing to share with others that they have diabetes
- want the pump themselves and are not being pressured by others
- are willing to do frequent blood sugar monitoring
- are either doing carb counting (Chapter 12) or are willing to learn

Final pre-pump visit

The person (and family) is trained to wear the pump and to give bolus dosages and to do set changes.

✔ If the family does not yet have their pump, an insulin pump may be lent to the person/family to use for one week. Only sterile saline (salt water) is used in the pump. They can wear it to see if they like it. They discover if they are able to do the required every two or three day infusion set changes. It is important to practice using the pump and to become comfortable with how it works.

✔ We recommend that the instructional video be viewed at least two times to learn all of the basic pump functions.

✔ Further instruction with the dietitian about carb counting is usually necessary.

✔ The social worker is available to discuss concerns about starting the pump.

Starting Insulin in the Pump (See Table 1)

The morning of the visit:

✔ We ask that NO INTERMEDIATE-ACTING INSULIN be taken on the morning when insulin is started in the pump. The normal dose of Humalog/NovoLog can be taken to cover breakfast prior to coming to the visit. If Lantus or Ultralente insulin are usually taken in the evening, the person may be asked to just take NPH insulin the night before starting the pump. Individual instructions are outlined in Table 1.

✔ *The person/family should bring:*

- the pump, case, batteries, etc.
- supplies for two or three insertions (in case needed)
- blood glucose meter and strips
- Humalog/NovoLog insulin
- calculator if needed
- significant other(s); as this person:

  ▼ may help with future pump problems

  ▼ may assist with blood sugar testing (particularly in the middle of the night)

  ▼ must be available to help with possible hypoglycemia

  ▼ should review glucagon administration

The support of the significant other(s) helps with success in pump use.

The Process:

1. The physician sets initial basal insulin dosages.

2. The dietitian again reviews carb counting (Chapter 12) and the food records.

3. The nurse educator or pump trainer usually does the technical training for the insulin pump.

4. The social worker is available to discuss concerns or fears.

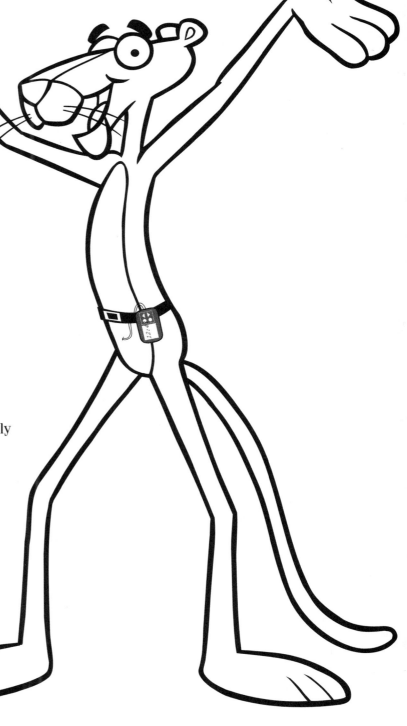

PRE-INSULIN PUMP START INSTRUCTIONS

Table 1

Name: _____ Saline Start Date: _____ Insulin Start Date: _____

The following instructions should be <u>discussed</u> with your physician at the <u>saline pump start</u>:

IF YOU ARE CURRENTLY ON <u>N</u> (NPH), <u>Lente, Ultralente or Lantus</u> in the evening, your physician recommends the following for the night before your insulin pump start (physician to check all that apply):

❏ Leave your evening dose as it is currently. No need to change anything.

❏ <u>Decrease</u> the <u>dinnertime</u> dose of <u>N</u> (NPH) to _____ units the evening before your dose.

❏ <u>Move</u> your <u>bedtime</u> dose of <u>N</u> (NPH) <u>to dinner</u>. The dose to take at dinner is _____ units.

❏ <u>Switch</u> your evening dose of Lantus, Lente or Ultralente to N (NPH) and take _____ units of NPH (N) at dinner.*

❏ Do not take any long acting insulin the evening before your pump start. Instead, supplement with _____ units of Humalog/NovoLog insulin every _____ hours through the evening and night.

* Get a prescription from your physician for Humulin or Novolin N (NPH).

If you are currently taking **Lantus** in the **morning**, you may take it the morning of the day <u>before</u> your pump start. **(Do not take it the morning of your insulin pump start!)**

The night before the insulin pump start:

▼ Give the usual insulin dose at dinner of Humalog/NovoLog and follow the directions prescribed above for your long acting insulin. Eat a regular meal.

▼ Get all of your supplies (see below) organized to take to the clinic.

▼ Watch the pump instructional video or use the interactive computer software one more time.

The morning of the insulin pump start:

<u>DO NOT</u> <u>give any intermediate-acting/long-acting insulin</u>; N (NPH), Lente, Lantus or Ultralente <u>this a.m.</u>

▼ Give the usual Humalog/NovoLog dose with breakfast. <u>If you are taking Regular</u> or a mixture of Humalog/NovoLog and Regular insulin in the morning, your physician may wish you to switch to (all) Humalog/NovoLog, recommending a total of _____ units.

▼ Bring your pump and pump supplies, Humalog/NovoLog, blood sugar testing equipment, snacks and written materials with you to the clinic.

If you have any questions, please contact your healthcare provider.

_____	_____	_____
Physician	Phone	Date
_____	_____	_____
Nurse	Phone	Date

Remember, you <u>must</u> call or <u>fax blood sugar records in daily</u> for the first 1-2 weeks after your pump start (see daily record form)! Discuss this with your physician or nurse at your insulin start.

❧ Post-pump Visits

✔ The person (or family member) faxes blood sugar results daily for the first week, then weekly for several weeks and then every two to four weeks. *Good communication at this time is essential.*

✔ After one to four weeks, another visit is scheduled. *The following activities and topics are covered:*

- Any problems the person/family is having with the pump.

- A food record may be brought to this visit to better determine the insulin-to-carbohydrate ratios with the dietitian. Other methods of preventing high blood sugars after meals (such as the square-wave or dual-wave bolus) are discussed.

- Sick-day management, site care and hypoglycemia are reviewed.

- Sometimes a second set of basal doses is programmed into the pump for high exercise days (lower basals) or for menses (higher basals).

- If the Sof-Set® or Quick Set™ is primarily being used, the Silhouette Infusion Set® may be demonstrated. The Silhouette set often stays in place better with heavy exercise.

- A physical exam is done including a careful eye check at this time (particularly if the blood sugar control is rapidly improving).

Insulin Infusion Sets

We do not recommend one infusion set over another. Every person is different and the favored set varies from person-to-person. Some of the sets most frequently used at present are shown in Table 2. However, new sets are becoming available all the time. For people who have difficulty with needles, it is fine to use EMLA® cream. This is a topical anesthetic cream which must be applied one hour before doing the insertion. The table indicates sets which have an automatic "inserter." These devices push the needle and plastic tube through the skin, usually with the push of a button. The needle is then removed, leaving the tube in the fatty layer under the skin.

PUMP INFUSION SET OPTIONS

 You have to find the tubing and sets that work for you. The variety has increased greatly and new options are appearing on the market about every six months. *Some of the current available sets are:*

Medtronic MiniMed Paradigm Pumps:	Automatic Inserter Available:
Paradigm Quick-Set - available with a 6mm or 9mm cannula	yes
Paradigm Sof-Set Ultimate QR® - 6mm (micro) or 9mm (ultimate) cannula	yes
Paradigm Silhouette™	yes
Medtronic MiniMed (508, 507c, 507, 506, 504, 407c)	
Quick Set – available with a 6mm or 9mm cannula	yes
Sof-Set Ultimate QR - 9mm	yes
Sof-Set Micro QR - 6 mm	yes
Silhouette™	yes
Bent Needle	no
Disetronic Pump Insertion Options:	
Ultraflex™ Soft	no
Tender	no
Rapid	no
Classic	no

Animas Pumps: Animas pumps can use any of the above infusion sets except for the Medtronic MiniMed Paradigm pump infusion sets. Automatic inserters can be used with the Medtronic MiniMed sets.

METHODS OF INSULIN DELIVERY BY PUMP

The pump delivers insulin in two ways:

1. *Basal dosages* that are programmed into the pump with the direction of the healthcare provider and remain the same day-after-day unless purposely changed. Table 3 can be used to direct initial pump insulin doses.

The basal rate:

✔ reflects the units of insulin per hour that would be needed if a person were not eating meals

✔ is similar to the small amount of insulin released by the pancreas every few minutes to turn off sugar production by the liver and to prevent fat breakdown

✔ usually consists of 50-60% of the total daily pump insulin dose

The number one goal in the first week is to calculate and fine-tune the desired basal dosages.

Dosing

✔ Most doctors reduce the total insulin dose (taken by shots) by about 30% when starting a pump. Then about half of the total daily dose is given as the basal dose. The other half is given as bolus doses.

✔ The number of basal dosages to be used varies between doctors. Some start with one or two basal rates and others with 8-12 basal rates.

✔ Many teenagers and young adults need more insulin in the early morning hours to cover the body's normal increase in growth hormone (the "dawn phenomenon").

✔ ALL people are different, and the use of different basal doses allows for individual fine-tuning.

✔ Once the basal rates are set they tend to stay quite consistent.

Exceptions are:

- large changes in body weight
- change of time zones
- injuries
- some medications (e.g., steroids)
- temporary reductions for exercise

✔ At a later date, basal rates can be checked by having the person not eat a meal. If the basal rate is correctly set, the person will not have a low sugar despite not having eaten. Skipping breakfast and checking the blood sugar at lunchtime is often the first step.

INITIAL INSULIN PUMP INSTRUCTIONS

Table 3

A. Check Blood Sugars:

1. <u>ALWAYS</u> before breakfast, lunch, dinner and bedtime.

2. Two hours after breakfast, lunch and/or dinner (pick two after meal checks the first week on the pump, one after meal check the second week on the pump and intermittently thereafter).

3. Between 12 midnight and 7 a.m. (every night for one week and intermittently thereafter).

B. Your Initial Basal Rates:

Time Period	U/hr	Total (U/hr x hrs)
1.	_____	_____
2.	_____	_____
3.	_____	_____
4.	_____	_____
5.	_____	_____
6.	_____	_____
7.	_____	_____
8.	_____	_____
9.	_____	_____
10.	_____	_____
		_____ = Total U's/24 hours

C. Initial Units of Insulin for Your Boluses (see example in Table 4):

	<u>Blood Sugar Level</u>			<u>Carb Intake(gms)</u>
For blood sugar (mg/dl) or (mmol/L):	< 100 mg/dl <u>< 5.5 mmol/L</u>	100-200 mg/dl <u>5.5-11.1 mmol/L</u>	> 200 mg/dl <u>> 11.1 mmol/L</u>	
Breakfast:				
Light*	_____	_____	_____	30-60
Standard	_____	_____	_____	60-90
Lunch:				
Light *	_____	_____	_____	45-60
Standard	_____	_____	_____	60-90
Dinner:				
Light *	_____	_____	_____	45-75
Standard	_____	_____	_____	75-105

*Also use lower dose if exercise is planned in next 1-2 hours.

D. If Using Insulin to Carbohydrate (CHO) Ratios*:

Breakfast ratio is: _____ unit(s) of insulin for each _____ gm of CHO
Lunch ratio is: _____ unit(s) of insulin for each _____ gm of CHO
Dinner ratio is: _____ unit(s) of insulin for each _____ gm of CHO
Snack ratio is: _____ unit(s) of insulin for each _____ gm of CHO

*For both of these methods, you will offset for high blood sugars by adding _____ units of insulin for each _____ mg/dl (____ mmol/L) above _____ mg/dl (____ mmol/L). For example, with a blood sugar of 241 mg/dl (13.3 mmol/L), you would add two units to your bolus if adding one unit for each 50 mg/dl (2.75 mmol/L) over 150 mg/dl (8.3 mmol/L).

2. *Bolus Dosages*

✔ These are taken before meals or when a blood sugar is high. The bolus must be programmed in by the user at the time the dose is taken, or it will not be given.

✔ Approximately 40-50% of the daily pump insulin doses are given as boluses before meals and snacks. (Some people give the bolus at the end of the meal when they can better judge the amounts eaten.) Others give multiple small doses as they decide to eat more.

✔ Everyone is different and boluses can be chosen to fit individual eating habits.

✔ The dietitian is an important member of the pump team and will need to review and reinforce carb counting. Changes are often suggested in **Insulin/Carb (I/C)** ratios for different meals after reviewing food records, insulin dosages taken and blood sugar levels two hours after meals.

• Most families attend carb counting classes prior to starting insulin pump therapy. However, dosages sometimes change after starting the pump. This is because an intermediate acting insulin (e.g., a.m. NPH acting at lunch time) is no longer peaking. Good recordkeeping in the period after beginning the pump is essential.

• Others bring records at the time of starting the pump which allow **I/C** ratios to be set.

• If the family has not had training in carb counting, or does not plan to use carb counting, they may decide to use a thinking scale as shown in Table 4. This table was developed for a 15-year-old boy and would vary with each person. A plan for initial boluses and basal insulin dosages is usually provided by the healthcare provider. It is usually done on the day of starting insulin in the pump. This may be on a form such as shown in Tables 3 and 4.

EXAMPLES OF BOLUS INSULIN DOSAGES

Blood Sugar Levels: mg/dl (mmol/L)

	< 100 (< 5.5)	100-200 (5.5-11.1)	> 200 (> 11.1)	Approximate Carbs (gms)
BREAKFAST				
Light*	3 units	4 units	5 units	30-60
Standard	4 units	6 units	8 units	60-90
LUNCH				
Light*	3 units	4 units	5 units	45-60
Standard	4 units	5 units	6 units	60-90
DINNER				
Light*	4 units	6 units	8 units	45-75
Standard	6 units	8 units	10 units	75-105

*** Or planned exercise (if heavy exercise, reduce more).**

3. *Correction Insulin Dosages*

Extra (unscheduled) insulin boluses are important to use if the blood sugar level is high. These can be determined in one of several ways and, once again, it is best to try different methods and see what works. Remember that larger dosages will be required if ketones are present. The healthcare team should be contacted if moderate or large urine ketones or blood ketones > 0.6 mmol/L are found. There are several ways to calculate correction boluses.

An example of a correction bolus:

▼ If one unit is used for every 50 mg/dl glucose above 150 mg/dl, and if the blood sugar level was 300 mg/dl, three units of insulin would be the bolus amount used to bring the blood sugar to 150 mg/dl (the goal blood sugar in this case). (This was determined by subtracting 150 from 300 = 150 and then dividing by 50 = 3 units of insulin.)

▼ For people using mmol/L for glucose values, one unit of insulin for every 2.7 mmol/L above 8.3 mmol/L could be used. For a level of 16.6 mmol/L with a desire to reach 8.3 mmol/L, divide 2.7 into 8.3 (16.6 minus 8.3) and give three units of insulin.

▼ The above calculation and a new bolus can be repeated after two hours if the blood sugar is still high using Humalog/NovoLog insulin.

▼ We generally suggest subtracting a unit if it is time for a meal bolus and the blood sugar is below 70 mg/dl (3.9 mmol/L). Similarly, a bolus at bedtime or during the night might be reduced by half. If a blood sugar during the day is high (> 300 mg/dl or 16.6 mmol/l), an extra unit of insulin is often added to the bolus. If moderate or large urine ketones or blood ketone level >1.6 mmol/L is present, we generally recommend doubling the correction insulin dose.

BLOOD SUGAR TESTING

More frequent blood sugar testing is required in the first week or two to help set the basal rates. The levels to aim for are the same as those shown for different ages in Chapter 7.

At a minimum:

✔ tests should be done prior to each meal

✔ before the bedtime snack

✔ two hours after eating one or two meals each day (to help with bolus doses)

✔ once during the night (start at 12 midnight and then test one hour later each succeeding night for one week)

This amounts to seven or eight tests per day. This number may be reduced in the second week to four or five per day. It is obvious that parents or a significant other are extremely helpful at this time to assist with testing. The minimum will eventually be four tests daily with occasional checks during the night. The form we like for reporting (faxing) blood sugar results is shown in Table 5 and may be copied as often as desired. It can be copied from this chapter on our website (http://www.barbaradaviscenter.org) for use in e-mailing blood sugars.

DAILY RECORD FOR INSULIN PUMP MANAGEMENT

Table 5

Day/Date	12MN	1AM	2AM	3AM	4AM	5AM	6AM	7AM	8AM	9AM	10AM	11AM	12 Noon	1PM	2PM	3PM	4PM	5PM	6PM	7PM	8PM	9PM	10PM	11PM	12MN	NOTES Including set change
BG																										
Carbs																										
Basal																										
Boluses: Food																										
Corrections																										

(This structure repeats for multiple days: BG / Carbs / Basal / Boluses: Food / Corrections)

Phone Numbers:

Family: Home _____ Work _____ Fax _____

Healthcare Team: Home _____ Work _____ Fax _____

This table may be copied as often as desired.

290   Chapter 26: Insulin Pumps

HYPOGLYCEMIA

The three main causes of low blood sugars for people using an insulin pump are all related to human (not pump) errors.

They are:

1. Too few blood sugars

Some people go through periods when they do not do the extra required work of more frequent blood sugar checking necessary for intensive diabetes management. They may be having lows and not be aware this is happening. They may then have a severe hypoglycemic event.

2. Incorrect bolus dose

This may be because carbohydrate counting is not being done, or because the person calculated wrong. It can also happen when a bolus is taken and a meal is then interrupted.

3. Wrong adjustment for exercise

Some people fail to think ahead and make needed changes in insulin dosage for exercise. At other times it may be a new exercise or one that is more intense than usual, and they just did not realize how much it would lower their blood sugar. The answer is to test blood sugars before, during and after exercise and to have extra drinks or food available.

Symptoms of Hypoglycemia

The symptoms and treatment of low blood sugar (hypoglycemia) are the same as those for people receiving insulin shots (Chapter 6). However, the symptoms may be somewhat less obvious when the blood glucose levels fall slowly over time from a mildly elevated level. Some keys to avoiding lows are given in Table 6.

Additional symptoms which should alert people/families to think of hypoglycemia during the nighttime (Chapter 6) are:

1. inability to sleep or waking up "alert"

2. waking up sweating

3. waking up with a fast heart rate

4. waking up with a headache

5. waking up feeling "foggy-headed" or with memory loss

6. unusually high morning blood sugar or with ketones (rebounding?)

IF ANY OF THESE DO OCCUR, DO A BLOOD SUGAR CHECK IMMEDIATELY. If low, treat appropriately and call the doctor or nurse the next day. Also think about what was different the previous day (extra exercise, bolus insulin, less food, etc.). This will allow planning ahead to prevent the low with a similar occurrence in the future. A summary of some key ideas for avoiding lows is given in Table 6.

Treatment

If hypoglycemia is suspected, the person with diabetes should be treated (see Chapter 6). If the blood sugar is below 60 mg/dl (3.25 mmol/L), we prefer 15 grams of "quick-acting" carbohydrate first (four ounces of juice or sugar pop or four glucose tablets). If it is still below 60 mg/dl (3.25 mmol/L) after 10 minutes, repeat this treatment. When it is above 60 mg/dl (3.25 mmol/L), give solid food.

If the glucose value is below 50 mg/dl (2.75 mmol/L), or if the person is "out of it" or unconscious, THE PUMP SHOULD BE PLACED ON "SUSPEND" OR DISCONNECTED for a period of at least 30 minutes. A parent or significant other must know how to do this, as the person with the low blood sugar may be confused. It must be remembered that insulin already infused will not yet have peaked, and so giving the sugar is essential. Instant Glucose (or cake decorating gel) and glucagon must be readily available by someone who knows how to give them (as for all people with diabetes).

KEYS TO AVOIDING LOWS

Table 6

▼ always do **AT LEAST** four blood sugars daily (and occasional checks during the night)

▼ count grams of carb to be eaten (or just eaten) to give correct bolus

▼ test before, during and after exercise

▼ recognize the symptoms of lows and treat promptly

▼ think ahead regarding variations in daily schedule which could result in low blood sugars

▼ if the blood sugar level is below 70 mg/dl (3.9 mmol/L) and it is time for a bolus dose, subtract one unit from the bolus amount

▼ reduce bedtime boluses or boluses during the night by half (the reduction may vary for different people)

HIGH BLOOD SUGARS

Some of the causes of high blood sugars for pump users are the same as for people taking their insulin by shots:

✔ extra food intake*

✔ lack of exercise*

✔ forgetting boluses*

✔ illnesses/infections*

✔ the pump not delivering insulin**

* In these cases, a correction insulin bolus can be taken as described earlier in this section.

** In this case it is often best to give Humalog/Novolog insulin with a syringe.

The most common causes of the pump not delivering insulin are:

▼ an empty reservoir (insulin syringe)

▼ a clogged infusion set

▼ leaks in the infusion set; a bead of insulin may be noted or the scent of insulin may be detected

▼ an infusion set which has come out

▼ a kinked cannula (soft tube in the body)

If there is still insulin in the syringe, changing the infusion set is usually a wise decision. In order to prevent running out of insulin, the syringe should be filled every 2-3 days as the set is changed. If more insulin has been used than usual (illness, driving in a car, etc.), correction doses can be taken using a syringe. Table 7 summarizes some possible pump problems. Remember that all pumps have a 1-800 number on the back to call for help 24 hours a day.

POSSIBLE PUMP PROBLEMS

Table 7

	Pump Alarm
Empty insulin reservoir (syringe)	Yes
Clogged infusion set	Yes
Partially blocked infusion set	No
Leaky infusion set	No
Weak or dead battery	Yes
Pump malfunction	Yes

EXERCISE

There are several options for altering the insulin dose with exercise. Experience is usually the best teacher to see which works. **Doing more frequent blood sugars to determine the effects of the exercise and the changes in insulin dosage is MOST helpful!** Many athletes find pumps are better than injections when exercising. It is generally not as necessary to eat and then perform on a full stomach.

1. If the exercise is mild to moderate (walking, golf, dancing, etc.), reducing the basal dosages by half during the exercise may be sufficient. Some people start the reduction 30 minutes before the exercise and continue it for 30 minutes after the exercise is over. Every person is different and will need to find what works best.

2. If it is intense exercise (jogging, football, basketball, etc.), most people just disconnect from the pump (some disconnect 30 minutes before the start of the exercise).

There are then several options for insulin adjustments:

▼ Estimate the amount of insulin to be missed while disconnected from the pump and take part of the dose before the exercise (particularly if the blood sugar is high) and the rest of the dose after the exercise. You may also consider using a temporary basal rate after an exercise of long duration and/or high intensity to lower the incidence of delayed hypoglycemia.

▼ do a blood sugar test and bolus after the exercise (particularly if the adrenaline put out with the exercise raises the blood sugar)

▼ use a bolus of the entire amount missed while disconnected

▼ use 1/2 of the amount missed AFTER the exercise

▼ Correction boluses given after exercise are also frequently reduced by half. This helps to prevent delayed hypoglycemia (Chapter 13).

In general, if the pump is to be disconnected for more than two hours, a blood sugar must be done. If the blood sugar is rising, it is easy to reconnect, take a small bolus and again disconnect.

3. If it is to be an all day exercise (e.g., a long hike), it may work best to reduce the basal rates (perhaps by half) and to not give any bolus doses. People must determine what works best for them.

4. With exercise, it is important to remember to stay hydrated and to take extra snacks (see Chapter 13). Drinking water or Gatorade (or other sports drinks) works for some people. The carbohydrates from the sports drinks will provide extra calories and energy. Snacks such as granola bars provide extra carbohydrates and calories. Make sure that coaches or others around at the time know that you have diabetes and wear an insulin pump.

SCHOOL

If the person using the pump is in school, the school nurse should have some knowledge of the pump. You may wish to copy the pump table in Chapter 23 on Schools (or this entire chapter) for the school nurse. (You have our permission to make copies as desired.)

SUMMARY

Insulin pumps have advantages and disadvantages. It is up to each person and family, working with their healthcare team, to decide if a pump would be good for an individual.

DEFINITIONS

Basal dose: A pre-set hourly rate of insulin as programmed into an insulin pump.

Bolus dose: An amount of insulin taken prior to a meal or when the blood sugar is high as entered at any time of the day by the person wearing the insulin pump.

Carbohydrate (carb) ratio (see Chapter 12): The number of units of insulin to be taken for a certain number of grams of carbohydrate eaten (e.g., one unit for 15 grams of carbohydrate).

Closed-loop pump: An insulin pump (not currently available) which would increase insulin given for high blood sugars or decrease insulin given for low blood sugars.

Correction bolus dose: A bolus of insulin used to correct a high blood sugar down to the desired level.

Insulin pump: A microcomputer with a syringe of insulin within the pager-sized device that can infuse a basal insulin dose at a pre-set hourly rate. Bolus insulin dosages can also be entered and given at any time by the person wearing the pump.

Additional Reading

1. *Pumping Insulin (Everything In A Book For Successful Use Of An Insulin Pump),* Second Edition, by John Walsh, PA, CDE and Ruth Roberts, MS Torrey Pines Press, 1030 West Upas Street, San Diego, CA 92103-3821

2. *Teens Pumping It Up! Insulin Pump Therapy* (Guide for Adolescents), by Elizabeth Boland, MSN, APRN, PNP, CDE. Medtronic MiniMed, 18000 Devonshire, Northridge, CA 91325, 1-800-933-3322

3. *The Insulin Pump Therapy Book.* Insights from the Experts, edited by Linda Fredrickson, MA, RN, CDE. Medtronic MiniMed, 18000 Devonshire, Northridge, CA 91325, 1-800-933-3322

4. *H-TRONplus® Advanced Insulin Pump Programming and Practices,* by Disetronic Medical System, Inc., 5201 East River Road, Ste. 312, Minneapolis, MN 55421-1014, 1-800-280-7801

5. *Pumper in the School!,* edited by Linda Fredrickson, RN, MA, CDE and Marilyn R. Graff, RN, BSN, CDE. Medtronic MiniMed, 18000 Devonshire, Northridge, CA 91325, 1-800-933-3322 or http://www.minimed.com

QUESTIONS (Q) AND ANSWERS (A) FROM NEWSNOTES

Q. **At what age should children with diabetes be considered for insulin pump therapy?**

A. This question is often asked. There is no "magic" age, although in general, teenagers tend to do better than pre-teens. *Other factors which are also important:*

a. the person must be faithful in doing at least four blood sugars daily

b. the desire of the patient, and not just the parents, to use a pump

c. the patient's maturity and ability to problem solve

d. the patient's ability to faithfully give the bolus dosages

e. the ability to use carbohydrate counting

f. family support

Some Considerations:

✔ Pumps are expensive at about $5,000 (U.S.), and it is important to make sure the insurance company will support this expense. The Diabetes Control and Complications Trial (DCCT) showed that the reduction in cost of caring for diabetes complications in later years more than makes up for this cost. However, not all insurance companies are willing to invest in prevention.

✔ Starting insulin pump therapy is time-consuming. We require an initial 3-7 day period of wearing the pump using saline (salt water). Then, if the person is still motivated, another half day is spent in the clinic to begin insulin treatment. We do NOT hospitalize people. Daily phoning and faxing of 6-8 blood sugars per day follows in the first week.

✔ Some people have said that starting the pump can be like getting diabetes all over again. Instead of taking shots in private, a pager-sized device is now constantly attached to the belt. This is removed during intensive exercise. People may ask questions such as, "What is that on your belt?"

✔ An additional drawback of pumps is that if the plastic catheter accidentally pulls out and insulin is not being infused, high sugars and ketones may develop in 3-6 hours. This is because only Humalog/NovoLog insulin is used in the pump, and it is a short-acting insulin.

The rewards are also plentiful:

✔ the HbA$_{1c}$ usually declines

✔ the likelihood of severe low blood sugars is now less than for three shots of insulin daily

✔ blood sugars are "smoothed out" with more consistent absorption of the Humalog insulin

✔ people may have more energy or feel better

✔ people may have more flexibility in the time they eat meals

✔ people may have more flexibility in the amount they eat

✔ people may be able to vary the time they arise in the morning

Although pumps are not for everyone, if it is something you want to know more about, ask your healthcare providers at the time of your clinic visit.

Q. **My son is going on a trip without other family members. He uses an insulin pump. Could you remind us of supplies he should be taking along?**

A. In case of pump malfunction, we generally recommend he take extra syringes and bottles of the intermediate-acting/long-acting insulin he was on prior to starting the pump. You should also look back in your records to send the dosages as well.

A summary of important items to include are:

1. clinic phone number
2. Humalog/NovoLog insulin
3. intermediate-acting/long-acting insulin
4. insulin syringes
5. extra pump batteries
6. glucose meter/strips
7. extra meter battery
8. extra infusion sets and inserter (if used)
9. extra pump syringe (reservoir)
10. alcohol pads
11. dressing, tape
12. glucose tablets/instant glucose
13. urine or blood ketone testing strips

Q. **Our teenage daughter is on an insulin pump and seems to forget to take some of her insulin mealtime bolus dosages. Do you have any suggestions?**

A. Missing bolus dosages with food is unfortunately fairly common. It is probably the number one cause of elevated HbA$_{1c}$ levels (> 8%) for people who receive insulin pump therapy.

When teens show signs of slipping, the parents must again get more involved. You may need to actually observe the breakfast and dinner boluses. Perhaps a friend or teacher can be found to make sure the noon bolus is taken.

One of our families found a Timex® watch called the "Iron Man Triathlon". It has five separate alarms and can store 10 messages. It can be set as a reminder for bolus dosages.

Chapter 27

TOPICS:

- Preconception Care, Management During Pregnancy and Gestational Management
- Monitoring
- Prevent, Detect and Treat Acute Complications
- Prevent, Detect and Treat Chronic Complications Through Risk Reduction

TEACHING OBJECTIVES:

1. Present the importance of preconceptual planning.

2. Define the aspects of intensive diabetes management.

3. Discuss the monitoring necessary to prevent complications.

LEARNER OBJECTIVES:

Learner (parents, significant other, relative or self) will be able to:

1. State the most important consideration when planning a pregnancy.

2. Name the four aspects of intensive diabetes management.

3. List the additional eye/kidney tests, clinic visits and monitoring required during pregnancy.

WITH SPECIAL THANKS FOR THE SUGGGESTIONS OF:

- Rick Abrams, MD
- Juan Frias, MD
- Satish Garg, MD
- Peter Gottlieb, MD

Chapter 27 PREGNANCY AND DIABETES

INTRODUCTION

This book has been used primarily by families of children with diabetes. Because of the increased readership, recently by people of all ages, this brief chapter on pregnancy has been added.

For a woman with diabetes, the best blood sugar control possible is most important before and during pregnancy. Normal or near-normal blood sugars reduces the risk of miscarriage and birth defects. Unfortunately, many women with (or without) diabetes do not plan their pregnancies.

High sugar levels can:

✔ increase the rate of birth defects (heart, spine, lips, etc.) during the first trimester

✔ result in the birth of large babies

✔ increase the risk for injury during delivery because of a baby's size

Proper planning for pregnancy will result in better HbA_{1c} values before the beginning of pregnancy. Pregnancy should be delayed until the HbA_{1c} is < 7.2% (or preferably < 6.5%) and folic acid has been started (see Section C).

1. GLUCOSE (SUGAR) CONTROL

Intensive diabetes management is essential during pregnancy. *As discussed in Chapter 8, this involves:*

A. insulin pump therapy or multiple daily injections (MDI)

B. frequent glucose monitoring

C. close attention to nutrition

D. frequent contact with the healthcare team

Although all four of these have been discussed in earlier chapters, some details related to pregnancy follow.

A. Insulin Pump Therapy or Multiple Daily Injections (MDI)

The two methods now usually used to normalize blood sugar levels are:

▼ the **insulin pump** (discussed in detail in Chapter 26). Early use of the pump was often recommended to improve sugar control during pregnancy.

▼ **multiple daily injections** (MDI - discussed under Intensive Diabetes Management in Chapter 8)

If NPH (N) insulin is used for the intermediate-acting insulin, three or four doses per day (in addition to Humalog) are often used (e.g., breakfast, lunch, bedtime).

Either method of intensive diabetes management is capable of achieving near-normal glucose levels. Standard diabetes care (2 shots a day, etc.) rarely achieves a normal or near-normal HbA_{1c}.

Insulins not approved by the FDA for use during pregnancy:

✔ Lantus (insulin-glargine): There is not yet adequate data on its safety during pregnancy. This insulin must be discontinued if pregnancy is being considered.

✔ NovoLog: Reports are not yet available.

✔ Humalog: There are a number of reports on the safety of Humalog and many doctors now recommend its use. Normalizing blood sugars after meals is very important. Numerous studies have shown Humalog to be more effective for this purpose than Regular insulin. Humalog should be taken whenever food is eaten. The Humalog Pen (Chapter 9) is a convenient way to do this for people choosing MDI.

B. Blood Glucose (Sugar) Testing

Some suggestions:

▼ blood sugar level goals are given in the Table

▼ it is best to do the 6 or 7 tests per day as outlined in the Table

▼ if HbA_{1c} values are between 5.0 and 6.5%, fewer tests may be OK

▼ the values two hours after meals (Table) are important for optimal glucose control

▼ Stay in close contact with the healthcare providers (see D in this Section). During pregnancy this should be at least weekly. (Tables for faxing or e-mailing are included in Chapters 7 and 26.)

▼ *Checking blood sugars frequently will:*

• allow the person to decrease their insulin dosages in the second half of the first trimester (9 to 12 weeks of pregnancy). It is not known why, but blood sugars seem to fall during this time.

• allow insulin dosages to be increased during the second and third trimesters. This is believed to be due to placental hormones.

C. Nutrition

Nutrition is important during pregnancy and lactation. Carbohydrate counting and the other methods of food management are discussed in Chapter 12.

Special goals:

1. to provide adequate calories for maternal and fetal weight gain. (This usually involves an additional 300 KCal/day during the 2nd and 3rd trimesters and during lactation.)

2. to provide adequate vitamins and minerals. All women capable of becoming pregnant should be certain they are taking 400 µg/day of folic acid. This helps to prevent birth defects.

3. alcohol must be avoided to prevent fetal alcohol syndrome and serious congenital defects

4. not smoking is important in reducing the risk for a premature infant

5. regular meals and snacks are important to prevent hypoglycemia. The evening snack is important to prevent lows during the night and ketone formation.

D. Frequent Contact with the Healthcare Team

▼ The blood sugars should be faxed or e-mailed weekly.

▼ Clinic visits will vary but are usually at least monthly.

▼ Care from a doctor with knowledge in the areas of diabetes as well as of pregnancy is essential.

▼ Frequent contact with the eye doctor or kidney specialist may also be important (see Section 3).

2. PREVENTING ACUTE COMPLICATIONS

Low Blood Sugar:

• The frequent blood sugar checking will help to prevent severe hypoglycemia.

• It is well recognized that severe insulin reactions occur more frequently with tight control (Chapter 6).

• There has not been evidence that low blood sugars are damaging to the fetus.

• They are not pleasant for the mom, however, and should be avoided, if possible.

Ketones:

• Frequent blood sugar checking will also help to prevent ketone formation and acidosis (Chapter 15).

• Acidosis has been related to miscarriage and is important to avoid.

Ketones should be checked:

▼ anytime a fasting blood sugar is above 240 mg/dl (13.3 mmol/L)

▼ if a random sugar is above 300 mg/dl (16.6 mmol/L)

• Some doctors advise checking for ketones every morning during pregnancy (see methods in Chapter 5).

- Acidosis is more common if insulin pump therapy is interrupted (Chapter 26). Humalog insulin lasts only four hours.

- It is important to check ketones sooner when pregnant.

3. PREVENTING CHRONIC COMPLICATIONS

A. Kidney (Renal) Damage

✔ Kidney damage does not usually worsen as a result of pregnancy in women who do not already have kidney damage. (This is in contrast to the movie, "Steel Magnolias".)

✔ Women planning a pregnancy can do a microalbumin test (and a blood creatinine) prior to pregnancy and after each trimester.

✔ If the person **does** have some kidney damage already present, it can get worse.

The following are then suggested:

▼ urine microalbumin and blood creatinine levels should be done every month

▼ **ACE-inhibitors (see Chapter 22) must be stopped (possible cause of birth defects) in any woman considering pregnancy**

▼ if blood pressure increases, other medicines should be used

✔ clinic visits every 2-4 weeks

B. Eye (Retinal) Complications

✔ Women who have had diabetes <5 years or who do not have eye (retinal) damage already present do not usually get eye damage due to pregnancy. They do need their eyes examined prior to the pregnancy and every 3 months.

✔ If a person already has moderate eye (retinal) damage from diabetes, this may worsen during pregnancy.

✔ If control (HbA$_{1c}$) has not been good and improves dramatically, there is more risk for eye (retinal) changes. These women must be followed closely. The time interval for visitis recommended by a retinal specialist is based on the amount of eye changes.

4. GESTATIONAL DIABETES

Gestational diabetes is diabetes which occurs as a result of the stress of pregnancy. After diagnosis, the care becomes similar to the care for the person who had diabetes prior to pregnancy.

Facts:

▼ Regular aerobic exercise and diet may help to lower blood sugars before and after meals.

▼ Insulin treatment may be necessary.

▼ Most women revert to normal glucose metabolism after pregnancy.

▼ There is still an increased risk of developing diabetes later in life.

TARGET VALUES FOR PLASMA BLOOD SUGARS AND HBA$_{1c}$ BEFORE AND DURING PREGNANCY

Blood Sugars	mg/dl	mmol/L
Fasting	60-100	3.3-5.5
Premeal	60-120	3.3-6.6
2 hours after meal	<130	<7.3
2:00 a.m. - 6:00 a.m.	70-140	3.9-7.7
Meter average	110-140	6.1-7.7
HbA$_{1c}$ (%)	**5.0-6.4 (must be <7.2%)**	

DEFINITIONS

ACE-inhibitor: A blood pressure medicine often used to treat people with early diabetic kidney disease (Chapter 22). *It must be discontinued if pregnancy is being considered.*

Birth defects: Abnormalities in the newborn baby such as heart malformations, spinal cord abnormalities or lip or palate defects. These are more common if glucose control for the mother was poor in the first trimester.

Folic acid: One of the B-vitamins that, when deficient in the pregnant mother, is related to birth defects in the baby.

Gestational diabetes: High glucose levels noted during pregnancy (most frequently in the last trimester). It is treated with diet exercise and sometimes insulin. It usually reverses after pregnancy is over.

Intensive diabetes management: Diabetes treatment directed toward the goal of having blood sugar and HbA_{1c} levels as close to normal as safely possible.

Microgram (µg): A common unit of weight in the metric system. It refers to one thousandth (0.001) of one gram.

Chapter 28

TOPICS:
- Prevent, Detect and Treat Chronic Complications Through Risk Reduction
- Psychosocial Adjustment

TEACHING OBJECTIVES:

1. Discuss current research related to type 1 and type 2 diabetes.

2. Present available research opportunities to families.

LEARNER OBJECTIVES:

Learner (parents, child, relative or self) will be able to:

1. List one current research study related to the individual's type of diabetes.

2. Name one research opportunity specific to the family.

Chapter 28   RESEARCH AND DIABETES

INTRODUCTION

Banting and Best received the Nobel prize for their discovery of insulin in 1921. It was believed that a "cure" for diabetes had been found. Before the discovery of insulin, people with the more severe form (now called type 1) lived only about one year. Insulin was not a "cure." but did save lives. Years later, we began to see and understand the long-term complications of diabetes.

Four Common Reseach Questions

The four questions about research asked most often are listed below:

1. When will there be a cure?

2. When will continuous glucose testing (no finger pokes) be available?

3. Can diabetes be prevented (type 1 or type 2)?

4. Are there advances in preventing diabetic complications?

There has been wonderful progress in diabetes research over the last ten years. The next ten years will likely show even more progress.

1. A CURE: ISLET/WHOLE PANCREAS TRANSPLANTS

The following research shows promise:

✔ ISLET TRANSPLANTATION

In 2001, successful islet cell transplants were done in Edmonton, Alberta, Canada. Drs. A.M.J. Shapiro, E.A. Ryan, R.V. Rajotte and team reported:

▼ 16 patients had received islet transplants

▼ the "cure" rate (off insulin) is 70% (11 of 16 patients)

▼ this rate is much better than the worldwide 11% success rate reported for the year 2001

▼ patients averaged 16 months post-transplant (time when last seen)

▼ four patients have had their islets for more than two years

All patients had "hard to manage" diabetes. For this reason they were willing to take the three medicines needed when receiving the transplant.

Major reasons for their success may have been:

• not using steroids as part of the treatment. Steroids have been helpful in preventing rejection of other organ transplants. Steroids cause insulin resistance and raise blood sugar levels.

• the medicine cyclosporine was not used

• their method of preparing the islets

• their use of new medicines that help the body accept the new islets

The procedure is simple compared with transplanting a whole pancreas:

A. A small plastic tube is put into a vein in the groin area.

B. It is then passed up to the liver.

C. Islets are then injected into the liver. Most patients required islets from two or more donors.

Dr. Bernhard Hering (University of MN) and his team have reported success for three patients using just one donor per patient. Their method of preparing the islets differs from the Canadian group. They are also using a new anti-CD3 antibody to help prevent rejection.

There are now many clinical research centers throughout the world with islet cell transplant programs (including the Barbara Davis Center). You can keep up to date on their progress at http://www.islet.org

These reports are very exciting and offer hope for the future.

However:

- there are not enough human islets

- the medicines used still cause side effects

- the medicines must be taken for the person's lifetime (at the time of this publication)

- the medicines are costly

This procedure is currently used only in people with diabetes that is hard to control. These people often have severe low blood sugars due to "hypoglycemic unawareness."

The main hopes for the future for islet transplantation involve:

▼ getting islets from an easier source (such as pig islets)

▼ use of new medicines which allow "tolerance" of the new cells

▼ protecting the transplanted islets from the immune system (so diabetes does not reoccur)

✔ **WHOLE PANCREAS TRANSPLANTATION**

Type 1 diabetes can be cured by a whole pancreas transplant. The medications needed are the same as those given after any organ is transplanted (e.g., kidney, liver, heart). The medicines have improved but still have harmful side effects.

Some side effects are:

- infections

- low white blood cell counts

- an increase in the risk for cancer

If a kidney transplant is needed due to kidney failure, a pancreas transplant may also be done.

In summary, the most important goal at this time is to keep in good sugar control. This will help prevent complications. Then, when a cure becomes routinely possible, the person will be able to benefit from this miracle.

2. CONTINUOUS GLUCOSE MONITORING (CGM)

We used to think it would be possible to put a finger in a hole of a box and get a precise sugar level. Researchers now doubt this will ever be possible. There are too many stumbling blocks (including water) which prevent the ability to get an accurate sugar result.

Two continuous testing devices have recently been approved by the FDA. Both measure glucose in the fluid under the skin rather than blood glucose levels. The glucose levels are very similar. The glucose levels under the skin are about 10 minutes behind the blood glucose levels. This does not seem to be a major problem.

The devices are:

1. The GlucoWatch®G2™ by Cygnus, Inc.

✔ It has a pad on the back of the watch that draws fluid from under the skin.

✔ It uses a small battery powered current. There is a little tingling or itching when you first start the watch. This soon goes away.

✔ A glucose level is given six times per hour (every 10 minutes).

✔ The watch requires a two hour warm up time.

✔ You must do a finger poke blood sugar at the end of the warm up period. It is then ready to give six readings per hour for the next 13 hours.

✔ If sweating or heat are present, the reading may be skipped.

✔ Glucose levels can be read on the watch.

✔ It has a memory to print out values.

✔ An alarm can be set to warn about low or high sugar values.

The drawbacks are:

- The watch may leave a mark under the pad.

- There may be skin irritation for some people around the outer edges of the sensor. These areas slowly disappear over 1-2 weeks.

- Families may decide not to have the child wear the watch every night unless methods are found to prevent the skin irritation.

It is likely the uses of the watch will be to:

▼ Check glucose levels in people thought to be having lows during the night.

▼ Use the alarm to alert people who have had seizures during the night.

▼ Wear on nights when children have had heavy daytime exercise.

2. Continuous Glucose Monitoring System™ (CGMS) by Medtronic MiniMed, Inc. It was the first device approved by the FDA.

The current monitor can:

✔ Read glucose levels 288 times in 24 hours (every five minutes).

✔ Be inserted under the skin using a plastic tube which can stay in place for up to three days.

✔ Provide a tracing (as shown in the Figure).

✔ Be useful as people change from standard diabetes management to intensive management (e.g., an insulin pump).

✔ Along with an insulin pump, be part of a "closed-loop" pump. This would be a "bionic pancreas." The CGM system would turn off or increase the insulin given by the pump. This would happen as glucose levels change. This may be possible within 5-10 years. It would transform the treatment of type 1 diabetes.

The initial device:

- Does not have an alarm system to warn of low or high glucose levels.

- Does not display the glucose levels.

- Must be taken to the doctor's office to have the values printed out.

The company will slowly make improvements. They must collect data to help persuade the FDA to allow advances.

Figure: EXAMPLE OF CGMS

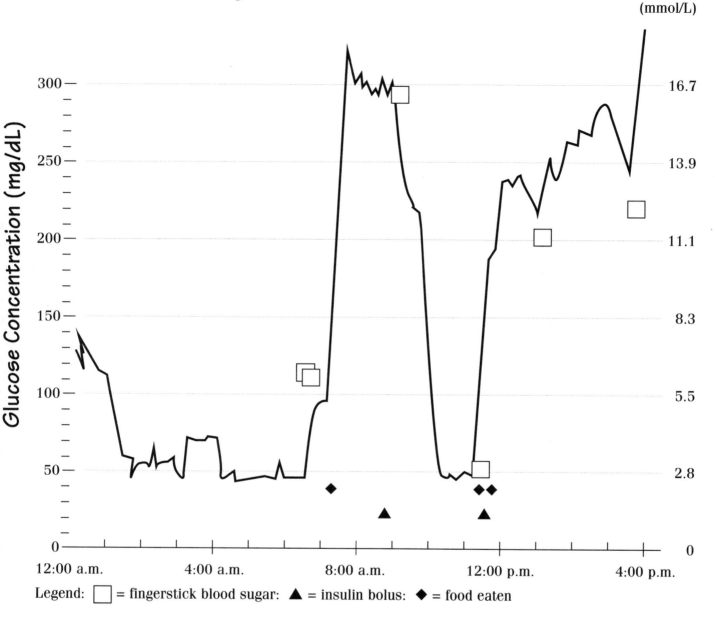

Legend: ☐ = fingerstick blood sugar: ▲ = insulin bolus: ◆ = food eaten

A graph of glucose levels using the Continuous Glucose Monitoring System (CGMS) by Medtronic MiniMed, Inc., and finger stick glucose readings (squares). This graph is from a boy who is on an insulin pump. His hemoglobin A$_{1c}$ is 8.5%, whch was above our desired level (<8.0%).

It can be seen that:

✔ The morning blood sugar level of 105 mg/dl (5.8 mmol/L) looked excellent (see meter value).

✔ The sensor graph, ith readings every five minutes, showed low glucose values (around 50 mg/dl [2.8 mmol/L]) from 1:00 a.m.-6:00 a.m.

✔ Low values are seen just before lunch (also shown by the meter).

✔ Sugars were high after meals due to forgetting to bolus.

Use of thisnformation:

▼ The basal dosages were decreased at night and late morning. This was done since two graphs were similar. Later CGMS graphs (not shown) showed the periods of low blood sugar were resolved.

▼ Adults began to help with meal boluses. (The diamonds represent bolus insulin given. The triangles represent food eaten [as entered by the boy].)

3. PREVENTION OF DIABETES

A. Prevention of Type 1 Diabetes

The first two large-scale prevention trials began in the 1990s. Both trials were possible as there are now methods to determine who is developing diabetes.

Antibodies are measured in both trials.

These are:

▼ the islet cell antibody (ICA) test

▼ the insulin autoantibody (IAA) test

Two other useful antibody tests:

• the GAD antibody*

• ICA-512 antibody test*

   * Neither was fully developed when these trials began.

The trials also require:

▼ An intravenous glucose tolerance test (IVGTT). This test can see if insulin is still made in normal amounts.

▼ An oral glucose tolerance test (OGTT) is also done. This is done to find if someone already has type 1 diabetes. Anyone found to have diabetes cannot enter the trial.

A summary of the tests is shown in the Table.

✔ THE DIABETES PREVENTION TRIAL – TYPE 1 (DPT-1)

***Part 1** (now completed):*

• required IV insulin once a year and two insulin shots a day

• showed that this way of giving insulin was not able to prevent or delay diabetes

Part 2:

• involves taking oral insulin or a placebo daily

• is still in progress

• the tests done to enter this trial are shown in the Table

• the basis for this trial is very different from *part 1;* the result could be different as well

People with a relative diagnosed with type 1 diabetes under age 40 can call 1-800-425-8361. They will give you the nearest site for the free screening.

The National Institutes of Health (NIH) is the largest research funding institute in the U.S. The NIH, JDRF and the ADA supported DPT-1. These organizations wish to help find a safe way to prevent type 1 diabetes. They have agreed to seven more years of study. This effort is under a new name, DPT/TrialNet.

It is likely that after 4,000 years, a method of prevention will be found in the next decade. (I have never made this prediction before.)

✔ EUROPEAN NICOTINAMIDE DIABETES INTERVENTION TRIAL (ENDIT)

The other trial began in Europe in 1994. It is under the direction of Dr. Edwin Gale of the U.K. They are using a B vitamin called nicotinamide. The study has all subjects entered. The results of this study will be available by the year 2003.

B. Prevention of Type 2 Diabetes

The Diabetes Prevention Program (DPP) is discussed in Chapter 13. The DPP studied 3,234 people with impaired (not diabetic) oral glucose tolerance tests. (They were close to having type 2 diabetes.) The results of the DPP were released in 2002.*

Results:

▼ 30 minutes of activity per day (five days per week) with a low-fat diet **reduced the risk for developing type 2 diabetes by 58%**

▼ taking metformin (glucophage) also reduced the chance of getting type 2 diabetes (by 31%)

People with a strong family history of type 2 diabetes now have a clear way to lessen their risk of getting this disease.

* (N Engl J Med 346:393-403, 2002)

4. CLINICAL ADVANCES IN DELAYING THE COMPLICATIONS OF DIABETES

The good news!

The life span for people with type 1 diabetes has increased. In the March, 1999 *Diabetes Care Journal,* an article indicated:

- **The well-being of patients with type 1 diabetes greatly improved in the last 50 years. This has been shown in studies from Europe and the U.S.**

- *The main reasons for this improvement are:*

  ▼ **the risk of developing diabetic kidney disease is less**

  ▼ **kidney disease is diagnosed at an earlier stage**

  ▼ **treatment with ACE-inhibitors or other high blood pressure medicines**

The bad news!

Families often do not bring in the two overnight urines for the microalbumin testing. The healthcare providers cannot always remember to ask you to do this.

If you or your child has had diabetes for:

✔ at least three years

      and

✔ has reached puberty (usually 11-13 years of age)

The two overnight urines should be collected every 12 months. Families must help by making sure these important tests are done yearly.

Directions for the collections can be found at the end of Chapter 22. There has been one change in how to collect them.

There have been too many large containers of urine in the lab. We now ask that you:

▼ measure the total volume of each of the two overnight collections at home

▼ take a small portion of each sample and place it in separate small containers

▼ bring the two containers to the clinic for testing

Urine is sterile. Measure the urine volume using a cooking measuring cup. Measuring containers and tubes can be picked up at the clinic during a routine clinic visit. Please label the tubes. Also fill out the form with the times and volumes. (The form can be found at the end of Chapter 22.)

In summary, the life span and quality of life for people with diabetes keeps getting better! Reducing the risk of kidney disease is the major reason.

There is less kidney disease because ...

✔ glucose control is better

✔ blood pressure control is better

✔ fewer people with diabetes are smoking

✔ with use of the **microalbumin test** kidney damage is found earlier

✔ early kidney damage can be reversed before it becomes permanent

We need each family to help!!! Then the news will all be good!!!

Data from Scandinavia shows that if people with diabetes do not develop diabetic kidney damage, they can live as long as any person who does not have diabetes.

THE DIABETES PREVENTION TRIAL: TYPE 1 (DPT-1)

Table

1. Screening: Islet cell antibody (ICA) test

More than 100,000 first degree relatives (3-45 years old) or second degree relatives (3-20 years old) of people who started insulin shots prior to age 40 years have been screened and more are needed. People can call 1-800-425-8361 to find out the nearest place to go to obtain the free ICA screening.

If the ICA test is positive, they can progress to "staging."

2. Staging: Testing done at first staging visit

- Intravenous glucose tolerance test (IV-GTT) x 1

- Repeat ICA

- Insulin autoantibody (IAA positive) x 1

- HLA 0602 protective gene absent (ineligible if present)

If all staging test results are as listed below, the person is then eligible for the Oral Insulin Trial.

▼ a positive ICA test (x2)

▼ a positive IAA (insulin autoantibody) test (x2)

▼ normal insulin production on one IVGTT

▼ no protective genes (HLA-DQ 0602)

▼ a normal oral glucose tolerance test (OGTT)

3. The Oral Insulin Trial

The participants have a 25-50% chance of developing diabetes in the next five years. The oral insulin trial is double-blinded so that participants will receive either 7.5 mg of insulin once daily or a placebo. The insulin does not have any hypoglycemic effect, as it is broken down into peptides by the stomach acid. Four-hundred-fifty subjects are being admitted to the trial.

DEFINITIONS

ADA: American Diabetes Association. They are involved with promoting care, education and research for type 1 and type 2 diabetes.

Bionic pancreas: A man-made device that would turn off or turn on insulin based on glucose levels.

DPT-1: Diabetes Prevention Trial-Type 1. The first large trial in the U.S. to see if type 1 diabetes can be prevented.

ENDIT: European Nicotinamide Diabetes Intervention Trial. The first large trial in Europe to test if diabetes can be prevented.

FDA: Food and Drug Administration.

JDRF: Juvenile Diabetes Research Foundation International. This organization helps to fund research on type 1 diabetes.

Tolerance: (As used in this chapter.) The body's acceptance of foreign tissue without needing medicines to prevent rejection.

QUESTIONS (Q) AND ANSWERS (A) FROM NEWSNOTES

Q. When is a cure coming?

A. I am asked this question almost daily in clinic. I do not know the answer other than to say that progress is being made.

Q. Which do you think will come first, a safe cure or the ability to prevent diabetes?

A. A cure is, of course, already possible if one is willing to take the medicines that may be risky. If enough people are willing to enter studies such as DPT/TrialNet, I would guess we will be able to prevent the onset of diabetes before we can cure those who already have it.

Some day, A CURE!

APPENDIX I

GLUCOSE CONVERSION BETWEEN
mg/dl and mmol/L

This is the third edition of this book to include all blood glucose levels in both mg/dl and mmol/L. Parts of the world use one system, and other parts use the other system. This will allow the book to now be used by both. An easy way to make the conversion from mmol/L to mg/dl is to multiply by 18 (or to divide if changing in the opposite direction). The table below may also help.

mg/dl		mmol/L	mg/dl		mmol/L	mg/dl		mmol/L
10	=	.6	190	=	10.5	370	=	20.6
15	=	.8	195	=	10.8	375	=	20.8
20	=	1.1	200	=	11.1	380	=	21.1
25	=	1.4	205	=	11.3	385	=	21.4
30	=	1.7	210	=	11.6	390	=	21.7
35	=	2.0	215	=	11.9	395	=	21.9
40	=	2.3	220	=	12.2	400	=	22.2
45	=	2.5	225	=	12.5	425	=	23.6
50	=	2.8	230	=	12.8	450	=	25.0
55	=	3.0	235	=	13.0	475	=	26.4
60	=	3.3	240	=	13.3	500	=	27.8
65	=	3.6	245	=	13.6	525	=	29.2
70	=	3.9	250	=	13.9	550	=	30.5
75	=	4.2	255	=	14.2	575	=	31.9
80	=	4.5	260	=	14.5	600	=	33.3
85	=	4.7	265	=	14.7	625	=	34.7
90	=	5.0	270	=	15.0	650	=	36.1
95	=	5.3	275	=	15.3	675	=	37.5
100	=	5.5	280	=	15.6	700	=	38.9
105	=	5.8	285	=	15.8			
110	=	6.1	290	=	16.1			
115	=	6.4	295	=	16.4			
120	=	6.7	300	=	16.7			
125	=	7.0	305	=	16.9			
130	=	7.3	310	=	17.2			
135	=	7.5	315	=	17.5			
140	=	7.8	320	=	17.8			
145	=	8.0	325	=	18.0			
150	=	8.3	330	=	18.3			
155	=	8.5	335	=	18.6			
160	=	8.9	340	=	18.9			
165	=	9.2	345	=	19.2			
170	=	9.5	350	=	19.4			
175	=	9.8	355	=	19.7			
180	=	10.0	360	=	20.0			
185	=	10.3	365	=	20.3			

APPENDIX II: ID TAGS

1. Medi-Check

Medi-Check International Foundation, Inc.
800 Lee Street
Des Plaines, Illinois 60016
847-299-0620

Please print or type

Name (First Name First)

1 2 3 4 5 6 7 8 9 10 11 12 13 14 15 16 17 18 19 20 21

Street Address

City   **State**   **Zip**

Area Code   **Phone**   **Age**

Religion (optional)

Notify in Emergency   **Name (First Name First)**

Area Code   **Phone**

Physician's Name (First Name First)

Area Code   **Phone**

Please send (check box)

❏ **Neck Tag**
❏ **Wallet Card**
❏ **Bracelet**

Medi-Check relies on its income through donations.
Please help if you can with your enclosure.

( ) $35 ( ) $30 ( ) $25 ( ) Other _____

It is suggested that a *minimum* donation of $20.00 or
more be offered for each neck tag, wallet card or bracelet.

For office use only

Date received

_____

Date shipped

_____

Code
A B C D E F G H I
J K L M N O P Q R
S T U V W X Y Z

3/91

313

2. MedicAlert

NOTE: IN FILLING OUT THE MEDICAL INFORMATION FORM BELOW, WE SUGGEST THAT YOU CONSULT YOUR DOCTOR.

1. MEDICAL INFORMATION (Please print or type):

Present medical problems _____

_____

_____

2. MedicAlert

To enroll by phone with credit card call 1-800-432-5378 anytime. Please have the following ready:
1. Member number
2. Credit card number and expiration date
3. Medical information
4. Name, telephone number and address of persons/physician/pharmacy to contact in an emergency
5. Bracelet size (when ordering bracelet)

To order by mail: Complete this form and mail with a check or money order to MedicAlert, Designer Department, 2323 Colorado Ave., Turlock, CA 95382. Or fax this form to: 209-669-2450.

Please print or type clearly. A separate application is needed for each person.

i. Are you or have you been a MedicAlert Member ❐ No ❐ Yes
If yes, enter member number _____

ii. Personal Information:

Last Name _____ First _____ Middle _____

Sex ❐ M ❐ F   Social Security Number _____

Mailing address _____ City _____ State ___ Zip _____

Phone _____ Date of Birth (m/d/y) _____

3. Emergency Contacts: Person, Physician, Pharmacy to contact

Person _____ Phone _____ Address _____

Physician _____ Phone _____ Address _____

Pharmacy _____ Phone _____ Address _____

4. Medical Information to be engraved on Emblem: Vital medical conditions and allergies. Allow one space between words. Emblem engraving space is limited. For help, call 1-800-432-5378. Medical professionals are on staff.

_____

_____

5. To be added to your computerized medical file, these vital medical facts: Additional medical conditions, allergies and medications. Dosage data not needed.

_____

_____

6. Membership Benefits: New members receive first-year membership including establishing and maintaining your computerized medical file with personal ID number, record summary, custom-engraved emblem and chain, 24-Hour Emergency Response Center, unlimited free record updates and member publications. Annual membership renewal after first year only $20

7. Emblem Selection:

A basic stainless steel (necklace, small bracelet, large bracelet) **$35.00**

Titanium steel two-toned (necklace, small bracelet, large bracelet) **$40.00**

Titanium coated stretch bracelet (small bracelet, large bracelet) **$45.00**

May 2002—Prices are for new members and are subject to change without notice. Please indicate if you are ordering a necklace or bracelet and the size (large sizes are an additional $5.00). Allow 4 weeks for delivery.

Emblem total from above: $ _____

8. Charitable Contribution (Medic Alert is a nonprofit organization that depends on fees and contributions to support a 24-Hour Emergency Response Center.) $ _____

9. Total Amount Enclosed $ _____

10. Method of Payment:

❏ Check   ❏ MasterCard   ❏ VISA   ❏ Discover   ❏ Money Order
No other cards accepted.

No COD's. Payment must accompany order. Send to:
Medic Alert, 2323 Colorado Ave., Turlock, CA 95382

Card Number _____-_____-_____-_____

Expiration Date: _____

Signature for Card Authorization: _____

IMPORTANT: When you receive your personalized MedicAlert emblem and the copy of your emergency medical file, please check both carefully for accuracy and call MedicAlert to report any errors. Also, please be sure to notify MedicAlert (1-800-432-5378) whenever your medical, address, or family physician information changes. MedicAlert believes that the information in your medical file is confidential and should only be released to protect or save a member's life. By accepting membership in MedicAlert, you do authorize MedicAlert to release information in emergencies or to healthcare personnel whom you authorize. We welcome you as a new member and will do our very best to serve you well.

11. Signature of Member _____ Date _____

----

3. Dog tags
(Please type or print clearly)

Line 1

Line 2

Line 3

Line 4

Line 5

Two each Genuine Dog Tags and Neck
Chain Set $7.50
Shipping and Handling $2.00
Optional Silencers 2 each $2.00
Total Enclosed $____

Return Address:

_____

_____

_____

Money Order to:
Dog Tags
P.O. Box 1337
Casper, WY 82602

APPENDIX III

SHOPPING LIST AND APPROXIMATE COST OF DIABETES SUPPLIES

Supplies	Cost in Dollars
Equipment for Injections	
Regular	26.00
NPH	26.00
Lente	26.00
Semi Lente	26.00
Ultra Lente	27.00
Humalog	50.00
Lantus	50.00
Alcohol Sponges (Box of 100)	2.50
BD Lo Dose Insulin Syringes (Box of 100)	25.00
Or	
Monoject 1cc Insulin Syringes (Box of 100)	30.00
Equipment for Urine Testing	
Ketodiastix #100	22.00
Ketodiastix #50	10.00
Ketostix #100	16.00
Ketostix #50	10.00
Ketostix #20 (foil wrapped)	7.00
Chemstrip uGK #100	13.00
Chemstrip K #25	20.00
Equipment for Blood Glucose Testing	
Finger stick device	10.00-25.00
Lancets (Box of 200)	11.00
One Touch Strips #50	40.00
Precision Strips #100	75.00
Blood Glucose Monitor (with memory)	70.00-140.00
Chemstrip BG #50	30.00
Miscellaneous Supplies	
Insta-Glucose	4.00
BD Glucose Tablets	2.50
Identification bracelet or necklace	2.50-20.00
Glucagon	70.00

INDEX

PUBLICATIONS

Additional copies of *Understanding Diabetes* may be purchased from The Guild of the Children's Diabetes Foundation at Denver (all orders must be pre-paid by credit card or check):

Make checks payable to:
The Guild-CDF at Denver

Mailing address:
The Guild of the
Children's Diabetes Foundation
777 Grant Street
Suite 302
Denver, CO 80203

All orders must be paid in full before delivery. Books are mailed Ground UPS. Allow one to three weeks for delivery.

Canadian and Foreign Purchasers: Please include sufficient funds to equal U.S. currency exchange rates.

The following are also available:

BOOKS

A Book for Coloring and Learning About Diabetes, a coloring book for children to create a better understanding of diabetes.

A First Book for Understnding Diabetes, a simplified book, in Spanish, for understanding diabetes.

Kids Cupboard, Chock Full of Treats for All Ages, a cookbook for diabetics and health conscious nibblers.

For current prices and additional information, please call:
(303)863-1200 or (800)695-2873
or visit our website at: www.ChildrensDiabetesFdn.org

PUBLICATIONS

Additional copies of *Understanding Diabetes* may be purchased from The Guild of the Children's Diabetes Foundation at Denver (all orders must be pre-paid by credit card or check):

Make checks payable to:
The Guild-CDF at Denver

Mailing address:
The Guild of the
Children's Diabetes Foundation
777 Grant Street
Suite 302
Denver, CO 80203

All orders must be paid in full before delivery. Books are mailed Ground UPS. Allow one to three weeks for delivery.

Canadian and Foreign Purchasers: Please include sufficient funds to equal U.S. currency exchange rates.

The following are also available:

BOOKS

A Book for Coloring and Learning About Diabetes, a coloring book for children to create a better understanding of diabetes.

A First Book for Understnding Diabetes, a simplified book, in Spanish, for understanding diabetes.

Kids Cupboard, Chock Full of Treats for All Ages, a cookbook for diabetics and health conscious nibblers.

For current prices and additional information, please call:
(303)863-1200 or (800)695-2873
or visit our website at: www.ChildrensDiabetesFdn.org

Notes

Notes

Notes

Notes